The Isolated City State

Why have the world's major cities experienced explosive growth? Why does the socio-economic status in North America roughly increase with distance from the city centre, while the socio-economic status in South America roughly decreases? What are the reasons behind the sudden decline of some large, central cities? Will recovery, if it happens, be equally rapid? The student of geography is faced with a bewildering range of major questions. Generally, in order to understand any particular phenomenon simplifications are made which make it impossible to understand other phenomena. The aim of this major study by a leading expert in the field is more ambitious. It synthesises a vast amount of theorising and individual research in an attempt to provide answers to the major questions of urban geography based on a single, coherent system of ideas. While those answers are necessarily incomplete and conditional, no serious student of urban economics and geography will be able to ignore them.

Yorgos Y Papageorgiou lectures in the Geography Department at McMaster University in Ontario, Canada.

The Isolated City State
An Economic Geography of Urban Spatial Structure

Yorgos Y Papageorgiou

ROUTLEDGE
London and New York

First published 1990
by Routledge
11 New Fetter Lane, London EC4P 4EE

Simultaneously published in the USA and Canada
by Routledge
a division of Routledge, Chapman and Hall, Inc.
29 West 35th Street, New York, NY 10001

© 1990 Yorgos Y Papageorgiou

Printed and bound in Great Britain by
Mackays of Chatham PLC, Chatham, Kent

All rights reserved. No part of this book may be reprinted or
reproduced or utilized in any form or by any electronic, mechanical, or
other means, now known or hereafter invented, including photocopying
and recording, or in any information storage or retrieval system, without
permission in writing from the publishers.

British Library Cataloguing in Publication Data

Papageorgiou, Yorgos Y. 1936-
  The isolated city state: an economic
  geography of urban spatial structure
  1. Urban regions. Economic conditions.
  Geographical aspects
  I. Title
  330.9173'3

ISBN 0-415-03032-3

Library of Congress Cataloging in Publication Data

Papageorgiou, Y.Y.
  The isolated city state : an economic geography of urban spatial
  structure / Yorgos Y. Papageorgiou. — 1st edn.
    p.   cm.
  Bibliography: p.
  Includes index.
  ISBN 0-415-03032-3
  1. Urbanization. 2. Land use, Urban. 3. City planning.
I. Title.
HT361.P36 1989
333.77'13—dc20   89-6180
                                                                 CIP

Contents

Dedication, ix
Prologue, xi
Acknowledgements, xxi

1 INTRODUCTION
   Appendix to the Introduction, 8. *Notes to the Introduction*, 31.

33 CHAPTER ONE: **Agglomeration**
   Appendix to Chapter One, 38. *Notes to Chapter One*, 42.

Part One: EQUILIBRIUM

47 CHAPTER TWO: Individual Behaviour
   Preferences, 47. *Expression of Preferences*, 48. *Mathematical Representation of Choice*, 49. *Theory and Reality*, 54. *Notes to Chapter Two*, 56.

60 CHAPTER THREE: Individual Behaviour in Space
   Spatial Structure, 60. *The Problem of Muth*, 61. *Equilibrium Conditions*, 68. *Example*, 71. *Appendix to Chapter Three*, 75. *Notes to Chapter Three*, 77.

Contents

80 CHAPTER FOUR: The Aggregation of Perfectly Rational Choices
Historical Background, 80. *Casetti Equilibrium*, 81. *Simple Urban Morphology*, 85. *Example*, 89. *Aggregate Relationships at Equilibrium*, 90. *Theory and Reality*, 93. *Appendix to Chapter Four*, 95. *Notes to Chapter Four*, 98.

102 CHAPTER FIVE: States of Urban Development
Historical Background, 102. *Response to Changing Conditions*, 103. *Example*, 115. *Theory and Reality*, 116. *Appendix to Chapter Five*, 118. *Notes to Chapter Five*, 133.

136 CHAPTER SIX: The Case of Income Variations
The Slope Test, 136. *Example*, 139. *Theory and Reality*, 141. *Response to Changing Conditions*, 142. *Appendix to Chapter Six*, 149. *Notes to Chapter Six*, 167.

169 CHAPTER SEVEN: The Case of Environmental Variations
Example, 173. *Density Craters*, 174. *The Slope Test Generalised*, 175. *Environmental Improvements and the Value of Land*, 176. *Notes to Chapter Seven*, 181.

184 CHAPTER EIGHT: Sudden Urban Growth
Historical Background, 184. *The Role of Production*, 185. *A Simple Case*, 191. *Complications*, 194. *Speculations*, 196. *Appendix to Chapter Eight*, 198. *Notes to Chapter Eight*, 203.

207 CHAPTER NINE: The Decline of Central Cities
Historical Background, 207. *Types of Suburbanisation*, 209. *A Simplified Framework*, 210. *The Cumulative Decay Process*, 215. *Revival?*, 223. *Notes to Chapter Nine*, 224.

Part Two: OPTIMUM

229 CHAPTER TEN: Public Choice
Collective Choice Rule, 229. *Social Choice and Individual Values*, 230. *The Impossibility of a Paretian Liberal*, 233.

Expression of Social Preferences, 235. *Mathematical Representation of Choice*, 237. *Allocation and Distribution*, 238. *Parametrising the Degree of Aversion to Inequality*, 240. *Traditional Misconceptions*, 244. *Appendix to Chapter Ten*, 248. *Notes to Chapter Ten*, 252.

259 CHAPTER ELEVEN: Simple Urban Optimum
Equilibrium and Optimality, 259. *The Problem of the Planner*, 259. *Optimal Conditions*, 264. *Appendix to Chapter Eleven*, 266. *Notes to Chapter Eleven*, 268.

270 CHAPTER TWELVE: Decentralisation
A. C. Pigou and the Correction Principle, 271. *Optimal Decentralisation Policy*, 274. *Theory and Reality*, 281. *Aggregate Relationships at the Optimum*, 284. *Theory and Reality*, 286. *Notes to Chapter Twelve*, 287.

290 CHAPTER THIRTEEN: Unequal Treatment of Equals
The Case of Environmental Variations, 290. *Explanation of Optimal Inequality*, 294. *Optimal Decentralisation Policy*, 297. *Urban Morphologies*, 300. *Theory and Reality* 303. *Notes to Chapter Thirteen*, 305.

Part Three: EXTERNALITIES

313 CHAPTER FOURTEEN: Conceptual Framework
Composition, 315. *Equilibrium*, 319. *A More General Point of View*, 325. *Appendix to Chapter Fourteen*, 328. *Notes to Chapter Fourteen*, 337.

341 CHAPTER FIFTEEN: Spatial Externalities and the City
Optimal Decentralisation Policy, 343. *Comparison Between Private Goods and Spatial Externalities*, 346. *Aggregate Relationships at the Optimum*, 350. *Adjustment to Spatial Externalities*, 352. *Discussion*, 356. *Notes to Chapter Fifteen*, 359.

Contents

362 **CHAPTER SIXTEEN: Prejudice**
Density-Response Specification, 362. *Integration*, 363. *Segregation*, 365. *Distance-Response Specification*, 369. *Money Counts*, 373. *Votes Count*, 374. *Comparisons*, 376. *Notes to Chapter Sixteen*, 377.

380 **CHAPTER SEVENTEEN: Industrial Pollution**
Equilibrium, 381. *Optimum*, 384. *Zoning*, 390. *Land-Development Projects*, 396. *A More General Point of View*, 399. *Notes to Chapter Seventeen*, 400.

405 **CHAPTER EIGHTEEN: Spatial Public Goods**
Conceptual Framework, 405. *The Model*, 409. *Classification*, 415. *Public Goods that Occupy Land*, 421. *The Mohring Paradox*, 429. *Aggregate Relationships at the Optimum*, 433. *Appendix to Chapter Eighteen*, 434. *Notes to Chapter Eighteen*, 439

445 **REFERENCES**

463 **CITATION INDEX**

του Σωτήρη

ωσει ανθος διηλθε
και ωσει χορτος των αγρων εξηρανθη

Prologue [1]

1

Consider the following questions.

1. Is suburbanisation, that is, the tendency of flattening population density gradients, the result of declining urban quality?
2. Why do some cities in underdeveloped countries exhibit patterns of population growth systematically different than those of some cities in developed countries?
3. Why does socioeconomic status in North America roughly increase with distance from the city centre, while socioeconomic status in South America roughly decreases?
4. Does the aggregate change in land values, generated by the opening of a new road, accurately reflect the corresponding social benefit or cost as measured by the aggregate willingness to pay for the improvement?
5. Why have all large cities in the world experienced, at one stage of their development, explosive growth?

Prologue

6. What are the reasons behind the sudden decline of some large, central cities? Will recovery, if it happens at all, also be sudden?
7. What is the long-run impact of an optimal public response to traffic congestion on the spatial structure of the city?
8. How does a theory of distributive justice affect the optimal distribution of urban population?
9. Can there be an optimal tax rate for residential land?
10. In what sense is the idea of an optimal urban population size both right and wrong?
11. Under what circumstances does the zoning proposed by a private land-developer coincide with the public interest?
12. Is optimal expenditure on public goods balanced by the corresponding receipts from optimal taxation?

The object of this book is to provide an answer to such questions based on a single, coherent system of ideas. Use of the term "an answer" instead of "the answer" is quite deliberate: some of these questions possess distinct answers generated by distinct theories; and there are many other fundamental questions about cities which cannot be properly answered within the framework of this book.

2

When one ponders about cities or, more generally, about social phenomena, matters often become so complicated that they require drastic simplification in order to be understood. What then remains to be understood is often general enough to discourage comprehensive quantification. In consequence, both quantitative and qualitative modes of analysis coexist in the social sciences, to support Thom's (1975) neat caricature of a distinction between theories that measure everything and explain nothing, and theories that measure nothing and explain everything. This book belongs to the second category. It is based on qualitative analysis, that is, on a mode of argument which falls deliberately short of precise measurement. For example, to deduce only that the density of urban population must be a strictly convex, decreasing function of distance from the city centre belongs to qualitative analysis. In consequence, no answer to the questions of the first section is supported by anything that resembles the power of a physical law. For example, even though we can explain why some cities in underdeveloped countries exhibit patterns of population growth systematically different from those of some cities in developed countries, we cannot yet predict the precise growth pattern of any city from the explanation available. It seems inevitable, therefore, that qualitative analysis may be suspect to some. The value and the validation of theory, they might say, comes essentially out of measurement. Since qualitative analysis falls short of measurement by construction, it can not be of essential value nor can it be validated in any proper sense. Yet they do accept as a matter of course verbal argument. Qualitative analysis, however, is nothing much more than an extreme case of verbal argument; and it should be treated as such. For this reason I maintain that if it is still intellectually legal to argue in English then it should also be legal to develop part of the argument in math. Hence, precisely as with verbal argument, the value of qualitative theory may simply stem from the conceptual clarification it affords. For example, an answer to question (5) suggests that, once explosive urban growth is under way, it would be futile to seek to contain it. In consequence the challenge of the future, far from being to stop explosive urban growth using various kinds of new town schemes, is rather to accept it and to plan for it. On the other hand, precisely as with verbal argument, the very nature of qualitative analysis does not preclude standard procedures of validation, ranging from casual empiricism to the development of formal tests. For example, to claim that the density of population must be a strictly convex, decreasing function of distance from the city centre is to invite well-defined, statistical schemes. Rejection of this claim would affect the structure of behavioural postulates upon which the corresponding equilibrium theory of spatial population distributions is founded.

Prologue

3

A preoccupation with qualitative analysis is not the exclusive domain of social sciences: physical sciences increasingly use qualitative argument in the case of complex systems. It is well understood by now that the power and success of the physical sciences does not stem only from measurement, and that detailed data gathering is not always necessary for the creation of theories. Taking this into account, can we maintain that the existing gap between the social and the physical sciences is cultural rather than real? Can we aspire to eventual unity? I believe that such expectations are rather empty for a considerable, and important, part of theoretical activity in the social sciences. It is possible to advance several reasons supporting this stance. Among those, (1) measurement as applied to humans and (2) normative theory seem to indicate that differences between the physical and the social sciences will continue to persist in the future.

1. Qualitative treatment in the physical sciences arises because of complexity. In contrast, qualitative treatment in the social sciences may arise because much of human nature and human relationships is about qualities, rather than quantities. In other words, much of human nature and human relationships unfolds in topological rather than metric spaces; and this is a characteristic of phenomena, not a limitation of the conceptual framework.

2. Physical sciences examine how part of our world *is*. So do the social sciences. In addition, however, social sciences examine how part of our world *should be*. For example, questions (1)–(6) belong to the former type of analysis, while questions (7)–(12) belong to the latter. It is well understood by now that the answer to any question about how part of our world should be entails some ethical position. More precisely, questions of this type are usually answered within the context of some constrained optimisation problem which cannot even be defined

unless the investigator adopts a particular theory of distributive justice. It may happen, of course, that the answer proves to be independent of the ethical position adopted. For example, an answer to questions (11) and (12) is unequivocal and, in this sense, objective. Typically however the traditional objectivity of science gives way to some softer, conditional kind of objectivity: I could display a continuum of answers explicitly related to a continuum of theories of distributive justice, and pass the burden of choice to you. For you, in turn, no particular choice of answer could be objective. To forget this is to shy away from the fundamental truth that objective social choice and therefore objective social action are, in your case, impossible.

4

Suppose that you were commissioned to draw the image of a statue. There are many pairs consisting of a pencil and a tablet scattered around the statue, each pair associated with a particular view of the statue. You can choose any single pair, in other words any particular view of the statue. But the pencil can be pressed only once. In consequence, all you can produce is a single-line drawing of the statue. There are others like you, and your collected works are now exhibited. The statue is in the middle. Upon entering the exhibition, I can compare any of the drawings with the statue. I can immediately see that the line in some of the drawings captures well some aspect of the statue, while the line in others simply deforms the statue. Having now physically discarded the bad drawings, I may rank and rearrange the rest according to their degree of correspondence with the statue; or even according to my personal view as to how important are the various aspects of the statue. Notice that during my evaluation I have never complained about the single-line restriction. I could of course hold that no true image of the statue consists of a single line, thereby dismissing the entire exhibition. This however, although true, would be a trivial statement; for even if the statue were removed, one could still learn a lot about it by visiting the exhibition.

You have been placed in the position of a theorist, that is, in the position of someone forced to deal with abstraction. This is necessary in order to meet the constraints imposed by the intellectual tools currently available. Therefore, to dismiss assumptions simply as being unrealistic is pointless. The decision must be based on whether or not assumptions lead to a single-line drawing that captures well some aspect of the statue. Only deforming assumptions should be dismissed. For example, the frictionless world of maximising behaviour in urban theory seems to be acceptable because it has provided us with considerable, experienced insight. On the other hand, the view of consumers as being entirely directed by minimum delivered price in location theory seems to be deforming because it implies a fundamental deglomerative force countered by experience.

Abstraction has often been attacked on the grounds that it forbids the adequate description of phenomena. Deep at the roots of the argument lies an intuitive belief about the realistic complexities necessary to reveal the order behind phenomena. Certainly this a priori thesis is no less subjective than the hope of understanding through generalized contours. Since no description is complete, the ongoing debate reduces to what is a meaningful degree of abstraction rather than to the use of abstraction itself. This is a matter of belief, of talent and of intuition, particular to the phenomenon examined, rather than a matter of an objective, permanent nature. Its resolution implies a fundamental tradeoff between detail and scope. You could, for example, spend your pencil on a generalized contour of the statue. Or you could concentrate on the eye of the statue. Then, of course, even if the detail of your drawing is exquisite, you should not expect it to reveal by itself anything of substance about the movement of the statue.

It is, perhaps, possible to discover some further analogies between a single-line drawing and theory construction. But differences are also important. Consider for example the pencil-tablet pair and its position relative to the statue. The pencil corresponds to the mode of expressing one's ideas, and the position to the particular aspect of the phenomenon considered. Now, in physical space, any single-line pencil can be used to draw any particular detail or generalised contour of the statue; and the various aspects of the statue can be seen equally well—provided that the studio is well lit. Thus, in the case of a single-line drawing, the choice of a pencil, level of detail and position relative to the statue are mutually independent. In the case of theory construction, however, all three choices are mutually interdependent. It is as if, upon entering the studio with a pencil to hand, the statue became invisible from certain positions while, from certain others, you could only see a single detail or some generalised aspect of the statue. Different pencils would reveal different views of the statue, suggesting that the mode of expression in theory, unlike the mode of expression in art, affects the very possibility of viewing the object itself. Evidently, your interest on a particular level of detail influences your point of view and, possibly, your choice of pencil; a particular point of view at a particular level of detail would require a type of pencil which, for now, may not even exist; and so on. For these reasons I believe that disagreements about the desired level of abstraction in theory are, for now, inevitable. I also believe in the progress of the human intellect, in other words, that it will eventually become possible to press the pencil more than once on the same tablet, thereby connecting the study of some detail with a generalised contour of the statue. Under these circumstances, I expect that the current range of views about the desired level of abstraction in theory will narrow. For example, in the present context, this may come when the dream of the behaviourists and of the emerging neobehaviourists is realised to provide us with the possibility of more realistic, and workable, models of man. Until then, however, the good-quality fragments available at any time will continue to provide meaningful, cumulative insight.

5

Being a model of models, the studio is subject to the very limitations it purports to illuminate. For example, the static image conveyed by the statue blurs the pervasive issue of dynamics. With this understanding, let the statue and its surrounding space stand for some "totality" of the system considered. Then the studio can be interpreted at different scales. At the scale of a particular theory, a drawing is a model while the statue and its surrounding space is the totality of what can be understood now within that theory. At the scale of a particular field, a drawing is a theory while the statue and its surrounding space is the totality of what can be understood now within the union of theories which define that field. One could even speak about an interdisciplinary scale. One should, however, remember that associations weaken at higher scales.

Consider the studio at the scale of a field. Differentiation does not arise only because of existing differences between individuals and their position around the statue, but also from the different modes of expression that these individuals use in order to describe an aspect of the statue. These, in turn, can be assembled to form a number of styles, each one characterising a particular group of individuals. Experience shows that communication across groups is rather difficult. For example, an applied mathematician rarely interacts with a humanist who studies the same subject. Furthermore, even within the same group, individuals tend to become differentiated by subject. Thus the studio portrays divergence between us. But it can also portray convergence: if someone makes the effort necessary to wander around the studio, he is bound to realize that your point of view illuminates an aspect of the statue invisible from his own. Thus one may operate on two levels, both, say, as a *model-builder* concerned with a particular aspect of our subject and as a *student* of our entire subject. For some there is but one level, that of a specialty. Many though are still concerned about this unsettling distinction, and about the ways in which different points of view may be composed into a more comprehensive kind of understan—

ding. Since it is still early for meaningful comprehensiveness in any one discipline, I am for now led to accept pluralism, that is, a fragmented world of missing links which invites the opposite of reconstruction—preconstruction; and to hope that the intuition gained around this studio, although prone to danger, will, somehow, improve my modelling. In the long run, this kind of feedback may lead us to comprehensiveness in a casual, gradual, almost imperceptible way. Meanwhile I must continue to produce single-line aspects of the statue. It is with such understanding that any book about cities should be read.

Notes to Prologue

1   This is based on Papageorgiou (1982).

Acknowledgements

Over the unreasonably long time it took me to complete this book, several institutions and many individuals gave me generous support and good advice. I wish to thank them all, especially those who might not be explicitly recognised here because of my short memory.

The Canada Council made it possible to spend my two sabbatical leaves entirely on this and other academic projects. This was fundamental to my development. The National Hellenic Research Foundation, especially Mr G. Antoniadis, offered me facilities during the early stages of my work. During the late stages, I wrote and rewrote chapters at the Institut de Mathématiques Economiques of the Université de Dijon. Professor C. Ponsard, its Director, J.-M. Huriot, J. Perreur, other friends and the geography of the region made all this an unforgettable experience. In between, I spent some time at the Institut de Science et Programmation Urbaines et Regionals of the Université Catholique de Louvain, and at the Department of Theoretical Spatial Economics of Erasmus Universiteit. At the former, under difficult personal circumstances, I enjoyed the kindness of and discussed aspects of my book with H. Zoller, H. Beguin and J.-F. Thisse. At the latter, I exploited the famous hospitality and brains of Professor J. Paelinck. The unforgettable

Acknowledgements

H. Mullally read patiently and commented on early chapters of my book. A. Brummel, P. Jones, S. Mestelman, P. Lesse and D. Peeters argued, corrected and gave ideas time and again. McMaster University provided me with everything one needs to complete such a project. J. Poon, B. Holdcroft, D. Maynard and M. Mirza suffered though various stages of the manuscript. M. Chan and R. Hamilton drew innumerable diagrams —some of them in vain. M. Rosati, who was charged with producing the camera-ready copy, still talks to me. Finally some things became easier through the good professionalism of Mr A. Jarvis, the Social Sciences Editor of Routledge.

If it were not for Sotiris, this would have been for Maria.

Introduction [1]

The city is multidimensionally complex. It has a physical and an abstract structure. The former is a continuous outcome of processes in the latter which, in turn, is a vector consisting of social, political, economic, cultural, institutional, technological and other variably obscure, closely intertwined substructures. This book pertains to some limited aspects of the abstract structure, fundamental in the sense that they transcend individual cities apparently differentiated by their idiosyncratic characteristics: if distinct abstract structures correspond to distinct branches of a tree, I am dealing with the trunk.

Given the complexity of the subject matter, it is not surprising that the theoretical literature about cities is diverse, somewhat unequal in depth and often difficult. One significant message implied throughout is that a typical analysis of urban structure nowadays carries with it a burden of theory which exists at different levels of abstraction, of which the city is probably the lowest. Hence our preoccupation with the city is not exclusive in the sense that, although everything said applies to the city, of many things said the city is only a subset. This is inevitable. The city, for example, as a society is subject to regularities existing beyond any spatial dimension. Although such regularities could be discussed in a context more general than the city, far from being irrelevant, they underline the simple truth that an analysis of urban structure is to be found within a context larger than mere spatial analysis.

The social, political, economic, cultural, institutional, technological and other components of spatial organisation are well reflected in human geography. Indeed human geography unfolds around that very theme, the spatial organisation of human activities, rather than around an approach as most other disciplines do. There is therefore considerable overlap between human geography and the other disciplines. For example, the economic aspects of our theme also belong to economics, the social aspects of our theme also belong to sociology, our models of spatial behaviour also belong to psychology, and so on. Each one of us exists on a margin, neither quite rejected by others with similar concerns in another discipline, nor quite accepted by others with different concerns in our own discipline.

The margin on which this book is to be found belongs to economics. During the past two decades, the economic literature about the geography of urban areas has grown at an astonishing rate. The dominant part of this literature forms a paradigm in urban economics, the new urban economics, closely related to some ideas of von Thünen (1826) and explicitly grounded on microeconomic theory. This paradigm, anticipated by Isard (1956), Beckmann (1957) and Wingo (1961), took off with Alonso (1964), who extended the model of maximising behaviour within a spatial context, and was propagated during its early stages by Beckmann (1969), Muth (1969), Casetti (1971) and Mills (1972) among others. The most important period in its development has been the seventies. By the end of that decade a large volume of urban theoretical studies, qualitative in nature and abstract in mode, was established. Although each one of these studies is rooted in the same ground, a comprehensive understanding of the whole field is difficult to obtain because of its sheer volume, the technicalities involved and the rich diversity of urban issues examined in ways which are often not directly comparable. It is therefore natural that the current state, accomplishments and limitations of the field are misunderstood by many geographers. Although there are several good books on the subject (see for example Henderson (1977) and Kanemoto (1980)), it is fair to characterise them as hybrids in the sense that they deal mainly with the accomplishments of their authors in the field, rather than with the field itself. This is natural since they were written during the period of highest growth. Now, however, that a period of consolidation and reevaluation is well under way, synthetic books on the subject have become feasible. My aim here is to provide one for geographers. Writing such a book, even a general one, presents considerable problems: in order to keep it within a reasonable length, one must discriminate. There is a number of possible choices to be made, resulting in a corresponding number of sophistication levels and areas of specialisation. Here I elected to reduce the size of the field by confining the analysis to the simplest case.[2] My aim is to provide a unified, consistent, as simple as possible account of what I believe to be the backbone around which the new urban economics has developed, especially during the seventies. Even within the realm I chose, I do not account for everything there—only what I perceive as being either fundamental and/or necessary for the development of a unified framework as I see it and at the level chosen. Such an eclectic view of the literature is bound to create omissions which in no way reflect the importance of what has been omitted.

It is perhaps useful at this point to relate the contents of this book with von Thünen (1826) who, in my opinion, provides a conceptual foundation for the entire new urban economics. In a nutshell, von Thünen's world is the following. There is an Isolated State consisting of a marketplace and a surrounding hinterland. The hinterland is perfectly homogeneous. It serves as the potential domain for a number of agricultural activities, each one endowed with known production character

3

istics. The product of agricultural activities is transported to the marketplace where it is sold at fixed prices. Hence distance from the marketplace differentiates the otherwise indistinguishable locations of the hinterland. There is competition for land between agricultural activities, and the use of land at any particular distance from the marketplace goes to the activity paying the highest positive rent. A land–use pattern is thus established around the marketplace, corresponding to the same (normal) profit per unit of land for every location of agricultural activity. The object of von Thünen's investigations is directed toward those particular land–rent and land–use patterns. The nature of the marketplace is of no concern. It simply serves to order locations and to absorb the entire agricultural production at fixed prices.

The world of this book, on the other hand, is the following. There is an isolated city–state consisting of an urban centre and a surrounding hinterland. The population of the city–state is partitioned into those individuals who interact regularly with the centre and those who do not. The partition may be determined in different ways, including migrations directed toward higher utility or the need for an optimal city size. Our attention is now confined to those who interact regularly with the centre. Since interaction is costly they locate around it, thus forming the city. The associated equilibrium and optimal land–rent and land–use patterns provide the main object of our investigation. The nature of the centre is of no concern. It simply serves to order locations and to satisfy the entire demand for urban goods at fixed prices.

Viewed from such a perspective, this book focusses on the physical complement of von Thünen's investigation with respect to the Isolated State. Our investigation will be directed toward land–rent and land–use patterns *within* the marketplace which, now, represents the city. The nature of the hinterland will be of no concern. It will simply serve as a convenient source or sink accommodating population movements to and from the city. Whereas the marketplace served to account for the product of agricultural activities in the world of von Thünen, the hinterland serves to account for migration flows in the world of this book. Clearly, since the population of the marketplace is irrelevant in the Isolated State, while the production of agricultural activities is irrelevant here, the two worlds do not fit. They remain partial and distinct, one involved with the spatial structure of agricultural activities, the other with the spatial structure of the city. Intuitively, the fundamental structure of the Isolated State is iterated once more to produce the city within the city–state; and the analysis remains partial not only relative to the rest of the city–state but also, at the city level, relative to the centre itself. Hence this book may further be taken to deal with the complement of location theory with respect to the city: whereas location theory investigates supply given demand, we shall investigate demand given supply.

In spite of the simplifications just described, what remains is sufficiently rich to provide considerable insight about urban structure. Furthermore, the analysis of what remains can become demanding on occasion. This is a serious problem, especially because the study of cities attracts a diverse geographical audience, with unequal backgrounds in the technical and conceptual details required. Awareness of this problem has gradually forced upon me simplicity as a metaphysical principle of organisation. Thus simplicity here is confined not only to the choice of the subject–matter, but also to the method of mathematical analysis and to the way such analysis is presented. The method consists of a discrete framework which is described in section 1 of the appendix. This lessens the burden of technique required. Yet the fact remains that the technical argument is often long and tedious. In such cases I confine the technical argument to an appendix: only the statement of related propositions appears in the text, supported by intuitive justification. An effort is made throughout toward unity and, to the extent of the reasonably possible, toward self–sufficiency. The former is sustained by a unified modelling framework which serves to develop the entire subject, and by consistent notation which appears in section 2 of the appendix. For the latter, elements of individual and public choice are described in separate chapters, and a partial list of definitions appears in section 3 of

Introduction

the appendix. Moreover links between theory and reality are often discussed, both to help intuition and to guard against one of the most ubiquitous sources of noise in theory—overinterpretation.

The outcome of all this can be approached at two levels of understanding. The first, casual approach, requires only the use of the text. In this manner, even those who systematically avoid technical argument could learn a lot about this particular style of looking at cities. The second, detailed approach, further requires the use of appendices. Beyond, this book could serve as a springboard to more sophisticated literature, including the important new field of urban dynamics: *it should be remembered throughout that what appears here does not exhaust the repertoire of urban economic theory; and that many of the assumptions made here have already been relaxed in more specialised works*. Thus, if one feels strongly about an assumption, one should not necessarily take it to imply a defect of the existing theory because such an assumption might well stem from my personal quest for simplicity.

The book is organized as follows. There is a first chapter serving to justify the agglomeration of urban economic activities into a single centre of the isolated city–state. This stands apart from everything else. The rest of the book, which is rather homogeneous, is partitioned into three groups of chapters dealing respectively with urban *equilibrium, optimality* and *spatial externalities*.

Equilibrium is a fundamental concept in urban economic theory. It has been extensively criticised for its unrealism. Yet, as discussed in the prologue, to dismiss assumptions and concepts as being unrealistic is pointless by itself. Evaluations must be based on whether or not such assumptions and concepts allow for simplified models of reality that capture well some of its essential aspects. Experience indicates that the use of equilibrium theory helps one to organise into a meaningful synthesis many essential aspects of urban phenomena. No one believes that there exist cities at equilibrium: cities are in a continuous flux. Yet, within a dynamic framework, it is useful to view urban changes at any moment as being directed by discrepancies between actual and equilibrium states of the system at the time. Suppose for example that you hold in your hands an invisible spherical bowl with a visible ball in it. As you walk, the ball moves inside the bowl. At any moment, given the characteristics of your walk, there is a point around the bottom of the bowl on which the ball would rest. This is the equilibrium of the moment. As it changes during your walk, the ball "tries" to follow it, never catching it except by chance, and then for a fleeting moment. You could, of course, describe in three dimensions the trajectory of the ball during your walk without any reference to the bowl: after all, the only thing you see is the ball. Yet a study of the relationships between the ball, the bowl and the characteristics of your walk may help you to understand better the object of your concern. The same is true for cities. In order to understand their behaviour, it is helpful to invoke the concept of urban equilibrium. Of course, this statement can only be justified in a fully dynamic framework, such as the one developed by Haag and Weidlich (1984). Therefore, since explicit dynamics are absent, one could maintain that this book remains essentially unfinished. Yet, even alone, many deductions of the equilibrium theory are strongly suggested by our experiences about cities: at the aggregate level and in the long run, cities behave as if they were near a moving equilibrium. In contrast, at the disaggregate level and in the short run, both observation and existing dynamic theory strongly suggest that cities are far more complex, and cannot be well understood through simple equilibrium arguments. Thus different scales of resolution generate different views about the nature of cities. These views need not contradict each other, precisely because they apply to different scales. It is with this motivation that the chapters about urban equilibrium should be approached.

Equilibrium analysis is based on the assumption that all decisions are taken by the individuals: the concept of State is absent. In contrast, the study of urban optimality in part two of this book is based on the assumption that all decisions are taken by a planner who personifies public institutions: the State is now all powerful. To fix ideas, one could think about the design of a new town where everything that

Introduction

pertains to the use of land is perfectly controlled. Once the planner begins to consider how the city *should* be, subjectivity enters via the need to decide about the meaning of distributive justice. Different such interpretations could give rise to different optimal patterns of land use. These stand on the one extreme of the continuum that describes the partitioning of power between the individual and the state. On the other extreme stand equilibrium patterns of land use. Comparison between the two extremes offers some intuition about what lies in between, that is, experienced urban patterns.

The central idea of part three is that the quality of the environment is created by the interaction of various urban activities. Such endogenous treatment, expressed in the form of spatial externalities, is fundamental to the understanding of cities.[3] Only at this stage, in my opinion, can the ideas of equilibrium and optimality be fully appreciated. The city here is viewed as the composition of comprehensively interdependent land uses. The nature of interdependence is wide, ranging from pollution and congestion to prejudice and the ways spatial public goods contribute to the creation of the urban environment. The deep effects of such interdependence on urban structure are the main object of the last group of chapters.

Appendix to the Introduction

1

This section of the appendix explains what is essential for understanding the discrete theoretical framework used in this book.

The backbone around which most arguments of this book develop is a constrained optimisation problem. The problem may be posed in the context either of urban equilibrium or of urban optimality. In the former case it pertains to the decisions of a "representative" individual, while in the latter case it pertains to the decisions of a planner who personifies public choice. In the context of urban equilibrium, the solution of the constrained optimization problem can be obtained through standard Kuhn–Tucker (1950) theory. On the other hand, in the context of urban optimality, more advanced methods such as the calculus of variations may be required. This stems from the need of the planner to aggregate over space in a way that individuals do not. For example the total population N of a circular city over some continuous landscape can be given as $N = \int_0^b 2\pi s \rho[s]ds$, where $\rho[s]$ is the (continuously distributed) population density of the city at distance s from the centre of the city, and b is the outer boundary of the city. Now if the planner must accommodate exactly N individuals, this integral equation will appear as a constraint of the associated optimisation problem. Integral constraints, in turn, cannot be handled by the Kuhn–Tucker theory. Thus, when space is treated as continuous, there is an asymmetry of method required to solve problems in the contexts of urban equilibrium and of urban optimality. On the other hand, if space were treated as discrete, so that $N = \sum_i n_i$ with n_i being the number of individuals in area i, the asymmetry disappears because summations of any length in the constraints are permissible for Kuhn–Tucker theory. Yet, another problem emerges: Kuhn–Tucker theory is about continuous variables. Therefore, in discrete space, those Kuhn–Tucker conditions for optimality which include differences instead of derivatives are only approximate, the approximation improving with finer partitions of the discrete space. Since summations of any length are permissible, appropriate partitioning of the discrete space can meet any standards of finite approximation. Such use of mathematical argument, however, remains heuristic irrespective of the accuracy of the approximation—hence potentially objectionable.

One therefore arrives at the following dilemma: either adopt standard mathematical reasoning at the expense of technical and conceptual simplicity; or promote simplicity at some loss of mathematical exactitude. Here, following the now classic paper of Strotz (1965), I elected for the second alternative. I found that treating physical space and population as discrete variables is sufficient to unify arguments under the simple and well-understood framework of Kuhn–Tucker theory—in the approximate sense already mentioned. For this reason, excepting chapter one which stands apart from the rest of the book, *physical space and population are discrete variables partitioned in units small enough to allow for the standard Kuhn–Tucker conditions to be treated as approximately true.* In this manner one can follow the arguments of this book even if one knows only the elements of constrained optimisation.[4] The notational and other consequences of this decision are detailed below. One is bound to observe in parts of this book a burden of indexing which could be avoided in a continuous framework, and which is fully justified only in the second half. Nevertheless, I believe that the consequent simple and unified manner of developing any argument is an advantage which, on the average, outweighs the disadvantages borne by the discrete theoretical framework.

It should be kept in mind that *here discreteness is a convention used to replace integrals with summations.* In all other respects all variables, including those under the summation symbol, are treated as continuous in the sense that Kuhn–Tucker conditions hold—even approximately. Thus the choice of discrete variables was strictly based on the decision to use the Kuhn–Tucker framework throughout. Treating physical space and population as discrete variables is sufficient for this purpose. In consequence all sources of approximation stem from those Kuhn–Tucker conditions which include location or population differences. To keep explicit all sources of approximation and, at the same time, produce the minimum number of changes in the standard continuous framework necessary to the purpose at hand, I use the following two rules:

1. *Changes due to a discrete variable are written as discrete.*

2. *Changes due to a continuous variable are written as continuous.*

Introduction

Before giving examples of how these two determinants of notation are applied, it is necessary to introduce the discrete equivalents of a derivative and of a total differential. Suppose that f is a function of a discrete variable x. Then

(1) $$\Delta_x f \equiv f[x+1] - f[x]$$

is called the *first difference of f with respect to x*. It is like the first derivative. The analogue of a partial derivative is obtained as follows. If, say, f is a function of x and y then

(2) $$\Delta_x f = f[x+1,y] - f[x,y].$$

If y is a discrete variable then we have $\Delta_y f$ similarly. If y is continuous (remember: a function can have both continuous *and* discrete variables) then we have $\partial f/\partial y$ as usual. Notice that there is no notational distinction between ordinary and partial differences here. Such distinction is not necessary as long as you remember whether the function you are dealing with has one or more variables. The *total difference* of $f[x,y]$, where x and y are discrete, is

(3) $$\delta f = \Delta_x f\, \delta x + \Delta_y f\, \delta y.$$

It is like the total differential. If y were continuous, the last term in (3) would have been replaced by $(\partial f/\partial y)dy$. Furthermore, dividing both sides of (3) by δx one obtains $\delta_x f$, the *total difference of f with respect to x*. It is like the total derivative. We can generalize all these for any number and for any mix of variables.

Whether to use discrete or continuous notation will be determined in each case by the two rules above. For example, taking into account that the only two discrete variables pertain to physical space and population, the change of land rents r as one moves from area i to area $i+1$ is $\Delta_i r$ by rule 1. Similarly, the change of land rents as an additional

Introduction

individual moves to area i is $\Delta_{ni} r$. On the other hand, analogous changes due to changes in per capita income y will be noted as dr/dy or $\partial r/\partial y$ by rule 2. Also by rule 2, the change of the border area b due to changes in per capita income is db/dy or $\partial b/\partial y$, even though physical space is discrete.

It remains to describe some discrete operations used throughout. Δ obeys the following laws.

1. The *commutative law* with respect to constants: if k is a constant then

(4) $$\Delta_x (kf) = k \Delta_x f,$$

because, from (1),

(5) $$\Delta_x (kf) = kf[x+1] - kf[x] = k(f[x+1] - f[x]) = k \Delta_x f.$$

2. The *distributive law*: if both f and g are functions then

(6) $$\Delta_x (f+g) = \Delta_x f + \Delta_x g,$$

because, from (1),

(7) $$\Delta_x (f+g) = (f[x+1] + g[x+1]) - (f[x] + g[x])$$
$$= (f[x+1] - f[x]) + (g[x+1] - g[x]) = \Delta_x f + \Delta_x g.$$

We can also easily find the first differences for products and for quotients of a function. Thus

(8) $$\Delta_x (fg) = f[x+1]\, g[x+1] - f[x]\, g[x]$$
$$= (f[x+1]\, g[x+1] - f[x+1]\, g[x]) + (f[x+1]\, g[x] - f[x]\, g[x])$$

$$= f[x+1](g[x+1] - g[x]) + g[x](f[x+1] - f[x])$$

$$= f[x+1] \mathop{\triangle}_{x} g + g[x] \mathop{\triangle}_{x} f,$$

which gives the difference of a product analogous to the corresponding formula for the derivative of a product. Also

(9) $$\mathop{\triangle}_{x} \frac{f}{g} = \frac{f[x+1]}{g[x+1]} - \frac{f[x]}{g[x]}$$

$$= (f[x+1] \, g[x] - g[x+1] \, f[x]) \div (g[x] \, g[x+1])$$

$$= (f[x+1] \, g[x] - f[x] \, g[x] + f[x] \, g[x] - g[x+1] \, f[x])$$

$$\div (g[x] \, g[x+1])$$

$$= ((g[x](f[x+1] - f[x]) - f[x](g[x+1] - g[x])) \div (g[x] \, g[x+1])$$

$$= (g[x] \mathop{\triangle}_{x} f - f[x] \mathop{\triangle}_{x} g) \div (g[x] \, g[x+1])$$

which gives the difference of a quotient, analogous to the corresponding formula for the derivative of a quotient.

The last type of rule for first differences to be used concerns differences of summations when the limits of the summation are concerned. The continuous equivalent of these rules is the rule of Leibnitz. In particular, if $g[x]$ is a discrete, increasing function of x,

(10) $$\mathop{\triangle}_{x} \sum_{j=1}^{g[x]} f_j[x] = \sum_{j=1}^{g[x+1]} f_j[x+1] - \sum_{j=1}^{g[x]} f_j[x]$$

$$= \sum_{j=1}^{g[x]} f_j[x+1] + \sum_{j=g[x]+1}^{g[x+1]} f_j[x+1] - \sum_{j=1}^{g[x]} f_j[x]$$

Introduction

$$= \sum_{j=1}^{g[x]} \underset{x}{\Delta} f_j[x] + \sum_{j=g\lfloor x\rfloor+1}^{g[x+1]} f_j[x+1]$$

gives the difference when the upper limit of the summation is concerned. On the other hand

(11) $$\underset{x}{\Delta} \sum_{j=g\lfloor x\rfloor}^{n} f_j[x] = \sum_{j=g\lfloor x+1\rfloor}^{n} f_j[x+1] - \sum_{j=g\lfloor x\rfloor}^{n} f_j[x]$$

$$= \sum_{j=g\lfloor x+1\rfloor}^{n} f_j[x+1] - \sum_{j=g\lfloor x+1\rfloor}^{n} f_j[x] - \sum_{j=g\lfloor x\rfloor}^{g[x+1]-1} f_j[x]$$

$$= \sum_{j=g\lfloor x+1\rfloor}^{n} \underset{x}{\Delta} f_j[x] - \sum_{j=g\lfloor x\rfloor}^{g[x+1]-1} f_j[x]$$

gives the difference when the lower limit of the summation is concerned.

Higher differences are also straightforward. For example $\Delta_x \Delta_x f \equiv \Delta_x^2 f$, $\Delta_y^2 f$, $\Delta_x \Delta_y f$, $\Delta_y \Delta_x f$ correspond to $\partial(\partial f/\partial x)/\partial x \equiv \partial^2 f/\partial^2 x$, $\partial^2 f/\partial y^2$, $\partial(\partial f/\partial y)/\partial x$, $\partial(\partial f/\partial x)/\partial y$. In particular it is easy to see that

(12) $$\underset{x}{\Delta}\underset{y}{\Delta} f = \underset{y}{\Delta}\underset{x}{\Delta} f,$$

because

(13) $$\underset{x}{\Delta}\underset{y}{\Delta} f = \underset{x}{\Delta}(f[x,y+1] - f[x,y])$$

$$= (f[x+1,y+1] - f[x,y+1]) - (f[x+1,y] - f[x,y])$$

$$= (f[x+1,y+1] - f[x+1,y]) - (f[x,y+1] - f[x,y])$$

$$= \underset{y}{\Delta} f[x+1,y] - \underset{y}{\Delta} f[x,y] = \underset{y}{\Delta}(f[x+1,y] - f[x,y])$$

$$= \Delta_y \Delta_x f.$$

Therefore, as in the case of partial differentiation, the order of differencing is immaterial.

2

This section of the appendix explains the principles of notation used in this book.

Square brackets relate primarily to the domain of a function (the only exception pertains to closed intervals). Parentheses are used for grouping operations. Curly brackets indicate sets. For example, $\mathscr{S} = \{x|P\}$ means that $\mathscr{S}$ is the set with elements x having property P. All sets are represented by capital, script letters.

Whenever possible, indices are avoided. Thus, if $f_i = f[x_1,..., x_n ;i]$, $\Delta_{x_i} f$, $\partial f/\partial x_i$ mean $\Delta_{x_i} f_i$, $\partial f_i/\partial x_i$. Only when there is a possibility of error, as in $\Delta_{x_i} f_j$, are indices explicitly shown.

Vector notation is the following. For $v,w \in \mathscr{R}^n$: $v \geq w$ means $v_i \geq w_i$ for $i = 1,...,n$; $v > w$ means $v_i \geq w_i$ for $i = 1,...,n$ and $v \neq w$; $v \gg w$ means $v_i > w_i$ for $i = 1,...,n$. All vectors are column vectors. Transposition is noted with a prime.

There is an effort to use symbols consistently. In the following list, symbols with variable meaning are only given their primary interpretation(s), noted by an asterisk.

Latin Symbols

a	The boundary area between production and residences.
A_i	The proportion of blacks in area i.
$\mathscr{A}$	A set describing individual allocations over the city.

Introduction

b	The boundary between the city and the alternative land use; the total number of distinct locations in the city.
B	A matrix.
c	Transportation costs of an individual.
C	Total urban transportation costs.
$\mathscr{c}$	Collective choice rule.
D	Deficit function.
e_i	Local traffic congestion in area i.
E	The total spatial externality effect.
E_i	Quality of the environment in area i.
f	A function.*
F	A function.
g	A function.*
G	The production function of a public good.
h	Index.*
H_i	The amount of land occupied by the public good in area i.
$\mathscr{H}_l$	The preference structure of individual l.
$\mathscr{H}$	The set of all possible vectors with components all $\mathscr{H}_l$.
i	Index.
I	The vector of locations in the city.
$\mathscr{I}$	The urban area as the set of locations in the city.
j	Index.
k	Index.
K	A state of society.
$\mathscr{K}$	The set of all possible states of society.
l	Index.
L	Lagrangean function.
LHS	The left-hand side of some relationship.
m	Number of income groups; number of land uses.*
M	Population of the city–state.
MEE	Marginal externality effects.
MLE	Marginal location effects.
MPB	Marginal private benefits.

MPC	Marginal private costs.
MRS	Marginal rate of substitution.
MSB	Marginal social benefits.
MSC	Marginal social costs.
n_i	The number of individuals in area i.
N	Population of the city.
$\mathcal{N}$	The domain of all feasible spatial distributions of the urban population.
NMSB	Net marginal social benefits.
NMSC	Net marginal social costs.
O_l	Preference ordering of individual l.
O	Social preference relation.
$\mathcal{O}$	The set of all possible preference relations.
p	Price.*
P	Public controls.
$\mathcal{P}$	The set of all possible vectors of prices.
q_i	Lot size for an individual in area i.
Q_i	The size of the area extending between the centre and boundary i.
r	Price per unit of land.
R	The total value of urban land.
$\mathcal{R}^n$	The n–dimensional Cartesian product of real numbers.
$\mathcal{R}_+$	The set of positive real numbers.
RHS	The right-hand side of some relationship.
s	Distance.
S	Total surplus value of urban production.
$\mathcal{S}$	Set of all possible sets of distances between agents.*
SWF	Social welfare function.
t	Time.
u_i	Utility of an individual in area i.
U	A vector with components that are all individual utility levels.

Introduction

$\mathcal{U}_l$	The set of all possible levels of utility associated with individual l.
v_l	Social valuation of the utility of individual l.*
W	Social welfare.
x_i	Consumption of the private good by an individual in area i.
x	A vector of quantities corresponding to that part of the state of society over which the individual is sensitive.
X	The value of what is produced in the city net of the associated transportation costs.
$\mathcal{X}$	The set of all possible vectors x.
y_i	The income of an individual in area i.
$\mathcal{Y}$	The set of incomes of income classes in the city.
z	A given level of utility.

Greek Symbols

α	Degree of aversion to inequality.*
β	A parameter.*
γ	A parameter.*
δ	Discrete differential.
Δ	First difference.
ζ_{ij}	Distance–response function.
$\eta_{x:y}$	The elasticity of x with respect to y.
θ	An angle.
λ_i	Lagrangean multiplier.*
μ_j	Lagrangean multiplier.*
ν	A number.*
ξ	Density–response function.
Π	Product.
ρ_i	Population density in area i.
σ	The bid–rent function.
Σ	Summation.

Introduction

v	The indirect utility function.
φ	Tax or subsidy.*
Φ^n	Total revenue from congestion taxes.
ψ	The expenditure function.*
ω_i	Public expenditure in area i.
Ω	Total amount of resources.

Other Symbols

∎	End of proof.
$\|\cdot\|$	The determinant of a matrix.*
$\approx$	Approximate equality.
$\equiv$	Identity.
$\subset$	Subset of.
$A \backslash B$	The complement of B relative to A.
$\in$	Element of.
$f\|_a$	A function evaluated at a.
$f\|_a^b$	A function evaluated between a and b.
$f : \mathscr{A} \to \mathscr{P}$	A function with domain $\mathscr{A}$ and range $\mathscr{P}$.
$\times$	Cartesian product.

3

This section of the appendix contains a partial list of definitions for concepts used in the book. A knowledge of elementary differential calculus is assumed throughout. Also necessary for some appendices is a knowledge of elementary linear algebra. Thus definitions of a derivative, a matrix, the determinant of a matrix etc. are assumed to be known. If not, there would be no point in giving a brief definition. On the other hand, several other elementary concepts used, and not requiring a considerable length of exposition in order to be explained, are included

Introduction

to help the memory. When necessary, differentiability of functions is implicitly assumed.

Bid demand function. A solution to the problem of maximizing land rent subject to utility and income constraints, with other prices held constant.

Bid-rent function. For a particular individual in the urban sector, it is that particular pattern of land rents which would generate a given maximum feasible level of utility over the entire urban area. The concept may also apply to any type of economic activity.

Bounded sets. Let $\mathscr{S} \subset \mathscr{R}^n$. If there exists x^* such that $x^* \leq x$ for all $x \in \mathscr{S}$ then $\mathscr{S}$ is bounded below. If there exists x^* such that $x^* \geq x$ for all $x \in \mathscr{S}$ then $\mathscr{S}$ is bounded above. If a set is bounded both below and above then it is bounded.

Brouwer's theorem. Let $\mathscr{S} \in \mathscr{R}^n$ be nonempty, compact and convex, and let $f : \mathscr{S} \to \mathscr{S}$ be continuous. Then there exists $x^* \in \mathscr{S}$ such that $f[x^*] = x^*$.

Cartesian product. Consider two sets $\mathscr{S}$ and $\mathscr{P}$. The set of ordered pairs (s,p) where $s \in \mathscr{S}$ and $p \in \mathscr{P}$ is their cartesian product $\mathscr{S} \times \mathscr{P}$.

Casetti equilibrium. A city where the maximum feasible level of utility is the same across the entire urban area.

Choice function. A choice function ascertains that, in every subset of alternatives that belong to its domain, there is at least one alternative at least as good as any other alternative in that subset.

Closed city. A city with variable equilibrium utility level and fixed equilibrium population.

Closure. A set is closed if and only if every point at zero distance from the set belongs to the set.

Compactness. A closed and bounded set is compact.

Compensated demand function. A solution to the problem of minimising expenditure subject to a utility constraint, with prices held fixed.

Completeness. For any $K^1, K^2 \in \mathcal{K}$, either K^1 is preferred to K^2, or K^2 to K^1, or there is indifference between K^1 and K^2.

Concave function. Let $\mathcal{S}$ be convex and $f: \mathcal{S} \to \mathcal{R}^n$. If, for all $x^1, x^2 \in \mathcal{S}$, and for $0 \le v \le 1$,

$$(1 - v)f[x^1] + vf[x^2] \le f[(1 - v)x^1 + vx^2]$$

then f is concave. Strict concavity means that the above condition holds with strict inequality.

Connected set. A set is connected if and only if it cannot be partitioned in two nonempty, closed subsets.

Constrained optimisation. Suppose that the problem is to

$$\underset{x}{maximise}\ f[x]\ subject\ to\ g[x] - y \le 0\ and\ x \ge a$$

where $f: \mathcal{S} \to \mathcal{R}$, g is a vector of m functions $g_i: \mathcal{S} \to \mathcal{R}$, with $\mathcal{S} \subset \mathcal{R}^n$, $a \in \mathcal{R}^n$ and $y \in \mathcal{R}^m$; and where a and y are fixed. Define the *lagrangean function*

$$L \equiv f[x] + \lambda'(y - g[x])$$

where $\lambda \in \mathscr{R}^m$ consists of lagrangean multipliers to be determined. A solution (x^*, λ^*) to the above problem satisfies the following $m + n$ necessary (Kuhn–Tucker) conditions, which may then be used to determine the $m + n$ unknowns:

$$\lambda \geq 0 \text{ and } \lambda_i(y_i - g_i[x]) = 0 \text{ for } i = 1,...,m$$

(*) $\quad \dfrac{\partial L}{\partial x_j} = \dfrac{\partial f}{\partial x_j} - \sum_{i=1}^{m} \lambda_i \dfrac{\partial g_i}{\partial x_j} \leq 0 \text{ and either } \dfrac{\partial L}{\partial x_j} = 0, \text{ or } x_j = a_j,$

or both for $j = 1,...,n$.

A solution may or may not exist. If it exists and if $x^* \gg a$ then it is called an interior solution. In that case the necessary conditions (*) for an optimum reduce to

$$\dfrac{\partial f}{\partial x_j} - \sum_{i=1}^{m} \lambda_i \dfrac{\partial g_i}{\partial x_j} = 0 \text{ for } j = 1,...,n.$$

When the problem is to

$$\underset{x}{minimise} \, f[x] \text{ subject to } g[x] - y \geq 0 \text{ and } x \geq a$$

then the inequality sign in (*) is reversed. In any case, when $\lambda^* \gg 0$, $g[x^*] - y = 0$. Then, applying the envelope theorem,

$$\lambda_i^* = \dfrac{\partial f^*}{\partial y_i} \text{ for } i = 1,...,m,$$

that is, lagrangean multipliers represent the marginal rate of change of the objective function at the optimum with respect to a change in the corresponding constraints. For sufficient conditions of constrained optimisation problems, as well as for a good overview of the field, see Dixit (1976).

Continuity of preferences. Strict preference between two states of society is not affected by sufficiently small changes in either or both.

Convex function. Let $\mathscr{S}$ be convex and $f: \mathscr{S} \to \mathscr{R}^n$. If, for all $x^1, x^2 \in \mathscr{S}$ and for $0 \leq v \leq 1$,

$$(1-v)f[x^1] + vf[x^2] \geq f[(1-v)x^1 + vx^2]$$

then f is convex. Strict convexity means that the above condition holds with strict inequality.

Convex set. Let $\mathscr{S} \subset \mathscr{R}^n$ with x and $y \in \mathscr{S}$. Then $\mathscr{S}$ is convex if and only if it owns the closed segment (x,y) for any x and y.

Cramer's rule. Consider a matrix A with elements a_{ij}. The corresponding elements of the inverse matrix are given by

$$a_{ij}^{-1} = \|A^{i,j}\|/\|A\|,$$

where $\|A^{i,j}\|$ is the determinant of a matrix obtained from A by replacing column i by a vector with a unit component in row j and zeros everywhere else.

Decisiveness. An individual is decisive over two states of society K^1 and K^2 if and only if, when the individual prefers K^1 to K^2 (or K^2 to K^1), so does society.

Dominant diagonal matrix. An $n \times n$ matrix A with elements a_{ij} has a dominant diagonal if there exist positive numbers $b_1,...,b_n$ such that

Introduction

$$|a_{ii}|b_i > \sum_{j \neq i} |a_{ij}|b_j \ for \ i = 1,...,n.$$

Elasticity of a function. Let $f : \mathscr{S} \to \mathscr{R}$ with $\mathscr{S} \subset \mathscr{R}^n$ and $x \in \mathscr{S}$. Then the elasticity of f with respect to x_i is

$$\eta_{f:xi} \equiv \frac{\partial f}{\partial x_i} \div \frac{f}{x_i}.$$

The elasticity denotes the relative change in f associated with a corresponding change in x_i. For discrete quantities,

$$\eta_{f:xi} \equiv \bigtriangleup_{x_i} f \div \frac{f}{x_i}.$$

Envelope theorem. Suppose that the problem is to

$$\underset{x}{maximise} \ f[x,b] \ subject \ to \ h[x,b] = 0$$

where x, h and b are vectors, with b fixed. The lagrangean function is

$$L \equiv f[x,b] + \lambda' h[x,b].$$

Denote by (x^*, λ^*) a solution to the problem and let $f^* \equiv f[x^*[b],b]$. Then it is true that

$$\frac{\partial f^*}{\partial b_j} = \frac{\partial L}{\partial b_j} = \frac{\partial f}{\partial b_j} + (\lambda^*)' \frac{\partial h}{\partial b_j}$$

for all b_j. See for example Dixit (1976, chapter three).

Externality. This occurs when the social conditions for optimal resource allocation are violated under a state of competitive equilibrium.

Homogeneous function. Let $x \in \mathscr{R}^n$ and $\lambda \in \mathscr{R}$. Then a function $f[x] = y$

is β–homogeneous with respect to its arguments if and only if $f[\lambda x] = \lambda^\beta y$. The Euler theorem for such functions states that

$$\sum_i \frac{\partial f}{\partial x_i} x_i = \beta y.$$

For a discussion see Chiang (1974, chapter twelve).

Hôpital's rule. Let $f[x]$ and $g[x]$ be continuous over an interval containing a. If $f[a]$ and $g[a]$ are both zero or infinite and if $\lim_{x \to a}(f'/g')$ exists then

$$\lim_{x \to a} \frac{f}{g} = \lim_{x \to a} \frac{f'}{g'}.$$

Independence of irrelevant alternatives. Social choice over a set of alternatives should only depend on individual preference orderings over this particular set of alternatives.

Indifference surface. For a utility function, this is the set of solutions $u[z] = \bar{u}$, where $\bar{u}$ is a constant. For an SWF, this is the set of solutions $W[u] = \bar{W}$, where $\bar{W}$ is a constant.

Indirect utility function. Let y be the income of an individual with (direct) utility function u, defined over a vector of commodities x with corresponding fixed prices p. Suppose that the problem of the individual is to

$$\underset{x}{maximise}\ u[x]\ subject\ to\ p'x - y \leq 0$$

with lagrangean function

$$L \equiv u[x] + \lambda(y - p'x).$$

Introduction

Let $(x^*[p,y], \lambda^*)$ be an interior solution. Replacing it in the utility function, one obtains the corresponding indirect utility function

$$u[x^*[p,y]] \equiv v[p,y]$$

which determines the optimal level of utility, given a level of income and a vector of prices. Using the envelope theorem, it is also true that

$$\frac{\partial v}{\partial p_i} = -\lambda^* x^*_i$$

for all i. Compare this with

$$\frac{\partial u}{\partial x_i}\bigg|_{x^*} = \lambda^* p_i$$

for all i, which represents the corresponding necessary conditions for an optimum.

Integration by parts. $\int_a^b f\, dg + \int_a^b g\, df = fg|_b - fg|_a$.

Interior solution. See "constrained optimisation".

Intervals. Let $\mathcal{K} \subset \mathcal{R}$. $\mathcal{K}$ is an interval if $x,y \in \mathcal{K}$ and $x \leq z \leq y$ implies $z \in \mathcal{K}$. When $a < x < b$ implies $x \in \mathcal{K}$ and $a,b \in \mathcal{K}$, the interval $[a,b]$ is closed. When $a < x < b$ implies $x \in \mathcal{K}$ but $a, b \notin \mathcal{K}$, the interval $]a,b[$ is open. Other types are the open–closed ($]a,b]$) and the closed–open ($[a,b[$). The concept can obviously be generalised to $\mathcal{K} \subset \mathcal{R}^n$.

Jacobian. Let $f : \mathcal{R}^m \to \mathcal{R}^n$ be differentiable. The matrix

$$\begin{bmatrix} \frac{\partial f_1}{\partial x_1} & \cdots & \frac{\partial f_1}{\partial x_m} \\ \vdots & & \vdots \\ \frac{\partial f_n}{\partial x_1} & \cdots & \frac{\partial f_n}{\partial x_m} \end{bmatrix}$$

is the Jacobian of f.

Kuhn-Tucker theory. See "constrained optimisation".

Leibnitz rule.

$$\frac{d}{da} \int_{g[a]}^{f[a]} h[x,a] \, dx = \int_{g[a]}^{f[a]} \frac{\partial h}{\partial a} \, dx + h[f,a] \frac{df}{da} - h[g,a] \frac{dg}{da}.$$

Lindahl price. Denotes the amount of money an individual is prepared to pay for increasing public investment by one dollar, thereby increasing the level of public good experienced, with utility held constant.

Marginal benefit. For some level of activity, it is the additional benefit realized by an additional unit of that activity.

Marginal cost. For some level of activity, it is the additional cost for an additional unit of that activity.

Marginal principle. The optimal size of some activity is where marginal costs are precisely balanced by marginal benefits.

Marginal rate of substitution. For a utility function u defined over a vector of commodities x, and along a given indifference surface, the ratio $(\partial u/\partial x_i)/(\partial u/\partial x_j)$ is the MRS of x_i with respect to x_j.

Nondictatorship. Social choice should not coincide with the preference ordering of any individual irrespective of the preference orderings of the rest.

"Open" city. A city with variable equilibrium population and fixed equilibrium utility level.

Opportunity cost of land. The bid–rent for the alternative (agricultural) sector.

Optimal decentralisation policy. A way of maintaining an optimum with the least possible public interference.

Ordinary demand function. A solution to the problem of maximizing utility subject to an income constraint, with prices held fixed.

Pareto efficiency. A state of society is Pareto efficient if and only if no one can increase his welfare without decreasing the welfare of someone else.

Pareto principle. For any $K^1, K^2 \in \mathcal{K}$, if every individual is indifferent between K^1 and K^2 then society should also be indifferent between K^1 and K^2. If at least one individual prefers K^1 to K^2, while the rest maintain that K^1 is at least as good as K^2, society should prefer K^1 to K^2.

Piecemeal policy. The application of only part of an optimal decentralisation policy.

Real-income compensated demand. For a particular commodity, it gives the demand at different price levels with income adjusted at the same time just enough to keep utility constant.

Rectangular set. One with elements belonging to intervals.

Reflexivity. A relation is reflexive if and only if every element over which this relation is defined is related to itself.

Returns to scale. Let a combination of inputs determine an output. Consider changes in a particular input with all other inputs held constant. If, as the input increases, associated costs increase relatively faster (slower) than benefits corresponding to the associated output change, the output exhibits decreasing (increasing) returns to scale with respect to that input—at that particular scale of the output. If the increase of costs is proportional to the corresponding increase of benefits, the output exhibits constant returns to scale with respect to that input—at that particular scale of the output.

Segments. Let $\mathscr{S} \subset \mathscr{R}^n$, and $x, y \in \mathscr{S}$. The closed segment (x,y) is the set with elements $(1 - v)x + vy$ for $0 \le v \le 1$. In two dimensions, this is the straight line between two points. An open segment is defined for $0 < v < 1$ and so on (see "intervals").

Shadow prices. These are associated with entities that do not have a direct money value, yet they influence choice. In chapter seven, for example, the shadow price of the quality of the environment is given by

$$\lambda \frac{\partial u}{\partial E} = \frac{dy}{d\bar{u}} \frac{\partial u}{\partial E},$$

which specifies the income rise necessary to attain a maximum possible level of utility precisely equal to that resulting from a unit rise in the quality of the environment. What a shadow price does is to make intangible factors directly comparable with commodities by attaching to the former a money value through the lagrangean multiplier. Notice for example that everything in (7.3) is expressed in terms of money, the last by virtue of λ.

Introduction

Strictly quasiconcave function. Let $f: \mathscr{S} \to \mathscr{R}^n$. If $x^1, x^2 \in \mathscr{S}$, $x^1 \neq x^2$ and $f[x^2] \geq f[x^1]$ imply $f[x] > f[x^1]$ for x belonging to the open segment (x^1, x^2) then f is strictly quasiconcave. Form the determinant of second-order partial derivatives

$$\begin{vmatrix} f_{11} & \cdots & f_{1n} \\ \vdots & & \vdots \\ f_{n1} & \cdots & f_{nn} \end{vmatrix}$$

The principal minors of order 2 to n are alternatively positive and negative, i.e.

$$\begin{vmatrix} f_{11} & f_{12} \\ f_{22} & f_{22} \end{vmatrix} > 0, \quad \begin{vmatrix} f_{11} & f_{12} & f_{13} \\ f_{21} & f_{22} & f_{23} \\ f_{31} & f_{32} & f_{33} \end{vmatrix} < 0, \ldots$$

For a discussion see, for example, Henderson and Quandt (1980, appendix A.3).

"Transient" city. A city with variable equilibrium levels of population and utility.

Transitivity. For any $K^1, K^2, K^3 \in \mathscr{K}$, if K^1 is preferred to or is indifferent to K^2, and K^2 is preferred to or is indifferent to K^3 then K^1 is also preferred to or is indifferent to K^3.

Unrestricted domain. The collective choice rule should be defined over all possible sets of individual preference orderings.

Utility–possibility frontier. For every possible combination of $n-1$ utility levels in a society of n individuals, the utility–possibility frontier gives the set of maximum possible utility levels for the remaining individual.

Weak libertarianism. Every individual is decisive over at least one pair of states of society.

Weak Pareto principle. For any $K^1, K^2 \in \mathcal{K}$, if every individual prefers K^1 to K^2 then society should also prefer K^1 to K^2.

Willingness to pay. Consider an individual having experienced an exogenous change in his utility level. His willingness to pay is that amount of money which, if taken away (given), will reduce (increase) his utility to the initial level.

Notes to the Introduction

1   This is drawn from Papageorgiou (1977).

2   The main simplifications and their consequences are as follows. Firstly, there is a single urban centre. In this manner one avoids the little-understood problems which arise within systems of cities (Henderson (1977)), including issues of central place theory at the interurban level (Christaller (1933)); the somewhat inflated literature on local political jurisdictions stemming from the classic paper of Tiebout (1956); and multicentric forms, including issues of central place theory at the interurban level. Secondly, residences are produced with land alone. In this manner one excludes the large field of housing (Muth (1969), Sweeney (1974)), with all its extensions to filtering (Ohls (1975)), urban renewal (Schall (1976)) and the like; and, since land alone does not age, one is able to eliminate dynamics altogether (Fugita (1976), Anas (1978), Arnott (1980)).

3   One definition of an externality is that it occurs when the social conditions for optimal resource allocation are violated under a state

of competitive equilibrium. A more explicit definition, which describes the economic conditions leading to such violation, is the following.

> "An externality is present whenever some individual's (say A's) *utility* or *production* relationships include real (that is, nonmonetary) variables, whose values are chosen by others (persons, corporations, governments) without particular attention to the effects on A's welfare.
>
> This definition should not be misunderstood to be a simple equation of externalities with economic interdependence. When I rely on the farmer for my food, no externality need be involved, for he does not decide for me how many zucchini I will consume, nor does my consumption enter directly into his utility function. Note also that the definition rules out cases in which someone *deliberately* does something to affect A's welfare ... If I purposely maneuver my car to splatter mud on a pedestrian whom I happen to dislike, he is given no choice in the amount of mud he 'consumes', but one would not normally regard this as an externality." (Baumol and Oates (1975, p. 17))

4   There is some incidental use of other mathematical tools, but they could be avoided without any significant loss of intuition. This happens because they are consistently associated with what here is considered to be peripheral, such as the existence of equilibria, stability and the like.

1

Agglomeration [1]

This book unfolds around a single centre—pivot of the city. One therefore is bound to seek at the very beginning a plausible reason for such agglomeration. The phenomenon is not well understood. Complexity renders futile any attempt to seek *the* model of agglomeration. In consequence each of a growing number of theoretical studies concentrates on some particular aspect, thereby contributing to the list of known, partially interconnected, reasons for the existence of cities.[2] Within this literature, three main classes of reasons for agglomeration may be identified: the city as a centre of production, the city as a public good and the city as a marketplace. It is intuitively clear that the reason behind the city as a centre of production is increasing returns, and that the reason behind the city as a public good is public investment. These matters will be discussed later. But the reason behind the city as a marketplace is not intuitively clear, as for example the persistence of periodic markets throughout history tends to suggest.[3] This is precisely the object of analysis here. In particular, out of the several possibilities already mentioned, I choose to discuss how certain market activities potentially benefit from physical proximity to each other, thus creating agglomeration in the long run—the centre.

Agglomeration

Consider a distribution of agents over some featureless landscape. The precise nature of agents is not yet defined. One may however take them as individuals, firms etc. The important feature of such spatial distributions now is the set of distances between agents, s_{jk} being the distance between agent j and agent k. The vector $s_j \equiv (s_{j1}, s_{j2}, ...)$ describes the position of agent j relative to the other agents in the landscape. The vector of vectors $s \equiv (s_1, s_2, ...)$ reflects any spatial distribution of agents with distances between agents s. All possible spatial distributions give rise to the set $\mathscr{S}$, $s \in \mathscr{S}$. If agents can float smoothly within the entire landscape and if the landscape is a closed set then $\mathscr{S}$ is also a closed set.

Agents engage in a number of economic activities involving spatial interaction between them. An agent may engage in any mix of such economic activities.[4] For economic activity i, p_i is the price per unit net of transportation costs. The vector $p \equiv (p_1, p_2, ...) \gg 0$ describes the prices of economic activities. All possible such vectors give rise to the set $\mathscr{P}$, $p \in \mathscr{P}$. If prices are constrained by some upper and lower bounds that belong to $\mathscr{P}$ and if they can assume any value within the consequent, corresponding, closed intervals then $\mathscr{P}$ is a closed rectangular set.[5]

The demand for economic activity i, f_i, is partitioned among agents, f_{ij} being that part of the demand for economic activity i which is satisfied by agent j. Obviously $\sum_j f_{ij} = f_i$. The vector $f_j \equiv (f_{1j}, f_{2j}, ...)$ defines the rôle of agent j in this economy. The vector $f \equiv (f_1, f_2, ...) = \sum_j f_j$ describes the demand for economic activities. Agents are also related to costs and profits, g_j and h_j being the cost incurred by the agent j and the profit of agent j respectively, where

$$(1.1) \quad h_j \equiv \sum_i p_i f_{ij} - g_j.$$

The vectors $g \equiv (g_1, g_2, ...)$ and $h \equiv (h_1, h_2, ...)$ describe the costs incurred by the agents and the profits of agents respectively. Since the pattern of demands, costs and profits depends both on prices and on the pattern of interaction between agents; and since, intuitively, the latter depends on the spatial distribution of agents, it follows that the pattern of demands, costs and profits depends on prices and on spatial distributions. In consequence it is reasonable to assert that f, g and h are continuous on $\mathcal{P} \times \mathcal{S}$.

What may draw agents together? Agents receive the product of others and distribute their product to others. With respect to the former, agents may agglomerate under an expectation of lower prices. With respect to the latter, they may agglomerate under an expectation of higher demand for their product. And, in any case, the tendency to agglomerate should be grounded on the expectation of higher profit. Of course, only some economic activities exhibit such desirable attributes with agglomeration.[6] One may indeed visualize economic activities grouped into sets according to whether they tend to agglomerate. Such economic activities are *compatible*.

I now restrict my attention to a set of economic activities characterized by the following properties. For every (p^1,s), $(p^2,s) \in \mathcal{P} \times \mathcal{S}$:

(1.2) $\qquad$ if $p^1 \leq p^2$ and $p^1_i = p^2_i$ then $f_i[p^1,s] \leq f_i[p^2,s]$,

in other words, if the price of an economic activity remains constant then the demand for this economic activity does not decrease because of other possible price increases;

(1.3) $\qquad$ if $p^1 < p^2$ and $p^1_i = p^2_i$ then there exists l such that

$$p^1_l = p^2_l \text{ and } f_l[p^1,s] < f_l[p^2,s],$$

in other words, if some prices increase while the rest remain constant then the demand for some economic activity (associated with an unchanged price) increases; and

(1.4)   if $p^1 \neq p^2$ then there exists i such that

$$(p_i^1 - p_i^2)(f_i[p^1,s] - f_i[p^2,s]) < 0,$$

in other words, if there is a change in prices then there is an economic activity with higher price and lower demand or vice versa.[7] It turns out that this set of economic activities becomes compatible if agglomeration reduces aggregate production costs.[8] This last desirable property, named *agglomeration economies*, is not strong enough to ensure agglomeration by itself. Its nature cannot be other than aggregate as the external effects of agglomeration may prove costly for some agents. On the other hand it has already been argued that, at least where location decisions rest with the agents of the economy, agglomeration advantages must in principle refer to these agents. Thus, given the distinction between aggregated agglomeration economies and disaggregated agglomeration advantages, there is nothing much at this stage to ascertain that the former lead to the latter. If however the set of economic activities under consideration obeys properties (1.2)–(1.4) then agglomeration economies lead to certain agglomeration advantages.

The precise nature of such agglomeration advantages is determined through comparisons of two states of the system, a *dispersed state* and an *agglomerated state*. These differ with respect to the spatial distribution of agents. In particular if $s, s^* \in \mathscr{S}$ and $s_j > s_j^*$ for all j then the state associated with s (s^*) is called a dispersed (agglomerated) state. Since the spatial distribution varies between states, demand is also expected to vary—even under the same system of prices. This affects the definition of agglomeration economies as follows. For every $p \in \mathscr{P}$ and $s, s^* \in \mathscr{S}$ such that $s_j > s_j^*$ for all j, if

(1.5) $f[p,s] \leq f[p,s^*]$ and $\sum_j g_j[p,s] > \sum_j g_j[p,s^*]$

then (p,s^*) is said to admit agglomeration economies with respect to (p,s). Property (1.5) asserts that the aggregate costs of production for the agglomerated state are lower than the aggregate costs of production for the dispersed state. This must be attributed to spatial proximity: the only other difference, related to total demand, is specified in a way that strengthens this conclusion.

I finish the description of circumstances under which agglomeration economies imply agglomeration advantages with two observations on the nature of cost and profit.

1. Externalities are fully taken into account since cost may well depend explicitly on both the entire pattern of demands and spatial arrangement as $g[f[p,s],s]$. The formulation is general enough to allow for the incredibly complex and subtle net of spatial interactions. This is important because significantly less remains to be understood of entities that shape urban form after externalities have been discounted.

2. There is no explicit mechanism for the determination of profits or indeed of prices. In consequence the same conclusions apply equally well to both market and to planned economies. This is also important because similar urban forms appear to transcend the entire gamut of socioeconomic systems.

Consider now any state (dispersed state) with given profits, prices and demands that corresponds to a nonempty set of states (agglomerated states). Then, for the kind of world described, the following proposition is true.[9]

1.1 *If there are agglomeration economies then any agglomerated state can support a higher aggregate profit and, for any economic activity, a lower price and a higher demand than those attained in the dispersed state.*

The aggregate nature of agglomeration economies has already been stressed. Yet the proposition demonstrates that such economies generate

Agglomeration

advantages specific to the agents of the economy: further to a higher potential for profit, agents as consumers face the possibility of a lower price for every single economic activity and agents as producers face the possibility of higher demand for all their products. Although strong, these represent potential rather than actual advantages because the attainment of such desirable conditions remains a matter of speculation.[10] This, in turn, implies the adoption of a somewhat Darwinian principle: if for certain classes of economic activity agglomeration is potentially more successful than dispersion then the former will eventually dominate the latter.

Based on these results, the isolated city–state will emerge as follows. There is a single class of compatible economic activities of the kind already discussed and there is a class of activities that do not agglomerate, which may represent agriculture. Agents can change from one class to another but they cannot be associated with both. Further, for the class of compatible economic activities, agglomeration economies persist. In this world agglomeration economies imply agglomeration. Then it must be that *there is a single, spatially compact node of economic activity associated with the class of compatible economic activities*. Otherwise agglomeration economies do not persist, a contradiction. This single node represents the centre around which the city will unfold. The entire book is based on that premise.

Appendix to Chapter One

This appendix contains a proof of the proposition that, with agglomeration economies on a set of compatible economic activities, any agglomerated state can support a higher aggregate profit and, for any economic activity, a lower price and a higher demand than those attained in the dispersed state.

If $\mathscr{A}$ is closed, if $\mathscr{P}$ is closed rectangular and if f, g and h are continuous on $\mathscr{P} \times \mathscr{S}$ then, for compatible economic activities, the following two lemmata are true.

1.2   *If $f[p^1,s] \le f[p^2,s]$ then there exists a continuous mapping $p : [0,1] \to \mathscr{P}$ such that*

$$p[0] = p^1$$
$$p[1] = p^2$$
$$(1 - v) f[p^1,s] + vf[p^2,s] = f[p[v],s] \text{ for } 0 \le v \le 1.\text{[11]}$$

1.3   *If $f[p^1,s] > f[p^2,s]$ then $p^1 \ll p^2$.*[12]

One may now claim the following intermediate proposition.

1.4   *For compatible economic activities, suppose that (p^1,s^*) admits agglomeration economies with respect to (p^1,s) and that $p^2 \in \mathscr{P}$. If $\sum_j h_j [p^1,s] > \sum_j h_j [p^2,s^*]$ and $f[p^1,s^*] \ll f[p^2,s^*]$ then there exists $(p,s^*) \in \mathscr{P} \times \mathscr{S}$ such that*

$$\sum_j h_j [p,s^*] = \sum_j h_j [p^1,s]$$

$$p \ll p^1$$

$$\sum_j f_j [p,s^*] \gg \sum_j f_j [p,s].\text{[13]}$$

Taking into account (1.1) and (1.5)

$$(1.6) \quad \sum_j h_j [p^1,s] = \sum_j \sum_i p^1_i f_{ij} [p^1,s] - \sum_j g_j [p^1,s]$$
$$< \sum_j \sum_i p^1_i f_{ij} [p^1,s] - \sum_j g_j [p^1,s^*]$$
$$\le \sum_j \sum_i p^1_i f_{ij} [p^1,s^*] - \sum_j g_j [p^1,s^*].$$

Agglomeration

Hence

$$(1.7) \quad \sum_j h_j [p^1,s^*] > \sum_j h_j [p^1,s].$$

Since $f[p^1,s^*] \ll f[p^2,s^*]$ then, according to lemma 1.2, there exists a continuous mapping $p : [0,1] \to \mathcal{P}$ such that

$$(1.8) \quad p[0] = p^1$$

$$(1.9) \quad p[1] = p^2$$

$$(1.10) \quad (1-v) f[p^1,s^*] + v f[p^2,s^*] = f[p[v],s^*]$$

for $0 \le v \le 1$. Now, with s^* fixed, $\sum_j h_j : [0,1] \to \mathcal{R}$ is continuous on [0,1]. Furthermore, using (1.7) and (1.8),

$$(1.11) \quad \sum_j h_j [p[0],s^*] > \sum_j h_j [p^1,s]$$

while

$$(1.12) \quad \sum_j h_j [p[1],s^*] < \sum_j h_j [p^1,s]$$

by premise and (1.9). In consequence there exists μ, $0 < \mu < 1$, such that

$$(1.13) \quad \sum_j h_j [p[\mu],s^*] = \sum_j h_j [p^1,s].$$

Also

$$(1.14) \quad f[p[\mu],s^*] = (1-\mu) f[p^1,s^*] + \mu f[p^2,s^*]$$

$$\gg (1-\mu) f[p^1,s^*] + \mu f[p^1,s^*]$$

by (1.10) and by premise. Thus

40

(1.15) $f[p[\mu],s^*] \gg f[p^1,s^*] = \sum_j f_j [p^1,s^*] \geq \sum_j f_j [p^1,s]$

by (1.5). Finally

(1.16) $p[\mu] \ll p^1$

according to lemma 1.3. ∎

It should be noted that the validity of proposition 1.4 depends on the existence of a hypothetical price vector p^2 with the following properties. The agglomerated state under the hypothetical price system would correspond to lower profits than those of the dispersed state under the existing price system. Furthermore, the demand in the agglomerated state under the hypothetical price system would be strictly higher than the corresponding demand under the existing price system. To postulate the existence of a hypothetical price system with these properties does not appear restrictive. One could for example lower the established prices of the dispersed state and apply them to the agglomerated state. Prices could be reduced to an extent that costs were not covered. In this case one would normally expect higher demand for the economic activities under consideration.

Proposition 1.4 describes advantages of agglomeration economies for situations of equal aggregate profit. It is easy however to strengthen these results by observing that, in conjunction with (1.13), there is $0 < \mu^* < \mu$ such that

(1.17) $\sum_j h_j [p[\mu^*],s^*] > \sum_j h_j [p^1,s]$

and such that the remaining assertions of the proposition are met. Hence at little additional cost the main conclusions of proposition 1.4 can be restated in the form of proposition 1.1.

Notes to Chapter One

1 This chapter draws upon Papageorgiou (1979). The whole idea is an extensive modification of Sandberg (1975).

2 See for example Stuart (1970), Starrett (1974), Baesemann (1977), Arnott (1979), Papageorgiou (1979), Ogawa and Fugita (1980), Shaked (1982), Wolinsky (1983), and Papageorgiou and Smith (1983).

3 It is perhaps interesting at this point to note a close correspondence between what belongs to the deductive urban literature and what belongs to the realm of the humanities. In the latter, four main classes of reasons for agglomeration have been identified (Carter (1977)): surplus theories, the city as a wall, the city as a temple and the city as a marketplace. Surplus theories arise in societies beyond subsistence agriculture. There, some may exist without being involved in primary production. Under these circumstances and under increasing returns to agglomeration, the city is born. Thus surplus theories correspond to the city as a centre of production. The wall and the temple on the other hand are specific instances of a public good.

4 This is a very general point of view. Labour may serve as a concrete example of an economic activity. If convenient, labour may be partitioned into distinct types, each type being a distinct economic activity. The retailing of feathers may serve as another concrete example of an economic activity. An agent on the other hand could labour to collect feathers to retail them.

5 This is not an excessive requirement: lower bounds can be as close to zero as desired and upper bounds can also be as large as desired.

6   Tourism and retail may tend to agglomerate. Tourism and heavy industry may not.

7   In other words the set of economic activities under consideration is exclusively formed by weak gross substitutes.

8   Such a phenomenon may for example be accounted for by consequent transportation savings.

9   The validity of the proposition depends on some additional technical requirements discussed in the appendix, which contains a proof.

10   This happens because the proposition says that there is a better state but it does not say what this better state is or how to arrive at it. Hence this better state may remain undiscovered for all time.

11   See Papageorgiou (1979). The proof is a modification of theorem 13.5.2 of Ortega and Rheinboldt (1970, pp. 464–466). It also draws upon theorem 5, part one of Gale and Nikaidô (1965, p. 87).

12   See Papageorgiou (1979).

13   This proof is based on theorem 2 of Sandberg (1976, p. 355).

Part One

EQUILIBRIUM

2

Individual Behaviour

There are several ways in which one could analyse urban phenomena. One such way is to view the city as a collection of individuals. In this context, it is necessary to provide a model of human behaviour that serves as the building–block of cities. Chapter two introduces the essentials of such a model, based on microeconomic theory, which provides the foundation for most arguments in this book. Chapter three transfers this model into an explicitly spatial framework.

Preferences [1]

Variations in human character imply variations in preference structure. Let $\mathcal{H}_1$ be the preference structure of individual l. Preferences cover everything, from choice of food to position in matters of art and politics. The expression of preference is constrained by existing conditions. Within a particular environment, expressed preferences reflect and sometimes reveal the character of individuals.

Particular preferences imply a particular preference ordering $\mathcal{O}_1$, $\mathcal{H}_1 \rightarrow \mathcal{O}_1$. Since preferences define our position on everything, a pref–

Individual Behaviour

erence ordering represents a natural choice rule. Hence preferences guide choice and this provides a theory of motivation needed to explain decision behaviour.

The theory has often been associated with hedonism, whereby human actions are driven by an incessant desire for pleasure. The error with such views is that the theory may apply to any motivation: even saints have (admittedly unusual) preference structures; and a propensity to sacrifice for the sake of society or for the sake of the future or for any other reasonable or unreasonable purpose, being irrelevant, does not present any conceptual difficulties. Thus the theory covers any purposive behaviour. Conversely any reasonable teleological approach is bound to consider human happiness and therefore human preferences.

Expression of Preferences

Preferences are expressed through choice. Choice refers to states of society, K being such a state,—a complete description of society at this state. All possible states of society give rise to the set $\mathcal{K}$, $K \in \mathcal{K}$. Clearly a state of society is beyond human comprehension. In consequence any individual is sensitive over a small part of the state of society and remains indifferent over the rest.

Preferences and their expression, choice, are extremely complex phenomena. Nevertheless if preference orderings obey *transitivity, completeness* and *continuity* then the expression of individual preferences becomes extremely simple. Transitivity of preferences means that, for any K^1, K^2 and $K^3 \in \mathcal{K}$, if an individual prefers K^1 to K^2 or is indifferent between the two and K^2 to K^3 or is indifferent between the two then he also prefers K^1 to K^3 or is indifferent between the two. Completeness of preferences means that, for any K^1 and $K^2 \in \mathcal{K}$, an individual either prefers K^1 to K^2 or K^2 to K^1 or is indifferent between the two. Continuity of preferences means that strict preference between two states of society is not affected by sufficiently small changes in

Individual Behaviour

either or in both states of society. Transitivity and completeness assert that individuals are able to rank any alternative states of society according to preference. Continuity on the other hand is not strictly necessary for the development of fundamental choice theory. If however all three attributes hold together then the following proposition is true.[2]

2.1 *Every preference ordering $\mathcal{H}_1$ which satisfies transitivity, completeness and continuity, and is defined over a convex set of states of society, can be represented by a continuous function $u_1 : \mathcal{H} \to \mathcal{R}$ such that, for any K^1 and $K^2 \in \mathcal{H}$, $u_1[K^1] \geq u_1[K^2]$ if and only if K^1 is preferred or is regarded indifferently to K^2.*[3]

The function u_1 is called a utility function. Under u_1, the expression of individual preferences becomes extremely simple, for, in order to determine individual preference of the first state of society over the second, one has simply to confirm that the utility index associated with the first state of society is greater than the utility index associated with the second. In this manner the obscure processes underlying the individual evaluation of complex phenomena collapse into a single, easily comparable index. This index does not represent numerically the intensity of preferences: the value of the index is meaningless beyond ordinal comparisons.[4]

Mathematical Representation of Choice

Since individuals are sensitive over a small part of the state of society, they will remain indifferent over most alternative states of society. If for example two states of society differ only by the colour of a particular room, almost every individual will remain indifferent between these two states. Moreover individuals have limited resources. In consequence only part of that over which they are sensitive is also feasible to them. This is precisely their domain of choice.

Consider a particular individual l. Let x be a vector of quantities corresponding to that part of the state of society over which he is sensitive. All such vectors give rise to the set $\mathscr{X}$, $x \in \mathscr{X}$. Let the behaviour of the individual be rational in the following sense. His acts are guided by his desire to use his limited resources in what, to him, is the best possible manner. This theory of motivation implies that the individual ranks feasible alternatives according to preference and selects one at least as good as any other feasible alternative. If he is able to rank any number of alternatives (that is, if his preference structure obeys transitivity and completeness) and if he knows all feasible alternatives then his choice behaviour will be perfectly rational in the sense that, for him, there is indeed no better choice than the one he has already taken. If, further, his preference structure obeys continuity and if the set of alternatives over which he is sensitive is convex then, according to proposition 2.1, his preferences are represented by a continuous utility function. Now if x^* is a feasible alternative that maximises his utility function it must be that it is also a perfectly rational choice. In other words, there is no other feasible alternative preferred to x^*. Otherwise, according to proposition 2.1, utility would not be maximised, a contradiction. Thus to determine perfectly rational behaviour is to find a feasible maximum of some continuous function. In this manner perfectly rational behaviour is translated into a simple analytic form.

Suppose that the preference ordering of individual l is defined over a set including commodities. Prices are represented by the vector p. Some components of this vector may be equal to zero. These are associated with components in x which are not commodities, as, for example, the quality of the environment. The limited resources of this individual are represented by a certain income y.[5] If prices are fixed, it is income that determines some combinations of quantities of goods as being feasible alternatives for individual l. Under these circumstances the desire of individual l to use his limited resources in what to him is the best possible manner may be expressed as the problem of determining a feasible consumption mix x such that

(2.1) $v_1[p,y] = max \{u_1[x] | p'x \le y\}, x \in \mathscr{X}$,

where v_1 is the *indirect* utility function of individual l.

We are now faced with a well-defined mathematical problem. Under what circumstances is a solution available? The following provides an answer to this fundamental question.

2.2   *If $\mathscr{X}$ is convex, closed and bounded below, and if utility is increasing over this set of alternatives, then there exists x^* that maximises utility subject to the income constraint. Further, if utility is strictly quasiconcave then x^* is unique.*[6]

It is important to understand what is intuitively implied by the assumptions of proposition 2.2.

If $\mathscr{X}$ is *convex* then it owns the closed segment (x^1, x^2) for any x^1, $x^2 \in \mathscr{X}$. If for example x^1 contains the entry "one car" and x^2 contains the entry "two cars" then the entry "1.64 cars" is admissible whenever x^1 and $x^2 \in \mathscr{X}$: convexity restricts choice to continuous quantities. Although this may appear to be an acceptable conceptual sacrifice for most indivisible goods, there is another, peculiarly geographic, kind of indivisibility which cannot be dismissed. It pertains to location itself and it emerges when goods are distinguished by location—a common practice in economic theory. According to this practice, not only is wheat distinguished from corn simply, but also as to whether it is available in London or New York. Wheat in London and wheat in New York are therefore two different commodities. Since it is physically impossible to be in London and New York at the same time, if both these commodities belong to $\mathscr{X}$, then this set of alternatives cannot be convex as it consists of two parts, one corresponding to consumption of wheat in

Individual Behaviour

London and another corresponding to consumption of wheat in New York.[7] If on the other hand commodities are not thus distinguished by location, so that wheat remains wheat no matter where it is, then this indivisibility evaporates. However, the relationship between consumption and location must be kept explicit. One way is to consider consumption of the same commodities at different locations. That is, *for any particular location i* there is a particular, convex $\mathscr{X}_i$ associated with individual l. If for example x_i^1 contains the entry "one acre" and refers to location i and x_i^2 contains the entry "two acres" and also refers to location i then the entry "1.64" acres that refers to location i is admissible whenever x_i^1 and $x_i^2 \in \mathscr{X}_i$. Acreage here pertains to the consumption of a particular commodity, land, and it belongs to the set of alternatives at any particular location.[8] If further every such set of alternatives is closed and bounded below then, according to proposition 2.2, for any particular location i there exists $x_i^* \in \mathscr{X}_i$ associated with individual l that maximizes utility subject to the income constraint. Under these circumstances one may conceive of spatial distributions x_i^* over the landscape.

If $\mathscr{X}_i$ is *closed* then it owns every point at zero distance from the set. If for example x_i^1 contains the entry "1.9 bushels of wheat", x_i^2 contains the entry "1.99 bushels of wheat", x_i^3 contains the entry "1.999 bushels of wheat" and so on, then the entry "two bushels of wheat" is admissible whenever the converging sequence $x_i^1, x_i^2, x_i^3,...$ belongs to $\mathscr{X}_i$. There is nothing restrictive in this assumption.

If $\mathscr{X}_i$ is *bounded below* then there exists a vector x^1 such that $x^1 \leq x_i^2$ for every $x_i^2 \in \mathscr{X}_i$. If for example $\mathscr{X}_i$ refers exclusively to consumption and given that you can consume only nonnegative quantities then x^1 could be any vector with negative elements. As with closure, there is nothing restrictive in this assumption.

Consider now the requirement that utility be *increasing* over every $\mathscr{X}_i$, in other words that more is better. For example, two chocolates are better than one, three chocolates are better than two, and so on ... up to a thousand chocolates and beyond—long after forcing chocolates down my throat has killed me. *Nonsatiation* (as this requirement is called) is indeed restrictive. But in order to say something beyond generalities about individual behaviour one has to live with it. However, one does not have to live with a situation as bad as the previous example tends to suggest. Indeed all that needs to be implicitly assumed is that nonsatiation holds around any x^*_i. That is, resources available are limited enough to preclude satiation when a choice is perfectly rational: once I make a feasible, perfectly rational choice, I would certainly enjoy a little more of everything. The only reason why I do not obtain it is that I cannot afford it. This is not a theory of millionaires.

We have now concluded the discussion about what is intuitively implied by the assumptions of proposition 2.2 which, at any location i, are sufficient to ensure the existence of an alternative x^*_i that maximises utility subject to the income constraint. But the mere knowledge about the existence of such an alternative is not sufficient for prediction because there may be an infinite number of diverse alternatives $x^*_i \in \mathscr{X}_i$. If however utility is *strictly quasiconcave* then prediction becomes certain because, under these circumstances, the perfectly rational choice is unique. Now strict quasiconcavity of the utility function implies that if $u_1[x^1_i] = u_1[x^2_i]$ and $x^1_i, x^2_i \in \mathscr{X}_i$ then $u_1[x^1_i] < u_1[(1-v)x^1_i + vx^2_i]$ for $0 < v < 1$. This

> "... is often considered as admissible owing to the fact that a complex x of the segment (x^1, x^2) has a composition which is intermediary to those of x^1 and x^2, and therefore is better balanced than either. It may fall down for example in certain choices relating to the consumer's chosen way of life. Any individual may be indifferent as between two complexes, one ensuring a comfortable life dedicated to the arts and the other an adventurous sporting life. But he may prefer one or (the) other of these to an intermediary third complex which does not allow full enjoyment of either way of life." [9]

Individual Behaviour

This is the last conceptual limitation implied by proposition 2.2 when the behaviour of individuals is assumed to be maximising.

Theory and Reality

Maximising behaviour as a model of choice implies a capacity to identify from a list of possible allocations of resources those deemed to be best with respect to some underlying preference structure. This is accomplished by direct comparison of entire possible allocations. Experience shows however that, under realistically complex circumstances, individuals do not possess the information processing capacity required for direct comparison of entire allocations.[10] Typically choice concerns allocation change. If for example I confronted you with a complete display of all the choices you made last month, together with a reasonable, for you, alternative display of choices, I doubt that you would be prepared to express a preference between the two. You would be prepared however to discuss the advantages of this brand of cereal over that brand, or the excessive amounts you spent last month on entertainment.

The emerging point of view is that of an individual who, with some allocation other than the best, reevaluates and readjusts allocation according to his preference structure. In principle, all that is necessary for this operation is a knowledge about marginal utilities, rather than about the utility function itself. Intuitively, this adjustment process may lead to some equilibrium that reflects stereotype choice behaviour. Accumulated evidence, however, indicates that individuals cannot perform properly even under this simplified choice framework: individuals cannot handle marginal utilities directly. Instead, individuals resort to *heuristics*, that is, simple rules–of–thumb which simplify and adapt choice behaviour to limitations in their processing capacity.[11] This introduces uncertainty in the choice of marginal allocation adjustment. For example, suppose that the distribution of marginal utilities at a particular moment of the allocation adjustment process has a single maximum. If the individual could handle marginal utilities perfectly well then his entire marginal allocation adjustment could be directed towards alternatives of highest marginal utility. If, though, the individual must resort to heuristics in order to compare the alternative marginal allocation adjustments then the direction of his allocation adjustment process remains uncertain. The choice of marginal allocation adjustment can now be associated with a set of transition probabilities. If there is a uniform distribution of these probabilities over alternatives of unequal marginal utility then there is no ability to be consistent with one's preference structure. As the quality of choice heuristics improves, so does consistency, and the distribution of transition probabilities around alternatives of higher marginal utility tightens until, at the limit, the individual adjusts only towards alternatives of highest marginal utility. The equilibrium of an individual using such perfect heuristics is, under certain conditions, equivalent to the outcome of maximising behaviour.[12] Thus, under these conditions, *perfect rationality is a limiting case of actual choice behaviour.*

The equivalence between the model of maximising behaviour and some equilibrium under perfect heuristics implies that any other structure of transition probabilities must correspond to a lower equilibrium utility level. The very idea that a typical individual at equilibrium enjoys a utility level below the highest possible implies *satisficing behaviour*. This, in turn, is associated with the concept of an aspiration level. One way in which an aspiration level may arise here is by considering utility at equilibrium as a random variable. Suppose that changes in heuristics generate a sequence of such random variables which are independent, identically distributed and of known probability distribution. Changing heuristics may now be interpreted as searching for larger utility values along the sequence. If there is a constant cost per observation and if the individual maximises the expected value of the difference between the largest utility value observed and the total costs of observation, then there is an aspiration level such that the individual stops changing heuristics as soon as he attains a level of utility at least equal to the aspiration level.[13] Thus the aspiration level separates equilibria into satisfactory and unsatisfactory types. An equilibrium is satisfactory if and only if it is associated with a value no less than the corresponding threshold level. Otherwise structural modifications such as an improvement in heuristics, or a lowering of aspirations ("I have learned to be satisfied with what I have"), or a change in preferences ("my hardships taught me to appreciate the simple things in life"), or a combination of these are bound to occur. Clearly such structural modifications must be related, and they may not be triggered only by a failure to meet aspirations: they may indeed operate during the adjustment process.

> "A vague principle would be that as the (decision-maker), in his exploration of alternatives, finds it *easy* to discover satisfactory alternatives, his aspiration level rises, as he finds it *difficult* to discover satisfactory alternatives, his aspiration level falls. Perhaps it would be possible to express the ease or difficulty of exploration in terms of the cost of obtaining better information about the mapping of (behaviour alternatives) on the (possible future states of affairs), or the combinatorial magnitude of the task of defining this mapping."[14]

All this implies that there may be feedback between the rate of the adjustment process, the rate at which choice heuristics improve or deteriorate and the rate of change in the critical threshold level. It seems conceptually straightforward to link combinations of these rates with alternative types of heuristic behaviour, ranging from the easy contentment of a good soul to the incessant driving of an overachiever.

Notes to Chapter Two

1 The first two sections of this chapter are taken from Papageorgiou (1977). The last section is taken from de Palma and Papageorgiou (1985). For a detailed exposition of microeconomic behaviour of individuals see any advanced textbook on microeconomic theory, for example Malinvaud (1972A, chapter two).

2 Although seemingly innocuous, these conditions imposed on the preference structure of individuals have been subjected to extensive criticism.

Transitivity postulates an absolute consistency of choices which is in conflict with experience in the case of sufficiently small differences. Yet experienced thresholds of perception do not really affect the reasonableness of this postulate.

> "It is observed that people more or less often make mistakes when they carry out arithmetical calculations. This, evidently, does not mean that these people do not accept the laws of arithmetic. Whenever they become aware of a mistake, they want to correct it. The same is true in decision making: it is observed that individuals make nontransitive decisions. But, as experiments show, individuals do wish to change their decisions when an intransitivity has been pointed out to them. Individuals want to behave transitively. These observations are due to Marschak (1950)." (Hildenbrand (1974, p. 86)).

The main objection to completeness is that many things cannot be compared. The reaction has been to treat completeness as the very foundation of choice theory, in other words, to narrow down the domain of choice theory to consideration of comparable situations. The imposed handicap is not nearly as great as first impressions tend to suggest. For even though you cannot compare the abstract idea of a pretty girl with that of writing a book, you can certainly face the problem of either going out on a date or staying at home to work.

Finally the restrictions imposed by continuity are limited. The main example of a preference ordering that fails to satisfy continuity is the so-called lexicographic ordering. Such preferences imply the existence of factors immeasurably more important than anything else. Little is lost in the way of realism by eliminating such preferences.

3   The proof of this proposition is in Arrow and Hahn (1971, pp. 82–87).

4   To say "I love you 5 units" does not make sense. To say, though, "I love you more than her" does. Further, proposition 2.1 says that there is a simple expression of individual preferences but it does not say *what* is the underlying utility function or *how* to arrive at it. Indeed, even though the expression of individual preferences becomes in principle extremely simple, the underlying utility function may be unimaginably complicated. Hence all this does not mean that one actually computes and compares utility indices as a matter of course. The great significance of this proposition is to be found in the simplification of mathematical analysis induced by the mere knowledge that individual preferences *can* be expressed as a function.

5   Time constraints could also be introduced. I believe however that nothing further of consequence would be gained within this essentially static framework if this complication was introduced.

6   A proof of this proposition is in Malinvaud (1972A, pp. 26–29). A more general proof is in Arrow and Hahn (1971, pp. 82–87). In

both cases it is required that the null vector belong to $\mathscr{X}$. This assumption is used to simplify proofs and is not repeated here. For although one may engage in a hunger strike, one must nevertheless occupy some space.

7   This difficulty is well known in spatial analysis. Mirrlees (1972) for example notes that if commodities are distinguished by location then a household is essentially assumed to distribute its consumption of housing over the entire landscape—a patently absurd premise. Schweizer, Varaiya and Hartwick (1976) respond to this difficulty within the context of general equilibrium theory.

8   The entry "one car" that refers to location i does not limit its use to that particular location. It simply means the use of one car by someone who is located at i.

9   Malinvaud (1972A, p. 26).

10 Block and Marschak (1960), for example, cite this as a possible reason for observed choice inconsistencies.

11 For a typology of heuristics see Bettman (1979, chapter seven).

12 These conditions include costless adjustment. See de Palma and Papageorgiou (1985).

13 See for example Radner (1975).

14 Simon (1957, p. 253).

3

Individual Behaviour in Space

Spatial Structure

We shall consider the simplest case of a closed region with a single node. The node arises from a class of compatible economic activities, and there is another class of activities that do not agglomerate.[1] The former class represents an urban sector and the latter an alternative sector, say, agriculture. Individuals may belong to either one and they may change sectors. But there is no other interaction whatsoever explicitly recognised between sectors; and *the only function of the alternative sector here is to provide a source or sink that captures population movements toward or away from the city.*

The single node is the only point of reference within the otherwise featureless landscape. I now partition the landscape into areas ranked according to distance from the node. Hereafter the node becomes the centre of the landscape. If I draw any sufficiently long segment with the centre as origin that belongs entirely to the landscape, areas will appear to be a string of unit intervals I_i, $i = 1, 2,...$ (figure 3.1). Each interval has an inner boundary toward the centre and an outer boundary away from the centre. The outer boundary of an area takes the name of that

Figure 3.1: Partition of the landscape into areas.

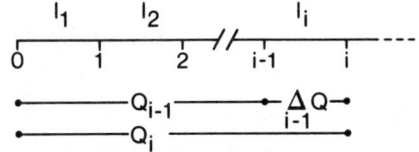

area. Since intervals are of unit length, the integer denoting the outer boundary of an area also denotes the distance between this outer boundary and the centre. By convention, it also denotes the distance between this area and the centre. All areas are connected sets, as indeed is the landscape. Intuitively, therefore, an area could be that defined between two concentric circles one unit of distance apart, in the case of a two-dimensional landscape extending over the entire plane; or that defined between two points one unit of distance apart, in the case of a one-dimensional landscape; or anything between zero and 2π radians. If Q_i is the size of the region extending between the centre and boundary i then

$$(3.1) \qquad Q_i - Q_{i-1} \equiv \bigwedge_{i-1} Q$$

is the size of area i (figure 3.1).

The Problem of Muth [2]

Consider a particular individual in the urban sector. His preferences are determined over the product of urban activity: for him, the product of activity in the alternative sector is irrelevant because there is no such interaction between sectors. Nevertheless, beyond his attitudes toward the product of urban activity, it is fundamental to recognise the spatial context of his decisions. I take it that this pertains to land occupancy and to location. Given that the landscape is featureless, there can be no explicit locational preference as the quality of the environment is

61

invariant throughout. Therefore, whereas land occupancy is explicitly included in his preference structure, location is not. But the decision where to locate is important because he must regularly interact with the centre, this being the characteristic that distinguishes those in the urban sector. In consequence the product of urban activity, land and location relative to the centre represent that part of the state of society over which the individual under consideration is sensitive.

There is a single product of urban activity at the centre. This is a composite named the private good and x is the quantity of it consumed by the individual.[3] Land occupancy is measured by the corresponding lot size q. Finally location is identified by a single area of residence, say i, and there is no distinction between locations in the same area. Hence (x_i, q_i) is an instance of the vector x_i discussed in the previous chapter —provided that there is no explicit locational preference. Then

(3.2) $\quad u_i = u[x_i, q_i]$

is now understood as the utility level of the individual under consideration who is located in area i.[4]

Consider the value an individual attaches to one of the two commodities at different levels of relative scarcity. In our context, it is natural to assume that the more he has of one, the less he values it relative to the other.[5] For example, if you already spend too much on housing in the sense of sacrificing on the consumption of everything else, improving the quality of your house a little further would seem to be less important than increasing your consumption of everything else a little more. If utility is twice differentiable (an assumption which I shall use throughout for reasons of mathematical convenience) then to assume that the more an individual has of one commodity the less he values it relative to the other is to maintain that, in addition to

(3.3) $\quad \dfrac{\partial u}{\partial x_i} > 0 \ and \ \dfrac{\partial u}{\partial q_i} > 0$

which expresses nonsatiation, it is also true that

(3.4) $\quad \dfrac{\partial}{\partial x_i}\left[\dfrac{\partial u}{\partial x_i}\right] < 0,\ \dfrac{\partial}{\partial q_i}\left[\dfrac{\partial u}{\partial q_i}\right] < 0\ \text{and}\ \dfrac{\partial}{\partial x_i}\left[\dfrac{\partial u}{\partial q_i}\right] > 0,$

in other words, utility increases at a decreasing rate with consumption; and the utility increase attributable to a particular lot size is more for higher levels of consumption of the private good.[6]

Assumptions (3.3) and (3.4) imply that the corresponding indifference curves are strictly convex.[7] Taking the total derivative of (3.2), we have

(3.5) $\quad du_i = \dfrac{\partial u}{\partial x_i} dx_i + \dfrac{\partial u}{\partial q_i} dq_i.$

Along an indifference curve, $du_i = 0$. In consequence, using (3.3) and (3.5),

(3.6) $\quad \dfrac{dx_i}{dq_i} = -\dfrac{\partial u}{\partial q_i} \div \dfrac{\partial u}{\partial x_i} < 0$

gives the slope of the indifference curve in terms of the corresponding marginal rate of substitution (MRS).[8] If, further, the MRS decreases with increasing q_i then the indifference curve is strictly convex. Differentiating (3.6),

(3.7) $\quad \dfrac{d^2 x_i}{dq_i^2} = -\left[\dfrac{\partial u}{\partial x_i}\dfrac{\partial}{\partial q_i}\left[\dfrac{\partial u}{\partial q_i}\right] - \dfrac{\partial u}{\partial q_i}\dfrac{\partial}{\partial q_i}\left[\dfrac{\partial u}{\partial x_i}\right]\right] \div \left[\dfrac{\partial u}{\partial x_i}\right]^2 > 0$

because of (3.3) and (3.4), as required.

Notice first that indifference curves cannot cross. Otherwise a single choice would be associated with two utility levels. Secondly, since no one can exist without eating or without occupying some space, $x_i > 0$ and $g_i > 0$ implying that indifference curves cannot cross the axes. Therefore indifference curves must appear as in figure 3.2.

Figure 3.2: A family of indifference curves.

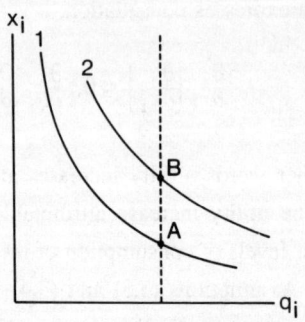

Consider points A and B. Both correspond to the same consumption of land, but the consumption of the private good is less for A than for B. Nonsatiation implies that A lies on a lower indifference curve than B. In consequence higher indifference curves are associated with higher utility levels. Using figure 3.3, where $u[\overset{1}{x}_i] = u[\overset{2}{x}_i]$ and $\overset{1}{x}_i, \overset{2}{x}_i \in \mathscr{X}_i$, it must be true that $u[\overset{1}{x}_i] < u[(1-v)\overset{1}{x}_i + v\overset{2}{x}_i]$ for $0 < v < 1$ because $\overset{1}{x}_i$ lies on a lower indifference curve than $(1-v)\overset{1}{x}_i + v\overset{2}{x}_i$. Thus assumptions (3.3) and (3.4) support the strict quasiconcavity of the utility function.

The price per unit of the private good at the centre, the only place where it is sold, is one unit. The price per unit of land r and the costs of transportation c vary between areas. The latter arises from a completely regular interaction of the individual with the centre. As no other type of spatial interaction is recognised, nothing can change this simple, stereotype travel behaviour. In consequence the individual takes all prices and costs of transportation parametrically, that is, he believes that none of his actions can change the observed pattern of prices and costs of transportation. He therefore perceives the price of land and the costs of transportation as being $r[i]$ and $c[i]$ respectively.[9] But there is a distinction to be made here. Even though the individual takes the observed $r[i]$ as fixed, its structure is to be determined later on. Indeed the ways urban land-value patterns are established is an issue of central concern. In contrast, if travel is uncongested then the structure of $c[i]$ may be treated as known. This structure often exhibits increasing returns to distance, in

Figure 3.3: Strictly convex indifference curve.

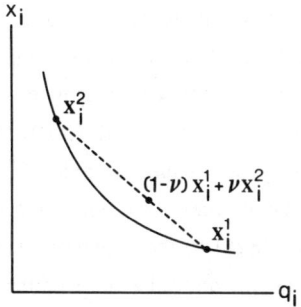

other words the cost of travel per unit of distance is smaller for longer distances. Now recall that areas and, therefore, locations are ordered according to distance from the centre; and that distances between consecutive locations along this order are precisely one unit. Hence one may write

(3.8) $\quad \triangle_i c > 0 \text{ and } \triangle_i^2 c < 0,$

that is, transportation costs increase at a decreasing rate with distance.

Within this context, (2.1) can be expressed as the problem of determining a feasible consumption mix (x_i, q_i) such that

(3.9) $\quad \upsilon[i; r[i], y] = max \{u_i \,|\, x_i + r[i]q_i + c[i] \leq y\}.$

Nevertheless, for every particular location, it is true that to maximise utility subject to an income constraint is to minimise expenditure subject to a utility constraint; and vice versa, provided that the given level of utility requires an expenditure above the minimum possible for sustenance.[10] Thus the two approaches are almost equivalent. In particular, the problem of someone in area i can be expressed as that of finding a feasible consumption mix (x_i, q_i) such that

(3.10) $\quad \psi[i; r[i], z] = min \{x_i + r[i]q_i + c[i] \,|\, z \leq u_i\}$

where ψ is the *expenditure* function and z is a given level of utility, and provided that the given level of utility requires an expenditure above the minimum possible for sustenance.

Problems (3.9) and (3.10) do not exhaust the possibilities for expressing optimising behaviour in our framework. There is a third, fundamental, alternative which reflects the important contribution of von Thünen (1826) to the economic geography of cities. In particular, it is true that to minimise expenditure subject to a utility constraint is equivalent to maximising land rent subject to income and utility constraints.[11] Hence the problem of someone in area i can be expressed as that of finding a feasible consumption mix (x_i, q_i) such that

$$(3.11) \qquad \sigma[i; y, z] = max \; \{(y - x_i - c[i]) \div q_i \, | \, z \le u_i\}$$

where σ is the *bid–rent* function, and y and z are given levels of income and utility; and provided that the given level of utility requires an expenditure above the minimum possible for sustenance.

It is perhaps useful at this point to further comment about the relationships between problems (3.9)–(3.11). Figure 3.4 pertains to these. Maximising utility subject to an income constraint appears in figure 3.4(1) where, with prices fixed, the objective is to find $x^* \in \mathcal{X}$ on the highest feasible indifference curve. Minimising expenditure subject to a utility constraint appears in figure 3.4(2) where, with prices fixed, the objective is to find $x^* \in \mathcal{X}$ on the lowest feasible budget line. Maximising land rent subject to income and utility constraints appears in figure 3.4(3) where, with the price of the private good fixed, the objective is to find $x^* \in \mathcal{X}$ on the steepest possible budget line. Lines AA and BB are identical in all three diagrams. Thus the point C, which defines the optimal solution in each case, is also the same.

Consider first problems (3.9) and (3.10). For the same utility function, there is a unique family of indifference curves; and for the same set of prices, there is a unique family of budget lines. Furthermore, for a given AA (BB) there is a unique BB (AA) tangent to it.

Behaviour in Space

Figure 3.4: Alternative individual choice problems.

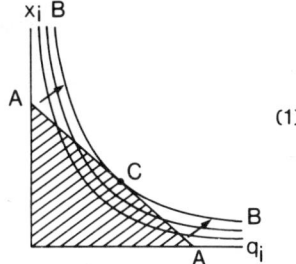
(1)

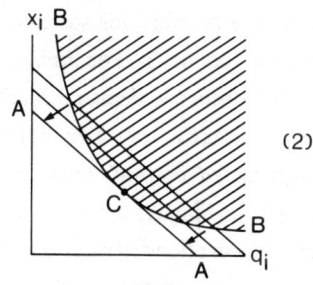
(2)

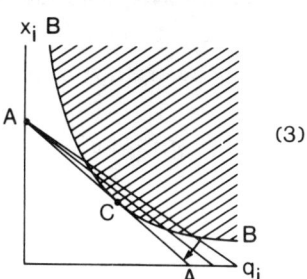
(3)

Therefore if lines AA (BB) coincide in the two diagrams, lines BB (AA) also coincide. That is, if $y = \psi[i;r[i],z]$ ($\upsilon[i;r[i],y] = z$) then $\upsilon[i;r[i],y] = z$ ($y = \upsilon[i;r[i],z]$). Introducing now problem (3.11), and using the same argument, if $r[i] = \sigma[i;y,z]$ then $\upsilon[i;r[i],y] = z$ and $\psi[i;r[i],z] = y$. These results can be summarised as

(3.12) $\qquad \upsilon[i;r[i],\psi[i;r[i],z]] = \upsilon[i;\sigma[i;y,z],y] = z,$

that is, the maximal utility from income $\psi[i;r[i],z]$, or from income y and land price $\sigma[i;y,z]$, is z; and

(3.13) $\qquad \psi[i;r[i],\upsilon[i;r[i],y]] = \psi[i;\sigma[i;y,z],z] = y,$

that is, the minimal expenditure to achieve utility $\upsilon[i;r[i],y]$, or to achieve utility z with land price $\sigma[i;y,z]$, is y.

If the optimal level of utility requires an expenditure above the

Behaviour in Space

minimum possible for sustenance, problems (3.9)–(3.11) give the same solution (point C). For problem (3.9) this solution is expressed in terms of the *ordinary* demand functions $x^*[i;r[i],y]$ and $q^*[i;r[i],y]$ which determine $\upsilon[i;r[i],y]$. For problem (3.10), it is expressed in terms of the *compensated* demand functions $x[r[i],z]$ and $q[r[i],z]$ which determine $\psi[i;r[i],z]$. Finally, for problem (3.11), it is expressed in terms of the *bid* demand functions $\bar{x}[i;y,z]$ and $\bar{q}[i;y,z]$ which determine $\sigma[i;y,z]$. Since point C is the same in all three cases, we have

(3.14) $\quad q^*[i;r[i],y] = q[r[i],\upsilon[i;r[i],y]]$

(3.15) $\quad q[r[i],z] = q^*[i;r[i],\psi[i;r[i],z]]$

(3.16) $\quad \bar{q}[i;y,z] = q^*[i;\sigma[i;y,z],y] = q[\sigma[i;y,z],z]$.

Analogous expressions hold for the consumption of the private good.

Equilibrium Conditions

From now on we shall treat problems (3.9)–(3.11) as equivalent and, therefore, interchangeable. In order to measure everything in terms of money rather than utils, individual behaviour will be discussed using expenditure minimisation rather than utility maximisation.

Equilibrium implies lack of any propensity to change. Here it implies lack of any propensity on the part of the individual to change either consumption, or location, or both. This must correspond to perfectly rational behaviour. Otherwise there is a preferable consumption, or location, or both and this creates a propensity to change. Hence to examine conditions under which the individual is at equilibrium with his environment is to find solutions to problem (3.10). Now *for any location i*, the set of alternatives (x_i, q_i) is certainly convex, closed and bounded below; utility is increasing over this set of alternatives by (3.3); and utility is strictly quasiconcave by (3.3) and (3.4). Thus, according to proposition 2.2 and for any location i, there is a unique (x_i^*, q_i^*) that maximises utility subject to the income constraint, in other words that minimises expenditure subject to a given level of utility. It follows immediately that, for any location i, the corresponding necessary conditions are also sufficient for the solution to problem (3.10). Since $x_i > 0$ and $q_i > 0$ by assumption, for any location i, the necessary and sufficient conditions for a unique solution to problem (3.10) are

(3.17) $\quad \lambda_i (z - u_i) = 0$

(3.18) $\quad 1 - \lambda_i \dfrac{\partial u}{\partial x_i} = 0$

(3.19) $\quad r[i] - \lambda_i \dfrac{\partial u}{\partial q_i} = 0$

where $\lambda_i = (\partial \psi / \partial z)|_i \equiv \partial \psi_i / \partial z$ is the lagrangean multiplier of problem (3.10).[12]

Since it must be that $\lambda_i > 0$ (otherwise either nonsatiation does not hold or individuals would dump income to enjoy the pleasures of poverty—a perfectly feasible type of behaviour but nevertheless one which is not admissible here), (3.17) implies that

(3.20) $\quad u_i = z$

at equilibrium. On the other hand (3.18) and (3.19) imply that the MRS between the private good and land is equal to the corresponding ratio of prices.

For every particular location, according to (3.20), to solve problem (3.10) is to associate a level of expenditure with a fixed level of utility. Since the landscape is bounded, there exists a location with a minimum level of expenditure related to that fixed level of utility. If location i exhibits such a property in the interior of $\mathcal{J}$ then it must satisfy

$$(3.21) \qquad q_i \triangle_i r + \triangle_i c = 0.^{13}$$

Furthermore, this location also corresponds to a maximum level of utility related to that particular level of expenditure. It is precisely within this context that condition (3.21) was first proposed by Muth (1969, chapter two). As it pertains to spatial decisions of individuals, it will hereafter be referred to as the *spatial equilibrium condition of Muth*. This concludes the list of conditions which characterise the equilibrium of an individual.

The spatial equilibrium condition of Muth has an intuitive meaning. Since $q_i \Delta_i r$ is the change in land costs associated with a unit-distance movement away from the centre, and since $\Delta_i c$ is the corresponding change in transportation costs, the spatial equilibrium condition of Muth implies that changes in land costs associated with short movements around an optimal location are balanced by the corresponding changes in transportation costs. In other words, it reveals a certain complementarity between the two types of location cost around an optimal location. This complementarity evolves as a manifestation of the marginal principle in space. Indeed, since transportation costs increase with distance, $\Delta_i c$ must represent marginal private costs (MPC). Then it must also be that land values decrease with distance so that $q_i \Delta_i r$ represent marginal private benefits (MPB). Possible relationships between these appear in figure 3.5 which, for simplicity, is drawn in continuous rather than discrete location space. In both cases the implied structure of transportation costs is compatible with assumption (3.8). However, in figure 3.5(1) the rate of decrease in marginal costs of land is slower than the corresponding rate of increase in marginal costs of transportation, while in figure 3.5(2) the opposite happens. Consider now short movements around the location i^*. In figure 3.5(1), a short movement toward the centre generates a decrease in transportation costs

Figure 3.5: Unstable and stable location equilibria.

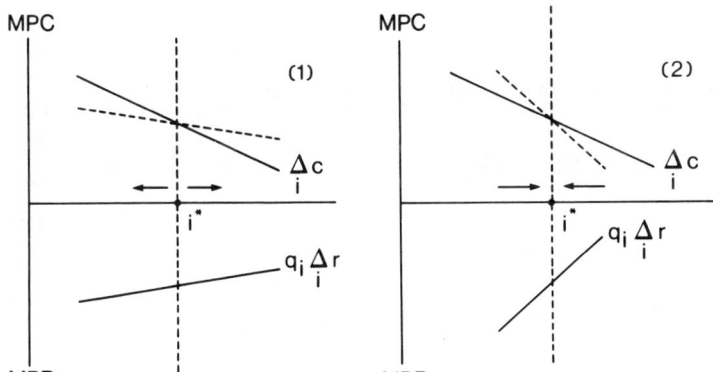

greater than the corresponding increase in land costs; and a short movement away from the centre generates a decrease in land costs greater than the corresponding increase in transportation costs. Therefore, in both cases, a small displacement from i^* creates an incentive to move away: i^* here is an expenditure–maximising, rather than an expenditure–minimising location. Only when the rate of decrease in the marginal costs of land is not slower than the corresponding rate of increase in the marginal costs of transportation, as for example in figure 3.5(2), will there be a stable location equilibrium which corresponds to the solution of problem (3.10) and satisfies condition (3.21).

Example

Let

$$u_i = x_i^\alpha q_i^\beta \text{ with } \alpha, \beta > 0 \text{ and } \alpha + \beta = 1.$$

Combining the first-order conditions (3.18) and (3.19),

$$\frac{\partial u}{\partial q_i} \div \frac{\partial u}{\partial x_i} = r[i] = \frac{\beta x_i}{\alpha q_i}.$$

This, in conjunction with the income constraint

$$y = x_i + r[i]q_i + c[i],$$

gives the ordinary demand functions

$$x^*[i,r[i],y] = \alpha(y - c[i]) \text{ and } q^*[i;r[i],y] = \frac{\beta}{r[i]}(y - c[i]).$$

Notice that, here, the ordinary demand for the composite good does not depend on the price of land. Then

$$v[i;r[i],y] = (\alpha(y - c[i]))^\alpha \left[\frac{\beta}{r[i]}(y - c[i])\right]^\beta$$
$$= \frac{\alpha^\alpha \beta^\beta}{r^\beta[i]}\left[y - c[i]\right].$$

On the other hand, in conjunction with the utility constraint

$$z = x_i^\alpha q_i^\beta,$$

the combined first-order conditions give the compensated demand functions

$$x[r[i],z] = \left[\frac{\alpha}{\beta}\right]^\beta r^\beta[i]z \text{ and } q[r[i],z] = \left[\frac{\beta}{\alpha}\right]^\alpha \frac{z}{r^\alpha[i]}.$$

Then

$$\psi[i;r[i],z] = \left[\frac{\alpha}{\beta}\right]^\beta zr^\beta[i] + r[i]\left[\frac{\beta}{\alpha}\right]^\alpha \frac{z}{r^\alpha[i]} + c[i]$$

$$= \frac{z}{\alpha^\alpha \beta^\beta} r^\beta[i] + c[i].$$

The bid–rent function can be obtained either by constraining the indirect utility function to be

$$\upsilon[i;\sigma[i;y,z],y] = z$$

using (3.12), or by constraining the expenditure function to be

$$\psi[i;\sigma[i;y,z],z] = y$$

using (3.13). In either case, we obtain

$$\sigma[i;y,z] = \left[\frac{\alpha^\alpha \beta^\beta}{z}(y - c[i])\right]^{1+\beta}.$$

Notice that

$$\upsilon[i;r[i],\psi[i;r[i],z]] = \frac{\alpha^\alpha \beta^\beta}{r^\beta[i]}\left[\left[\frac{z}{\alpha^\alpha \beta^\beta} r^\beta[i] + c[i]\right] - c[i]\right] = z$$

and

$$\psi[i;r[i],\upsilon[i;r[i],y]] = \left[\frac{\alpha^\alpha \beta^\beta}{r^\beta[i]}(y - c[i])\right]\frac{1}{\alpha^\alpha \beta^\beta} r^\beta[i] + c[i] = y,$$

as expected from (3.12) and (3.13) respectively. Also notice that

$$x[r[i],\upsilon[i;r[i],y]] = \left[\frac{\alpha}{\beta}\right]^\beta r^\beta[i]\left[\frac{\alpha^\alpha \beta^\beta}{r^\beta[i]}(y - c[i])\right]$$

$$= \alpha(y - c[i]) = x^*[i;r[i],y]$$

and

$$x^*[i;r[i],\psi[i;r[i],z]] = \alpha\left[\left[\frac{z}{\alpha^\alpha\beta^\beta}r^\beta[i] + c[i]\right] - c[i]\right]$$
$$= \left[\frac{\alpha}{\beta}\right]^\beta r^\beta[i]z = x[r[i],z].$$

The verification of (3.14) and (3.15) is similar. Finally, the bid demand function for the composite good can be obtained by inserting the bid–rent either in the corresponding ordinary demand function

$$\bar{x}[i;y,z] = x^*[i;\sigma[i;y,z],y],$$

which in our case is a trivial operation, or in the corresponding compensated demand function

$$\bar{x}[i;y,z] = x[\sigma[i;y,z],y].$$

In either case, we obtain

$$\bar{x}[i;y,z] = \alpha(y - c[i]).$$

Similarly,

$$\bar{q}[i;y,z] = \left[\frac{z}{\alpha^\alpha\beta^\beta}(y - c[i])^{-\alpha}\right]^{1+\beta}$$

which is consistent with (3.16). The bid–rent and bid demand functions thus obtained will correspond to that location in $\mathcal{J}$ for which the indirect utility function is maximal given y or, equivalently, the expenditure function is minimal given z.

Appendix to Chapter Three

1

This section of the appendix contains a proof of the statement that, for every particular location, to maximise utility subject to an income constraint is to minimise expenditure subject to a given level of utility; and that to minimise expenditure subject to a given level of utility is to maximise utility subject to an income constraint—provided that the given level of utility requires an expenditure above the minimum possible for sustenance. The proof for both parts of the statement is taken from Arrow and Hahn (1971, p. 81).

3.1 *If x^* maximises u subject to an income constraint $p'x^* - y \leq 0$ then x^* minimises $p'x$ subject to the constraint $u[x^*] - u[x] \leq 0$.*

Suppose that the conclusion is false. Then there exists x^1 such that $u[x^1] \geq u[x^*]$ and $p'x^1 < p'x^*$. By (3.3) there exists x^2 arbitrarily close to x^1 for which $u[x^2] > u[x^1]$ and, therefore, $u[x^2] > u[x^*]$. We now may select x^2 close enough to x^1 to guarantee $p'x^2 \leq p'x^* \leq y$ which contradicts the hypothesis that x^* maximises u subject to the income constraint. ∎

3.2 *If x^* minimises $p'x$ subject to the constraint $z - u[x] \leq 0$ and if $p'x^* > p'x^1$ for some $x^1 \in \mathcal{X}$ then x^* maximises u subject to the income constraint $p'x - p'x^* \leq 0$.*

Consider any x^2 for which $p'x^2 \leq p'x^*$. Let

(3.22) $\quad x[v] = vx^1 + (1 - v)x^2.$

Then

(3.23) $p'x[v] = vp'x^1 + (1-v)p'x^2 < p'x^*$

for $0 < v \leq 1$. If $u[x[v]] \geq z$ then by hypothesis $p'x^* \leq p'x[v]$. This, by (3.23), is a contradiction. Therefore $z > u[x[v]]$ and

(3.24) $x[v] \in \{x \mid z \geq u[x]\}$.

Since this last set is closed, it contains $\lim_{v \to 0} x[v] = x^2$. Since $u[x^*] \geq z$ it follows that $u[x^*] \geq u[x^2]$ for any x^2 for which $p'x^2 \leq p'x^*$. ∎

2

This section of the appendix demonstrates that the problem of minimising expenditure subject to a given level of utility is equivalent to the problem of maximising some price subject to a given level of income and utility.

3.3   *If x^* minimises $p'x$ subject to the constraint $z - u[x] \leq 0$ then x maximises*

$$\bar{p}_i = \left[p'x - \sum_{j \neq i} p_j x_j\right] \div x_i$$

subject to the constraint $z - u[x] \leq 0$.

From (3.20), it is true that $u[x^*] = z$. If the proposition is false then there exists $p^1 \equiv (p_1, \ldots, p_{i-1}, p^1_i, p_{i+1}, \ldots, p_m)$ such that

(3.25) $p^1_i > p_i = \left[p'x^* - \sum_{j \neq i} p_j x^*_j\right] \div x^*_i$

which, for the given level of expenditure $(p^1)'x^1 = p'x^*$, would satisfy $u[x^1] \geq z$. This however is impossible because $p'x^* \leq p'x^1$, which holds by definition, together with $p'x^1 < (p^1)'x^1$, which holds by (3.25), would imply $(p^1)'x^1 < (p^1)'x^1$. ∎

3.4   *If x^* maximises*

$$\bar{p}_i = \left[p'x - \sum_{j \neq i} p_j x_j\right] + x_i$$

subject to the constraint $z - u[x] \leq 0$ then x^* minimises $p'x$ subject to the constraint $z - u[x] \leq 0$.

Let $\bar{p} \equiv (p_1, ..., p_{i-1}, \bar{p}_i, p_{i+1}, ..., p_m)$. By definition, for any x^1 such that $u[x^1] \geq z$, if $\bar{p}'x^* = (p^1)'x^1$ then $\bar{p}_i \geq p_i^1$. It follows immediately that $\bar{p}'x^* \leq \bar{p}'x^1$. ∎

Notes to Chapter Three

1   See discussion at the end of chapter one.

2   This section describes in some detail the circumstances under which individuals make choices within a spatial framework. The origin of all this, of course, is the classic work of Alonso (1964). Here though I adopt the spirit of the variation developed by Muth (1969, chapter two) which embodies the first simple, explicit analysis of the decision where to locate. Hence the title. I must also mention a curiously unnoticed article by Long (1971) which directly extends the microeconomic tradition in space.

3   It is possible to consider any number of private goods. But nothing further of consequence would be gained if this essentially notational complication was introduced.

4   Notice that utility here is not indexed by individual as in chapter two. This more restricted point of view is necessary in order to aggregate individual decisions simply, an issue discussed in chapter four.

5   In a general context, Shylock would provide us with the inevitable exception.

6   Since $\partial(\partial u/\partial q_i)/\partial x_i = \partial(\partial u/\partial x_i)/\partial q_i$, it is also true that the utility increase attributable to the consumption of a particular quantity of the private good is greater for larger lot sizes.

7   An indifference surface is the locus of elements in $\mathcal{X}_i$ that corresponds to a particular level of utility. In general, since utility is continuous and $\mathcal{X}_i$ is closed, this locus is also continuous.

8   The marginal rate of substitution of x_i with respect to q_i is equal to $(\partial u/\partial q_i) \div (\partial u/\partial x_i)$ with u_i held constant. This can be generalised for any two components of x.

9   In reality individuals generate complex patterns of spatial interaction. Nevertheless, although individuals travel in all directions, transportation costs of an average individual do depend upon the distance between his residence and the centre. Therefore one may determine a transportation cost function that incorporates both direct and indirect costs of travel, and depends on distance from the centre. This is the context in which the assumption about stereotype travel behaviour should be understood.

10 See appendix.

11 See appendix.

12 Condition (3.13) is the Kuhn–Tucker condition for inequality constraints. The lagrangian function of problem (3.10) is

$$L_i \equiv x_i + r[i]q_i + c[i] + \lambda_i(z - u[x_i, q_i]).$$

Conditions (3.14) and (3.15) are obtained upon partial differentiation of the lagrangean function in terms of x_i and q_i respectively. Finally, using the envelope theorem,

$$\frac{\partial \psi_i}{\partial z} = \frac{\partial L_i}{\partial z} = \lambda_i.$$

13 Since i is a parameter in problem (3.10), we may use the envelope theorem to obtain

$$\bigtriangleup_i \psi = \bigtriangleup_i L = q_i \bigtriangleup_i r + \bigtriangleup_i c.$$

This is only approximate with respect to its continuous counterpart $q_i dr/di + dc/di$, the approximation improving as the unit width of areas decreases. If $\psi[i;r[i],z]$ unfolds smoothly over $\mathcal{J}$, a necessary condition for the minimum expenditure being associated with area i in the interior of $\mathcal{J}$ is $\partial \psi/\partial i = 0$ which, in the discrete approximation, becomes $\Delta_i \psi = 0$.

4

The Aggregation of Perfectly Rational Choices

Historical Background

In 1892 Bleicher observed that the spatial distribution of population in Frankfurt am Main could be described by a negative exponential function of distance from the centre

(4.1) $\quad \rho[i] = \rho[0]e^{-\gamma i}$

where $\rho[i]$ denotes population density in area i, and $\rho[0]$ and γ are parameters. Bleicher's observation was forgotten and rediscovered by Clark (1951) within a different context. Since Clark's formula, as (4.1) came to be known, is independent of orientation, it implies that the population density at locations on the circumference of any circle centred at the centre will be the same. Evidently, this is not true for actual cities. In consequence, the empirical interpretation of $\rho[i]$ has been consistently given by

(4.2) $\quad \rho[i] = \varphi^{-1} \int_0^\varphi \rho[i,\theta]\, d\theta;\ 0 < \varphi \leq 2\pi$

Aggregation

where (i,θ) are the polar coordinates of a location with respect to the centre: Clark's formula is a statement concerning the population density averaged over locations equidistant from the centre.

In addition to (4.1), a number of different functions have been used to describe the phenomenon.[1] Excepting some, mentioned in chapter seven, the crucial property shared by the rest is a negative first difference (derivative) and a positive second difference. This property has been repeatedly tested in several cases for different parts of the world and for the past 150 years.[2] Whenever examined, it has proved to be statistically significant and, most often, strong. Similar statements apply to the spatial distribution of land values. The main purpose of this chapter is to provide an explanation for these phenomena.

Casetti Equilibrium

Name $\mathcal{J}$ the city-related part of the landscape. According to (3.16), at every location where expenditure is minimised, utility equals a fixed level z. The special case where expenditure is minimised everywhere within the city-related part of the landscape, in other words where

(4.3) $\quad \upsilon[i;r[i],y] = z \ for \ i \in \mathcal{J}$

is called a *Casetti equilibrium*. Then, using (3.13), $\psi[i;r[i],z] = y$ for $i \in \mathcal{J}$ and

(4.4) $\quad q_i \triangle_i r + \triangle_i c = 0 \ for \ i \in \mathcal{J}$

by (3.21). One can always construct a Casetti equilibrium here. For example, one could select $\bar{r}[i]$ that satisfies (4.3) and (4.4) as follows.[3] Firstly, MPB in figure 3.5(1) or 3.5(2) is rotated on i^* and adjusted until the reflection of MPB about the abscissa coincides with MPC as in figure 4.1, that is, until (4.4) is satisfied. Intuitively, for the same level

Aggregation

Figure 4.1: Conditions for locational indifference.

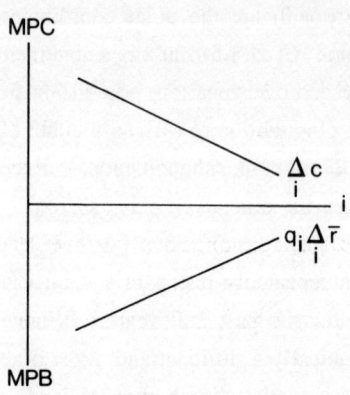

of expenditure, this generates an infinite number of land-value patterns, each one associated with a distinct level of utility at the optimum. One then chooses that pattern of prices, $\bar{r}[i]$, which satisfies (4.3). Obviously $\bar{r}[i]$ is the maximum possible over $\mathcal{J}$ given particular levels of utility and expenditure, i.e.

(4.5) $\qquad \bar{r}[i] = \sigma[i;y,z] \;\; for \; i \in \mathcal{J}.$

This is called an *equilibrium bid-rent* function.[4]

There are two main interpretations of a Casetti equilibrium.

1. Consider a particular individual with a particular utility level z. The associated equilibrium bid-rent function is a schedule of prices that generates z everywhere within $\mathcal{J}$ under perfectly rational behaviour. If for example he is now located in area 1, the bid-rent function defines circumstances under which he would evaluate other areas within $\mathcal{J}$ as equally attractive to area 1; in other words, circumstances under which he would become indifferent as to where he should locate. This interpretation is due to Alonso (1964). It provides a simple criterion for spatial choice. Namely, if an observed land value is lower than the

Aggregation

corresponding value of the bid–rent function the individual will change location because he can improve his utility level. Otherwise he will not.

2. Consider a class of individuals, identical as to income and tastes, with a particular utility level z. Then there is a single equilibrium bid–rent function common to all. Further, under perfectly rational behaviour, consumption in any area will be the same for all individuals in that area. One may visualise in every area $i \in \mathcal{J}$ the precise number of individuals necessary to partition the land available into lots of size q_i, precisely equal to that required under perfectly rational behaviour. The result is a population of identical individuals suitably arranged over $\mathcal{J}$ with no incentive to move because everyone is indifferent between locations. Hence the city at equilibrium emerges as a composite of identical, perfectly rational choices. This interpretation is due to Casetti (1971). It provides the single most effective instrument of aggregation available within this framework.[5]

Under what circumstance does the city emerge as a Casetti equilibrium? Suppose that a distribution of identical individuals and a corresponding pattern of land values are somehow established over $\mathcal{J}$. Under perfectly rational behaviour, for every area in $\mathcal{J}$, one observes a particular consumption and utility level. Suppose that the distribution of utility (in continuous rather than discrete location space) appears as z^1 in

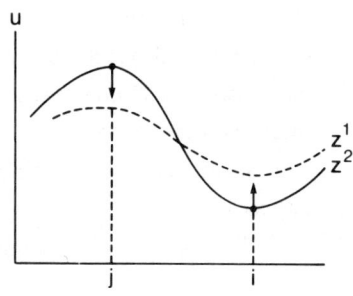

Figure 4.2: Impact of the competitive process on the spatial distribution of utility.

Aggregation

figure 4.2. Consider first the city as a closed system. If the market for land is competitive, someone in a low-utility area, say i, will find it profitable to bid a slightly higher rent than the one established in a high-utility area, say j. Moving from i to j, even under a slightly higher rent, will improve his condition. Higher prices in area j will lower the corresponding utility level; and lower demand for land in area i will lower prices which, in turn, will raise the corresponding utility level. This process of adjustment will create a smoother distribution of utility z^2; and if the market for land is perfectly competitive, it will continue to operate until a certain bid-rent function, associated with a particular level of utility, has been established over $\mathcal{J}$.[6]

A simple location adjustment process consistent with these ideas is given by

$$(4.6) \qquad \frac{d}{dt} n_i = \begin{cases} u_i - \bar{u} \text{ for } n_i > 0 \\ max\{0, u_i - \bar{u}\} \text{ for } n_i = 0, \end{cases}$$

where n_i represents the population in area i and $\bar{u}$ the average utility level.[7] That is, the population of a zone increases (decreases) if the utility of the zone is higher (lower) than average. Of course, in an already depopulated zone, the population cannot decrease any further.

4.1 *If the total population is fixed, a Casetti equilibrium exists and is globally stable under (4.6).*[8]

Global stability means that the equilibrium is unique. The requirement of a fixed total population can be interpreted in two ways. Firstly, the city itself is a closed system. Secondly, the city is an open system, individuals in the alternative sector attain a common utility level and the adjustment process (4.6) operates over the city-state, rather than over the city itself.

To propose such an adjustment process is to assume a distinct class of agents, landowners. It is probably worthwhile at this point to emphasise that particular quality of distinctiveness. An individual in the urban sector cannot be a landowner because he cannot have any source of income other than y. Now the single criterion that guides the behaviour of landowners is profit: it is always true that the highest bidder captures their land. *This is the general principle according to which land use is determined within the city-state*; and this is their only function: namely, to justify the general principle and to provide an infinite sink where all rent proceeds may vanish.[9] The sink in fact is conveniently extended to absorb all other proceeds, those collected from the distribution of the private good and those from the use of transportation. One may visualise a black box into which all such proceeds enter and from which income for those in the urban sector is, somehow, generated.

In this manner the city may emerge as a Casetti equilibrium under the auspices of a perfectly competitive land-market. For some, this connection is sufficient to identify the theory itself with perfect competition. The error in such views is a failure to distinguish between the theory and one of its models. A counter example will suffice. Consider a planner who desires to achieve a state of absolute equity in the sense of some fixed utility level common to all individuals within $\mathcal{J}$. He sets a unit-price of the private good and an appropriate income. Given these, he must now define that distribution of land values over $\mathcal{J}$ which, under perfectly rational behaviour, will generate the desired utility level. In other words he must construct a Casetti equilibrium entirely devoid of competition.

Simple Urban Morphology

It is now possible to describe the city at equilibrium in some detail. I begin with the distribution of the urban and the alternative land uses over the landscape. Using (4.4),

Aggregation

(4.7) $$\bigtriangleup_i \bar{r} = -\frac{1}{\bar{q}_i} \bigtriangleup_i c < 0$$

because $\bigtriangleup_i c > 0$ by (3.8). Therefore equilibrium bid–rents decrease away from the centre. Observe that both the equilibrium bid–rent and land demand have been noted explicitly. For the latter, using (3.16) and (4.5), $q[\bar{r}[i],z] = q[\sigma[i;y,z],z] = \bar{q}[i;y,z] \equiv \bar{q}_i$. What about land prices in the alternative sector? I take it that *production in this sector occurs under constant returns to scale for land*. This, together with the assertions that (1) activities in the alternative sector do not agglomerate and that (2) there is no interaction whatsoever between activities in the alternative sector and the centre, is sufficient to justify an analogous bid–rent for the alternative sector, $\check{r} > 0$, constant over the entire landscape. Since the urban bid–rent function decreases away from the centre, one may imagine it as a cone centred at the centre. This cone intersects the plane of the alternative bid–rent function at some distance from the centre.[10] Since the highest bidder captures the land, it follows immediately that the city is compacted around the centre. Its spatial extent must be finite—provided that transportation costs increase over distance without bound. This is an immediate consequence of the income constraint and of the requirement that, over the urban area, urban bid–rents must be positive as they cannot be lower than the alternative bid–rents. If b is the area over which the urban bid–rent function intersects with the alternative bid–rent function, that is where

(4.8) $\bar{r}[b] = \check{r},$

then the city–related part of the landscape may be written as

(4.9) $\mathcal{J} \equiv \{I_1, ..., I_b\}.$

Area I_b is the only one where a land–use mix is possible. If, by convention, every area is occupied by a single type of land use and if I allocate area b to the urban land use then $\mathcal{J}$ belongs entirely to the city while its complement relative to the landscape, $\setminus \mathcal{J}$, belongs entirely to the alternative land use. I thus obtain a compact, connected urban area that owns the centre, surrounded by the alternative land use.

Using (3.16) and (4.7),

$$(4.10) \quad \underset{i}{\triangle} \bar{q} = \frac{\partial q}{\partial r[i]} \underset{i}{\triangle} \sigma \bigg|_{r[i]=\bar{r}[i]} \equiv \frac{\partial q}{\partial \bar{r}[i]} \underset{i}{\triangle} \sigma > 0$$

because $\partial q / \partial r[i] < 0$ holds generally in the case of compensated demand functions.[11]

To determine completely the spatial structure of urban bid–rents, take the difference of (4.7) with respect to i and rearrange:

$$(4.11) \quad \underset{i}{\triangle}^2 \bar{r} = -\frac{1}{\bar{q}_{i+1}} \left[\underset{i}{\triangle} \bar{q} \underset{i}{\triangle} \bar{r} + \underset{i}{\triangle}^2 c \right] > 0$$

according to (3.8) and (4.10). Under these circumstances the bid–rent gradient appears as in figure 4.3. Furthermore, taking the difference of

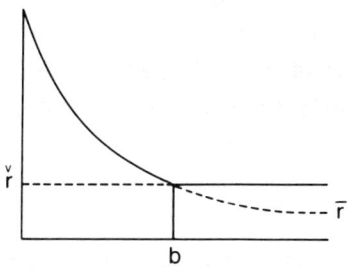

Figure 4.3: Bid–rent gradient.

(4.10) with respect to i, one may conclude that

$$(4.12) \quad \underset{i}{\triangle}^2 \bar{q} = \left[\underset{i}{\triangle} \frac{\partial q}{\partial \bar{r}[i]} \right] \underset{i+1}{\triangle} \bar{r} + \frac{\partial q}{\partial \bar{r}[i]} \underset{i}{\triangle}^2 \bar{r}$$

from (4.7). Taking into account (4.10) and (4.11), $\triangle_i^2 \bar{q}$ is negative if

87

Aggregation

(4.13) $$\bigwedge_i \frac{\partial q}{\partial \bar{r}[i]} \geq 0,$$

in other words if the decrease in the compensated demand for land associated with increased equilibrium bid–rents does not increase away from the centre. Under these circumstances the spatial distribution of the demand for land appears as in figure 4.4.[12]

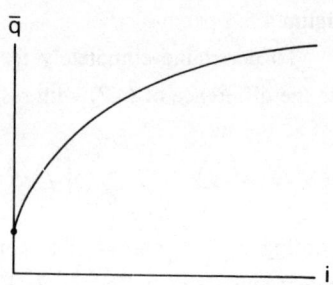

Figure 4.4: Spatial distribution of the demand for land.

It has been established that land uses are completely segregated over the landscape so that an urban area is occupied only by individuals in the urban sector. If transportation is spaceless (or if the size of areas is net of land allocated to streets) then the entire area i is equally subdivided between the individuals in that area as

(4.14) $$q_i = \frac{1}{n_i} \bigwedge_{i-1} Q$$

where n_i is the number of individuals in area i. The density, on the other hand, of area i is by definition

(4.15) $$\rho_i \equiv n_i \div \bigwedge_{i-1} Q$$

and, obviously,

(4.16) $$q_i \rho_i = 1.$$

In other words lot size is the inverse of population density. This, together with (4.10), (4.12) and (4.43), implies directly that

(4.17) $\quad \triangle_i \bar{p} < 0 \text{ and } \triangle_i^2 \bar{p} > 0$

where $\bar{p}$ is the inverse of the compensated demand $\bar{q}$. Thus the spatial

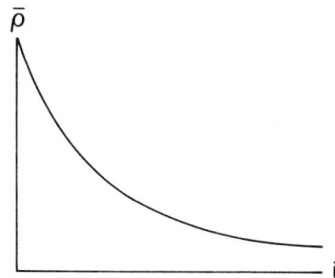

Figure 4.5: Spatial distribution of population density.

distribution of population density at equilibrium appears as in figure 4.5: bid–rents and population densities have qualitatively the same spatial structure over the urban area. This is supported by experience.[13]

Example

The example of chapter three can also be used here. In that example, the bid–rent and bid demand functions pertained to that location in $\mathcal{J}$ for which the indirect utility function was maximal given y or, equivalently, the expenditure function was minimal given z. Now that every location in $\mathcal{J}$ is utility maximising or, equivalently, expenditure minimising, the bid–rent and bid demand functions in the example of chapter three apply everywhere in $\mathcal{J}$. Thus

$\bar{x}_i = \alpha(y - c[i])$

Aggregation

$$\bar{q}_i = \left[\frac{z}{\alpha^\alpha \beta^\beta}(y-c[i])^{-\alpha}\right]^{1+\beta}$$

$$\bar{r}[i] = \left[\frac{\alpha^\alpha \beta^\beta}{z}(y-c[i])\right]^{1+\beta}$$

for $i \in \mathcal{J}$. Using (4.17),

$$\bar{\rho}_i = \left[\frac{\alpha^\alpha \beta^\beta}{z}(y-c[i])^\alpha\right]^{1+\beta}$$

It is straightforward to establish that these functions satisfy the properties discussed in the previous section.

Aggregate Relationships at Equilibrium [14]

This section describes a class of remarkably simple relationships between the total cost of urban transportation and the total value of urban land net of its opportunity cost, both estimated at equilibrium. In order to specify the latter, let $\bar{R}$ be the total value of urban land at equilibrium and $\check{R}$ the total opportunity cost of urban land.[15] Then $\bar{R} - \check{R}$ represents the total value of urban land net of its opportunity cost at equilibrium, which corresponds to the shaded area of figure 4.6. Intuitively, whereas the total cost of urban transportation, C, represents disbenefits created by agglomeration, the total value of urban land net of its opportunity cost must reflect corresponding benefits. The relationship between these two aggregate measures of the city at equilibrium is directed by two elasticities, the elasticity of transportation costs with respect to distance, $\eta_{c:i}$, and the elasticity of the urban area with respect to distance, $\eta_{Q:i}$.[16] The second elasticity is a measure of shape. For a linear city, where the size of areas is one unit,

Figure 4.6: The value of urban land net of its opportunity cost.

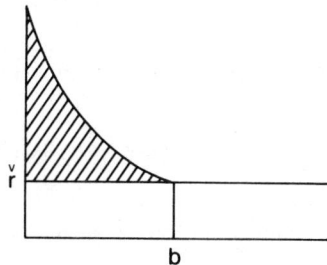

(4.18) $\quad \eta_{Q:i} \equiv \underset{i-1}{\triangle} Q \div (Q_i/i) = 1 \div (i/i) = 1$

whereas for a circular city

(4.19) $\quad \eta_{Q:i} \equiv \underset{i-1}{\triangle} Q \div (Q_i/i) = \pi(i^2 - (i-1)^2) \div (\pi i^2/i) = (2i-1) \div i \approx 2$

provided that distance partitions are small. The linear city corresponds to a measure of zero radians and the circular city corresponds to a measure of 2π radians. These are the two extremes of shape. In between there is a continuum of urban shapes and related elasticities: as the measure of radians gradually increases from zero to 2π, the elasticity of the urban area with respect to distance gradually increases from one to two.[17]

4.2 *If the elasticity of the urban area with respect to distance is constant over distance, then the ratio between the total cost of urban transportation and the total value of urban land net of its opportunity cost is smaller than (equal to, greater than) the elasticity of the urban area with respect to distance if the elasticity of transportation costs with respect to distance is greater than (equal to, smaller than) unity.*

Applying proposition 4.2 to the case of a linear city one obtains

91

Aggregation

(4.20) $\quad \bar{R} - \check{R} >(=,<) C \quad \text{if} \quad \eta_{c:i} >(=,<) 1;$

and applying it to the case of a circular city

(4.21) $\quad \bar{R} - \check{R} >(=,<) \frac{1}{2} C \quad \text{if} \quad \eta_{c:i} >(=,<) 1.$

Over the continuum of urban shapes between the linear and the circular, as the measure of radians gradually increases from zero to 2π, the coefficient that multiplies the total cost of urban transportation gradually decreases from one to one-half. Suppose now that the elasticity of transportation costs with respect to distance is equal to unity. Then, for a linear city at equilibrium, the total value of urban land net of its opportunity cost is precisely equal to the total cost of urban transportation; and, for a circular city at equilibrium, the total value of urban land net of its opportunity cost equals one-half the total cost of urban transportation. Over the continuum of urban shapes, the total value of urban land net of its opportunity cost gradually decreases from being equal to the total cost of urban transportation to one-half of that cost. The simplicity of this class of relationships is, indeed, striking. Intuitively, variations within this class must relate to variations in the efficiency of shapes. One may observe for example that the linear shape, being here the least efficient of urban shapes, corresponds to the highest total cost of urban transportation relative to the total value of urban land net of its opportunity costs; and that the circular shape, being here the most efficient of urban shapes, corresponds to the lowest total cost of urban transportation relative to the total value of urban land net of its opportunity cost. As efficiency gradually increases, the total cost of urban transportation gradually decreases relative to the total value of urban land net of its opportunity cost. Stated otherwise, as efficiency gradually increases, centrality becomes less important on average. In consequence the total value of urban land net of its opportunity cost, which reflects centrality, also decreases.

The same intuitive observations can be extended to cases where the elasticity of transportation costs with respect to distance is other than unity. It remains now to interpret this elasticity. What it actually measures is economies of scale in transportation with respect to distance. A value greater than unity implies decreasing returns to scale in transportation with respect to distance because costs increase relatively faster than distance. Similarly, a value equal to (smaller than) unity implies constant (increasing) returns to scale in transportation with respect to distance. Consider the case of a linear city at equilibrium. When there are decreasing returns to scale in transportation, the value of centrality is relatively high. Since this is reflected in the total value of urban land net of its opportunity cost, $\bar{R} - \check{R} > C$ at the optimum. On the other hand, when there are increasing returns to transportation, the value of centrality is relatively low and, consequently, $\bar{R} - \check{R} < C$. When assumption (3.8) applies, that is, when there are increasing returns to scale in transportation, the class of relationships displayed in proposition 4.2 is reduced to cases where the elasticity of transportation costs with respect to distance is actually smaller than unity.

Theory and Reality [18]

No city is purely monocentric. It is a rather high concentration of various order centres within a relatively small area. A simple way of treating this complexity is to assume, as Christaller (1933) did, that the centres form an h–order hierarchy such that a centre of order j operates in effect as a centre of order 1, 2,..., j; and that the interaction between any individual and the centres is regulated by a set of frequencies which denote the individual's number of trips per unit of time for the purpose of acquiring goods and services of order j. These frequencies of interaction decrease as the order increases. If the quality of goods and services of order j is the same throughout, individuals are expected to interact with the closest centre that contains goods and services of that order.

Aggregation

Since a higher-order centre contains all lower-order functions, distances travelled to acquire goods and services of order j cannot be shorter than distances travelled to acquire goods and services of order lower than j. It follows that every residential location within this system can be related to one vector of frequencies and one vector of distances, where the former may depend on the latter. In any case, since the distance vector is defined over every location once the distribution and the hierarchical properties of the centres are fixed and known, any residential location within this system can be characterised by a single vector of distances. One could then replace the scalar in the exponent of (4.1) with an h-dimensional vector to obtain a model of point, rather than area, estimates.

This model captures well some aspects of the morphological complexity characterising land-value and population density surfaces over a multicentre environment. In particular: (1) it attains a maximum at the location of the highest-order centre; (2) its values that correspond to the locations of centres of a given order j decrease as distances between these centres and centres of order higher than j increase; (3) local maxima correspond to the locations of centres (other than the highest order); (4) there may be centres that do not correspond to local maxima; and (5) maxima correspond only to the locations of centres. Figure 4.7 illustrates these principles in the case of a three-level hierarchy with one third-order centre, two second-order centres and four first-order centres. Now any such structure can be approximated by a single-centre model which coincides with the location of the highest-order centre. This happens because, in reality, the spacing of lower-order centres depends on average upon their proximity to higher-order centres: their density decreases as the distance from higher-order centres increases.[19] One may therefore express average distance to lower-order centres in terms of distance to successively higher-order centres, until locations in the model are described by a single distance to the highest-order centre capturing an average overall centrality of locations. This is the reason why (4.1) has proven to be so successful.

Aggregation

Figure 4.7: Population density and land–value distribution in a multicentre framework.

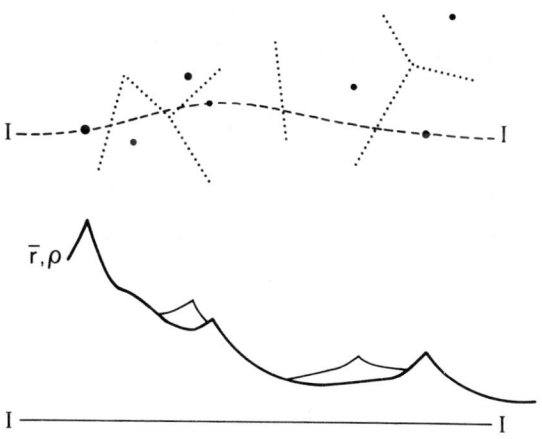

Appendix to Chapter Four

This appendix contains a proof of the proposition that, if the elasticity of the urban area with respect to distance is constant over distance, then the ratio between the total cost of urban transportation and the total value of urban land net of its opportunity cost is smaller than (equal to, greater than) the elasticity of the urban area with respect to distance if the elasticity of transportation costs with respect to distance is greater than (equal to, smaller than) unity.

It is true that

$$(4.22) \qquad \triangle_i \bar{r}Q = \bar{r}_{i+1} \triangle_i Q + Q_i \triangle_i \bar{r}.$$

Aggregating over the city

95

Aggregation

(4.23) $$\sum_i \triangle_i \bar{r}Q = \sum_i \bar{r}_{i+1} \triangle_i Q + \sum_i Q_i \triangle_i \bar{r},$$

where the LHS of (4.23) may be written as

(4.24) $$\sum_i \triangle_i \bar{r}Q \equiv \bar{r}_2 Q_2 - \bar{r}_1 Q_1 + \ldots + \bar{r}_{b+1} Q_{b+1} - \bar{r}_b Q_b$$
$$= -\bar{r}_1 Q_1 + \bar{r}_{b+1} Q_{b+1} = -\bar{r}_1 \triangle_0 Q + \bar{r}_{b+1} Q_{b+1};$$

the first term on the RHS of (4.23) may be written as

(4.25) $$\sum_{i=1}^{b} \bar{r}_{i+1} \triangle_i Q = \sum_{i=2}^{b} \bar{r}_i \triangle_{i-1} Q + \bar{r}_{b+1} \triangle_b Q;$$

and the second term on the RHS of (4.23) may be written as

(4.26) $$\sum_i Q_i \triangle_i \bar{r} = -\sum_i \left[Q_i \bar{n}_i \triangle_i c \right] \div \triangle_{i-1} Q$$

because, at equilibrium, (4.4) holds and (4.14) is true by definition. Here $\bar{n}_i$ corresponds to $\bar{q}_i$. Upon substitution of (4.24), (4.25) and (4.26) into (4.23) and rearrangement,

(4.27) $$\bar{r}_1 \triangle_0 Q + \sum_{i=2}^{b} \bar{r}_i \triangle_{i-1} Q - \bar{r}_{b+1}(Q_{b+1} - \triangle_b Q)$$
$$= \sum_i \bar{r}_i \triangle_{i-1} Q - \bar{r}_{b+1} Q_b = \sum_i \left[Q_i \bar{n}_i \triangle_i c \right] \div \triangle_{i-1} Q.$$

Now $\bar{r}_i \triangle_{i-1} Q$ is the total value of urban land in area i at equilibrium. Hence $\sum_i \bar{r}_i \triangle_{i-1} Q$ is the total value of urban land at equilibrium. Moreover, since $\bar{r}_{b+1}$ is approximately equal to the bid–rent for the alternative sector, $\bar{r}_{b+1} Q_b$ is approximately equal to the total opportunity cost of urban land. Then (4.25) may be written as

Aggregation

(4.28) $$\bar{R} - \check{R} = \sum_i \left[Q_i \bar{n}_i \bigtriangleup_i c \right] \div \bigtriangleup_{i-1} Q.$$

On the other hand the total cost of urban transportation at equilibrium is

(4.29) $$C \equiv \sum_i \bar{n}_i c[i].$$

Comparisons between the total value of urban land net of its opportunity cost and the total cost of urban transportation can be made through the RHSs of (4.28) and (4.29). Now

(4.30) $$\eta_{c:1} > (=,<) \; 1$$

may be written as

(4.31) $$\bigtriangleup_i c \div (c[i]/i) > (=,<) \frac{1}{\eta_{Q:i}} \bigtriangleup_{i-1} Q \div (Q_i/i),$$

or as

(4.32) $$Q_i \bar{n}_i \bigtriangleup_i c \div \bigtriangleup_{i-1} Q > (=,<) \frac{1}{\eta_{Q:i}} \bar{n}_i c[i].$$

Then, since it is true that

(4.33) $$\left[Q_i \bar{n}_i \bigtriangleup_i c \right] \div \bigtriangleup_{i-1} Q > (=,<) \frac{1}{\eta_{Q:i}} \bar{n}_i c[i]$$

if and only if $\eta_{c:i} > (=,<) \; 1$,

it must also be true that

(4.34) $$\sum_i \left[Q_i \bar{n}_i \bigtriangleup_i c \right] \div \bigtriangleup_{i-1} Q > (=,<) \sum_i \frac{1}{\eta_{Q:i}} \bar{n}_i c[i]$$

if $\eta_{c:i} > (=,<) \; 1$

which, upon comparison with (4.28) and (4.29) implies

Aggregation

(4.35) $C+(\bar{R} - \check{R}) <(=,>) \eta_{Q:i}$ *if* $\eta_{c:i} >(=,<) 1$

because the elasticity of the urban area with respect to distance is constant over distance, and hence it may be taken out of the summation symbol in (4.34). ∎

Notes to Chapter Four

1   See for example Casetti (1969).

2   For a good review of empirical tests see Berry, Simmons and Tennant (1963).

3   In his original paper Casetti (1971) proposed the following alternative method for the construction of a Casetti equilibrium. For every pair $(i,r[i])$ the individual selects an appropriate (x_i,q_i) that maximises utility subject to an income constraint. The necessary and sufficient conditions for this problem are (3.18) and (3.19) respectively. Since they hold for every $(i,r[i])$, they must also hold for $(i,\bar{r}[i])$ where the individual is equally satisfied everywhere within $\mathcal{J}$. Then, using the above necessary and sufficient conditions, one may seek the $\bar{r}[i]$ that satisfies (4.3).

4   In chapter three, $r[i]$ was fixed. Thus $\lambda_i = dy_i/d\bar{u}$. Here however $\bar{r}[i]$ is sensitive to variations in utility. Consequently, application of the envelope theorem on the lagrangean function in footnote 3.12 gives

$$\frac{\partial \psi_i}{\partial z} = \frac{\partial L_i}{\partial z} = q_i \frac{\partial \sigma_i}{\partial z} + \lambda_i.$$

That is, the income change necessary to bring about an exogenous

Aggregation

utility change is modified to take into account related adjustments in the bid–rent function.

5   Nevertheless it carries with it the assumption of identical individuals. This requirement will be relaxed later on, where classes of individuals characterised by different income levels are considered. However, identical tastes will persist throughout. To treat preference variations effectively would involve stochastic utility functions, an issue not discussed any further.

   The dilemma of a theorist now becomes clear: either to accept different tastes and forsake aggregation because different tastes imply different bid–rents and different consumptions within the same area; or to aggregate, assuming that taste differences are small enough to be reasonably subsumed under the guise of some "representative" individual.

6   The level of utility and the associated bid–rent function will be determined by forces outside the scope of our discussion, that is, aspirations, bargaining power, institutional controls, etc.

7   See Ginsburgh, Papageorgiou and Thisse (1985).

8   A proof of this statement must wait until chapter fourteen. An additional requirement for the validity of proposition 4.1 is that population be represented by a continuous density.

9   It is customary in the literature to name them "absentee landowners".

10 The cone of course could be everywhere lower than the plane. But then there would be no city, a case which is assumed away.

11 For a proof see Malinvaud (1972A, p. 38). In figure 3.4(2), a rise

Aggregation

in the land rent will steepen line AA. Since the new AA will be a tangent to BB, q_i must decrease.

12 Inequality (4.13) is sufficient but not necessary for inequality (4.12). Consider two locations, one closer to the centre (the "central" location) and one further away (the "peripheral" location). Consider the same consumption of land at the same price in both locations. Then (4.13) implies that the decrease in the consumption of land at the central location should be no less than the corresponding decrease at the peripheral location. This is intuitively plausible: given that the consumption of land increases away from the centre at equilibrium, the same consumption of land in both locations would imply either that the consumption at the central location is more than it should be, or that the consumption at the peripheral location is less than it should be, or both. In any case, one would expect that (4.13) holds.

13 It is also possible to infer something about the spatial distribution of consumption of the private good. Using bid demand functions at equilibrium, the total difference of u with respect to distance from the centre is

$$\frac{\partial u}{\partial \bar{x}_i} \Delta_i \bar{x} + \frac{\partial u}{\partial \bar{q}_i} \Delta_i \bar{q} = 0$$

because of (4.3). This, together with (3.3) and (4.10), implies $\Delta_i \bar{x} < 0$. The sign of the second difference remains undetermined.

14 This section is based on some ideas in Arnott and Stiglitz (1979).

15 The opportunity cost per unit of land equals the bid–rent for the alternative sector.

16 The elasticity of the urban area with respect to distance is the ratio between the relative change in the urban area enclosed within a certain distance from the centre and the relative change in that distance. Similarly, the elasticity of transportation costs with respect to distance is the ratio between the relative change in transportation costs and the relative change in the corresponding distance.

17 The classification based on radians implies urban areas of regular shape. Then the elasticity of the urban area with respect to distance is constant over distance. This is not the case with irregular shapes where the above elasticity varies over distance.

18 This section draws from Papageorgiou (1971).

19 See for example Isard (1956, pp. 270–274), especially the diagram on page 272.

5

States of Urban Development

Historical Background

In a comparative study of ten Western and four Eastern European countries, van den Berg, Drewett, Klaasen, Rossi and Vijverberg (1982) conclude that different urban systems progress through similar stages of development. Urbanisation, the first stage, is replaced by suburbanisation which gathers momentum, diffuses into adjacent nonmetropolitan areas and eventually causes the decline of metropolitan regions.

> "Urban decline, particularly in the nations first to industrialize, thus becomes a development stage neatly explained by economic progress. The Industrial Revolution's boom areas, such as Ghent, Glasgow, Liège, Liverpool, Manchester, and Saarbrucken were the first evidencing wholesale decline. The larger European industrial cities and capitals, such as Amsterdam, Budapest, Copenhagen, London, Sofia, Vienna, and Zurich are situated at later stages of the development spectrum than their lower-order counterparts. The lower-order centers, in turn, are still experiencing the earlier stage of suburbanization. In the earliest development stage of all

are the East European regions that, not coincidentally, were also the last to industrialize."[1]

Evidence available for other parts of the world supports these conclusions.[2] In terms of (4.1), the first stage, urbanisation, corresponds to $\rho[0]$ increasing and γ constant, while the second stage, suburbanisation, to both $\rho[0]$ and γ decreasing. During the last stage, the process of flattening population density gradients continues. Such evidence indicates that the order behind urban development transcends social, political, economic and cultural differences. An attempt toward explaining the first two stages of this order is presented here. Evidently, the forces behind urban development are complex and impossible to condence within a simple model. This will become clear in subsequent chapters, especially chapters eight and nine, where the consequences of examining some aspects of the phenomenon in more detail will be explored. It should be borne in mind however that a study of overall metropolitan decline is missing because it would require at least an understanding of how technological developments affect industrial productivity between regions—an issue not pursued any further.

Response to Changing Conditions

The spatial distributions of consumption, land occupancy and land values in the city are given by the solution to a Casetti equilibrium as

(5.1) $\quad \bar{x}_i = \bar{x}[i;y,z]$

(5.2) $\quad \bar{q}_i = \bar{q}[i;y,z]$

(5.3) $\quad \bar{r}[i] = \sigma[i;y,z]$

respectively; the equilibrium population of the city is

(5.4) $$\sum_j \bar{n}_j = N;$$

and the spatial extent of the city is determined by the border condition

(5.5) $\sigma[b;y,z] = \check{r}.$

Equations (5.1)–(5.5) completely describe the city under a Casetti equilibrium.

Urban form depends on prevailing conditions external to the city. According to equations (5.1)–(5.5) such conditions include income, the cost of transportation (through the explicit dependence on i), the value of land in the alternative sector, utility attained and population of the city. Of these, the first three are primarily set by technology (or productivity) while the last two reflect the type of interaction between the urban and the alternative sector. Now utility attained and population of the city are related through the type of interaction between the urban and the alternative sector in the following manner. *Whenever there is a utility difference between the urban and the alternative sector, costless migrations occur until this discrepancy is eliminated.* This has already been argued in the previous chapter. Therefore, if $\bar{v}$ is the utility in the alternative sector and if M is the population of the city-state then

(5.6) $\bar{u}[N] = \bar{v}[M - N]$

at equilibrium. It follows that one may study the relationship between utility and population in the urban sector at equilibrium through the relationship between utility and population in the alternative sector. One may intuitively believe that a migration flow toward the city implies higher urban utility; and that higher urban utility implies a migration flow toward the city. Both beliefs are substantially true at equilibrium —but not quite. The first breaks down in the case of an "open" city and the second in the case of a "closed" city.[3]

Consider figure 5.1. It represents both urban utility as a function

Figure 5.1: Utility as a function of population partitions.

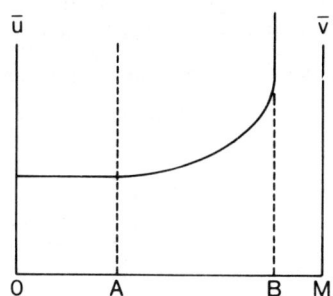

of urban population *at equilibrium* (measured from left to right) and the utility in the alternative sector as a function of the corresponding population (measured from right to left). Otherwise utility in the two sectors would not be equal, a contradiction. When the city is small relative to the alternative sector, small changes in the population of the city do not affect utility in the alternative sector in any significant manner because such changes are very small relative to the population in the alternative sector. Thus, over OA, urban utility at equilibrium may be treated as a constant:

$$(5.7) \qquad \triangle_N \bar{u} = - \triangle_{M-N} \bar{v} = 0.$$

Beyond A however changes in population do affect utility. If labour in the alternative sector becomes more valuable as population in that sector decreases then an increase of the city size beyond A would imply higher utility in the alternative sector. Thus, beyond A, urban utility at equilibrium increases with the urban population:

$$(5.8) \qquad \triangle_N \bar{u} = - \triangle_{M-N} \bar{v} > 0.$$

If $\bar{u}[N]$ has an inverse then one may claim from (5.8) that, beyond A, higher urban utility levels at equilibrium attract more individuals from the alternative sector. This may continue until complete urbanisation or it may be that there is a limit B beyond which further reductions in the population of the alternative sector are impossible. In any case there is a city size beyond which no more individuals from the alternative sector can be attracted for any increase of the urban utility level at equilibrium:

$$(5.9) \qquad \bigtriangleup_{N} \bar{u}\Big|_B = - \bigtriangleup_{M-N} \bar{v}\Big|_B = \infty.$$

Within OA, where utility is fixed and city population varies, the city is "open". Within AB, where both utility and city population vary, the city is "transient". Finally at B, where utility varies and city population is fixed, the city is "closed". This urban typology follows in a natural manner urban evolution from its "open", underdeveloped stage to its "closed", developed one.

What has just been argued is that prevailing conditions external to the city vary with the stage of development. For example whereas utility is a condition external to the "open" city, it is not external to the "transient" or to the "closed" city. It follows that the response of the city to changing conditions must also vary with the stage of development. I now turn to the description and the comparison of such responses when only one condition external to the city varies, with all other external conditions remaining fixed.[4] These results are based on the additional premise that both x_i and q_i have positive income effects for $i \in \mathcal{S}$ (figure 5.2).[5]

Figure 5.2: Positive income effects.

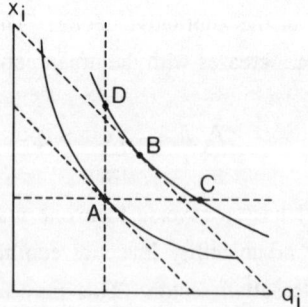

Figure 5.3: The effect of changing external conditions on an individual in an "open" city.

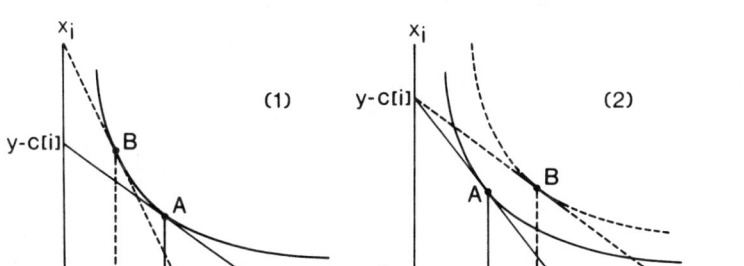

The conditions external to an "open" city pertain to disposable income, utility and the opportunity cost of land.

Consider figure 5.3(1). The indifference curve represents the exogenous utility level of the "open" city. The straight line tangent to the indifference curve at A represents the income constraint of an individual at i. Using the definition of income constraint, the y intercept of this straight line is the disposable income $y - c[i]$ and the corresponding slope is $-\bar{r}[i]$. Point A is the solution to the problem of an individual at i because it belongs to the highest indifference curve compatible with the income constraint. Consider a rise in disposable income. The y intercept will move upward but the tangency between the income constraint and the same, fixed, indifference curve at B will require a higher bid-rent (steeper slope of the straight line) and lower consumption of land. Since the same conclusion holds everywhere in the city, it must be that bid-rent and density will rise everywhere. In consequence the city becomes larger in terms of both population and spatial extent, more congested and more expensive. These changes are shown in figure 5.4(1) where, for simplicity, the natural logarithm of (4.1) is taken to represent the structure of bid-rent and density gradients at equilibrium. What essentially happens in this case is that the effect of

Urban Development

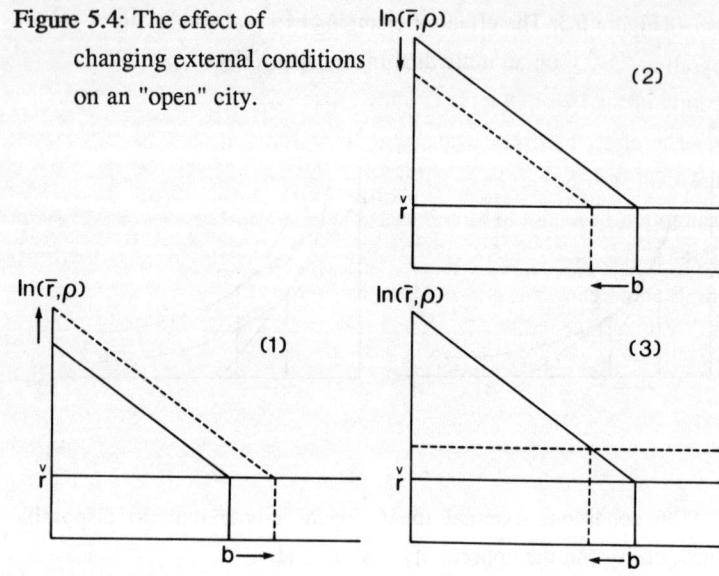

Figure 5.4: The effect of changing external conditions on an "open" city.

rising urban disposable income is eliminated by immigration of people expecting a better life in the city.

Consider figure 5.3(2). It represents a rise in the exogenous utility level. As a result of this rise, the point of tangency between the indifference curve and the income constraint will move from A to B. This corresponds to lower bid-rent and higher consumption of land. Since the same conclusion holds everywhere in the city, it must be that bid-rent and density will fall everywhere. In consequence the city becomes smaller in terms of both population and spatial extent, less congested and less expensive (figure 5.4(2)). The reason behind this effect is that utility increases with disposable income held constant. Then higher utility can only be justified through lower land values leading to higher per capita consumption of land. In other words land values and densities are reduced because emigration is faster than the conversion from the urban to the alternative land use at the border. Observe that the effect of rising utility is precisely the opposite to the effect of rising disposable income: whereas the former is eliminated by emigration, the latter is eliminated by immigration. In any case the direction of the flow points toward the new, exogenous, advantage.

The effect of rising land value in the alternative sector appears in figure 5.4(3). Since both disposable income and utility are fixed, consumption of land and bid–rent in (5.2) and (5.3) do not change while emigration in the urban fringe reduces the aggregate demand for urban land. Summarising these results

5.1 *For an "open" city at equilibrium, increasing income implies increasing urban area, population, land values and densities; increasing utility implies decreasing urban area, population, land values and densities; and increasing opportunity cost of land implies decreasing urban area and population, with land values and densities over the urban area remaining unaffected.*

The conditions external to a "transient" city pertain to disposable income, and the opportunity cost of land.

Consider figures 5.5(1) and 5.5(2). They correspond to an individual at the centre and near the border respectively of a "transient" city. The difference is that disposable income in the former case is higher because transportation cost is lower. Points A are the solutions to the problem of these individuals. Now, unlike in the case of an "open" city, the advantages of rising disposable income are not completely eliminated by immigration. During the early stages of a "transient" city, however, the consequent rise in utility will be small because the migratory mechanism is still effective. When such utility shifts are small as in figure 5.5(1) and 5.5(2), the new solutions B will require higher bid–rent and lower consumption of land everywhere within the city. In consequence the city becomes larger in terms of both population and spatial extent, more congested and more expensive. During this process the migratory mechanism becomes gradually less effective, so that rising

Figure 5.5: The effect of rising disposable income on an individual in a "transient" city.

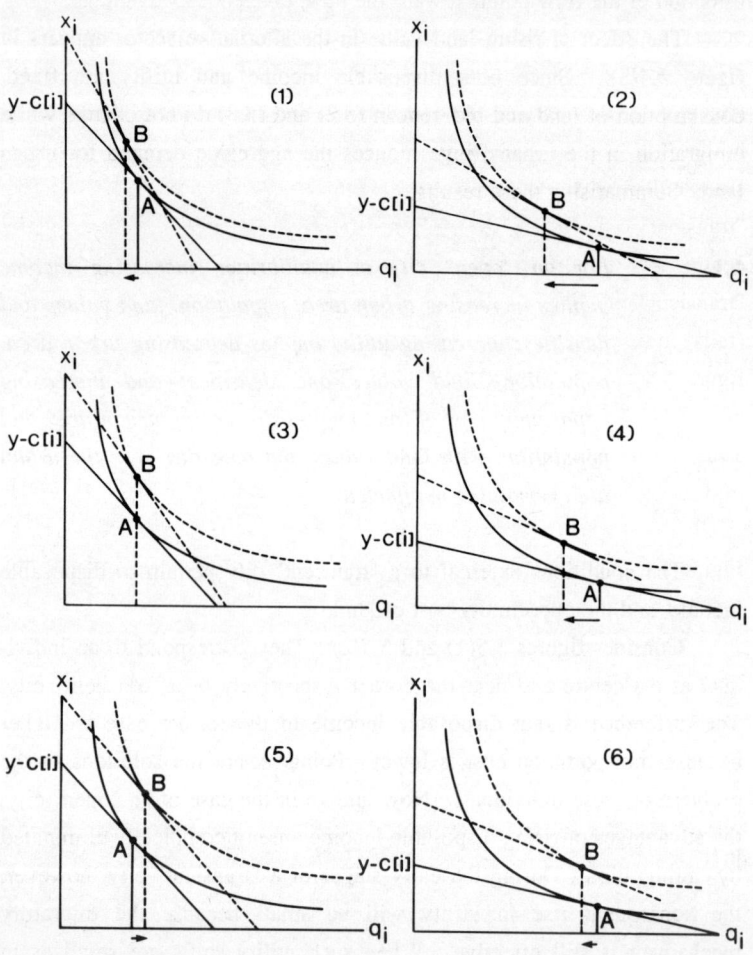

disposable income induces gradually stronger upward shifts in utility. When such utility shifts become large enough, as in figures 5.5(3) and 5.5(4), there is a qualitative change in the response to rising disposable income: namely, whereas the consumption of land near the border of the "transient" city continues to drop as before (figure 5.5(4)), it remains unaffected at the centre (figure 5.5(3)). As the upward shifts in utility become even stronger during the late stages of the "transient" city, one observes a complete reversal in the response to rising disposable income at the centre: the consumption of land at the centre now increases (figure 5.5(5)) while the trend toward more intensive land use near the border still persists (figure 5.5(6)). It turns out that analogous conclusions hold for the value of land at the centre. Precisely as there is a "transient" city size N^* below (above) which population density at the centre rises (falls) in response to rising disposable income, there is also a "transient" city size N^{**} below (above) which bid-rent at the centre rises (falls) in response to rising disposable income. These are summarised in figure 5.6. As in the case of an "open" city, rising disposable income creates a city larger in terms of both population and spatial extent. There is however an important difference: namely, although during the initial stages both land value and population density continue to increase

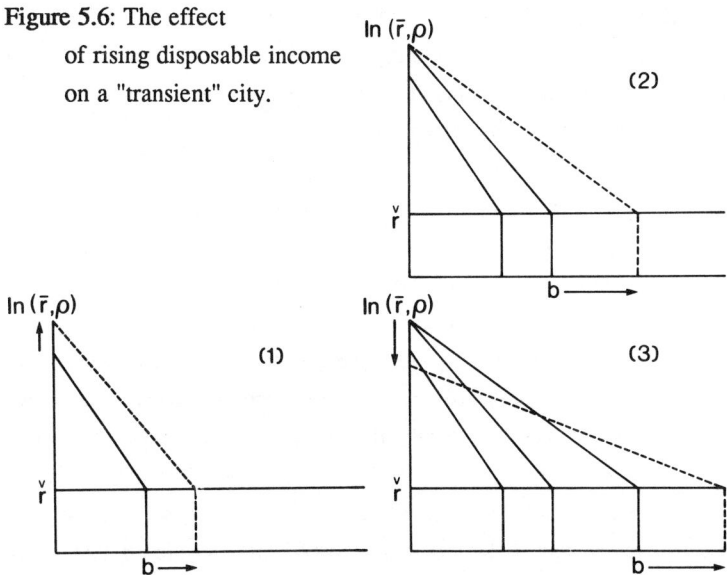

Figure 5.6: The effect of rising disposable income on a "transient" city.

everywhere (figure 5.6(1)), there comes a stage, probably distinct to each, during which they remain invariant at the centre (figure 5.6(2)) and beyond which they gradually begin to decrease at the centre (figure 5.6(3)). Since at the same time the city continues to expand, it must be the case that although land value and population density decrease at the centre, they increase at the periphery: this stage marks the beginning of suburbanisation. Nevertheless the corresponding disadvantages such as longer average distance from the centre and stronger competition for land do not completely eliminate the effect of rising income so that utility also increases.

The effect of rising land value in the alternative sector on an individual in a "transient" city appears in figure 5.7. The pressure for land–use conversion at the periphery is not completely eliminated through outmigration as in the case of an "open" city. For this reason, although the population of the city decreases, the value of urban land increases, the slope of the income constraint steepens and the solution to the problem of an individual moves from A to B, which corresponds to lower utility and higher density. The same conclusions hold for every location in the city. Thus higher land value in the alternative sector creates a city smaller not only in terms of population but also in spatial extent (figure 5.8). Summarising these results

5.2   *For a "transient" city at equilibrium, increasing disposable income implies increasing urban area, population and utility, and increasing (constant, decreasing) central land values and densities, each for an urban population smaller than (equal to, greater than) a particular size; and increasing opportunity cost of land implies decreasing urban area, population and utility, and increasing land values and densities.*

The conditions external to a "closed" city pertain to disposable income, population of the city and the opportunity cost of land.

Figure 5.7: The effect of rising opportunity cost of land on an individual in a "transient" city.

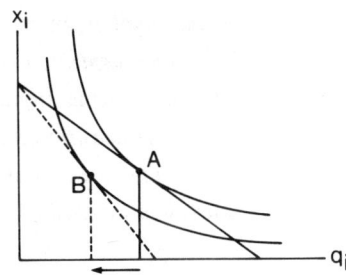

Figure 5.8: The effect of rising opportunity cost of land on a "transient" city.

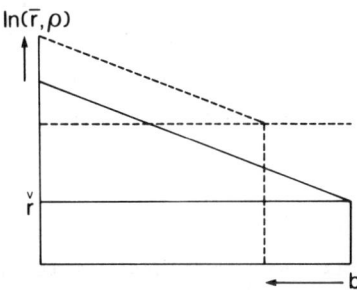

The "transient" city should be seen as a link between the "open" and the "closed": whereas during its early stages it resembles the "open", during its late stages it resembles the "closed". Thus increasing disposable income continues to cause suburbanisation and higher utility after the city has attained its "closed" form. Rising urban population, on the other hand, will create higher urban land values which, in turn, will affect individuals precisely as in figure 5.7. Then the effect of rising urban population on a "closed" city will be as in figure 5.4(1). At this point one should be cautious about the implication that rising urban population implies lower utility. Taken literally, it means that smaller cities are better and this counters intuition. The error with such an implication is that here one does not simply compare cities of different size, but cities of different size under a given level of income. Finally the effect of higher land value in the alternative sector is that of the "transient" city (figures 5.7 and 5.8). Summarising these results

Urban Development

5.3　　　*For a "closed" city at equilibrium, increasing disposable income implies increasing urban area and utility, and decreasing central land values and densities; increasing population of the city implies increasing urban area, land values and densities, and decreasing utility; and increasing opportunity cost of land implies decreasing urban area and utility, and increasing land values and densities.*

Changes in disposable income arise as changes either in income or in the cost of transportation. A difference between the two types of change is the following. When income changes, the consequent change in disposable income is the same for everyone in the city. When the cost of transportation per mile changes, the consequent change in disposable income increases away from the centre because the change per mile is weighted by distance at each location. This difference however does not affect the main implication here: that, since to increase income (transportation costs) is to increase (decrease) disposable income, the qualitative impact of the two types of change on the city is precisely the opposite. Now, the impact of changes in income itself is already described by the three propositions of this chapter. Using the same source, the impact of changes in the cost of transportation is the following. For an "open" city at equilibrium, increasing cost of transportation implies decreasing urban area, population, land values and densities; for a "transient" city at equilibrium, it implies decreasing urban area, population and utility, and decreasing (constant, increasing) central land values and densities for an urban population smaller than (equal to, greater than), a particular size;[6] and for a "closed" city at equilibrium it implies decreasing urban area and utility, and increasing central land values and densities.

I now imagine the following abstract process of urban development. I hold $\bar{r}$ and $\bar{v}[M-N]$ fixed. As technology develops over time, income rises and transportation conditions improve. These effects compound each other. Initially urban land values and densities increase

Figure 5.9: Process of urban development.

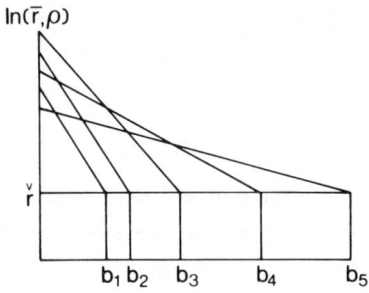

everywhere as immigration completely eliminates the effect of rising income and improved transportation ("open" city, b_1 and b_2 in figure 5.9). Eventually immigration weakens and utility begins to increase while urban land values and densities, although continuing to increase everywhere, begin to spread out ("transient" city, b_3). Beyond a certain stage central land values and densities begin to decrease while urban population and utility continue to increase. This is probably the period of strongest suburbanisation ("transient" city, b_4). Finally, immigration ceases altogether while utilities increase and the suburbanisation trend continues ("closed" city, b_5).

Example

Using the example of chapter four the description of the city at equilibrium given in (5.1)–(5.5) becomes

$$\bar{x}_i = \alpha(y - c[i])$$

$$\bar{q}_i = \left[\frac{z}{\alpha^\alpha \beta^\beta}(y - c[i])^{-\alpha}\right]^{1+\beta}$$

$$\bar{r}[i] = \left[\frac{\alpha^\alpha \beta^\beta}{z}(y - c[i])\right]^{1+\beta}$$

$$\sum_{j=1}^{b} \bar{n}_j = \sum_{j=1}^{b} \bar{p}_j \bigwedge_{j=1}^{b} Q = \sum_{j=1}^{b} \left[\frac{\alpha^{\alpha}\beta^{\beta}}{z}(y-c[j])^{\alpha}\right]^{1+\beta} \bigwedge_{j-1} Q = N$$

$$\left[\frac{\alpha^{\alpha}\beta^{\beta}}{z}(y-c[b])\right]^{1+\beta} = \check{r}.$$

In the case of an "open" city, the unknowns are $\bar{x}_i$, $\bar{q}_i$, $\bar{r}[i]$, N and b. On the other hand, the exogenous factors are $y - c[i]$, z, $\check{r}$, α, β and $\Delta_{j-1} Q$. The first three unknowns are already expressed in terms of parameters. From the last equation, we obtain the equilibrium boundary of the city. Substituting this into the population relationship we determine the equilibrium population of the city.

In the case of a "closed" city, N becomes a parameter and z becomes an unknown. Solving the population relationship for z, we have

$$z = \bar{u}[N] = \frac{\alpha^{\alpha}\beta^{\beta}}{N^{\beta}}\left[\sum_{j=1}^{b}(y-c[j])^{\alpha+\beta}\bigwedge_{j-1} Q\right]^{\beta}.$$

Substituting this into the boundary relationship, we obtain once more the equilibrium boundary of the city. At this point, the equilibrium utility level given by the last equation is also known. Substituting next the value of z into the second and third equations, we obtain

$$\bar{q}_i = \frac{1}{N}(y-c[i])^{-\alpha+\beta}\sum_{j=1}^{b}(y-c[j])^{\alpha+\beta}\bigwedge_{j-1} Q$$

$$\bar{r}[i] = N(y-c[i])^{1+\beta} \div \sum_{j=1}^{b}(y-c[j])^{\alpha+\beta}\bigwedge_{j-1} Q.$$

In the case of a "transient" city, we need to specify $\bar{u}[N]$ a priori. The derivation of the remaining unknowns is similar.

Theory and Reality

It must be remembered that the theory in this book is static and furthermore, that land is completely malleable, in other words that one could continuously adjust one's consumption of land in a way that optimal consumption dictates. A first step toward relaxing such assumptions is to consider preferences determined on housing, rather than simply on land. Housing is produced using land, labour and capital, which implies a supply side of the model far richer than the market for land as discussed here.

Once housing is introduced, it is possible to treat urban dynamics as an incremental process. Suppose that housing is perfectly durable and that urban development, occurring in successive zones away from the centre, proceeds under myopic foresight.[7] Then Anas (1978) has shown (1) that declining population densities can only be accounted for by sufficiently rising income and declining transportation costs; and (2) that, under these circumstances, an ever-increasing amount of central housing becomes abandoned. According to the first conclusion, observed density gradients are not the outcome of a balance between housing and transportation costs but rather the result of rising incomes and declining costs of transportation. The second, unrealistic conclusion is a direct consequence of imposing perfect durability. When this assumption is relaxed to allow for replaceable housing capital, both conclusions cease to be necessarily true and the general trend of density gradients becomes quite similar to that of the static model (Wheaton, (1982)). Clearly, the idea of durable, but replaceable, housing capital stands in between the perfectly flexible conditions of the static model and the perfectly inflexible conditions of the Anas (1978) model. In the light of these recent developments, the results of this chapter must be understood as partially correct, although oversimplifying the complexities involved in urban development. *The city at a macro-level and in the long run behaves as if it were close to equilibrium and land were completely malleable.* The city at a micro-level and in the short run, however, behaves in an entirely different manner.

Urban Development

Appendix to Chapter Five

It is probably useful here to restate some conventions used throughout. The variables q_i and ρ_i, although functions of n_i by (4.14) and (4.15) respectively, are treated as continuous. Thus the only discrete variables refer to population and distance from the centre. Furthermore, changes due to a discrete variable are explicitly treated as discrete; and changes of a discrete variable due to a continuous variable are treated as continuous.

Sections 1, 2 and 3 of this appendix are based on Wheaton (1974).

1

This section of the appendix contains some preliminary results to be used for the proofs of the three propositions stated in chapter five.

Consider figure 5.2. Since indifference curves are strictly convex (see chapter three) it must be that dx_i/dq_i is greater at point C than at point B, and hence also at point A. At point C, q_i has increased while x_i has been kept constant relative to point A. This immediately implies

(5.10) $$\frac{\partial}{\partial q_i}\left[\frac{dx_i}{dq_i}\right]\bigg|_{u_i=z} > 0.$$

From (3.6)

(5.11) $$\frac{dx_i}{dq_i}\bigg|_{u_i=z} = -\frac{\partial u}{\partial q_i} \div \frac{\partial u}{\partial x_i}$$

which, together with (5.10) implies

(5.12) $$\frac{\partial}{\partial q_i}\left[\frac{\partial u}{\partial q_i} \div \frac{\partial u}{\partial x_i}\right] < 0.$$

A similar argument leads to

(5.13) $$\frac{\partial}{\partial x_i}\left[\frac{\partial u}{\partial \bar{q}_i} \div \frac{\partial u}{\partial \bar{x}_i}\right] > 0$$

It is now possible to calculate the impact of changing parameters upon the solution of problem (3.11) for a given location i. From the definition of the budget constraint, (3.18) and (3.19), we have

(5.14) $$\bar{q}_i \frac{\partial u}{\partial \bar{q}_i} + \frac{\partial u}{\partial \bar{x}_i} = y - (\bar{x}_i + c_i).$$

Holding the transportation cost fixed, totally differentiate (3.20) and (5.14) to obtain

(5.15) $$\begin{bmatrix} \frac{\partial u}{\partial \bar{x}_i} & \frac{\partial u}{\partial \bar{q}_i} \\ \bar{q}_i \frac{\partial}{\partial \bar{x}_i}\left[\frac{\partial u}{\partial \bar{q}_i} \div \frac{\partial u}{\partial \bar{x}_i}\right] + 1 & \bar{q}_i \frac{\partial}{\partial \bar{q}_i}\left[\frac{\partial u}{\partial \bar{q}_i} \div \frac{\partial u}{\partial \bar{x}_i}\right] + \frac{\partial u}{\partial \bar{q}_i} \div \frac{\partial u}{\partial \bar{x}_i} \end{bmatrix} \begin{bmatrix} d\bar{x}_i \\ d\bar{q}_i \end{bmatrix}$$

$$= \begin{bmatrix} dz \\ dy \end{bmatrix}.$$

Holding z fixed and solving (5.15)

(5.16) $$\frac{\partial}{\partial y} \bar{x}[i;y,z] = \left[\left[\frac{\partial u}{\partial \bar{q}_i} \div \frac{\partial u}{\partial \bar{x}_i}\right] \div \bar{q}_i\right]$$

$$\div \left[\left[\frac{\partial u}{\partial \bar{q}_i} \div \frac{\partial u}{\partial \bar{x}_i}\right] \frac{\partial}{\partial \bar{x}_i}\left[\frac{\partial u}{\partial \bar{q}_i} \div \frac{\partial u}{\partial \bar{x}_i}\right] - \frac{\partial}{\partial \bar{q}_i}\left[\frac{\partial u}{\partial \bar{q}_i} \div \frac{\partial u}{\partial \bar{x}_i}\right]\right] > 0$$

(5.17) $$\frac{\partial}{\partial y} \bar{q}[i;y,z] = -(1 \div \bar{q}_i)$$

$$\div \left[\left[\frac{\partial u}{\partial \bar{q}_i} \div \frac{\partial u}{\partial \bar{x}_i}\right] \frac{\partial}{\partial \bar{x}_i}\left[\frac{\partial u}{\partial \bar{q}_i} \div \frac{\partial u}{\partial \bar{x}_i}\right] - \frac{\partial}{\partial \bar{q}_i}\left[\frac{\partial u}{\partial \bar{q}_i} \div \frac{\partial u}{\partial \bar{x}_i}\right]\right] < 0$$

by (3.3), (5.12) and (5.13). For a given location, to increase the cost of transportation is to decrease disposable income and vice versa. Therefore, using (5.16) and (5.17),

(5.18) $\quad \dfrac{\partial}{\partial c[i]} \bar{x}[i;y,z] < 0$

(5.19) $\quad \dfrac{\partial}{\partial c[i]} \bar{q}[i;y,z] > 0.$

From (5.17) and (5.19) together with (4.16)

(5.20) $\quad \dfrac{\partial}{\partial y} \bar{\rho}[i;y,z] > 0$

(5.21) $\quad \dfrac{\partial}{\partial c[i]} \bar{\rho}[i;y,z] < 0.$

Holding income fixed and solving (5.15)

(5.22) $\quad \dfrac{\partial}{\partial z} \bar{x}[i;y,z] = - \left[\dfrac{\partial u}{\partial \bar{q}_i} \left[\dfrac{\partial u}{\partial \bar{q}_i} \div \dfrac{\partial u}{\partial \bar{x}_i} \right] + \left[\dfrac{\partial u}{\partial \bar{q}_i} \div \dfrac{\partial u}{\partial \bar{x}_i} \right] \div \bar{q}_i \right]$

$\quad \div \left[\dfrac{\partial u}{\partial \bar{x}_i} \left[\left[\dfrac{\partial u}{\partial \bar{q}_i} \div \dfrac{\partial u}{\partial \bar{x}_i} \right] \dfrac{\partial}{\partial \bar{x}_i} \left[\dfrac{\partial u}{\partial \bar{q}_i} \div \dfrac{\partial u}{\partial \bar{x}_i} \right] - \dfrac{\partial}{\partial \bar{q}_i} \left[\dfrac{\partial u}{\partial \bar{q}_i} \div \dfrac{\partial u}{\partial \bar{x}_i} \right] \right] \right]$

which from (3.3), (5.12) and (5.13) implies

(5.23) $\quad \dfrac{\partial}{\partial z} \bar{x}[i;y,z] >(=,<) 0$ *if and only if*

$\quad \dfrac{\partial}{\partial \bar{q}_i} \left[\dfrac{\partial u}{\partial \bar{q}_i} \div \dfrac{\partial u}{\partial \bar{x}_i} \right] \div \left[\dfrac{1}{\bar{q}_i} \left[\dfrac{\partial u}{\partial \bar{q}_i} \div \dfrac{\partial u}{\partial \bar{x}_i} \right] \right] <(=,>) -1.$

This is a condition on the elasticity of the MRS of land for the private good with respect to land. Also

(5.24) $$\frac{\partial}{\partial z} \bar{q}[i;y,z] = \left[\frac{\partial}{\partial \bar{x}_i}\left[\frac{\partial u}{\partial \bar{q}_i} + \frac{\partial u}{\partial \bar{x}_i}\right] + \frac{1}{\bar{q}_i}\right.$$

$$\left. \div \left[\frac{\partial u}{\partial \bar{x}_i}\left[\left[\frac{\partial u}{\partial \bar{q}_i} + \frac{\partial u}{\partial \bar{x}_i}\right]\frac{\partial}{\partial \bar{x}_i}\left[\frac{\partial u}{\partial \bar{q}_i} + \frac{\partial u}{\partial \bar{x}_i}\right] - \frac{\partial u}{\partial \bar{q}_i}\left[\frac{\partial u}{\partial \bar{q}_i} + \frac{\partial u}{\partial \bar{x}_i}\right]\right]\right] > 0$$

again from (3.3), (5.12) and (5.13). Therefore, using (4.16) and (5.24)

(5.25) $$\frac{\partial}{\partial z} \bar{\rho}[i;y,z] < 0.$$

Using the envelope theorem on the rent maximisation problem (3.11), it is true that

(5.26) $$\frac{\partial}{\partial y} \sigma[i;y,z] = \frac{\partial}{\partial y}\left[\frac{1}{\bar{q}_i}(y - (x_i + c[i])) + \lambda_i(z - u_i)\right]$$

$$= \frac{1}{\bar{q}_i} > 0$$

(5.27) $$\frac{\partial}{\partial c[i]} \sigma(i;y,z) = \frac{\partial}{\partial c[i]}\left[\frac{1}{\bar{q}_i}(y - (x_i + c[i])) + \lambda_i(z - u_i)\right]$$

$$= -\frac{1}{\bar{q}_i} < 0.$$

From the definition of the budget constraint, (3.18) and (3.19)

(5.28) $$\frac{\partial}{\partial z} \sigma[i;y,z] = -\frac{1}{\bar{q}_i}\left[\frac{\partial \bar{x}_i}{\partial z} + \bar{r}[i]\frac{\partial \bar{q}_i}{\partial z}\right]$$

$$= -\frac{1}{\bar{q}_i}\left[\frac{\partial \bar{x}_i}{\partial z} + \left[\frac{\partial u}{\partial \bar{q}_i} + \frac{\partial u}{\partial \bar{x}_i}\right]\frac{\partial \bar{q}_i}{\partial z}\right],$$

where $\partial \bar{x}_i/\partial z \equiv \partial \bar{x}[i;y,z]/\partial z$, etc. Comparing (5.22) and (5.24), it is true that

Urban Development

(5.29) $\quad \dfrac{\partial \bar{x}_i}{\partial z} = 1 + \dfrac{\partial u}{\partial \bar{x}_i} - \left[\dfrac{\partial u}{\partial \bar{q}_i} \div \dfrac{\partial u}{\partial \bar{x}_i}\right] \dfrac{\partial \bar{q}_i}{\partial z}$

which, in conjunction with (5.28), gives

(5.30) $\quad \dfrac{\partial}{\partial z} \sigma[i;y,z] = -1 + \left[\bar{q}_i \dfrac{\partial u}{\partial \bar{x}_i}\right] < 0$

because of (3.3). This concludes the description of the impact of changing parameters upon the solution of problem (3.11).

The final result of this section pertains to the behaviour of $\partial u / \partial \bar{x}_i$ over space:

(5.31) $\quad \delta_i \left[\dfrac{\partial u}{\partial \bar{x}_i}\right] = \dfrac{\partial}{\partial \bar{x}_i}\left[\dfrac{\partial u}{\partial \bar{x}_i}\right] \delta_i \bar{x} + \dfrac{\partial}{\partial \bar{q}_i}\left[\dfrac{\partial u}{\partial \bar{x}_i}\right] \delta_i \bar{q}$

$\quad = \underset{i}{\Delta}\, c \left[\dfrac{\partial}{\partial \bar{x}_i}\left[\dfrac{\partial u}{\partial \bar{x}_i}\right]\dfrac{\partial \bar{x}}{\partial c[i]} + \dfrac{\partial}{\partial \bar{q}_i}\left[\dfrac{\partial u}{\partial \bar{x}_i}\right]\dfrac{\partial \bar{q}}{\partial c[i]}\right] > 0$

by (3.4), (5.18) and (5.19).

2

This section of the appendix contains a proof of the proposition that, for an "open" city at equilibrium, increasing disposable income implies increasing urban area, population, land values and densities; increasing utility implies decreasing urban area, population, land values and densities; and increasing opportunity cost of land implies decreasing urban area and population, with land values and densities over the urban area remaining unaffected.

In this case utility is a parameter and urban population is a variable. Totally differentiate (5.4) and (5.5) to obtain

$$\text{(5.32)} \quad \begin{bmatrix} \bar{n}_{b+1} + \underset{b}{\Delta} \bar{n} & -1 \\ \underset{b}{\Delta} \sigma & 0 \end{bmatrix} \begin{bmatrix} db \\ dN \end{bmatrix} = \begin{bmatrix} -\sum_j \frac{\partial \bar{n}}{\partial y}j \, dy - \sum_j \frac{\partial \bar{n}}{\partial z}j \, dz \\ -\frac{\partial \sigma_b}{\partial y} dy - \frac{\partial \sigma_b}{\partial z} dz + d\check{r} \end{bmatrix},$$

where $\partial \sigma_b / \partial y \equiv \partial \sigma[b;y,z]/y$, etc.

Holding $\bar{u}$ and $\check{r}$ constant, observe that for every location in $\mathcal{J}$ the only parameter of the bid–rent and population gradients that changes is the one being altered. In consequence

$$\text{(5.33)} \quad \frac{d\sigma_i}{dy} = \frac{\partial \sigma_i}{\partial y} > 0$$

$$\text{(5.34)} \quad \frac{d\bar{n}_i}{dy} = \frac{d\bar{\rho}_i}{dy} \underset{i-1}{\Delta} \varrho = \frac{\partial \bar{\rho}_i}{\partial y} \underset{i-1}{\Delta} \varrho > 0$$

from (5.26) and (5.20) respectively. Now solving (5.32)

$$\text{(5.35)} \quad \frac{db}{dy} = -\frac{\partial \sigma_b}{\partial y} + \underset{b}{\Delta} \sigma > 0$$

from (4.7) and (5.33), and

$$\text{(5.36)} \quad \frac{dN}{dy} = \left[-(\bar{n}_{b+1} + \underset{b}{\Delta} \bar{n}) \frac{\partial \sigma_b}{\partial y} + \underset{b}{\Delta} \sigma \sum_j \frac{\partial \bar{n}_j}{\partial y} \right] + \underset{b}{\Delta} \sigma > 0$$

from (4.7), (5.33) and (5.34), provided that

$$\text{(5.37)} \quad \bar{n}_{b+1} \geq \frac{1}{2} \bar{n}_b .$$

Holding y and $\check{r}$ constant, observe that for every location in $\mathcal{J}$ the only parameter of the bid–rent and population gradients that changes is the one being altered. In consequence

Urban Development

(5.38) $$\frac{d\sigma_i}{dz} \equiv \frac{\partial \sigma_i}{\partial z} < 0$$

(5.39) $$\frac{d\bar{n}_i}{dz} = \frac{d\bar{\rho}_i}{dz} \bigtriangleup_{i-1} Q = \frac{\partial \bar{\rho}_i}{\partial z} \bigtriangleup_{i-1} Q < 0$$

from (5.30) and (5.25) respectively. Now solving (5.32)

(5.40) $$\frac{db}{dz} = -\frac{\partial \sigma_b}{\partial z} \div \bigtriangleup_b \sigma < 0$$

from (4.7) and (5.38), and

(5.41) $$\frac{dN}{dz} = \left[-(\bar{n}_{b+1} + \bigtriangleup_b \bar{n}) \frac{\partial \sigma_b}{\partial z} + \bigtriangleup_b \sigma \sum_j \frac{\partial \bar{n}_j}{\partial z} \right] \div \bigtriangleup_b \sigma < 0$$

from (4.7), (5.38) and (5.39) provided that (5.37) is true.

Holding y and z constant, observe that since the arguments of the bid–rent and population gradients are exogenous they remain unchanged. Solving (5.32) once more

(5.42) $$\frac{db}{d\check{r}} = 1 \div \bigtriangleup_b \sigma < 0$$

(5.43) $$\frac{dN}{d\check{r}} = \left[\bar{n}_{b+1} + \bigtriangleup_b \bar{n} \right] \div \bigtriangleup_b \sigma < 0$$

from (4.7) if (5.37) is true. ∎

It should be noted that the conclusions concerning the effect of rising income, utility and the opportunity cost of land on the population of the city depend on the validity of (5.37), a requirement additional to those stated in conjunction with proposition 5.1. This requirement seems reasonable because $\Delta_{b-1} Q \leq \Delta_b Q$ and, intuitively, the density gradient is not steep at the border.

Urban Development

3

This section of the appendix contains a proof of the proposition that, for a "closed" city at equilibrium, increasing disposable income implies increasing urban area and utility, and decreasing central land values and densities; increasing population of the city implies increasing urban area, land values and densities, and decreasing utility; and increasing opportunity cost of land implies decreasing urban area and utility, and increasing land values and densities.

In this case utility is a variable and urban population is a parameter. Rearranging (5.32), we obtain

$$(5.44) \quad \begin{bmatrix} \bar{n}_{b+1} + \underset{b}{\Delta} \bar{n} & \sum_j \frac{\partial \bar{n}_j}{\partial z} \\ \underset{b}{\Delta} \sigma & \frac{\partial \sigma_b}{\partial z} \end{bmatrix} \begin{bmatrix} db \\ dz \end{bmatrix} = \begin{bmatrix} -\sum_j \frac{\partial \bar{n}_j}{\partial y} dy + \delta N \\ -\frac{\partial \sigma_b}{\partial y} dy + d\check{r} \end{bmatrix}.$$

Holding N and $\check{r}$ constant, solve (5.44) for

$$(5.45) \quad \frac{dz}{dy} = \left[-\frac{\partial \sigma_b}{\partial y}(\bar{n}_{b+1} + \underset{b}{\Delta} \bar{n}) + \underset{b}{\Delta} \sigma \sum_j \frac{\partial \bar{n}_j}{\partial y} \right]$$

$$\div \left[\frac{\partial \sigma_b}{\partial z}(\bar{n}_{b+1} + \underset{b}{\Delta} \bar{n}) - \underset{b}{\Delta} \sigma \sum_j \frac{\partial \bar{n}_j}{\partial z} \right] > 0$$

from (4.7), (5.26), (5.30), (5.34) and (5.39), if (5.37) is true. Totally differentiating the equilibrium border condition (5.5) and rearranging

$$(5.46) \quad \frac{\partial b}{\partial y} = -\left[\frac{\partial \sigma_b}{\partial y} + \frac{\partial \sigma_b}{\partial z} \frac{dz}{dy} \right] \div \underset{b}{\Delta} \sigma$$

$$= -\frac{\partial \sigma_b}{\partial y} \left[1 + \frac{\partial \sigma_b / \partial z}{\partial \sigma_b / \partial y} \frac{dz}{dy} \right] \div \underset{b}{\Delta} \sigma$$

$$= -\frac{\partial \sigma_b}{\partial y} \left[1 + \frac{-1 + (\bar{q}_b(\partial u / \partial \bar{x}_b))}{1 + \bar{q}_b} \frac{dz}{dy} \right] \div \underset{b}{\Delta} \sigma$$

$$= -\frac{\partial \sigma_b}{\partial y}\left[1 - \frac{dz}{dy} \div \frac{\partial u}{\partial \bar{x}_b}\right] \div \bigwedge_b \sigma$$

from (5.26) and (5.30). Totally differentiating (5.3) at the city centre

(5.47) $$\frac{d\sigma_1}{dy} = \frac{\partial \sigma_1}{\partial y} + \frac{\partial \sigma_1}{\partial z}\frac{dz}{dy} = \frac{\partial \sigma_1}{\partial y}\left[1 + \frac{\partial \sigma_1/\partial z}{\partial \sigma_1/\partial y}\frac{dz}{dy}\right]$$

$$= \frac{\partial \sigma_1}{\partial y}\left[1 - \frac{dz}{dy} \div \frac{\partial u}{\partial \bar{x}_1}\right]$$

as in the derivation of (5.46). Totally differentiating (5.2) at the city centre

(5.48) $$\frac{d\bar{q}_1}{dy} = \frac{\partial \bar{q}_1}{\partial y} + \frac{\partial \bar{q}_1}{\partial z}\frac{dz}{dy} = \frac{\partial \bar{q}_1}{\partial y}\left[1 + \frac{\partial \bar{q}_1/\partial z}{\partial \bar{q}_1/\partial y}\frac{dz}{dy}\right].$$

Now

(5.49) $$\frac{\partial \bar{q}_1}{\partial z} \div \frac{\partial \bar{q}_1}{\partial y} = \left\{\left[\frac{\partial}{\partial \bar{x}_1}\left[\frac{\partial u}{\partial \bar{q}_1} \div \frac{\partial u}{\partial \bar{x}_1}\right] + \frac{1}{\bar{q}_1}\right]\right.$$

$$\left. \div \left[\frac{\partial u}{\partial \bar{x}_1}\left[\left[\frac{\partial u}{\partial \bar{q}_1} \div \frac{\partial u}{\partial \bar{x}_1}\right]\frac{\partial}{\partial \bar{x}_1}\left[\frac{\partial u}{\partial \bar{q}_1} \div \frac{\partial u}{\partial \bar{x}_1}\right] - \frac{\partial}{\partial \bar{q}_1}\left[\frac{\partial u}{\partial \bar{q}_1} \div \frac{\partial u}{\partial \bar{x}_1}\right]\right]\right]\right\}$$

$$\div \left[-1 \div \bar{q}_1\left[\left[\frac{\partial u}{\partial \bar{q}_1} \div \frac{\partial u}{\partial \bar{x}_1}\right]\frac{\partial}{\partial \bar{x}_1}\left[\frac{\partial u}{\partial \bar{q}_1} \div \frac{\partial u}{\partial \bar{x}_1}\right] - \frac{\partial}{\partial \bar{q}_1}\left[\frac{\partial u}{\partial \bar{q}_1} \div \frac{\partial u}{\partial \bar{x}_1}\right]\right]\right]$$

$$= -\left[\bar{q}_1\frac{\partial}{\partial \bar{x}_1}\left[\frac{\partial u}{\partial \bar{q}_1} \div \frac{\partial u}{\partial \bar{x}_1}\right] + 1\right] \div \frac{\partial u}{\partial \bar{x}_1}$$

from (5.17) and (5.24). Combining (5.48) and (5.49)

(5.50) $$\frac{d\bar{q}_1}{dy} = \frac{\partial \bar{q}_1}{\partial y}\left\{1 - \left[\bar{q}_1\frac{\partial}{\partial \bar{x}_1}\left[\frac{\partial u}{\partial \bar{q}_1} \div \frac{\partial u}{\partial \bar{x}_1}\right] + 1\right]\left[\frac{dz}{dy} \div \frac{\partial u}{\partial \bar{x}_1}\right]\right\}.$$

The signs of db/dy, $d\sigma_1/dy$ and $d\bar{q}_1/dy$ depend on $(dz/dy) \div (\partial u/\partial \bar{x})$

evaluated at the centre and at the periphery of the city. In order to evaluate these quantities recall that

(5.51) $$\bar{n}_j = -\left[\underset{j}{\Delta}\sigma + \underset{j}{\Delta}c\right]\underset{j-1}{\Delta}\varrho$$

from (4.4) and (4.14). Upon substitution of (5.51) into (5.4)

(5.52) $$\sum_j \left[\underset{j}{\Delta}\sigma + \underset{j}{\Delta}c\right]\underset{j-1}{\Delta}\varrho = -N.$$

I now approximate the LHS of (5.52) as the discrete equivalent of integration by parts to obtain

(5.53) $$\check{r}\left[\underset{b-1}{\Delta}\varrho + \underset{b}{\Delta}c\right] - \sum_j \check{r}[j]\underset{j}{\Delta}\left[\underset{j-1}{\Delta}\varrho + \underset{j}{\Delta}c\right] = -N.^8$$

Totally differentiating (5.53) with respect to income

(5.54) $$\check{r}\underset{b}{\Delta}\left[\underset{b-1}{\Delta}\varrho + \underset{b}{\Delta}c\right]\frac{db}{dy}$$
$$= \sum_j \left[\frac{\partial\sigma_j}{\partial z}\frac{dz}{dy} + \frac{\partial\sigma_j}{\partial y}\right]\underset{j}{\Delta}\left[\underset{j-1}{\Delta}\varrho + \underset{j}{\Delta}c\right] - \check{r}\underset{b}{\Delta}\left[\underset{b-1}{\Delta}\varrho + \underset{b}{\Delta}c\right]\frac{db}{dy}$$
$$= -\sum_j \left[\frac{\partial\sigma_j}{\partial z}\frac{dz}{dy} + \frac{\partial\sigma_j}{\partial y}\right]\underset{j}{\Delta}\left[\underset{j-1}{\Delta}\varrho + \underset{j}{\Delta}c\right] = 0.^9$$

This implies

(5.55) $$\frac{dz}{dy} = \left[\sum_j \frac{\partial\sigma_j}{\partial y}\underset{j}{\Delta}\left[\underset{j-1}{\Delta}\varrho + \underset{j}{\Delta}c\right]\right]$$
$$\div \left[-\sum_j \frac{\partial\sigma_j}{\partial z}\underset{j}{\Delta}\left[\underset{j-1}{\Delta}\varrho + \underset{j}{\Delta}c\right]\right] =$$
$$\left[\sum_j \frac{\partial\sigma_j}{\partial y}\underset{j}{\Delta}\left[\underset{j-1}{\Delta}\varrho + \underset{j}{\Delta}c\right]\right] \div \left[\sum_j \frac{\partial\sigma_j}{\partial y} \div \frac{\partial u}{\partial \bar{x}_j}\right]\underset{j}{\Delta}\left[\underset{j-1}{\Delta}\varrho + \underset{j}{\Delta}c\right]$$

from (5.26) and (5.30). It follows that

Urban Development

$$(5.56) \quad \frac{dz}{dy} \div \frac{\partial u}{\partial \bar{x}_1} = \left[\sum_j \frac{\partial \sigma_j}{\partial y} \bigtriangleup_j \left[\bigtriangleup_{j-1} Q + \bigtriangleup_j c \right] \right]$$
$$+ \left[\sum_j \frac{\partial u}{\partial \bar{x}_1} \div \frac{\partial u}{\partial \bar{x}_j} \right] \frac{\partial \sigma_j}{\partial y} \bigtriangleup_j \left[\bigtriangleup_{j-1} Q + \bigtriangleup_j c \right] \right] > 1$$

$$(5.57) \quad \frac{dz}{dy} \div \frac{\partial u}{\partial \bar{x}_b} = \left[\sum_j \frac{\partial \sigma_j}{\partial y} \bigtriangleup_j \left[\bigtriangleup_{j-1} Q + \bigtriangleup_j c \right] \right]$$
$$+ \left[\sum_j \frac{\partial u}{\partial \bar{x}_b} \div \frac{\partial u}{\partial \bar{x}_j} \right] \frac{\partial \sigma_j}{\partial y} \bigtriangleup_j \left[\bigtriangleup_{j-1} Q + \bigtriangleup_j c \right] \right] < 1$$

because

$$(5.58) \quad \bigtriangleup_j \left[\bigtriangleup_{j-1} Q + \bigtriangleup_j c \right] > 0$$

according to (3.8);[10] and because

$$(5.59) \quad \frac{\partial u}{\partial \bar{x}_1} \div \frac{\partial u}{\partial \bar{x}_j} < 1$$

$$(5.60) \quad \frac{\partial u}{\partial \bar{x}_b} \div \frac{\partial u}{\partial \bar{x}_j} > 1$$

for $j \in]1, b[$ according to (5.31).

It is now possible to assess the signs of db/dy, $d\sigma_1/dy$ and $d\bar{q}_1/dy$. From (4.7), (5.26), (5.46) and (5.57)

$$(5.61) \quad \frac{db}{dy} > 0.$$

From (5.26), (5.47) and (5.56)

$$(5.62) \quad \frac{d\sigma_1}{dy} < 0.$$

From (5.13), (5.17), (5.50) and (5.56)

(5.63) $\quad \dfrac{d\bar{q}_1}{dy} > 0.$

Hence

(5.64) $\quad \dfrac{d\bar{\rho}_1}{dy} < 0.$

Holding y and $\check{r}$ constant and solving (5.44)

(5.65) $\quad \underset{N}{\delta} b = \dfrac{\partial \sigma_b}{\partial z} + \left[\dfrac{\partial \sigma_b}{\partial z} (\bar{n}_{b+1} + \underset{b}{\triangle} \bar{n}) - \underset{b}{\triangle} \sigma \sum_j \dfrac{\partial \bar{n}_j}{\partial z} \right] > 0$

(5.66) $\quad \underset{N}{\delta} z = - \underset{b}{\triangle} \sigma \div \left[\dfrac{\partial \sigma_b}{\partial z} (\bar{n}_{b+1} + \underset{b}{\triangle} \bar{n}) - \underset{b}{\triangle} \sigma \sum_j \dfrac{\partial \bar{n}_j}{\partial z} \right] < 0$

from (4.7), (4.15), (5.25) and (5.30) if (5.37) is true. Further, for every location in $\mathcal{J}$, income and travel cost are fixed as N changes z. In consequence

(5.67) $\quad \underset{N}{\delta} \sigma_i = \dfrac{\partial \sigma_i}{\partial z} \underset{N}{\delta} z > 0$

(5.68) $\quad \underset{N}{\delta} \bar{\rho}_i = \dfrac{\partial \bar{\rho}_i}{\partial \bar{u}} \underset{N}{\delta} z > 0$

from (4.15), (5.25), (5.30) and (5.66) if (5.37) is true.

Holding y and N constant and solving (5.44)

(5.69) $\quad \dfrac{db}{d\check{r}} = - \sum_j \dfrac{\partial \bar{n}_j}{\partial z} \div \left[\dfrac{\partial \sigma_b}{\partial z} (\bar{n}_{b+1} + \underset{b}{\triangle} \bar{n}) - \underset{b}{\triangle} \sigma \sum_j \dfrac{\partial \bar{n}_j}{\partial z} \right] < 0$

(5.70) $\quad \dfrac{dz}{d\check{r}} = (\bar{n}_{b+1} + \underset{b}{\triangle} \bar{n})$

$\qquad \div \left[\dfrac{\partial \sigma_b}{\partial z} (\bar{n}_{b+1} + \underset{b}{\triangle} \bar{n}) - \underset{b}{\triangle} \sigma \sum_j \dfrac{\partial \bar{n}_j}{\partial z} \right] < 0$

from (4.15), (5.25), (5.30) and (5.66) if (5.37) is true. Further, for every

Urban Development

location in $\mathcal{J}$, income and travel cost are fixed as $\check{r}$ changes z. In consequence

(5.71) $\quad \dfrac{d\sigma_i}{d\check{r}} = \dfrac{\partial \sigma_i}{\partial z}\dfrac{dz}{d\check{r}} > 0$

(5.72) $\quad \dfrac{d\bar{\rho}_i}{d\check{r}} = \dfrac{\partial \bar{\rho}_i}{\partial z}\dfrac{dz}{d\check{r}} > 0$

from (4.15), (5.25), (5.30) and (5.70) if (5.37) is true. ∎

It should be noted that, similarly to the case of an "open" city, the conclusions concerning the effects of rising urban population and the opportunity cost of land on the urban area, utility, land values and densities depend on the validity of (5.37), a requirement additional to those stated in conjunction with proposition 5.3.

4

This section of the appendix contains a proof of the proposition that, for a "transient" city at equilibrium, increasing disposable income implies increasing urban area, population and utility, and increasing (constant, decreasing) central land values and densities, each for an urban population smaller than (equal to, greater than) a particular size; and increasing opportunity cost of land implies decreasing urban area, population and utility, and increasing land values and densities.

In this case both utility and urban population are variables. Totally differentiate (5.4), (5.5) and (5.6) to obtain

Urban Development

$$
(5.73) \quad \begin{bmatrix} \bar{n}_{b+1} + \underset{b}{\Delta} \bar{n} & -1 & \sum_j \frac{\partial \bar{n}_j}{\partial z} \\ \underset{b}{\Delta} \sigma & 0 & \frac{\partial \sigma_b}{\partial z} \\ 0 & \underset{M-N}{\Delta} \bar{v} & 1 \end{bmatrix} \begin{bmatrix} db \\ dN \\ dz \end{bmatrix} = \begin{bmatrix} -\sum_j \frac{\partial \bar{n}_j}{\partial y} dy \\ -\frac{\partial \sigma_b}{\partial y} dy + d\check{r} \\ 0 \end{bmatrix}
$$

Holding $\check{r}$ constant and solving (5.73)

$$
(5.74) \quad \frac{db}{dy} = \left[-\frac{\partial \sigma_b}{\partial y} - \underset{M-N}{\Delta} \bar{v} \left(-\frac{\partial \sigma_b}{\partial z} \sum_j \frac{\partial \bar{n}_j}{\partial y} + \frac{\partial \sigma_b}{\partial y} \sum_j \frac{\partial \bar{n}_j}{\partial z} \right) \right]
$$

$$
\div \left[\underset{b}{\Delta} \sigma - \underset{M-N}{\Delta} \bar{v} \left[\frac{\partial \sigma_b}{\partial z} (\bar{n}_{b+1} + \underset{b}{\Delta} \bar{n}) - \underset{b}{\Delta} \sigma \sum_j \frac{\partial \bar{n}_j}{\partial z} \right] \right].
$$

In order to calculate the sign of (5.74), solve (5.44) for db/dy holding N and $\check{r}$ constant:

$$
(5.75) \quad \frac{db}{dy} = \left[-\frac{\partial \sigma_b}{\partial z} \sum_j \frac{\partial \bar{n}_j}{\partial y} + \frac{\partial \sigma_b}{\partial y} \sum_j \frac{\partial \bar{n}_j}{\partial z} \right]
$$

$$
\div \left[\frac{\partial \sigma_b}{\partial z} (\bar{n}_{b+1} + \underset{b}{\Delta} \bar{n}) - \underset{b}{\Delta} \sigma \sum_j \frac{\partial \bar{n}_j}{\partial z} \right].
$$

From (4.7), (4.15), (5.25), (5.30), (5.61) and (5.75) it must be that

$$
(5.76) \quad -\frac{\partial \sigma_b}{\partial z} \sum_j \frac{\partial \bar{n}_j}{\partial y} + \frac{\partial \sigma_b}{\partial y} \sum_j \frac{\partial \bar{n}_j}{\partial z} < 0
$$

if (5.37) is true. Then

$$
(5.77) \quad \frac{db}{dy} > 0
$$

from (4.7), (4.15), (5.8), (5.25), (5.26), (5.30), (5.74) and (5.76) if (5.37) is true. Furthermore, also from (5.73),

Urban Development

(5.78) $$\frac{dN}{dy} = \left[-(\bar{n}_{b+1} + \bigtriangleup_b \bar{n}) \frac{\partial \sigma_b}{\partial y} + \bigtriangleup_b \sigma \sum_j \frac{\partial \bar{n}_j}{\partial y} \right]$$

$$+ \left[\bigtriangleup_b \sigma - \bigtriangleup_{M-N} \bar{v} \left[\frac{\partial \sigma_b}{\partial z} (\bar{n}_{b+1} + \bigtriangleup_b \bar{n}) - \bigtriangleup_b \sigma \sum_j \frac{\partial \bar{n}_j}{\partial z} \right] \right] > 0$$

(5.79) $$\frac{dz}{dy} = \left[-\bigtriangleup_{M-N} \bar{v} \left[-(\bar{n}_{b+1} + \bigtriangleup_b \bar{n}) \frac{\partial \sigma_b}{\partial y} + \bigtriangleup_b \sigma \sum_j \frac{\partial \bar{n}_j}{\partial y} \right] \right]$$

$$+ \left[\bigtriangleup_b \sigma - \bigtriangleup_{M-N} \bar{v} \left[\frac{\partial \sigma_b}{\partial z} (\bar{n}_{b+1} + \bigtriangleup_b \bar{n}) - \bigtriangleup_b \sigma \sum_j \frac{\partial \bar{n}_j}{\partial z} \right] \right] > 0$$

from (4.7), (4.15), (5.8), (5.20), (5.25) and (5.30) if (5.37) is true.

Consider now the behaviour of $d\bar{p}_1/dy$, $d\sigma_1/dy$, as $-\Delta_{M-N}$ changes with population. Initially, when $-\Delta_{M-N} \bar{v}$ equals zero, these derivatives are positive. Eventually, when $-\Delta_{M-N} \bar{v}$ is infinite, these derivatives are negative. Since all functions here are considered to be smooth for smooth changes of the parameters, the change of these derivatives must also be smooth as the change in population is approximated by a smooth change. Hence there are population sizes N^* and N^{**} of the "transient" city such that

(5.80) $$\frac{d\bar{p}_1}{dy} >(=,<) 0 \text{ for } N <(=,>) N^*$$

(5.81) $$\frac{d\sigma_1}{dy} >(=,<) \text{ for } N <(=,>) N^{**}.$$

Holding y constant and solving (5.73)

(5.82) $$\frac{db}{d\check{r}} = \left[1 + \bigtriangleup_{M-N} \bar{v} \sum_j \frac{\partial \bar{n}_j}{\partial z} \right]$$

$$+ \left[\bigtriangleup_b \sigma - \bigtriangleup_{M-N} \bar{v} \left[\frac{\partial \sigma_b}{\partial z} (\bar{n}_{b+1} + \bigtriangleup_b \bar{n}) - \bigtriangleup_b \sigma \sum_j \frac{\partial \bar{n}_j}{\partial z} \right] \right] < 0$$

(5.83) $$\frac{dN}{d\check{r}} = (\bar{n}_{b+1} + \bigtriangleup_b \bar{n})$$

$$\div \left[\bigtriangleup_b \sigma - \bigtriangleup_{M-N} \bar{v} \left[\frac{\partial \sigma_b}{\partial z}(\bar{n}_{b+1} + \bigtriangleup_b \bar{n}) - \bigtriangleup_b \sigma \sum_j \frac{\partial \bar{n}_j}{\partial z} \right] \right] < 0$$

(5.84) $$\frac{dz}{dr} = - \bigtriangleup_{M-N} \bar{v} (\bar{n}_{b+1} + \bigtriangleup_b \bar{n})$$

$$\div \left[\bigtriangleup_b \sigma - \bigtriangleup_{M-N} \bar{v} \left[\frac{\partial \sigma_b}{\partial z}(\bar{n}_{b+1} + \bigtriangleup_b \bar{n}) - \bigtriangleup_b \sigma \sum_j \frac{\partial \bar{n}_j}{\partial z} \right] \right] < 0$$

from (4.7), (4.15), (5.8), (5.25), (5.26) and (5.30) if (5.37) is true. Further, for every location in $\mathcal{J}$, income and travel cost are fixed as $\check{r}$ changes z. In consequence

(5.85) $$\frac{d\bar{p}_i}{d\check{r}} = \frac{\partial \bar{p}_i}{\partial z}\frac{dz}{d\check{r}} > 0$$

(5.86) $$\frac{d\sigma_i}{d\check{r}} = \frac{\partial \sigma_i}{\partial z}\frac{dz}{d\check{r}} > 0$$

from (4.15), (5.25), (5.30) and (5.84) if (5.37) is true. ∎

With the exception of the conclusions concerning the effects of rising income on central land values and densities, all other conclusions depend on the validity of (5.37), a requirement additional to those stated in conjunction with proposition 5.2.

Notes to Chapter Five

1   Burns (1982, pp. 1618–1619).

2   See for example Clark (1951), and Berry, Simmons and Tennant (1963).

Urban Development

3   The "open"–"closed" dichotomy was first introduced by Wheaton (1974), this being the original source for most of the subsequent results stated in this chapter. Part of the diagrammatic exposition is due to Thrall (1980).

4   The technique is comparative statics. It must be clearly understood that, within this context, an urban response to a changing condition is the derivative of some variable with respect to some parameter. Hence changes to be examined are small and statements about consequent responses hold only within the close vicinity of the equilibrium under consideration. For a discussion of the technique see, for example, Samuelson (1970, chapter two).

5   There are some other secondary requirements discussed in the appendix. To define positive income effects consider figure 5.2. For given i, suppose that the solution to problem (3.10) is represented by point A. Suppose now that utility increases and that point B on the corresponding higher indifference curve has the same slope as point A on the original lower indifference curve. Then if point B lies within the upper right quadrant of point A, x_i and q_i have positive income effects.

6   It should be noted that the urban population size that marks the beginning of suburbanisation for increasing income does not necessarily coincide with that for decreasing transportation cost.

7   Myopic foresight means that a decision–maker takes into account only current variables.

8   Let

$$f \equiv \bigwedge_{j-1} Q \div \bigwedge_{j} c \text{ and } dg \equiv \bigwedge_{j} \sigma.$$

Then

$$\int_0^b f\,dg = fg|_b - \int_0^b g\,df$$

is the continuous prototype of (5.53), with $\bar{r}[b] = \check{r}$ by (5.5).

9   Differentiation under the sum of (5.53) is approximated as the discrete equivalent of the rule of Leibnitz, namely, following the notation of note 8

$$\frac{d}{dy}\int_0^b g\,df = \int_0^b \frac{d}{dy}g\,df + \frac{db}{dy}g\,df|_b \,.$$

10 Taking the difference of (5.58)

$$\underset{j}{\Delta}\left[\underset{j-1}{\Delta}Q + \underset{j}{\Delta}c\right] = \left[\underset{j}{\Delta}c\underset{j-1}{\Delta^2}Q - \underset{j-1}{\Delta}Q\underset{j}{\Delta^2}c\right] + \left[\underset{j}{\Delta}c\underset{j+1}{\Delta}c\right],$$

which immediately confirms its sign because $\Delta^2_{j-1}Q \geq 0$ given that the city has a regular shape as discussed in chapter four.

6

The Case of Income Variations

The Slope Test [1]

Chapters four and five dealt with a population of identical individuals. Now this assumption is partially relaxed through income variations. Preferences however remain identical throughout.

If one allows for income variations then, in principle, both bid-rent and transportation cost must vary with income. The former may be confirmed by (5.3) and the latter may be argued on the grounds that transportation cost not only depends on the direct money cost of travel but also on the related indirect time cost. If time is more valuable for the rich then the unit cost of transportation must rise with income:

(6.1) $$\frac{\partial}{\partial y} \Delta_i c > 0 \quad \text{for } i \in \mathcal{J}.$$

Differences between the bid-rent functions of different income classes determine the spatial distribution of these classes over the urban area in the following manner. If one class is more centrally located than another then it must necessarily be that the slope of the bid-rent function of the former is steeper than that of the latter (figure 6.1). This ob–

Figure 6.1: Bid-rents for two income classes.

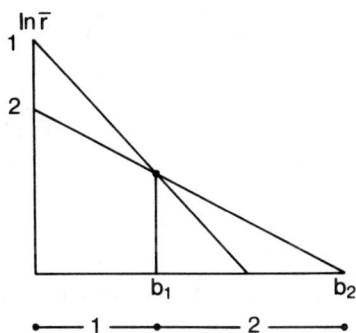

servation gives rise to the idea of the slope test, whereby the variation of slope steepness with income provides a description of how existing income classes are spatially distributed. In order that the rich live near the centre it must be that the slope of the bid-rent function decreases as income increases:

(6.2) $$\frac{\partial}{\partial y} \underset{i}{\Delta} \bar{r} < 0 \text{ for } i \in \mathcal{J}.$$

On the other hand, in order that the poor live near the centre it must be that the slope of the bid-rent function increases as income increases:

(6.3) $$\frac{\partial}{\partial y} \underset{i}{\Delta} \bar{r} > 0 \text{ for } i \in \mathcal{J}.$$

Conditions (6.2) and (6.3) are necessary but not sufficient for the emergence of a concentric land-use pattern. This happens because, although the bid-rent function of one class may be steeper than that of another, the steep bid-rent gradient may be everywhere lower than the flat one. In this case the former class will be outbid everywhere. To ascertain the existence of both classes within the urban area one needs, further to either (6.2) or (6.3), $0 < b_1 < b_2$ in figure 6.1; and in the case of more than two classes, one needs $0 < b_1 < b_2 < b_3 \ldots$. Under these circumstances, using (4.7),

Income Variations

(6.4) $\quad \dfrac{\partial}{\partial y} \underset{i}{\triangle} \bar{r} = -\dfrac{1}{\bar{q}_i}\dfrac{\partial}{\partial y}\underset{i}{\triangle} c + \dfrac{1}{\bar{q}_i^2}\dfrac{\partial q_i}{\partial y}\underset{i}{\triangle} c$

$\quad\quad = -\dfrac{1}{\bar{q}_i\, y}\underset{i}{\triangle} c \left[\dfrac{\partial}{\partial y}\underset{i}{\triangle} c \div \left[\dfrac{1}{y}\underset{i}{\triangle} c\right] - \dfrac{\partial \bar{q}_i}{\partial y} \div \dfrac{\bar{q}_i}{y}\right]$

$\quad\quad \equiv -\dfrac{1}{\bar{q}_i\, y}\underset{i}{\triangle} c \left[\eta_{c:y} - \eta_{q:y}\right]$

where $\eta_{c:y}$ is the income elasticity of the unit cost of transportation and $\eta_{q:y}$ is the income elasticity of the demand for land at equilibrium. From (3.8), (6.1) and the assumption of a positive income effect for q_i (figure 5(2)), both these elasticities must be positive. Furthermore, using (3.8) and (6.4)

(6.5) $\quad \dfrac{\partial}{\partial y}\underset{i}{\triangle}\bar{r} <(=,>) 0 \;\;\textit{if and only if}\;\; \eta_{c:y} >(=,<) \eta_{q:y}\,.$

Condition (6.5) is intuitively revealing. It connects the urban land-use pattern with two elasticities. The former, $\eta_{c:y}$, reflects how important centrality is to individuals because it describes how fast costs to overcome the friction of distance increase relative to income. The latter, $\eta_{q:y}$, reflects how important land is to individuals because it describes how fast the demand for land increases relative to income. In consequence, the land-use pattern depends upon the importance individuals place on centrality relative to the consumption of land. If centrality is more important then the rich live near the centre. If, on the other hand, land occupancy is more important, then the poor live near the centre. Generalising these concepts somewhat, so that centrality also reflects intangibles such as a quest for urban qualities of life, while the demand for land reveals a sense of value for property, (6.5) becomes still another facet of the well known "community versus privacy" issue: if the city as a public good is more important then the rich live near the centre. If, on the other hand, individualism prevails then the poor live near the centre.

These conclusions hold for any income distribution, ranging from two distinct income classes to a continuum. In any case, condition (6.5) normally suggests a segregated pattern of land use, one where income either increases or decreases away from the centre. The only significant exception occurs when there is a balance between centrality and the demand for land in the sense that

(6.6) $\quad \eta_{c:y} = \eta_{q:y}$.

Under these circumstances, there is a state of locational indeterminacy over the land, whereby a random mix of different income classes is observed. This of course presumes identical bid–rent functions. Otherwise a single income class would dominate completely.

Example

Consider two income groups, group one representing the poor and group two the rich. Preferences are the same for both groups, and so are transportation costs. Thus, in this example,

$$\frac{\partial}{\partial y} \underset{i}{\Delta} c = 0$$

and condition (6.5) gives

$$\frac{\partial}{\partial y} \underset{i}{\Delta} \bar{r} > 0,$$

that is, the poor must live around the centre at equilibrium. In order to see this, using the example of chapter four,

$$\bar{r}^1[i] = \left[\frac{\alpha^\alpha \beta^\beta}{z^1} \left[y^1 - c[i] \right] \right]^{1+\beta}$$

Income Variations

$$\bar{r}^2[i] = \left[\frac{\alpha^\alpha \beta^\beta}{z^2}\left[y^2 - c[i]\right]\right]^{1+\beta}$$

where

$y^1 < y^2$ and $z^1 < z^2$.

Using figure 6.1, $\bar{r}^1[b_1] = \bar{r}^2[b_1]$ implies

$$\frac{y^1 - c[b_1]}{z^1} = \frac{y^2 - c[b_1]}{z^2}.$$

Solving for $c[b_1]$, we obtain

$$c[b_1] = \frac{z^1 y^2 - z^2 y^1}{z^1 - z^2}$$

which must be positive if both groups have a place in the city at equilibrium. Since $z^1 < z^2$, it must be that $z^1 y^2 < z^2 y^1$ also, or

$$\frac{1}{z^1} y^1 > \frac{1}{z^2} y^2.$$

This is equivalent to

$$\left[\frac{\alpha^\alpha \beta^\beta}{z^1} y^1\right]^{1+\beta} > \left[\frac{\alpha^\alpha \beta^\beta}{z^2} y^2\right]^{1+\beta}.$$

Given that transportation costs at zero distance from the centre are equal to zero, the last inequality can be interpreted as

$\bar{r}^1[0] > \bar{r}^2[0]$

which, using figure 6.1, implies that the poor occupy the centre in this example—as expected.

Theory and Reality

There is little reliable evidence connecting income variation with distance from the centre. It is known however that systematic locational differences do exist. For example, whereas the typical urban poor in North America live at the centre, those in Latin America live at the periphery.[2] Similarly, socioeconomic status decreases away from the city centre in several other non-Western countries. In India, for example, the influence of the caste system appears in the concentration of higher castes around the centre and in the dispersion of lower castes over the periphery. On the other hand, in several western countries, socioeconomic status increases away from the city centre. It is interesting to note how such differences may be attributed to historical and cultural factors, rather than to pure economics. It should be borne in mind however that such conclusions must be applied to cities beyond a certain stage of development. At the beginning, when the city is sufficiently small, there is no significant tradeoff between accessibility and privacy so that the distinction cannot arise.

Suburbanisation is a strong characteristic of urban development in Western cities where socioeconomic status increases away from the centre. On the other hand, in non-Western cities,

> "any income improvements lead to greater demands for central locations, and increased overcrowding. Sprawl reflects projection of the overall surface outward as densities increase throughout, in a periphery of degrading and depressing slums. Degree of compactness of the non-Western city remains, therefore, relatively unchanged, with the least mobile groups located at the periphery. In spite of reductions of transport costs in non-Western cities, the groups located where the possibilities of saving are greatest are the

Income Variations

groups least able to take advantage of the possibilities. Changes on the supply side occasioned by transport improvements are of little utility. Differences in movements of central densities and density gradients through time are a function of the invested locational patterns of socio-economic groups within Western and non-Western cities, and attendant contrasts in demands for residential land." [3]

Cast in terms of this book, development implies lower transportation costs and higher incomes. The former causes a flattening of population density and land-value surfaces in both Western and non-Western cities. The effects of the latter vary. In Western cities where (6.3) holds, higher incomes compound the effect of transportation improvements. On the other hand, in non-Western cities where (6.2) holds, higher incomes and transportation improvements work in the opposite direction. Thus population density and land-value surfaces in large non-Western cities behave approximately as in the "open" model, while their Western counterparts behave as in the "closed" model. According to the previous arguments, such differences should be attributed not only to differences in the stage of urban development, as in chapter five, but also to cultural differences which may account for reverse location patterns.

Response to Changing Conditions [4]

Suppose that there are m distinct income classes in the city arranged so that

(6.7) $\quad y^1 < y^2 < ... < y^m.$

Further suppose that the transportation cost depends only on distance. Then $\eta_{c:y}$ must be zero and (6.5) implies that the slope of the bid-rent function increases with income, in other words that the rich live further away. The emerging income zones are defined in the following manner. Since the bid-rent functions of two consecutive income classes differ in slope, locational indeterminacy occurs only in a single area between the two classes, where individuals of both classes are assumed to bid identically. To eliminate such indeterminacy, I take it that this area belongs entirely to the lower income class. Thus the transition between income zones is marked by the boundary between two adjacent areas. Invoking once more the difference in slope between the bid-rent functions of two consecutive income classes, income zones must be connected. Thus the income zone j is

(6.8) $\qquad \mathcal{J}^j = \,]b_{j-1}, b_j\,]$

where b_{j-1} and b_j are the outer boundaries for income classes $j-1$ and j respectively, and where

(6.9) $\qquad \mathcal{J} = \underset{j}{\cup} \mathcal{J}^j .^5$

The spatial relationships between income zones $\mathcal{J}^j$, outer *boundary areas* b^j and outer *boundaries* b_j are shown in figure 6.2 which follows the principles of figure 3.1.

Figure 6.2: Partition of the urban area into income zones.

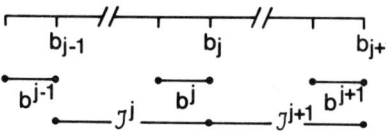

For each income class, the spatial distributions of consumption, land occupancy and land values in the corresponding income zone are given by the solution to a Casetti equilibrium as

(6.10) $\bar{x}_i^j = \bar{x}[i;y^j,z^j]$

(6.11) $\bar{q}_i^j = \bar{q}[i;y^j,z^j]$

(6.12) $\bar{r}_i^j = \sigma[i;y^j,z^j]$

respectively; the population distribution of income classes at equilibrium is

(6.13) $\sum_{i \in \mathcal{J}^j} \bar{n}_i^j = N^j$;

and the spatial extent of income zones is determined by the m border conditions

(6.14) $\sigma[b^j;y^j,z^j] = \sigma[b^j;y^{j+1},z^{j+1}]$ for $j < m$

(6.15) $\sigma[b^m;y^m,z^m] = \check{r}$.

Equations (6.10)–(6.15) completely describe the multiclass city under a Casetti equilibrium.

Consider the case of a "closed" city. In particular, consider the effect that the rising income and population of a class k have on the spatial extent of the city and on the welfare of the various classes in the city.

When the income of a class rises it is possible to distinguish the following two spatial effects. Firstly, there is a rise in the demand for land which creates pressure along the boundaries with the adjacent classes. Secondly, there is a preference for more distant locations (richer individuals live further away) which creates a void along the inner boundary and a pressure along the outer boundary. These effects are shown in figure 6.3. When the transportation cost does not depend on income, the location effect dominates and both boundaries associated with class k move outward. Since there is now more space available for

Income Variations

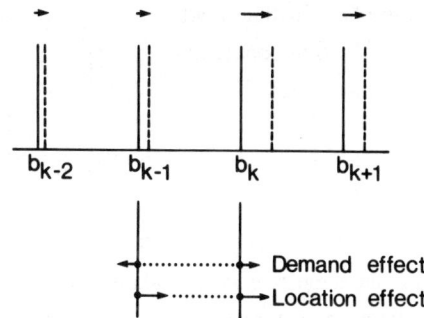

Figure 6.3: Spatial effects of rising income of class k.

class $k - 1$, $\bar{r}^{k-1}$ falls so that b_{k-2} moves outward and so on, until the zone of the class surrounding the centre is similarly affected. On the other hand, since there is now less space available for class $k + 1$, $\bar{r}^{k+1}$ rises so that b_{k+2} moves outward and so on, until the zone of the richest class surrounded by the alternative sector is similarly affected.[6] The welfare implications of such spatial adjustments are immediate. Class k will enjoy higher utility because of higher income; every class poorer than class k will also enjoy higher utility because of lower bid–rents caused by more available land; and every class richer than class k will suffer a loss in utility because of higher bid–rents caused by less available land. In consequence

(6.16) $\qquad \dfrac{db^j}{dy^k} > 0$ for all j and k; $\dfrac{dz^j}{dy^k} > (<) \; 0 \; for \; j \leq (>) \; k$

where db^j does not mean a change in the size of the boundary area, but rather a change in its location.

When the population of a class rises, the only spatial effect is a consequent rise in the demand for land which creates pressure along the boundaries with the adjacent classes through higher bid–rents. This effect is shown in figure 6.4. Since there is now less space available for class $k - 1$, $\bar{r}^{k-1}$ rises so that b_{k-2} moves inward and so on, until the zone of the poorest class surrounding the centre is similarly affected.

145

Income Variations

Figure 6.4: Spatial effect of rising population of class k.

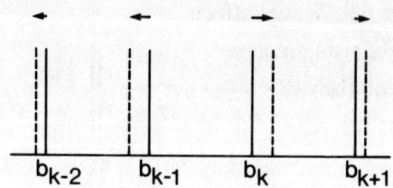

For the same reason, boundaries beyond b_k move outward. As for the welfare implications of such spatial adjustments, every class will suffer a loss in utility because of a general rise in bid-rents. In consequence

(6.17) $\delta_{N^k} z^j < 0$ *for all j and k;* $\delta_{N^k} b^j <(>) 0$ *for* $j <(\geq) k$.

Summarising these results

6.1 *If, in a "closed" city, the income of a class rises then all boundaries move away from the centre, the welfare of poorer classes increases together with that of the class under consideration and the welfare of richer classes decreases. If, on the other hand, the population of a class rises then the welfare of all classes decreases, boundaries between the centre and the class under consideration move toward the centre and the remaining boundaries move away from the centre.*

The perfect asymmetry of these conclusions, clearly displayed in (6.16) and (6.17), is remarkable. That a rise in the income of one class causes an increase in the utility of all lower-income classes and a decrease in the utility of all higher-income classes is disturbing because it implies that the most innocuous rise is that of the highest-income class. In other words, greater inequality implies greater welfare for everyone.[7] Therefore, if motives of individuals are selfish, it is clear that the change to be met with the greatest resistance is a rise in the income of the poorest. The foundation upon which such conclusions are built is the dominance of the location effect over the demand effect in figure 6.3 which causes all boundaries to move away from the centre. Stated differently, these conclusions are predicated on a strong preference for more distant locations as income rises. This certainly is the case when the transportation cost is independent of income. If though the transportation cost depends on income then the preference for more distant locations weakens because transportation becomes more expensive according to (6.1). In consequence, if the effect of income on transportation is strong enough, increasing the income of the rich may worsen the condition of the poor. Under these circumstances, encouragement of income homogeneity will probably be easier to achieve.

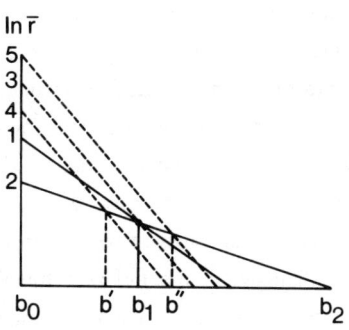

Figure 6.5: Adjustments of bid–rent to changing conditions.

In order to explain the previous argument in more detail, consider the following two cases, both referring to figure 6.5. Assume first that there are two bid–rent functions, 1 and 2, defining two income zones with common boundary b_1. For some reason, suppose that the bid–rent function of the first class rotates clockwise to 3, thus causing individuals of the first class to pay higher rent everywhere within their income zone. If the reason behind that change does not generate a demand for land sufficiently higher to compensate for the rent increase, the bid–rent function will shift downward to 4 where the demand and supply of land

Income Variations

are equal. The new boundary b' allows more space for individuals of the second class. In consequence, after the process of readjustment has been completed, the individuals of the second class will enjoy greater welfare. With the first class representing the poor and the second class representing the rich, this describes the main result of this section: that decreasing (increasing) the income of the poor will augment (reduce) the welfare of the rich.

Suppose now that the cost of transportation depends on income and it is such that the income elasticity of the unit cost of transportation is greater than the income elasticity of the demand for land. Then, according to (6.5), the first class represents the rich and an obvious reinterpretation of the preceding paragraph describes once more the main result of this section: that increasing the income of the rich will augment the welfare of the poor. It is conceivable however that higher income can generate a demand for land sufficiently higher to compensate for the rent increase. Then bid–rent function 3 will be observed and the welfare of the poor will remain unaffected. An even stronger effect of rising income upon the demand for land will shift the bid–rent function upward to 5. The new boundary b'' allows less space for the poor. In consequence, after the process of readjustment has been completed, the poor will suffer a loss of welfare instead of a gain as before.

Changes in the bid–rent function 2 can also be described in an analogous manner. When the transportation cost did not depend on income,

"... increasing the income of the peripherally located rich flattened their bids sufficiently so that the higher price of land outweighed the impact of greater income, and land demands were reduced (near b_1). This naturally benefited the inner located poor."[8]

The flattening of the bid–rent function is precisely the reason behind the so-called location effect in figure 6.3. Therefore, when transportation cost depends on income, this flattening weakens because

Income Variations

transportation becomes more expensive. Then it is possible that the demand effect dominates, and we observe a movement of the boundary toward b' with all its adverse consequences on the welfare of the poor.

Appendix to Chapter Six

1

This section of the appendix establishes that income zones are homogeneous, connected and arranged so that income rises away from the centre. In conjunction with figure 6.2, if bid–rents intersect only once, it is sufficient to show that within every $\mathcal{J}^j$ the income class j outbids all other income classes. The following lemma is necessary as an intermediate step.

6.2   *If $j < k$ then there is b such that $\bar{r}^j_i > (<) \bar{r}^k_i$ for $i < (>) b$.*

Suppose that there is no such b. Then bid–rents of one income class must be below those of the other everywhere in $\mathcal{J}$ and therefore the former cannot locate anywhere in $\mathcal{J}$, which contradicts the hypothesis that all income classes exist in $\mathcal{J}$. If, on the other hand, there is b such that $\bar{r}^j_i > (<) \bar{r}^k_i$ for $i > (<) b$ then

(6.18) $$\frac{\partial}{\partial y} \bigtriangleup_i \bar{r} > 0$$

is contradicted, which stems from the assumption that transportation costs do not depend on income together with condition (6.5). ∎

6.3   *If $i \in \mathcal{J}^j$ then $\bar{r}^j_i = max\{\bar{r}^1_i,...,\bar{r}^m_i\}$.*

The argument proceeds in stages. The first stage is to notice that, for $i < b_m$, $\overset{m}{\bar{r}}_i > \check{r}$ because of (4.7). For $i > b_{m-1}$ lemma 6.2 ensures that $\overset{m}{\bar{r}}_i > \overset{m-1}{\bar{r}}_i$. This lemma also ensures that $\overset{m}{\bar{r}}_i > \overset{j}{\bar{r}}_i$ for $j < m - 1$. Otherwise there is $b_j > b_{m-1}$, a contradiction. Hence, using (6.8), if $i \in \mathscr{J}^m$ then $\overset{m}{\bar{r}}_i = \max\{\overset{1}{\bar{r}}_i,...,\overset{m}{\bar{r}}_i\}$ and the first stage is complete. The remaining stages are similar. ∎

2

This section of the appendix contains some preliminary results to be used for the proof of proposition 6.1. Lemmata 6.4 and 6.5 are based on Hartwick, Schweizer and Varaiya (1976). Lemma 6.6 is based on Lancaster (1962).

From (6.15) one may solve for z^m as a function of y^m and b^m. Then, by induction, one may solve for z^j as a function of $y^j,...,y^m$ and $b^j,...,b^m$ through (6.14). The following lemma gives signs of the derivatives of this function.

6.4 $\qquad \dfrac{\partial z}{\partial y^k} > 0$ and $\bigwedge_{b^k} z^j < 0$ for $j \leq k$.

The argument proceeds by induction. Holding b^m constant, totally differentiate (6.15) to obtain

(6.19) $\qquad \dfrac{\partial \sigma^m}{\partial y^m} + \dfrac{\partial \sigma^m}{\partial z^m} \dfrac{\partial z^m}{\partial y^m} = 0$

where, from now on, $\sigma[i;y^j,z^j]$ will be denoted σ^j in partial differentiation. Because of (5.26) and (5.30), (6.19) implies

(6.20) $\qquad \dfrac{\partial z^m}{\partial y^m} > 0.$

Suppose that this lemma holds for $j + 1$. Varying only y^j, (6.14) gives

(6.21) $$\frac{\partial \sigma^j}{\partial y^j} + \frac{\partial \sigma^j}{\partial z^j}\frac{\partial z^j}{\partial y^j} = 0$$

so that, as before,

(6.22) $$\frac{\partial z^j}{\partial y^j} > 0.$$

Varying only y^{j+1}, (6.14) gives

(6.23) $$\frac{\partial \sigma^j}{\partial z^j}\frac{\partial z^j}{\partial y^{j+1}} = \frac{\partial \sigma^{j+1}}{\partial y^{j+1}} + \frac{\partial \sigma^{j+1}}{\partial z^{j+1}}\frac{\partial z^{j+1}}{\partial y^{j+1}} = \frac{1}{\bar{q}_i^{j+1}}\left[1 - \frac{\partial z^{j+1}}{\partial y^{j+1}} + \frac{\partial u^{j+1}}{\partial \bar{x}_i^{j+1}}\right] < 0$$

by (5.30) and (3.3). Therefore

(6.24) $$\frac{\partial z^j}{\partial y^{j+1}} > 0.$$

Varying utilities in (6.14), one obtains

(6.25) $$\frac{\partial \sigma^j}{\partial z^j}\frac{\partial z^j}{\partial z^{j+1}} = \frac{\partial \sigma^{j+1}}{\partial z^{j+1}}$$

so that

(6.26) $$\frac{\partial z^j}{\partial z^{j+1}} > 0$$

because of (5.30). Then

(6.27) $$\frac{\partial z^j}{\partial y^k}\frac{\partial z^j}{\partial z^{j+1}}\frac{\partial z^{j+1}}{\partial y^k} > 0 \text{ for } j+1 < k$$

Income Variations

by (6.26) and by hypothesis, so that the first part of this lemma has been proved.

For the second part, holding y^m constant, totally differentiate (6.15) to obtain

$$(6.28) \qquad \underset{b^m}{\triangle} \sigma^m + \frac{\partial \sigma^m}{\partial z^m} \underset{b^m}{\triangle} z^m = 0$$

which, because of (4.7) and (5.30), implies

$$(6.29) \qquad \underset{b^m}{\triangle} z^m < 0.$$

Suppose once more that this lemma holds for $j+1$. Varying only b^j, (6.14) gives

$$(6.30) \qquad \underset{b^j}{\triangle} \sigma^j + \frac{\partial \sigma^j}{\partial z^j} \underset{b^j}{\triangle} z^j = \underset{b^j}{\triangle} \sigma^{j+1}$$

or

$$(6.31) \qquad \underset{b^j}{\triangle} z^j = \left[\underset{b^j}{\triangle} \sigma^{j+1} - \underset{b^j}{\triangle} \sigma^j \right] \div \frac{\partial \sigma^j}{\partial z^j} < 0$$

because of (5.30), (6.7) and (6.18). Finally,

$$(6.32) \qquad \underset{b^k}{\triangle} z^j = \frac{\partial z^j}{\partial z^{j+1}} \underset{b^k}{\triangle} z^{j+1} < 0 \; \text{for } j < k$$

because of (6.26) and the induction hypothesis. ∎

From (4.14), (6.8), (6.11), (6.13) and the argument preceding lemma 6.4, note that N^j is a function of $y^j,...,y^m$ and $b^{j-1},...,b^m$. The following lemma gives signs of the derivatives of this function.

(6.5) $\quad \dfrac{\partial N^j}{\partial y^k} < 0, \bigwedge_b {}^{j-1} N^j < 0 \text{ and } \bigwedge_b {}^k N^j > 0 \text{ for } j \le k.$

From (4.12), (5.17), (5.24) and (6.13) we obtain

(6.33) $\quad \dfrac{\partial N^j}{\partial y^j} = - \sum_{i \in \mathcal{J}^j} \bigwedge_{i-1} Q \left[\dfrac{\partial \bar{q}_i^j}{\partial y^j} + \dfrac{\partial \bar{q}_i^j}{\partial z^j} \dfrac{\partial z^j}{\partial y^j} \right] \div (\bar{q}_i^j)^2$

$= - \sum_{i \in \mathcal{J}^j} \bigwedge_{i-1} Q \left\{ -\dfrac{1}{\bar{q}_i^j} \left[1 - \dfrac{\partial z^j/\partial y^j}{\partial u^j/\partial \bar{x}_i^j} \right] + \dfrac{\partial}{\partial \bar{x}_i^j} \left[\dfrac{\partial u^j}{\partial q_i^j} + \dfrac{\partial u^j}{\partial \bar{x}_i^j} \right] \dfrac{\partial z^j/\partial y^j}{\partial u^j/\partial \bar{x}_i^j} \right.$

$\left. + (\bar{q}_i^j)^2 \left[\left[\dfrac{\partial u^j}{\partial q_i^j} + \dfrac{\partial u^j}{\partial \bar{x}_i^j} \right] \dfrac{\partial}{\partial \bar{x}_i^j} \left[\dfrac{\partial u^j}{\partial q_i^j} + \dfrac{\partial u^j}{\partial \bar{x}_i^j} \right] - \dfrac{\partial}{\partial \bar{q}_i^j} \left[\dfrac{\partial u^j}{\partial q_i^j} + \dfrac{\partial u^j}{\partial \bar{x}_i^j} \right] \right] \right\}.$

The first term in the numerator is positive by (6.23). The second term is also positive by (3.3), (5.13) and (5.45). The denominator is also positive by (3.3), (5.12) and (5.13). Hence

(6.34) $\quad \dfrac{\partial N^j}{\partial y^j} < 0.$

For $j < k$, again from (6.13), we obtain

(6.35) $\quad \dfrac{\partial N^j}{\partial y^j} = \sum_{i \in \mathcal{J}^j} \dfrac{\partial n_i^j}{\partial z^j} \dfrac{\partial z^j}{\partial y^k} < 0$

because of (4.15), (5.25) and lemma 6.4. Now

(6.36) $\quad \bigwedge_b {}^{j-1} N^j = - n^j [i; y^j, z^j] \Big|_b {}^{j-1} < 0$

from (6.13). Also

(6.37) $$\bigtriangleup_{b^j} N^j = n^j[i;y^j,z^j]\Big|_{b^j} + \sum_{i \in \mathcal{J}^j} \frac{\partial n_i^j}{\partial z^j} \bigtriangleup_{b^j} z^j > 0$$

by (4.15), (5.25) and lemma 6.4. Finally, for $j < k$, again from (6.13), we obtain

(6.38) $$\bigtriangleup_{b^j} N^j = \sum_{i \in \mathcal{J}^j} \frac{\partial n_i^j}{\partial z^j} \bigtriangleup_{b^k} z^j > 0$$

by (4.15), (5.25) and lemma 6.4. ∎

Taking the total differential of N^j as a function of $y^j,...,y^m$ and $b^{j-1},...,b^m$

(6.39) $$\delta N^j = \sum_{k=j}^{m} \frac{\partial N^j}{\partial y^k} dy^k + \sum_{k=j-1}^{m} \bigtriangleup_{b^k} N^j \, \delta b^k \quad \text{for } j=1,...,m$$

which in matrix notation becomes

(6.40) $$\delta N = -A\delta y + \beta \delta b^0 + B \delta b$$

where, using lemma 6.5, the sign pattern of A, β and B is

(6.41) $$A = \begin{bmatrix} + & \cdots & + \\ 0 & \ddots & \vdots \\ \vdots & \ddots & \vdots \\ 0 & \cdots & 0 & + \end{bmatrix} ; \beta = \begin{bmatrix} - \\ 0 \\ \vdots \\ 0 \end{bmatrix} ; B = \begin{bmatrix} + & \cdots & + \\ - & \ddots & \vdots \\ 0 & \ddots & \vdots \\ \vdots & \ddots & \vdots \\ 0 & \cdots & 0 & - & + \end{bmatrix}.$$

The following lemma describes the sign of the determinant of B and the sign pattern of the inverse of B.

6.6 $\quad \|B\| > 0 \text{ and } B^{-1} = \begin{bmatrix} + & - & & & ? \\ \vdots & \ddots & \ddots & & \\ \vdots & & \ddots & \ddots & \\ \vdots & & & \ddots & - \\ + & \cdots & \cdots & & + \end{bmatrix}.$

Consider an $m \times m$ matrix

(6.42) $\quad B = \begin{bmatrix} \beta_{11} & \cdots\cdots & \beta_{1m} \\ -\gamma_2 & \ddots & & \vdots \\ 0 & \ddots & \ddots & \vdots \\ \vdots & \ddots & \ddots & \vdots \\ 0 \cdots & 0 & -\gamma_m & \beta_{mm} \end{bmatrix}$

where $\beta_{jk} > 0$ and $\gamma_j > 0$. Using a row operation

(6.43) $\quad \|B\| = \|\bar{B}\| = \begin{vmatrix} \bar{\beta}_{11} & \cdots\cdots & \bar{\beta}_{1m} \\ 0 & \ddots & & \vdots \\ \vdots & \ddots & \ddots & \vdots \\ 0 & \cdots & 0 & \bar{\beta}_{mm} \end{vmatrix} = \prod_{j=1}^{m} \bar{\beta}_{jj}$

where

(6.44) $\quad \bar{\beta}_{1k} = \beta_{1k} \text{ and } \bar{\beta}_{jk} = \beta_{jk} + \bar{\beta}_{j-1,k} (\gamma_j \div \bar{\beta}_{j-1,j-1})$

which implies $\bar{\beta}_{jj} > 0$ and hence, by (6.43),

(6.45) $\quad \|B\| > 0.$

Let B^{-1} have elements B_{jk}. By Cramer's rule

(6.46) $\quad B_{jk} = \|B^{j,k}\| \div \|B\|$

where $B^{j,k}$ is obtained from B by replacing column j by a vector with a unit component in row k and zeros everywhere else. Then for $j \geq k$

Income Variations

$$(6.47) \quad \|B^{j,k}\| = \begin{vmatrix} \begin{matrix} + & \cdots & +0 \\ - & & \vdots \\ 0 & \ddots & \vdots \\ \vdots & \ddots & +\vdots \\ 0 & \cdots & 0 & -0 \end{matrix} \begin{matrix} 1 \end{matrix} & \begin{matrix} + & \cdots & + \\ \vdots & & \vdots \\ + & \cdots & + \end{matrix} \\ \hline 0 & \begin{matrix} + & \cdots & + \\ 0 & \ddots & \vdots \\ \vdots & \ddots & \vdots \\ 0 & \cdots & 0 & -+ \end{matrix} \end{vmatrix}$$

$$= \begin{vmatrix} + & \cdots & + \\ - & & \vdots \\ 0 & \ddots & \vdots \\ \vdots & \ddots & +\vdots \\ 0 & \cdots & 0 & -+ \end{vmatrix} \begin{vmatrix} + & \cdots & + \\ - & & \vdots \\ 0 & \ddots & \vdots \\ \vdots & \ddots & \vdots \\ 0 & \cdots & 0 & -+ \end{vmatrix}.$$

Using a row operation on the first determinant

$$(6.48) \quad \begin{vmatrix} + & \cdots & +0 \\ - & & \vdots \\ 0 & \ddots & \vdots \\ \vdots & \ddots & +\vdots \\ 0 & \cdots & 0 & -0 \end{vmatrix} = \begin{vmatrix} + & \cdots & +0 \\ 0 & \ddots & \vdots \\ \vdots & \ddots & +\vdots \\ \vdots & \ddots & +\vdots \\ 0 & \cdots & 0 & + \end{vmatrix} > 0,$$

whereas the last determinant in (6.47) has dimensions $(m-j) \times (m-j)$ and, as before, it is positive with the same structure as B. In consequence

$$(6.49) \quad B_{jk} > 0 \text{ for } j \geq k.$$

It now remains to examine the case $j = k - 1$. In this case

$$
(6.50) \quad \|B^{jk}\| = \left\|\begin{array}{cccc|cccc}
+ & \cdots & + & 0 & + & \cdots & \cdots & + \\
\overline{0} & \ddots & \vdots & \vdots & \vdots & & & \vdots \\
\vdots & \ddots & + & \vdots & \vdots & & & \vdots \\
0 & \cdots & 0 & -0 & + & \cdots & \cdots & + \\
\hline
0 & \cdots & 0 & 1 & + & \cdots & \cdots & + \\
\vdots & & & 0 & \overline{0} & \ddots & & \vdots \\
\vdots & & & \vdots & \vdots & \ddots & \ddots & \vdots \\
0 & \cdots & 0 & 0 & 0 & \cdots & 0 & -+
\end{array}\right\|
$$

$$
= \left\|\begin{array}{cccc|cccc}
+ & \cdots & + & 0 & + & \cdots & \cdots & + \\
0 & \ddots & \vdots & \vdots & \vdots & & & \vdots \\
\vdots & \ddots & + & \vdots & \vdots & & & \vdots \\
0 & \cdots & 0 & 0 & + & \cdots & \cdots & + \\
\hline
0 & \cdots & 0 & 1 & + & \cdots & \cdots & + \\
\vdots & & & 0 & 0 & \ddots & & \vdots \\
\vdots & & & \vdots & \vdots & \ddots & \ddots & \vdots \\
0 & \cdots & 0 & 0 & 0 & \cdots & 0 & +
\end{array}\right\|
$$

$$
= \left\|\begin{array}{ccc|ccc}
+ & \cdots & + & + & \cdots & + \\
 & \ddots & \vdots & \vdots & & \vdots \\
 & & + & + & \cdots & + \\
\hline
 & & & - & \cdots & - \\
 & & & + & \cdots & + \\
 & & & & \ddots & \vdots \\
 & & & & & +
\end{array}\right\|
$$

$$
= \left\|\begin{array}{ccc}
+ & \cdots & + \\
 & \ddots & \vdots \\
 & & +
\end{array}\right\| \cdot \left\|\begin{array}{ccc}
- & \cdots & - \\
+ & \cdots & + \\
 & \ddots & \vdots \\
 & & +
\end{array}\right\|
$$

Income Variations

$$= - \begin{vmatrix} + & \cdots & + \\ & \ddots & \vdots \\ & & \ddots & \vdots \\ & & & + \end{vmatrix} < 0.$$

Therefore

(6.51) $B_{jk} < 0$ for $j = k - 1$. ∎

3

This section of the appendix contains a proof of the proposition that if, in a "closed" city, the population of a class rises then the welfare of all classes decreases, boundaries between the centre and the class under consideration move toward the centre and the remaining boundaries move away from the centre. The entire section is based on Hartwick, Schweizer and Varaiya (1976).

I begin with the impact of population changes on the spatial pattern. Using (6.40)

(6.52) $\delta b = B^{-1} \delta N^1 \gamma^1 > 0,$

where $\gamma^1 \equiv (1,0,...,0)'$, provided that only δN^1 varies. In consequence, using (6.41) and lemma 6.6

(6.53) $\delta_{N^1} b^j > 0$ for $j = 1,...,m$

if $\delta N^1 > 0$. Further

(6.54) $\delta_{N^1} z^j = \bigwedge_{b^j} z^j \delta_{N^1} b^j < 0$ for $j = 1,...,m$

because of lemma 6.4 and (5.53).[9]

To determine the effects of a change in N^j for $j > 1$, it is necessary to employ an indirect approach. Let b^m in (6.15) become exogenous and $\check{r}$ endogenous. This interchange implies that z^m is no longer determined by y^m and b^m through (6.15) so that, holding incomes constant, z^j is a function of $b^j,...,b^{m-1}$ and z^m, while N^j is a function of $b^{j-1},...,b^m$ and z^m, and

$$(6.55) \qquad \sum_{k=j-1}^{m-1} \Delta_{b^k} N^j \, \delta b^k + \frac{\partial N^j}{\partial z^m} dz^m = -\Delta_{b^m} N^j \, \delta b^m \quad \text{for } j > 1$$

provided that $\delta N^j = 0$. Dividing by $\Delta_{b^m} N^j$, (6.55) becomes

$$(6.56) \qquad \tilde{B} \begin{bmatrix} dz^m \\ \delta b^{j-1} \\ \vdots \\ \delta b^{j-1} \end{bmatrix} = \begin{bmatrix} -\delta b^m \\ 0 \\ \vdots \\ 0 \end{bmatrix}.$$

In general (say, $j = 2$) the sign pattern of $\tilde{B}$ can be shown to have the form

$$(6.57) \qquad \tilde{B} = \begin{bmatrix} -- & 0 & \cdots & 0 \\ + &   &   &   \\ \vdots & \ddots & & 0 \\ & & & - \\ -+ & \cdots & & + \end{bmatrix}$$

through an argument similar to that of lemma 5. Applying Cramer's rule to (6.56) as in lemma 6.6, we conclude that

$$(6.58) \qquad \begin{bmatrix} dz^m \\ \delta b^{m-1} \end{bmatrix} = \begin{bmatrix} + \\ + \end{bmatrix} \delta b^m.$$

Now if we fix b^{m-1} and consider only income classes $j \leq b^{m-1}$

Income Variations

(6.59) $$\begin{bmatrix} dz^{m-1} \\ \delta b^{m-2} \end{bmatrix} = \begin{bmatrix} + \\ + \end{bmatrix} \delta b^{m-1} = \begin{bmatrix} + \\ + \end{bmatrix} \delta b^m,$$

where the last equality follows from (6.58). Continuing in the same manner, one concludes that

(6.60) $$\begin{bmatrix} dz^m \\ \vdots \\ db^1 \end{bmatrix} = \begin{bmatrix} + \\ \vdots \\ + \end{bmatrix} \delta b^m \text{ and } \begin{bmatrix} \delta b^{m-1} \\ \vdots \\ \delta b^1 \end{bmatrix} = \begin{bmatrix} + \\ \vdots \\ + \end{bmatrix} \delta b^m,$$

with the last step of the induction being $dz^1 = (+)\delta b^m$ since $\delta b^0 = 0$ by assumption. Thus when the city boundary is shifted outward, all income classes become more suburbanised and their welfare improves because the effect of the additional consumption of land is stronger than the related effect of higher transportation costs.

Let $\delta N^k = 0$ for $k \neq j$, $dy = 0$ and $\delta b^0 = 0$. Then (6.40) becomes

(6.61) $$B\,\delta b = \begin{bmatrix} 0 \\ \vdots \\ \delta N^j \\ \vdots \\ 0 \end{bmatrix}$$

and using lemma 6.6

(6.62) $$\begin{bmatrix} \delta b^{j-1} \\ \delta b^j \\ \vdots \\ \delta b^m \end{bmatrix} = \begin{bmatrix} - \\ + \\ \vdots \\ + \end{bmatrix} \delta N^j \text{ for } j > 1$$

while, using lemma 6.4 and (6.62),

$$(6.63) \quad \begin{bmatrix} dz^j \\ \vdots \\ dz^m \end{bmatrix} = \begin{bmatrix} - \\ \vdots \\ - \end{bmatrix} \delta N^j \text{ for } j > 1$$

because $dz^j = \Delta_{b_j} z^j \, \delta b^j$. The remaining income classes $(1,...,j-1)$ behave as if they lived in a city with boundary area b^{j-1} which was shifted outward. In consequence, using (6.60) and (6.62),

$$(6.64) \quad \begin{bmatrix} \delta b^1 \\ \vdots \\ \delta b^{j-2} \end{bmatrix} = \begin{bmatrix} + \\ \vdots \\ + \end{bmatrix} \delta b^{j-1} = \begin{bmatrix} - \\ \vdots \\ - \end{bmatrix} \delta N^j$$

$$(6.65) \quad \begin{bmatrix} d\bar{u}^1 \\ \vdots \\ d\bar{u}^{j-1} \end{bmatrix} = \begin{bmatrix} + \\ \vdots \\ + \end{bmatrix} \delta b^{j-1} = \begin{bmatrix} - \\ \vdots \\ - \end{bmatrix} \delta N^j. \quad \blacksquare$$

4

This section of the appendix contains a proof of the proposition that if, in a "closed" city, the income of a class rises then all boundaries move away from the centre, the welfare of poorer classes increases together with that of the class under consideration and the welfare of richer classes decreases. The entire section is based on Hartwick, Schweizer and Varaiya (1976).

Using (6.40),

$$(6.66) \quad \delta b = B^{-1} A(dy^1)\gamma^1 > 0$$

where $\gamma^1 \equiv (1, 0,...,0)'$, provided that only dy^1 varies. In consequence, using (6.41) and lemma 6.6

$$(6.67) \quad \frac{db^j}{dy^1} > 0 \text{ for } j = 1,...,m$$

Income Variations

if $dy^j > 0$. Furthermore

$$(6.68) \qquad \frac{dz^j}{dy^1} = \bigtriangleup_{b^j} z^j \frac{db^j}{dy^1} < 0 \quad for \ j = 2,\ldots,m$$

using lemma 6.4 and (6.67). For $j = 1$, (6.68) does not hold because it would require y^1 fixed, a contradiction. In order to determine this case, totally differentiate (6.13) holding N^1 and b^0 constant to obtain

$$(6.69) \qquad 0 = n^1[i;y^1,z^1]\Big|_{b^1} \frac{db^1}{dy^1} + \sum_{i \in \mathcal{J}^1} \left[\frac{\partial n_i^1}{\partial y^1} + \frac{\partial n_i^1}{\partial z^1} \frac{\partial z^1}{\partial y^1} \right].$$

Since the first term in (6.69) is positive by virtue of (6.67), there exists $i \in \mathcal{J}^1$ such that

$$(6.70) \qquad \frac{\partial n_i^1}{\partial y^1} + \frac{\partial n_i^1}{\partial z^1} \frac{dz^1}{dy^1} < 0.$$

It follows that

$$(6.71) \qquad \frac{dz^1}{dy^1} > 0$$

because of (4.15), (5.20) and (5.25). This concludes the description of effects when the income of the poorest varies.

To determine the effects of a change in y^j for $j > 1$, it is necessary to prove first the following lemma:

6.7 $\qquad \dfrac{\partial \sigma^1}{\partial y^1}\Big|_{b^0} < 0.$

From (4.7) and (6.13)

(6.72) $$N^j = \sum_{i \in \mathcal{J}^j} -\underset{i}{\Delta} \bar{r}^j + \underset{i}{\Delta} c.$$

From the identity

(6.73) $$\underset{i}{\Delta} \frac{\bar{r}^j_i}{\Delta c_i} = \bar{r}^j_{i+1} \underset{i}{\Delta} \frac{1}{\Delta c_i} + \underset{i}{\Delta} \bar{r}^j + \underset{i}{\Delta} c$$

it follows that

(6.74) $$\frac{\bar{r}^j_i}{\Delta c_i}\bigg|_{b_{j-1}}^{b_j} = \sum_{i \in \mathcal{J}^j} \bar{r}^j_{i+1} \underset{i}{\Delta} \frac{1}{\Delta c_i} + \sum_{i \in \mathcal{J}^j} \underset{i}{\Delta} \bar{r}^j + \underset{i}{\Delta} c$$

which, in conjunction with (6.72), implies

(6.75) $$N^j = \sum_{i \in \mathcal{J}^j} \bar{r}^j_{i+1} \underset{i}{\Delta} \frac{1}{\Delta c_i} - \frac{\bar{r}^j_i}{\Delta c_i}\bigg|_{b_j} + \frac{\bar{r}^j_i}{\Delta c_i}\bigg|_{b_{j-1}}.$$

Upon total differentiation of (6.75)

(6.76) $$0 = \sum_{i \in \mathcal{J}^j} \frac{\partial \bar{r}^j_{i+1}}{\partial y^1} \underset{i}{\Delta} \frac{1}{\Delta c_i} - \frac{1}{\Delta c_i} \frac{\partial \bar{r}^j_i}{\partial y^1}\bigg|_{b_j} + \frac{1}{\Delta c_i} \frac{\partial \bar{r}^j_i}{\partial y^1}\bigg|_{b_{j-1}}.$$

Now

(6.77) $$\frac{\partial \bar{r}^j_{i+1}}{\partial y^1} = \frac{\partial \bar{r}^j_{i+1}}{\partial z^1} \frac{\partial z^j}{\partial y^1} > 0$$

by (5.30) and (6.68). Also

(6.78) $$\underset{i}{\Delta} \frac{1}{\Delta c_i} = -\underset{i}{\Delta}^2 c + (\underset{i}{\Delta} c \underset{i+1}{\Delta} c) > 0$$

by (3.8). Therefore the first term in (6.76) is positive, so that

Income Variations

(6.79) $$\frac{1}{\underset{i}{\Delta c}}\frac{\partial \bar{r}_i^j}{\partial y^1}\Big|_{b_{j-1}} < \frac{1}{\underset{i}{\Delta c}}\frac{\partial \bar{r}_i^j}{\partial y^1}\Big|_{b_j}.$$

Since $\partial \bar{r}_i^m/\partial y^1|_{b_m} = 0$, it follows from (6.79) that $\partial \bar{r}_i^{m-1}/\partial y^1|_{b_{m-1}} < 0$, ..., $\partial \bar{r}_i^1/\partial y^1|_{b_1} < 0$. From (6.3), which is true because the rich live further away,

(6.80) $$\underset{i}{\Delta} \frac{\partial \bar{r}_i^j}{\partial y^1} > 0.$$

In consequence, if it were true that $\partial \bar{r}_i^1/\partial y^1|_{b_0} \geq 0$ then $\partial \bar{r}_i^1/\partial y^1|_{b_1} > 0$ which contradicts (6.79). ∎

If in (6.40) N and y are held constant then

(6.81) $$\beta\, \delta b^0 + B\, \delta b = 0$$

which, in conjunction with (6.41) and lemma 6.6, implies

(6.82) $$\begin{bmatrix} \delta b^1 \\ \vdots \\ \delta b^m \end{bmatrix} = \begin{bmatrix} + \\ \vdots \\ + \end{bmatrix} \delta b^0.$$

Thus, from (6.82) and lemma 6.4

(6.83) $$\begin{bmatrix} dz^1 \\ \vdots \\ dz^m \end{bmatrix} = \begin{bmatrix} - \\ \vdots \\ - \end{bmatrix} \delta b^0.$$

If in (6.40) N, y^k for $k \neq j$ and b^0 are held constant then, from (6.41),

(6.84) $$B \begin{bmatrix} \delta b^1 \\ \vdots \\ \vdots \\ \delta b^m \end{bmatrix} = \begin{bmatrix} + \\ \vdots \\ + \\ 0 \\ \vdots \\ 0 \end{bmatrix} dy^j$$

Income Variations

where the last $j-1$ components on the RHS of (6.84) are zero. From (6.84) and lemma 6.6

$$(6.85) \qquad \begin{bmatrix} \delta b^j \\ \vdots \\ \delta b^m \end{bmatrix} = \begin{bmatrix} + \\ \vdots \\ + \end{bmatrix} dy^j$$

while from (6.85) and lemma 4

$$(6.86) \qquad \begin{bmatrix} dz^{j+1} \\ \vdots \\ dz^m \end{bmatrix} = \begin{bmatrix} - \\ \vdots \\ - \end{bmatrix} dy^j.$$

For z^j, (6.86) does not hold because it would require y^j fixed, a contradiction. The remaining income classes $1,...,j-1$ behave as if they lived alone in a city with boundary area b^{j-1}. Hence, from (6.60)

$$(6.87) \qquad \begin{bmatrix} \delta b^1 \\ \vdots \\ \delta b^{j-2} \end{bmatrix} = \begin{bmatrix} + \\ \vdots \\ + \end{bmatrix} \delta b^{j-1} \text{ for } j > 1$$

$$(6.88) \qquad \begin{bmatrix} dz^1 \\ \vdots \\ dz^{j-1} \end{bmatrix} = \begin{bmatrix} + \\ \vdots \\ + \end{bmatrix} \delta b^{j-1} \text{ for } j > 1.$$

Further, notice that income classes $j,...,m$ behave as if they lived alone in a city with central radius b^{j-1}. In this sense z^j is determined by b^{j-1} and y^j as

$$(6.89) \qquad z^j = f[b^{j-1}, y^j]$$

and, since the income class j is the lowest amongst $j,...,m$, it is true that

$$(6.90) \qquad \frac{\partial f}{\partial y^j} > 0 \text{ and } \bigwedge_{b^{j-1}} f < 0$$

165

Income Variations

from (6.71) and (6.83) respectively. We now totally differentiate the equilibrium condition (6.14), with z^{j-1} being a function of only b^{j-1}, to obtain

$$(6.91) \qquad \bigwedge_{b^{j-1}} \sigma^{j-1} \delta b^{j-1} + \frac{\partial \sigma^{j-1}}{\partial z^{j-1}} \delta_{b^{j-1}} z^{j-1} \delta b^{j-1}$$

$$= \bigwedge_{b^{j-1}} \sigma^{j} \delta b^{j-1} + \frac{\partial \sigma^{j}}{\partial y^{j}} dy^{j} + \frac{\partial \sigma^{j}}{\partial z^{j}} \left[\frac{\partial f}{\partial y^{j}} dy^{j} + \bigwedge_{b^{j-1}} f \delta b^{j-1} \right]$$

or

$$(6.92) \qquad \left[\frac{\partial \sigma^{j}}{\partial y^{j}} + \frac{\partial \sigma^{j}}{\partial z^{j}} \frac{\partial f}{\partial y^{j}} \right] dy^{j}$$

$$= \bigwedge_{b^{j-1}} \left[\sigma^{j-1} - \sigma^{j} \right] + \left[\frac{\partial \sigma^{j-1}}{\partial z^{j-1}} \delta_{b^{j-1}} z^{j-1} - \frac{\partial \sigma^{j}}{\partial z^{j}} \bigwedge_{b^{j-1}} f \right] \delta b^{j-1}.$$

Now

$$(6.93) \qquad \frac{\partial \sigma^{j}}{\partial y^{j}} \bigg|_{b^{j-1}} = \frac{\partial \sigma^{j}}{\partial y^{j}} + \frac{\partial \sigma^{j}}{\partial z^{j}} \frac{\partial f}{\partial y^{j}} < 0$$

by lemma 6.7. The RHS of (6.92) is negative by (5.30) and (6.88), by (6.3), and by (5.30) and (6.90). Therefore

$$(6.94) \qquad \frac{db^{j-1}}{dy^{j}} > 0 \text{ for } j > 1.$$

Finally, from (6.91),

$$(6.95) \qquad \frac{\partial \sigma^{j}}{\partial z^{j}} dz^{j} = \frac{\partial \sigma^{j}}{\partial z^{j}} \left[\frac{\partial f}{\partial y^{j}} dy^{j} + \bigwedge_{b^{j-1}} f \delta b^{j-1} \right]$$

$$= \frac{\partial \sigma^{j-1}}{\partial z^{j-1}} \delta_{b^{j-1}} z^{j-1} \delta b^{j-1} + \bigwedge_{b^{j-1}} (\sigma^{j-1} - \sigma^j) \delta b^{j-1} - \frac{\partial \sigma^j}{\partial y^j} dy^j$$

which implies

(6.96) $\quad \dfrac{dz^j}{dy^j} > 0 \;\; for \;\; j > 1$

by (6.94), and by (5.26), (5.30), (6.3) and (6.88). ∎

Notes To Chapter Six

1   This section is based on Pines (1975).

2   Ingram and Carrol (1981) report that, although high–status groups are still somewhat concentrated in the central cities of Latin American metropolitan areas, their concentrations are declining. Some reasons for this phenomenon will be examined in chapter nine.

3   Berry, Simmons and Tennant (1963, p. 404).

4   This section is based on Hartwick, Schweizer and Varaiya (1976). It also draws upon Wheaton (1976). The analysis of limitations imposed by the assumption that transportation costs are independent of income, as elaborated in the closing paragraphs of this section, is based on Arnott, Mackinnon and Wheaton (1978).

5   See appendix, section 1.

6   This is only the first round of adjustments. Re–adjustments to the first round will continue until the new equilibrium is attained.

7   This however does not take into account the possible direct effects of social inequality on the welfare of individuals.

8   Arnott, MacKinnon and Wheaton (1978, p. 135).

9   Equation (6.54) uses the chain rule as an approximation in the discrete case when differences are small.

7

The Case of Environmental Variations

Implicit until now has been the assumption that the quality of the environment is invariant over the landscape, because only then could it be argued that the quality of the environment is not a factor in the location decision, as described by the spatial equilibrium condition of Muth (3.21). Clearly, if the quality of the environment varies over the urban area then individuals must have an explicit preference for location. Under these circumstances, location affects choice not only indirectly as before through the cost of transportation, but also directly as

(7.1) $\quad u_i = u[x_i, q_i, E_i]$

where E_i is the quality of the environment in area i. One should visualise the quality of the environment as a surface unfolding over the landscape—"peaks" corresponding to high-quality urban areas and "valleys" corresponding to low-quality urban areas. Intuitively, it is a composite index that reflects a variety of natural, man-made and social factors. The question of what determines it will be left for later on. Suffice it to say that, here, its spatial distribution is known as

Environmental Variations

(7.2) $\quad E_i = E[i]$

and that, since individuals prefer higher rather than lower quality of the environment,

(7.3) $\quad \dfrac{\partial u}{\partial E_i} > 0.$

If this generalised utility function is introduced in problem (3.10), it is easy to see that the equilibrium conditions (3.17)–(3.19) remain unchanged.[1] The only difference is associated with the decision of an individual where to locate. Namely, the spatial equilibrium condition of Muth (3.21) now becomes

(7.4) $\quad q_i \triangle_i r + \triangle_i c - \lambda_i \dfrac{\partial u}{\partial E_i} \triangle_i E = 0.$

Since λ_i measures the marginal value of utility then

(7.5) $\quad \lambda_i \dfrac{\partial u}{\partial E_i} = \left[\dfrac{\partial \psi_i}{\partial z} - q_i \dfrac{\partial \sigma_i}{\partial z} \right] \dfrac{\partial u}{\partial E_i}$

represents the *shadow price* of the quality of the environment in area i.[2] In other words, for an individual in area i, it specifies the income rise necessary to attain an optimal level of utility precisely equal to that resulting from a unit rise in the quality of the environment in the same area. Thus the generalised spatial equilibrium condition of Muth represents a balance between marginal changes with respect to the optimal location in the cost of land occupied, the cost of transportation and the value of the quality of the environment. When the quality of the environment is invariant over the landscape, $\Delta_i E = 0$, the generalised condition (7.4) reduces to the original (3.21).

If the quality of the environment decreases away from the centre then

(7.6) $\quad -\lambda_i \frac{\partial u}{\partial E_i} \underset{i}{\Delta} E > 0.$

Under these circumstances, a change in the quality of the environment becomes a marginal private cost for moves further away, added to the corresponding marginal increase in the cost of transportation (figure 7.1(1)). As a consequence, the optimal location i^* will be found closer to

Figure 7.1: Location equilibria
under variable quality of the environment.

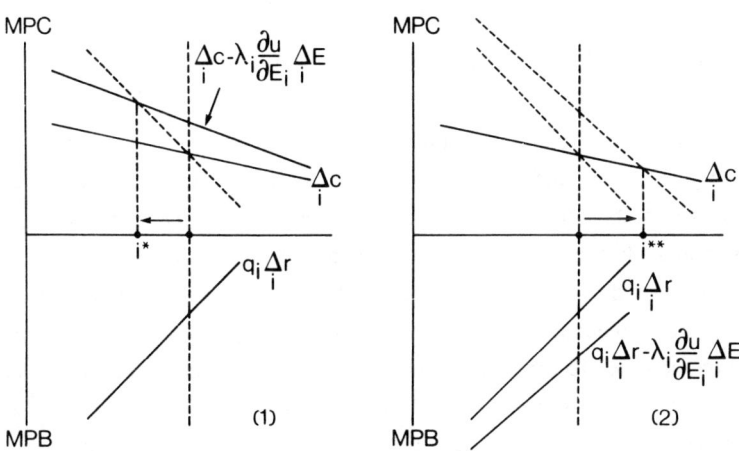

the centre than when the quality of the environment is invariant. If, on the other hand, the quality of the environment increases away from the centre then

(7.7) $\quad -\lambda_i \frac{\partial u}{\partial E_i} \underset{i}{\Delta} E > 0.$

Under these circumstances, the change in the quality of the environment becomes a marginal private benefit for moves further away, added to the

Environmental Variations

corresponding decrease in the cost of land occupied (figure 7.1(2)). As a consequence, the optimal location i^{**} will be found further away from centre than when the quality of the environment is invariant. In any case, higher quality of the environment attracts individuals.

How is the spatial structure of bid–rents affected by variations in the quality of the environment? Using (7.4) in the context of a Casetti equilibrium one obtains

(7.8) $$\bigtriangleup_i \bar{r} = -\frac{1}{\bar{q}_i} \left[\bigtriangleup_i c - \lambda_i \frac{\partial u}{\partial E_i} \bigtriangleup_i E \right].$$

Therefore

(7.9) $$\bigtriangleup_i \bar{r} >(=,<) 0 \text{ if and only if } \bigtriangleup_i c <(=,>) \lambda_i \frac{\partial u}{\partial E_i} \bigtriangleup_i E.$$

From (7.9), the spatial structure of bid–rent emerges as the resultant of two forces. For moves away from the centre, as long as the marginal change in the cost of transportation is larger than the corresponding marginal change in the value of the quality of the environment, the bid–rent gradient will be negative. If though the value of the quality of the environment increases faster than the associated cost of transportation then the bid–rent will increase away from the centre. Furthermore, if environmental variations are strong enough over the city, there may be an area $i < b$ associated with a bid–rent lower than the opportunity cost of land. It is always possible to obtain such conditions by decreasing the exogenous quality of the environment in area i sufficiently. It follows that Casetti equilibria may be spatially discontinuous in the case of environmental variations. This possibility is not examined any further: I simply assume that the quality of the environment for $i < b$ is high enough to preclude $\bar{r}[i] < \check{r}$.

Example

Let

$$u[x_i, q_i, E_i] = x_i^\alpha q_i^\beta E_i^\gamma \text{ with } \alpha, \beta, \gamma > 0 \text{ and } \alpha + \beta = 1.$$

It has already been argued that, in this case, the equilibrium conditions (3.17)–(3.19) remain. Therefore, using the example of chapter three,

$$x_i^* = \alpha(y - c[i])$$

$$q_i^* = \frac{\beta}{r[i]}(y - c[i]).$$

Upon replacement of these optimal values in the utility function, we have

$$\upsilon[i, E_i; r[i], y] = (\alpha(y - c[i]))^\alpha \left[\frac{\beta}{r[i]}(y - c[i])\right]^\beta E_i^\gamma$$

$$= \frac{\alpha^\alpha \beta^\beta}{r^\beta[i]}(y - c[i])E_i^\gamma.$$

Constraining the indirect utility function to equal z everywhere, we obtain the equilibrium bid–rent function

$$\bar{r}[i] = (\frac{\alpha^\alpha \beta^\beta}{z}(y - c[i])E_i^\gamma)^{1+\beta}.$$

The behaviour of the equilibrium bid–rent over $\mathscr{J}$ will depend on

$$\text{sign} \bigwedge_i ((y - c[i])E^\gamma[i]).$$

If this sign is positive (negative) then the equilibrium bid–rent increases

Environmental Variations

(decreases) away from the centre. As in condition (7.9), which it expresses here, the sign of the equilibrium bid–rent is determined by the interplay between the change in transportation costs and the change in the quality of the environment over $\mathcal{J}$.

Density Craters

It has been observed that residential density craters develop at the centre of some large cities. This may be accounted for by systematic variations of environmental quality around such centres. Consider for example a polluted city. Since there is a strong distance decay of pollution away from the centre, there must also be a corresponding rise in the quality of the environment (figure 7.2(1)). Marginal changes in the quality of the environment appear in figure 7.2(2). The components on the RHS of (7.8), together with their sum $\Delta_i \bar{r}$, appear in figure 7.2(3). They describe a situation where the environmental component is dominant in the vicinity of the centre. Thus between the centre and A in figure 7.2(4) the bid–rent increases, thereby forming a crater. Between A and B, although decreasing, the structure of the bid–rent still differs from that described in chapter three because $\Delta_i^2 \bar{r} < 0$. Only beyond B does the bid–rent attain its standard, convex appearance. In general an increasing quality of the environment decelerates or even reverses the downward trend of the bid–rent gradient, while a decreasing quality of the environment accelerates it.

In view of (4.10) and (4.16), the spatial behaviour of bid–rent and population density gradients is essentially the same. It follows that variations in the quality of the environment may generate population density craters and other deformations precisely as in the case of the bid–rent gradient.

Environmental Variations

Figure 7.2: Determination of a bid–rent crater.

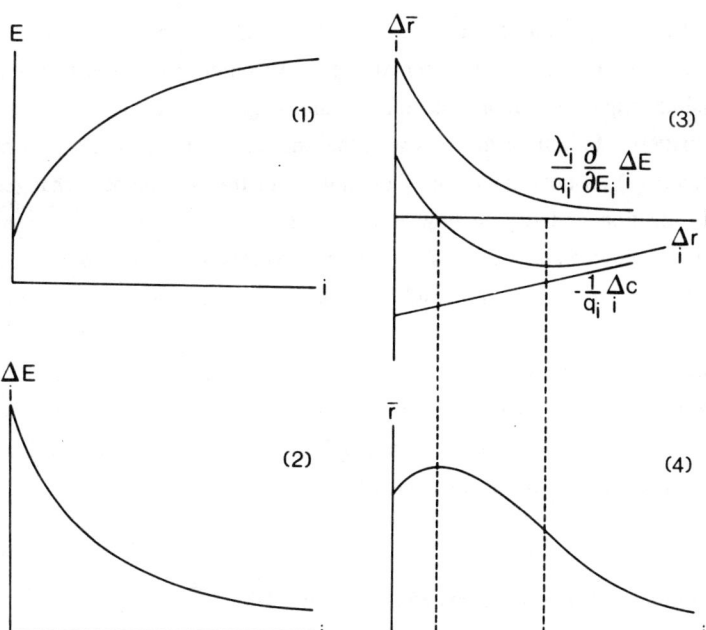

The Slope Test Generalised [3]

When the quality of the environment varies, (7.8), rather than (4.7), provides a basis for the slope test. Differentiating with respect to income

$$(7.10) \quad \frac{\partial}{\partial y} \triangle_i \bar{r} = -\frac{1}{\bar{q}_i} \left[\frac{\partial}{\partial y} \triangle_i c - \frac{\partial}{\partial y} \left[\lambda_i \frac{\partial u}{\partial E_i} \triangle_i E \right] \right]$$
$$+ \frac{1}{\bar{q}_i^2} \frac{\partial \bar{q}_i}{\partial y} \left[\triangle_i c - \lambda_i \frac{\partial u}{\partial E_i} \triangle_i E \right]$$

175

Environmental Variations

$$= \frac{1}{\bar{q}_i\, y}\left[\eta_{c:y} - \eta_{q:y}\right] - \frac{1}{\bar{q}_i^2}\lambda_i \frac{\partial \bar{q}_i}{\partial y}\frac{\partial u}{\partial E_i}\triangle_i E + \frac{1}{\bar{q}_i}\frac{\partial}{\partial y}\left[\lambda_i \frac{\partial u}{\partial E_i}\triangle_i E\right].$$

The first component on the RHS of (7.10) has already been discussed in the context of (6.4). The remaining two components represent the possible impact of environmental variations upon the residential land-use pattern. In both terms, it is seen that the residential land-use pattern depends (1) on how the value of the quality of the environment changes with location and (2) on how important such changes are relative to different income classes. Thus, even if transportation costs do not depend on income ($\eta_{c:y} = 0$), the results of the generalised slope test, unlike those of chapter six, are far from determinate. Indeed, whenever the quality of the environment varies, the residential land-use pattern may become very complicated. Then different cities will exhibit different residential land-use patterns corresponding to different spatial distributions of the quality of the environment over the landscape.

Environmental Improvements and the Value of Land [4]

How is the value of land at equilibrium precisely affected by the quality of the environment? In order to answer this question, consider the system of equations (5.1)–(5.5) generalised for variations in the quality of the environment. Clearly now

(7.11) $\qquad \bar{x}_i = \bar{x}[i, E_i; y, z]$

(7.12) $\qquad \bar{q}_i = \bar{q}[i, E_i; y, z]$

(7.13) $\qquad \bar{r}_i = \bar{r}[i, E_i; y, z]$

(7.14) $$\sum_j n_j = N$$

(7.15) $$\bar{r}[b, E_b; y, z] = \check{r}$$

describes the city under a Casetti equilibrium. Consider (7.13) in the context of an "open" city. Since the level of utility is fixed, the value of land in area i will be completely determined by the quality of the environment in that area. Hence the quality of the environment in other parts of the city is irrelevant from this point of view.[5] Indeed (7.1), (7.3) and (7.13) suggest that an improvement in the quality of the environment in area i must force an increase of the bid–rent in the same area. Otherwise utility would increase, a contradiction. This purely local effect of the quality of the environment on land value is confined to the "open" city. For when the city is either "transient" or "closed", utility is endogenous and (7.13) suggests that the bid–rent in area i is determined not only by the quality of the environment in that area but also by the equilibrium level of utility. Thus (7.13) now contains two unknowns rather than one, and another equation must be considered simultaneously. If, for example, (7.12) and (7.13) are considered simultaneously then the number of unknowns increases to three; and so on. It is easy to see that the system closes only when (7.12)–(7.15) are considered for all areas simultaneously. Therefore, when the city is either "transient" or "closed", the value of land in area i will be affected by the entire distribution of the quality of the environment over the urban area. This is supported by intuition because the bid–rent depends on utility and utility, in turn, as determined by the process toward equilibrium, must be affected by everything that happens over the urban area.

Changes in the quality of the environment imply aggregate benefits or disbenefits. One way to represent these is through the idea of an *aggregate willingness to pay*. For a particular individual, willingness to pay is that amount of money which, if taken away (given), will reduce (increase) his welfare to some initial level. Summation over all individuals gives the aggregate willingness to pay, the sign of which determines whether the net impact of changes in the quality of the environment is positive or negative with respect to aggregate welfare. Since in our case there are two homogeneous classes, landowners and renters, willingness to pay may be partitioned accordingly. Consider a change in the quality of the environment. For landowners, willingness to pay is determined by the difference between the new and the old bid–rent induced by the environmental change. For renters, on the other hand, willingness to pay is determined by the corresponding difference in utility expressed in money terms. Summing up over the two classes gives the aggregate willingness to pay for the change in the quality of the environment.

The aggregate willingness to pay represents an indirect measure of change. A more direct measure, one that has been used to assess the social impact of environmental improvements, is the aggregate change in the value of urban land. The question is, *do aggregate changes in the value of urban land accurately reflect the aggregate benefit (or disbenefit) of related changes in the quality of the environment*? In other words, do such aggregate changes in the value of urban land equal the related aggregate willingness to pay? To answer this question observe that the component of the aggregate willingness to pay generated by landowners is by definition equal to the aggregate change in the value of urban land. Thus only when the component generated by the renters is zero will aggregate changes in the value of urban land be equal to the related aggregate willingness to pay. This happens in the case of an "open" city where the utility of individuals must remain fixed, and therefore their willingness to pay is zero. Nevertheless, when the city is either "transient" or "closed" the equilibrium level of utility will vary so that individuals will be prepared to pay (will have to be compensated by) an amount which would reduce (increase) their utility to its original equilibrium level. Such amounts belong to the second component of the aggregate willingness to pay and are therefore quite distinct from changes in bid–rent. It follows immediately that if, in a "transient" or "closed" city, the equilibrium utility level increases (decreases) then aggregate changes in the value of urban land will understate (overstate) the aggregate willingness to pay.[6]

We have seen that, when the city is either "transient" or "closed", the bid–rent in area i depends on the quality of the environment both in that area and elsewhere in the city. It follows that changes of the bid–rent in area i may be decomposed into a *direct* component associated with changes in the quality of the environment in area i and an *indirect* component associated with changes in the quality of the environment everywhere else. In order to study this decomposition, write the condition for a Casetti equilibrium (4.3) using the indirect utility function relationship (3.12):

(7.16) $\upsilon[i, E_i; \bar{r}[i], y] = z.$

Suppose that the quality of the environment improves only in area i. If this area is small relative to that of the city, the equilibrium level of utility will remain virtually unaltered. Then, by (7.16), the bid–rent in area i must increase. This is a direct effect because the change in bid–rent is attributable only to a local change in the quality of the environment. Suppose now that the quality of the environment improves everywhere else but in area i. Further suppose that the equilibrium level of utility also increases because of environmental improvements. Then, by (7.16), the bid–rent in area i must decrease because the rest of the city is now relatively better off. Clearly this is an indirect effect.[7]

Let the quality of the environment in area i depend on, say, the total amount Ω of resources used for this purpose. Then

(7.17) $\dfrac{dE_i}{d\Omega} > 0,$

in other words, the quality of the environment improves as more resources are put to use. Since the equilibrium level of utility depends on the

Environmental Variations

entire distribution of the quality of the environment, it must be a function of the total amount of resources used for this purpose. Obviously, the more resources that are put to use the higher is expected the equilibrium level of utility:

(7.18) $\quad \dfrac{\partial v}{\partial E_i} > 0.$

Upon total differentiation of (7.16) with respect to Ω

(7.19) $\quad \dfrac{\partial v}{\partial E_i}\dfrac{dE_i}{d\Omega} + \dfrac{\partial v}{\partial \bar{r}[i]}\dfrac{d\bar{r}[i]}{d\Omega} = \dfrac{dz}{d\Omega}$

which implies

$$
\begin{aligned}
(7.20)\quad \dfrac{d\bar{r}[i]}{d\Omega} &= \left[1 + \dfrac{\partial v}{\partial \bar{r}[i]}\right]\left[\dfrac{dz}{d\Omega} - \dfrac{\partial v}{\partial E_i}\dfrac{dE_i}{d\Omega}\right] \\
&= \left[\dfrac{z}{\Omega} + \dfrac{\partial f}{\partial \bar{r}[i]}\right]\left[\dfrac{dz}{d\Omega}\div\dfrac{z}{\Omega} - \left[\dfrac{\partial v}{\partial E_i}\div\dfrac{z}{E_i}\right]\left[\dfrac{dE_i}{d\Omega}\div\dfrac{E_i}{\Omega}\right]\right] \\
&= \left[\dfrac{z}{\Omega} + \dfrac{\partial v}{\partial \bar{r}[i]}\right]\left[\eta_{z:\Omega} - \eta_{v:E_i}\eta_{E_i:\Omega}\right]
\end{aligned}
$$

where $\eta_{z:\Omega}$ is the elasticity of the equilibrium level of utility with respect to resources available, $\eta_{v:E_i}$ is the elasticity of utility attained by an individual in area i with respect to the quality of the environment in that area and $\eta_{E_i:\Omega}$ is the elasticity of the quality of the environment in area i with respect to resources available. Using (7.16) and (7.20)

(7.21) $\quad \dfrac{d\bar{r}[i]}{d\Omega} > (=,<) \; 0 \;\; \text{if and only if} \;\; \eta_{z:\Omega} < (=,>) \; \eta_{v:E_i}\eta_{E_i:\Omega}\,.$

Environmental Variations

The direct effect of the quality of the environment on the bid–rent corresponds to $\eta_{\upsilon:E_i}\eta_{E_i:\Omega}$ in (7.21): the bid–rent in area i will be likely to increase the more important is the quality of the environment to the welfare of individuals ($\eta_{\upsilon:E_i}$) and the more sensitive is the quality of the environment to resources available ($\eta_{E_i:\Omega}$). The indirect effect of the quality of the environment on the bid–rent corresponds to $\eta_{z:\Omega}$ in (7.21): the bid–rent in area i will be likely to decrease the more sensitive is the equilibrium level of utility to resources available— hence to the entire distribution of the quality of the environment over the city.[8] The outcome of these two opposing forces will determine whether bid–rents increase or decrease in response to improvements in the quality of the environment. When the city is "open", $\eta_{z:\Omega}$ is zero by definition so that (7.21) implies $d\bar{r}/d\Omega > 0$ because $\eta_{\upsilon:E_i}\eta_{E_i:\Omega} > 0$ by (7.3) and (7.18). That is, when the city is "open", the direct effect completely dominates.

Notes to Chapter Seven

1 The lagrangean function of the generalised problem (3.10) is

$$L_i = x_i + r[i]q_i + c[i] + \lambda_i(z - u[x_i, q_i, E_i]).$$

Since the new factor, quality of the environment, depends only on location, the partial derivatives with respect to x_i and q_i are given once more by (3.18) and (3.19) respectively.

2 See note 4 in chapter four.

3 This section is based on Pines (1975).

4   This section is based on Polinsky and Shavell (1976). Literature associated with this issue includes Mohring (1961), Strotz (1968), Lind (1973), Getz (1975), Polinsky and Shavell (1975), Pines and Weiss (1976), Arnott and MacKinnon (1977A), Courant and Rubinfeld (1978), and Diamond (1980).

5   Here one must distinguish carefully between the quantity E_i and how this quantity is determined. The statement that "the quality of the environment in other parts of the city is irrelevant" is meant to emphasise that only E_i determines $\bar{r}[i]$. The quantity E_i itself, in turn, may well be affected by what happens in other areas through spillovers.

6   In order to illustrate this point Polinsky and Shavell (1976) have constructed an example of a "closed" city where land values remain fixed, although the quality of the environment increases everywhere and the equilibrium level of utility also increases. It is the example already used in this chapter. Suppose that the quality of the environment doubles everywhere. Then the ratio between land values in any two areas i and j,

$$\bar{r}^\beta[i] \div \bar{r}^\beta[j] = (y - c_i)E_i^\gamma \div (y - c_j)E_j^\gamma,$$

remains the same before and after the increase in the quality of the environment. Hence bid–rents increase or decrease together. If they increase then the demand for land per capita falls so that total population rises, a contradiction to the "closedness" of the city. If they decrease then the demand for land per capita rises so that total population falls, another contradiction. Therefore bid–rents must remain fixed. If so, the condition for a Casetti equilibrium implies that utility has also increased: in this example the zero aggregate change in the value of urban land dramatically understates the corresponding aggregate willingness to pay.

7 In the example of note 6 bid-rents remained fixed because the two effects precisely balanced each other.

8 "Holding $\eta_{\upsilon:E_i}$ and $\eta_{E_i:\Omega}$ constant, as $\eta_{z:\Omega}$ becomes larger, the new equilibrium level of utility becomes larger. But to achieve this higher equilibrium level of utility, bid-rents will have to fall (or rise less than otherwise) in order to maintain the higher equilibrium level of utility given the new distribution of the quality of the environment."

Here I could do no better than to paraphrase Polinsky and Shavell (1976, pp. 127), using my notation.

8

Sudden Urban Growth [1]

Historical Background

In 1860 there were five cities of over one million inhabitants (Berlin, London, Paris, Peking and Vienna). In 1960 there were one hundred and nine, in 1975 one hundred and ninety one. To–day there must be well over two hundred of them, gaining faster in a world of fast growth. Indeed, world population in large cities has now become a significant part of the total world population and it will continue to increase its share until, probably, it will become dominant in the not too distant future (figure 8.1). All these large cities underwent sudden urban growth, a phenomenon that transcends political, cultural and regional barriers.[2] Its global nature and some of its astonishing force are reflected in the examples of figure 8.2. One may envisage silent urban "explosions" of increasing frequency around the earth. In combination, figures 8.1 and 8.2 illustrate one of the greatest challenges humanity must face: if to–day sudden urban growth causes the gravest (and, to many, insurmountable) urban problems ever encountered anywhere, then what about to–morrow when it will accumulate precisely as an avalanche

Figure 8.1: World population trends.

1. Rural settlements
2. Cities less than 1 million
3. Cities more than 1 million

Sources: Doxiadis (1968, p.217)
United Nations (1974, pp.36, 64)

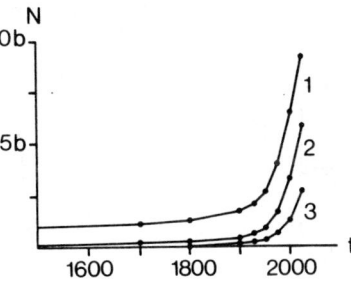

does? The question about what drives this phenomenon is taken by chapter eight.

The Role of Production

Sudden urban growth feeds on migration. This suggests a clear advantage of the city over the existing alternatives, an advantage that must be created suddenly and must persist with city growth. Hence in order to explain this phenomenon one is bound to begin with a study of the relationship between urban opportunities and urban size. Related is the analysis in chapter five, which involved utility adjustments around equilibrium partitions of population between the urban and the alternative sector, in other words, adjustments along the line of figure 5.1 which represents both urban utility as a function of urban population at equilibrium (measured from left to right) and the utility in the alternative sector as a function of the corresponding population (measured from right to left). Of particular interest here is the quantity $\delta_N \bar{u}$ in appendix 5.3. One may now reinterpret this quantity in the following manner. *For any given urban population level $\delta_N \bar{u}$ describes the direction of $\bar{u}[N]$.* Then, taking into account (5.66), one obtains figure 8.3 which combines $\bar{u}[N]$ with $\bar{v}[M - N]$ of figure 5.1. In a manner analogous to figure 3.5(2) and

Figure 8.2: Examples of sudden urban growth.

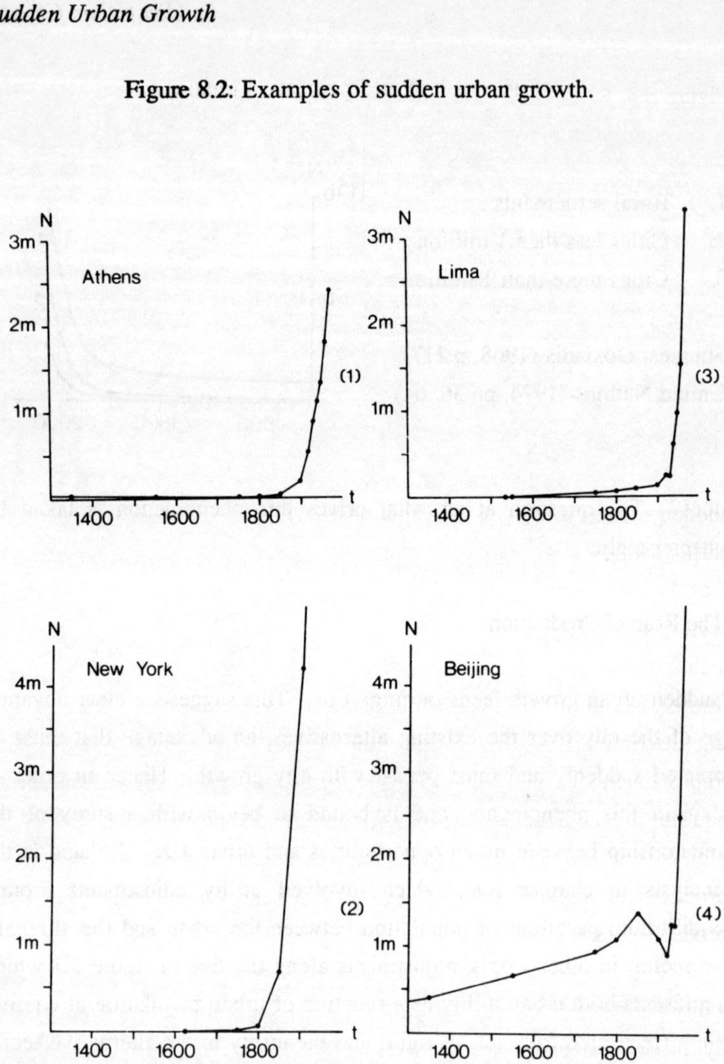

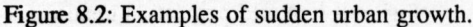

following Casetti (1980), we conclude that the intersection between $\bar{u}[N]$ and $\bar{v}[M - N]$ marks a stable equilibrium partition of population between the urban and the alternative sector. It is obvious now that the structure of $\bar{u}[N]$ as it emerges from the analysis in chapter five cannot produce

Figure 8.3: Partial equilibrium city size.

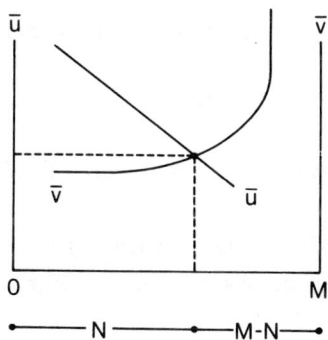

sudden urban growth. To see this observe that both curves in figure 8.3 shift upwards with the development of technology. Then, if one asserts that the city is more responsive to such development than the alternative sector, one may obtain a growing city. Nevertheless, under smooth technological improvements, growth will be smooth whereas the structure of sudden urban growth in figure 8.2 clearly suggests a corresponding discontinuity. The gist of the difficulty (hence the potential for improvement) is the shape of $\bar{u}[N]$ which holds for fixed y: the partial equilibrium approach of chapter five excludes returns to scale in agglomeration and therefore fails to capture the relationship between urban productivity and urban size. For this reason I now introduce urban production explicitly.

The simplest construct sufficient to explain sudden urban growth is a city partitioned into two concentric zones, $[1,a]$ and $[a + 1, b]$, occupied by production and residences respectively.[3] Production refers to the private good and uses labour and land. Everyone in the city works to produce the private good and no outside labour is used for production. The output of production is concentrated at the centre where it is sold. If there is a surplus (deficit) in production then the necessary quantities are exported (imported) at the same, fixed price. Production is organised in accordance with the principle of minimising the difference between the value of what is used for production and the value of what is produced. Thus the problem is to determine a level of employment, N, and a size of the area allocated to production, a, such that

(8.1) $\quad D[r^0,y] =$

$$min\left\{\left[\sum_{j=1}^{a} r^0_j \underset{j-1}{\Delta} Q + yN + C^0\,[f]\right] - f[N,N[a],a]\right\},$$

where D is a deficit function; f is the production function of the private good; r^0 has components r^0_j, the price of land in area j used for production; and C^0 is the total cost of transporting the output of production from where it is produced to the centre where it is sold. The function $N[a]$ in the production function is such that $\Delta_a N = -n_{a+1}$. This reflects the truth that, when the area of production expands, one must also take into account the loss in manpower that the corresponding displacement of individuals entails. For simplicity, suppose that income, population and the observed pattern of land values in the zone of production are treated parametrically with respect to changes in a. Then the solution to problem (8.1) gives

(8.2) $\quad y = \underset{N}{\Delta} X$

(8.3) $\quad r^0_{a+1} = \underset{a}{\Delta} X + \underset{a}{\Delta} Q$

where

(8.4) $\quad X \equiv f - C^0$

is the value of what is produced net of the associated transportation costs.[4] Every individual travels to work along the radius passing through his residence. He then travels toward the centre along the same radius, purchases the private good and returns to his residence. Hence problem (3.11) and therefore (5.1)–(5.3) remain unaffected. However, (5.4) is replaced by

(8.5) $$\sum_{j=a+1}^{b} \bar{n}_j = N$$

while

(8.6) $$\sigma[a+1;y,z] = r_{a+1}^{0}$$

represents an interior border condition analogous to (5.5).

Under these circumstances the relationship between urban opportunities and urban size is given by the following proposition.

8.1 *If* $\bigtriangleup_{a+1} \sigma + \bar{r}[a+1] + \bigtriangleup_{a}^{2} Q \div \bigtriangleup_{a} Q > 0$

then

$$\left[\alpha_1 - \alpha_2 \bigtriangleup_{N} \bigtriangleup_{a} X - \alpha_3 \bigtriangleup_{a}^{2} X \right] \delta \bar{u}_{N}$$
$$= - \alpha_4 - \alpha_5 \bigtriangleup_{N} \bigtriangleup_{a} X + \alpha_6 \bigtriangleup_{N}^{2} X + \alpha_7 \bigtriangleup_{a}^{2} X$$
$$- \alpha_8 \left[\left[\bigtriangleup_{a}^{2} X \right] \left[\bigtriangleup_{N}^{2} X \right] - \left[\bigtriangleup_{N} \bigtriangleup_{a} X \right]^2 \right] \text{ with } \alpha_1,...,\alpha_8 > 0.$$

Since this proposition represents the basis for everything that follows, it is important to understand what is intuitively implied by the assumptions and definitions related to it. According to problem (8.1), equation (8.2) describes urban population as a function of income. In other words urban population is treated as endogenous. Recall however that our objective is to determine utility as a function of urban population. In other words urban population must be treated as exogenous. Hence, in (8.2), it is necessary to consider y as endogenous, that is, to assume that y can be expressed as a function of N. Furthermore, in addition to the strict quasiconcavity of the utility function and to the positive income effects for x_i and q_i, which continue to be necessary as before, there is

$$(8.7) \qquad \Delta_{a+1} \sigma + \bar{r}[a+1] + \Delta_a^2 Q + \Delta_a Q > 0$$

as a further requirement. Since the city is circular,

$$(8.8) \qquad \Delta_a Q = \pi((a+1)^2 - a^2) = \pi(2a+1)$$

$$(8.9) \qquad \Delta_a^2 Q = \pi((2(a+1)+1) - (2a+1)) = 2\pi$$

so that

$$(8.10) \qquad \Delta_a^2 Q + \Delta_a Q = 2\pi + (\pi(2a+1)) \approx 1 + (a+1)$$

which, if substituted into (8.7), yields

$$(8.11) \qquad \eta_{\bar{r}[a+1]:a+1} > -1.^5$$

Inequality (8.11) is a condition on the elasticity of residential bid–rent at the interior border area with respect to this border. It states that the residential bid–rent at the interior border area must decrease relatively more slowly than the movement of this border away from the centre. Figure 8.4 describes this condition. Point A represents the residential bid–rent at the interior border $a + 1$. The continuous downward–sloping line that begins at A represents the residential bid–rent function. The slope OA represents the ratio $\bar{r}[a+1] \div (a+1)$. The steepness of AD is precisely the same as that of OA. Now suppose that the interior border moves to $a + 2$. If, in consequence, A moves to C then the slope AD represents the ratio $\sigma + \Delta_a(a+1) = \Delta_{a+1}\sigma$. Since the slopes OA and AD have the same steepness, it follows that a movement of the residential bid–rent at the interior border from A to C implies $\eta_{\bar{r}[a+1]:a} = -1$.

Figure 8.4: Adjustments of residential bid–rent to movements of the interior border.

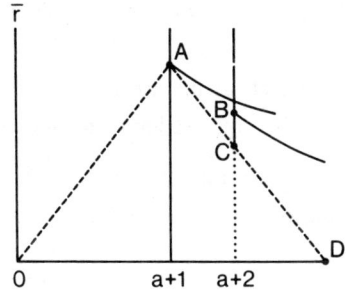

Hence condition (8.11) restricts such adjustments to points above C, say, B.

The constants $\alpha_1, ..., \alpha_8$ in proposition 1 are known functions of individual characteristics such as marginal utilities and of observables such as the opportunity cost of land. Therefore knowledge of these characteristics would permit the direct computation of these constants. The quantity $\Delta_N \Delta_a X$ describes how the marginal value of land used for production is affected by the number of individuals working on it. The quantity $\Delta_a^2 X$ describes returns to scale in land as a factor of production. A value greater than (equal to, smaller than) zero represents increasing (constant, decreasing) returns to scale. Finally $\Delta_N^2 X$ describes how the marginal value of labour changes with urban population.

A Simple Case

I begin to examine the implications of proposition 8.1 in the simplest possible case compatible with sudden urban growth. If $\Delta_N \Delta_a X = 0$, in other words if the marginal value of land used for production is not affected by a change in the number of individuals working on it (or, alternatively, if the marginal value of labour is not affected by a change in the amount of land used for production); and if $\Delta_a^2 X = 0$, in other words if there are constant returns to scale in land as a factor of production; then proposition 8.1 implies

Sudden Urban Growth

(8.12) $\alpha_1 \delta_N \bar{u} = -\alpha_4 + \alpha_6 \Delta_N^2 X.$

Suppose that, as the urban population increases, the structure of advantages in the organisation of production causes $\Delta_N X$ to increase initially at an increasing rate (figure 8.5(1)). Then if $\alpha_4 + \alpha_1$ is large enough proposition 8.1 implies $\delta_N \bar{u}$ as in figure 8.5(1) and, therefore, $\bar{u}[N]$ as in

Figure 8.5: Variation of utility with city size.

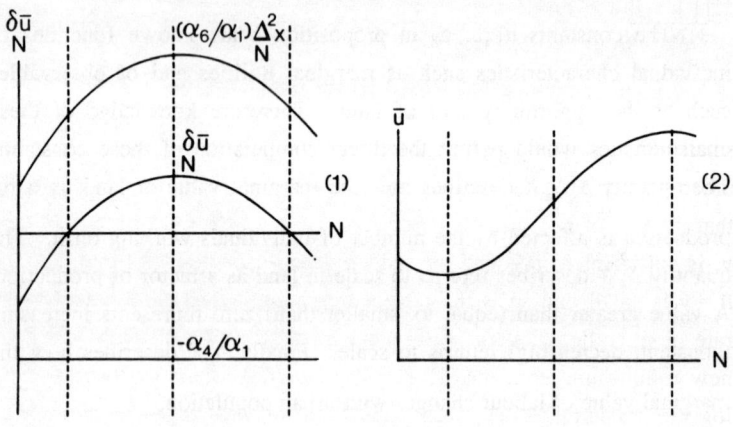

figure 8.5(2). Unlike its appearance in figure 8.3, the structure of $\bar{u}[N]$ is now relatively complex. It is precisely this complexity that generates sudden urban growth.

Consider figure 8.6.[6] Both $\bar{u}$ and $\bar{v}$ shift upwards with the development of technology. Suppose however that the city is more responsive to such development than the alternative sector. Figure 8.6(1) indicates shifts of $\bar{u}$ relative to $\bar{v}$. Until period three, smooth changes in technology cause smooth changes in the stable partition of the equilibrium population. Period three however marks a critical point beyond which a

Figure 8.6: Equilibrium path of urban population.

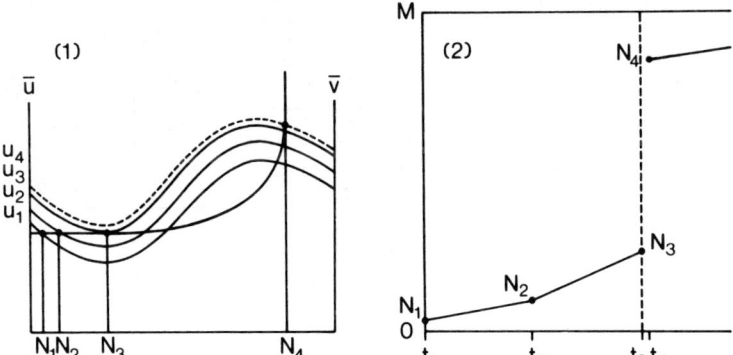

small relative upward shift in $\bar{u}$ creates a discontinuity in the equilibrium urban population path (figure 8.6(2)). This, together with an assumption that the rate of migration is proportional to the difference between $\bar{u}$ and $\bar{v}$, is sufficient to account for sudden urban growth as follows. At t_4, $\bar{u} - \bar{v}$ is small and so is the rate of migration. Over time however the rate of migration first increases with $\bar{u} - \bar{v}$ and then declines until the new equilibrium is reached (figure 8.6(1)). One therefore may expect a logistic structure of the urban population trajectory. Furthermore, one may also imagine the unobservable equilibrium path in figure 8.6(2) as guiding the urban population trajectory.

Sudden urban decline may happen as well. Consider for example a city with diminishing hinterland. Then u shifts gradually downward relative to $\bar{v}$ and the reverse phenomenon materialises, provided that the decline is persistent enough.[7]

The assumptions used to construct $\bar{u}[N]$ do not generate qualitatively unique outcomes. If for example the negative term in figure 8.5(1) is initially smaller in absolute value than the corresponding positive term, then $\bar{u}[N]$ initially increases to create the extreme case of sudden urban growth within a completely agrarian society (figure 8.7).

Figure 8.7: Sudden urban growth in an agrarian society.

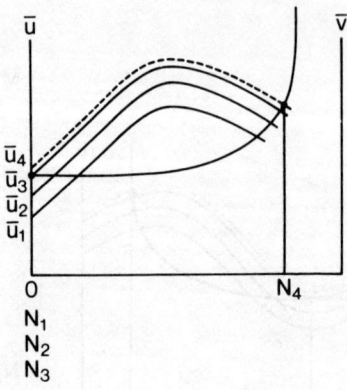

Furthermore, it is easy to describe cases (consistent with these assumptions) that fail to produce a discontinuity in the equilibrium urban population path: sudden urban growth hinges upon a combination of circumstances fully realised only in some cities.

Complications

The analysis of the previous section was based on the premise that the marginal value of land used in the production of the private good is invariant with city size and that there are constant returns to scale in land as a factor of production. Suppose now that the marginal value of land used in production varies with city size, while constant returns to scale in land as a factor of production are still retained. Then proposition 8.1 implies

$$(8.13) \quad \left[\alpha_1 - \alpha_2 \triangle_N \triangle_a X \right] \delta \bar{u} = \\ - \alpha_4 - \alpha_5 \triangle_N \triangle_a X + \alpha_6 \triangle_N^2 X + \alpha_8 \left[\triangle_N \triangle_a X \right]^2.$$

Intuitively, the marginal value of land used in production must increase

Figure 8.8: Alternative utility variation paths.

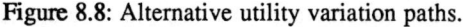

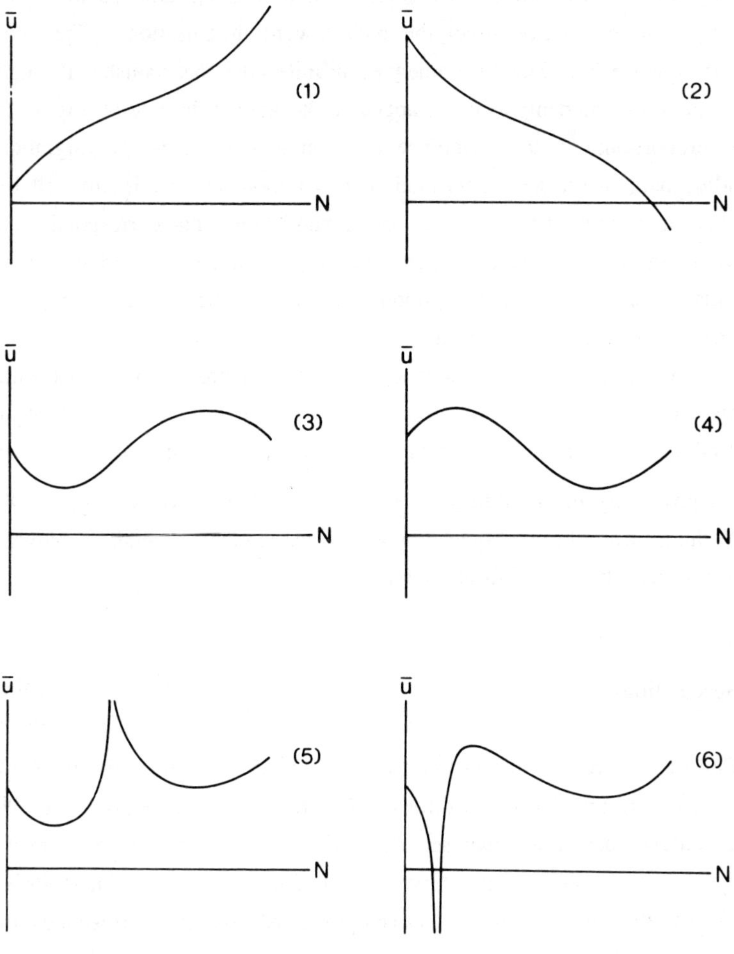

with city size. If so, the qualitative behaviour of (8.13) appears in figure 8.8.[8] It seems that these alternative utility variation paths represent the main types of urban development. Gradual urbanisation corresponds to figure 8.8(2). Sudden urban growth as in figure 8.6 corresponds to

Sudden Urban Growth

figure 8.8(3). The extreme case of cities suddenly created as in figure 8.7 corresponds to figures 8.8(1) and 8.8(4).[9] Unbounded values of $\bar{u}[N]$ may also occur. Those that correspond to a maximum, as in figure 8.8(5), do not really affect the path toward urbanisation. The only consequence is a fleeting moment of infinite bliss that vanishes through migration as suddenly as it has appeared, because if the rate of migration is proportional to the difference between $\bar{u}$ and $\bar{v}$ then the migration adjustment in the neighbourhood of this unbounded maximum will be close to instantaneous. On the other hand those that correspond to a minimum, as in figure 8.8(6), stop the path toward further urbanisation. This represents the case of population-stable cities amidst a rapidly growing regional environment.

When the marginal value of land used in production varies with city size and there are variable returns to scale in land as a factor of production, $\delta_N u$ is described by proposition 8.1. This, in general, implies the possibility of an additional bend in the utility curves of figure 8.8. Nothing further of consequence would be gained from a detailed analysis of this case, hence I shall not pursue it.

Speculations

Consider figure 8.9. It contains two stable (N_1, N_3) and one unstable (N_2) equilibrium population partitions. Intuitively, N_1 corresponds to an underdeveloped, low-urbanised state while N_3 corresponds to a developed, high-urbanised state. Given population homogeneity, this tends to suggest that all is well with development because N_3 corresponds to higher welfare for everyone relative to N_1. If however the urban population is heterogeneous then figure 8.9 should be interpreted as indicating average welfare, so that the issue of welfare distribution becomes relevant. What can be said about this issue now? In chapter six we have seen that increasing the size of a class (with everything else

Figure 8.9: Equilibrium population partitions.

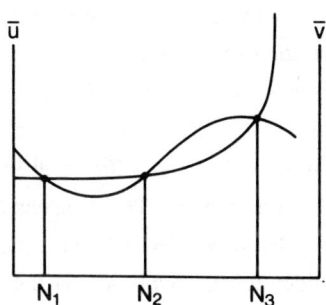

being held constant) decreases the utility of all classes, whereas increasing the income of a class (with everything else being held constant) may increase the utility of the poorer classes and decrease the utility of the richer classes. Here, that both urban population and utility have increased as the system moves from its underdeveloped to its developed state implies a positive overall income effect on the average utility stronger than the corresponding negative population effect. But if the income of the poorer half has increased relative to the income of the richer half then the utility of the richer half has decreased which, together with the urban population increase, tends to suppress average utility as the system moves from N_1 to N_3. Hence development in laissez-faire economies may increase rather than decrease social inequality.

What may happen in a system of cities? Then $\bar{u}_i$ relates to a particular city i and $\bar{v}_i$ relates to the rest of the economy relative to that city. For smaller cities, where the economy is relatively larger, the slope of $\bar{v}_i$ must flatten. For very large central place systems, migration to and from city i cannot affect the general level of utility because it involves a relatively insignificant part of the total population: $\bar{v}_i$ becomes horizontal over the population range of city i as determined by $\bar{u}_i$.

Complexity multiplies if one allows for interdependences between cities.[10] In consequence the position of $\bar{u}_i$ relative to $\bar{v}_i$ remains virtually unknown. For some cities, it may well be that a discontinuity is imminent: *regional policies aimed to alter, even slightly, the relative configuration of advantages in the system may be prone to unexpectedly catastrophic population shifts unless they are supported by effective controls on migration.* Furthermore, once sudden urban growth is well under way, it is very difficult to stop it by means other than direct controls on migration. This happens because a fast rate of urban growth implies a large positive difference between $\bar{u}$ and $\bar{v}$. Thus, in order to stop sudden urban growth and at the same time avoid direct controls on migration, one has to eliminate this large difference either by substantially reducing the opportunities in city i, or by substantially increasing the opportunities in the rest of the economy, or both; and all this within a prohibitively short period. The case of direct controls on migration is also difficult to support. This happens because to maintain a large difference between $\bar{u}$ and $\bar{v}$ is to create a (probably unmanageable) political problem. Hence, following Doxiadis (1967), I am led to believe that the challenge of the future, far from being to stop sudden urban growth, is rather to accept it and to plan for it.

Appendix to Chapter Eight

1

This section of the appendix contains a proof of the proposition that if

(8.14) $$\bigwedge_{a+1} \sigma + \bar{r}[a+1] + \bigwedge_{a}^{2} Q + \bigwedge_{a} Q > 0$$

then

(8.15) $$\left[\alpha_1 - \alpha_2 \bigwedge_{N} \bigwedge_{a} X - \alpha_3 \bigwedge_{a}^{2} X \right] \delta \bar{u}_{N} =$$
$$- \alpha_4 - \alpha_5 \bigwedge_{N} \bigwedge_{a} X + \alpha_6 \bigwedge_{N}^{2} X + \alpha_7 \bigwedge_{a}^{2} X$$

$$-\alpha_8\left[\left[\underset{a}{\Delta^2} X\right]\left[\underset{N}{\Delta^2} X\right] - \left[\underset{N}{\Delta}\underset{a}{\Delta} X\right]^2\right]$$

with $\alpha_1,...,\alpha_8 > 0$.

Using (3), the total differentials of (8.5), (8.6) and (5.5) yield

$$(8.16) \begin{bmatrix} -\bar{n}_{a+1} + \sum_{j=a+1}^{b} \frac{\partial \bar{n}_j}{\partial y} \underset{a}{\Delta}\underset{N}{\Delta} X & \bar{n}_{b+1} & \sum_{j=a+1}^{b} \frac{\partial \bar{n}_j}{\partial z} \\ \underset{a+1}{\Delta} \sigma + \frac{\Delta_a^2 Q}{\Delta_a Q} r_{a+1}^0 + \frac{\partial \sigma_{a+1}}{\partial y} \underset{a}{\Delta}\underset{N}{\Delta} X - \frac{\Delta_a^2 X}{\Delta_a Q} & 0 & \frac{\partial \sigma_{a+1}}{\partial z} \\ \frac{\partial \sigma_b}{\partial y} \underset{a}{\Delta}\underset{N}{\Delta} X & \underset{b}{\Delta} \sigma & \frac{\partial \sigma_b}{\partial z} \end{bmatrix}$$

$$\cdot \begin{bmatrix} \underset{N}{\delta a} \\ \underset{N}{\delta b} \\ \underset{N}{\delta \bar{u}} \end{bmatrix} = \begin{bmatrix} 1 - \sum_{j=a+1}^{b} \frac{\partial \bar{n}_j}{\partial y} \underset{N}{\Delta^2} X \\ \frac{1}{\underset{a}{\Delta} Q} \underset{a}{\Delta}\underset{N}{\Delta} X - \frac{\partial \sigma_{a+1}}{\partial y} \underset{N}{\Delta^2} X \\ - \frac{\partial \sigma_b}{\partial y} \underset{N}{\Delta^2} X \end{bmatrix} . \quad {}^{11}$$

Solving for $\delta_N \bar{u}$ one obtains (8.15) where

$$(8.17) \quad \alpha_1 \equiv -\left[\left[\sum_{j=a+1}^{b} \frac{\partial \bar{n}_j}{\partial z}\left[\underset{a+1}{\Delta}\sigma + \frac{\Delta_a^2 Q}{\Delta_a Q} r_{a+1}^0\right] + \frac{\partial \sigma_{a+1}}{\partial z} \bar{n}_{a+1}\right]\left[-\underset{b}{\Delta}\sigma\right]\right.$$

$$\left. + \frac{\partial \sigma_b}{\partial z} \bar{n}_{b+1}\left[\underset{a+1}{\Delta}\sigma + \frac{\Delta_a^2 Q}{\Delta_a Q} r_{a+1}^0\right]\right]$$

$$(8.18) \quad \alpha_2 \equiv \bar{n}_{b+1}\left[\frac{\partial \sigma_{a+1}}{\partial y}\frac{\partial \sigma_b}{\partial z} - \frac{\partial \sigma_b}{\partial z}\frac{\partial \sigma_{a+1}}{\partial z}\right]$$

$$- \underset{b}{\Delta}\sigma \sum_{j=a+1}^{b}\left[\frac{\partial \bar{n}_j}{\partial z}\frac{\partial \sigma_{a+1}}{\partial y} - \frac{\partial \bar{n}_j}{\partial y}\frac{\partial \sigma_{a+1}}{\partial z}\right]$$

Sudden Urban Growth

$$(8.19) \quad \alpha_3 \equiv \frac{1}{\Delta_a Q}\left[-\bar{n}_{b+1}\frac{\partial \sigma_b}{\partial z} + \bigtriangleup_b \sigma \sum_{j=a+1}^{b}\frac{\partial \bar{n}_j}{\partial z}\right]$$

$$(8.20) \quad \alpha_4 \equiv -\left[\bigtriangleup_{a+1}\sigma + \frac{\Delta_a^2 Q}{\Delta_a Q}\overset{0}{r}_{a+1}\right]\bigtriangleup_b \sigma$$

$$(8.21) \quad \alpha_5 \equiv \bigtriangleup_b \sigma \left[\frac{\bar{n}_{a+1}}{\Delta_a Q} + \frac{\partial \sigma_{a+1}}{\partial y}\right]$$

$$(8.22) \quad \alpha_6 \equiv -\sum_{j=a+1}^{b}\frac{\partial \bar{n}_j}{\partial y}\left[\bigtriangleup_{a+1}\sigma + \frac{\Delta_a^2 Q}{\Delta_a Q}\overset{0}{r}_{a+1}\right]\bigtriangleup_b \sigma - \frac{\partial \sigma_{a+1}}{\partial y}\bar{n}_{a+1}\bigtriangleup_b \sigma$$

$$+ \frac{\partial \sigma_b}{\partial y}\bar{n}_{b+1}\left[\bigtriangleup_{a+1}\sigma + \frac{\Delta_a^2 Q}{\Delta_a Q}\overset{0}{r}_{a+1}\right]$$

$$(8.23) \quad \alpha_7 \equiv \frac{\Delta_b \sigma}{\Delta_a Q}$$

$$(8.24) \quad \alpha_8 \equiv \frac{1}{\Delta_a Q}\left[\bar{n}_{b+1}\frac{\partial \sigma_b}{\partial y} - \bigtriangleup_b \sigma \sum_{j=a+1}^{b}\frac{\partial \bar{n}_j}{\partial y}\right].$$

One may now use some results of chapter five in order to determine the signs of these coefficients. From (5.26) and (5.30),

$$(8.25) \quad \frac{\partial \sigma_{a+1}}{\partial y}\frac{\partial \sigma_b}{\partial z} - \frac{\partial \sigma_b}{\partial y}\frac{\partial \sigma_{a+1}}{\partial z}$$

$$= \frac{1}{\bar{q}_{a+1}}\left[-\frac{1}{\bar{q}_b(\partial u \div \partial \bar{x}_b)}\right] - \frac{1}{\bar{q}_b}\left[-\frac{1}{\bar{q}_{a+1}(\partial u \div \partial \bar{x}_{a+1})}\right]$$

$$= -\frac{1}{\bar{q}_{a+1}\bar{q}_b}\left[\frac{1}{\partial u \div \partial \bar{x}_b} - \frac{1}{\partial u \div \partial \bar{x}_{a+1}}\right] > 0$$

because $\bar{x}_{a+1} > \bar{x}_b$ according to note 4.12, hence because $0 < \partial u \div \partial \bar{x}_{a+1} < \partial u \div \partial \bar{x}_b$ according to (3.3) and (3.4). Taking into account (8.25), together with (4.7), (4.8), (5.20), (5.25) and (5.30), the proposition follows because $\overset{0}{r}_{a+1} = \bar{r}[a+1]$ at equilibrium. ∎

2

This section of the appendix examines the behaviour of $\delta_N \bar{u}$ in (8.13). It also briefly touches upon the most general case (8.15).

Equation (8.13) applies when the marginal value of land used in the production of the private good varies with city size and there are constant returns to scale in land as a factor of production. Under these circumstances it is reasonable to assume that the marginal value of land used in production increases with city size. It is however unclear whether it increases at an increasing, constant, or decreasing rate. In consequence let

(8.26) $$\Delta_N \Delta_a X = \beta_1 \pm \beta_2 N$$

where $\beta_1 > 0$ and $\beta_2 \geq 0$. Also let

(8.27) $$\Delta_N^2 X = \beta_3 + (\beta_4 - \beta_5 N)N$$

which is consistent with figure 8.5. Upon substitution of (8.26) and (8.27) in (8.13) one obtains

(8.28) $$(\gamma_1 \mp \gamma_2 N) \delta_N \bar{u} = -\gamma_3 + (\gamma_4 - \gamma_5 N)N$$

where

(8.29) $$\gamma_1 \equiv \alpha_1 - \alpha_2 \beta_1$$

(8.30) $$\gamma_2 \equiv \alpha_2 \beta_2$$

(8.31) $$\gamma_3 \equiv \alpha_4 + (\alpha_5 - \alpha_8 \beta_1)\beta_1 - \alpha_6 \beta_3$$

(8.32) $$\gamma_4 \equiv \alpha_6 \alpha_4 \mp (\alpha_5 - 2\alpha_8 \beta_1)\beta_2$$

(8.33) $\quad \gamma_5 \equiv \alpha_6 \beta_5 - \alpha_8 \beta_2^2.$

The qualitative structure of $\bar{u}[N]$ now depends on the combination of three factors: the sign behaviour of the LHS of (8.28), the sign of γ_3 and the signs of γ_4 and γ_5.[12] Alternative combinations of these factors lead to alternative utility variation paths. A detailed classification of those leads to the types shown in figure 8.8.

When the marginal value of land used in production varies with city size and there are variable returns to scale in land as a factor of production then $\delta_N \bar{u}$ is described by (8.15). Even now it is possible to use a procedure similar to the previous one, because if $\Delta_a^2 X$ is a positive (increasing returns) or a negative (decreasing returns) constant then (8.15) remains qualitatively similar to (8.28) and the previous analysis holds. If, on the other hand, $\Delta_a^2 X$ is linear in N, that is, if returns to scale in land as a factor of production vary with city size in this particular manner, then the LHS of (8.15) is qualitatively similar to the LHS of (8.28), whereas the RHS of (8.15) becomes a third-degree polynomial. This implies an additional change in the direction of $\bar{u}[N]$, and hence an additional equilibrium configuration.

In general, the realised path toward urbanisation depends on the particular combination of factors that drives (8.28). These, in turn, depend on the prevailing characteristics of individuals and of the existing technology embodied in (8.17)–(8.24) and (8.29)–(8.33) respectively, as well as on the characteristics of land used in production. Hence, given a knowledge of these characteristics, it would be possible to explain the path toward urbanisation. Different outcomes would then be attributed to different behavioural and technological circumstances. Prediction, however, would require a theory concerning $\bar{v}[M-N]$ at the same level of detail as that of $\bar{u}[N]$, and a theory about how $\bar{v}$ shifts relative to $\bar{u}$ through time: to simply assert that agricultural societies enjoy a lower standard of living than urbanised ones and that the city is more responsive to the development of technology than the alternative sector, although both seemingly reasonable and sufficient to account for sudden urban growth, is nevertheless too abstract to be used for drawing conclusions about particulars.

Notes to Chapter Eight

1. This chapter is taken from Papageorgiou (1980).

2. Sudden urban growth does not imply fast total population growth. It may happen in population–stable regions (Athens, Greece, provides such an example). Total population growth, however, compounds it.

3. This implies that the slope of the bid–rent associated with production is taken to be steeper than that associated with the individuals.

4. Parametric treatment of land values here means the following. When land used for production expands, the existing pattern of land values may, in principle, be affected. If such indirect consequences of expansion are small, they may not be taken into account by the production manager. That is, the existing pattern of land values may be taken as fixed (parametric) by the production manager when he ponders expansion. Under these circumstances, for $I_j \in [1,a]$,

$$\triangle_a r_j^0 = 0.$$

Conditions (8.2) and (8.3) are obtained by differencing D with respect to N and a, and by setting the expressions thus obtained to zero. Hence (8.2) and (8.3) approximate the continuous equivalent to problem (8.1). Differencing with respect to a yields

$$\underset{a}{\Delta} D = \sum_{j=1}^{a} \underset{a}{\Delta} r_j^0 \underset{j-1}{\Delta} Q$$
$$+ r_{a+1}^0 \underset{a}{\Delta} Q + \sum_{j=a+2}^{b} n_j \underset{a}{\Delta} y - n_{a+1} y + \delta_a C^0 - \delta_a f$$
$$= \sum_{j=1}^{a} \underset{a}{\Delta} r_j^0 \underset{j-1}{\Delta} Q$$
$$+ r_{a+1}^0 \underset{a}{\Delta} Q + \sum_{j=a+2}^{b} n_j \underset{a}{\Delta} y + n_{a+1} \left[\underset{N}{\Delta} X - y \right] - \underset{a}{\Delta} X = 0$$

using the discrete rule of Leibnitz and noting that $N = \Sigma_{j=a+1}^{b} n_j$. Condition (8.3) follows because the first and third terms are zero under a parametric treatment of r^0 and y respectively, and because the fourth term is also zero because of (8.2). The term $1+\Delta_a Q$ occurs in (8.3) because the value of land is measured per unit of area.

5   More generally, notice that since the first term in (8.7) is negative the second term must be positive. This implies that proposition 8.1 may hold on a subset of city shapes, because for linear cities $\Delta_a^2 Q = 0$.

6   The commentary on this figure borrows from the ideas of Casetti (1980).

7   Rome toward the end of antiquity would serve as an example.

8   See appendix, section 2.

9   It is easy to draw such conclusions through comparison of $\bar{u}$ and $\bar{v}$ about their intersection. If $\bar{u}$ is greater (smaller) than $\bar{v}$ before (after) their intersection then there is gradual change, as in figure 8.6(1) for $0 \leq N \leq N_3$, because the equilibrium population partition

is stable. If on the other hand $\bar{u}$ is smaller (greater) than $\bar{v}$ before (after) their intersection then there is catastrophic change, as in figure 8.6(1) for $N_3 < N \le N_4$ or as in figure 8.7 for $0 \le N \le N_4$, because the equilibrium population partition is unstable.

10   See Henderson (1977) chapter three.

11   The total differential of (8.5) is obtained as follows. Since

$$\sum_{j=a+1}^{b} \bar{n}_j = g[a,b;y,z]$$

then

$$\delta N = \bigtriangleup_a g\, \delta a + \bigtriangleup_b g\, \delta b + \frac{\partial g}{\partial y} dy + \frac{\partial g}{\partial z} d\bar{u}$$

$$= -\bar{n}_{a+1}\, \delta a + \bar{n}_{b+1}\, \delta b + \sum_{j=a+1}^{b} \frac{\partial \bar{n}_j}{\partial y} d\bigtriangleup_N X + \sum_{j=a+1}^{b} \frac{\partial \bar{n}_j}{\partial z} d\bar{u}$$

by means of the discrete method of Leibnitz and by (8.2), where

$$d\bigtriangleup_N X = \bigtriangleup_N^2 X\, \delta N + \bigtriangleup_a \bigtriangleup_N X\, \delta a$$

and $z = \bar{u}[N]$. The total differential of (8.6) is obtained as follows. From (8.3)

$$\bigtriangleup_a Q\, dr^0_{a+1} + r^0_{a+1} \bigtriangleup_a^2 Q\, \delta a = d\bigtriangleup_a X$$

hence

$$\frac{\partial \sigma_{a+1}}{\partial y} dy + \bigtriangleup_{a+1} \sigma\, \delta a + \frac{\partial \sigma_{a+1}}{\partial z} d\bar{u} = dr^0_{a+1}$$

$$= \frac{1}{\bigtriangleup_a Q} \left[d\bigtriangleup_a X - r^0_{a+1} \bigtriangleup_a^2 Q\, \delta a \right]$$

where

$$d \bigwedge_a X = \bigwedge_N \bigwedge_a X \, \delta N + \bigwedge_a^2 X \, \delta a.$$

12 Suppose, for example, that the LHS of (8.28) remains positive for all feasible values of N. Then, although variable, it does not affect the qualitative structure of $\delta_N \bar{u}$ as determined by the RHS of (8.28). Further suppose that all coefficients of the RHS of (8.28) are positive. Then, if $-\alpha_4 + \alpha_6 \beta_3 < 0$, the qualitative structure of the RHS of (8.28) is the same as that of (8.12) and figure 8.8(3) applies. If, on the other hand, the LHS of (8.28) remains negative for all feasible values of N, while all the coefficients of the RHS of (8.28) are positive and $-\alpha_4 + \alpha_6 \beta_3 < 0$, then the utility shape of figure 8.8(3) will be reversed to create one stable and two unstable equilibria as in figure 8.8(4).

9

The Decline of Central Cities [1]

Historical Background

Chapter eight dealt with catastrophic population movements from the alternative sector to the city. This chapter deals with analogous movements within the city.

During the recent past, metropolitan developments in North America have been characterised by an exodus of the middle class from the central city to the suburbs. Since the middle class in North America is mostly white and since central cities in the United States have become increasingly black, it remains unclear whether such exodus was initially triggered by a quest for a better physical environment or by an aversion to blacks. Whatever the reasons, they were strong enough to reverse the spatial distribution of whites around the United States metropolitan centres completely during the span of a single decade (figure 9.1). Similar trends persisted through the seventies (table 9.1)—but with a difference: the white flight of the sixties now became mixed. At the same time, even in the devastated inner–city landscapes of the United

Decline of Central Cities

Figure 9.1: Average distribution of blacks (B) and whites (W) in 33 US metropolitan areas for (1) 1960 and (2) 1970.

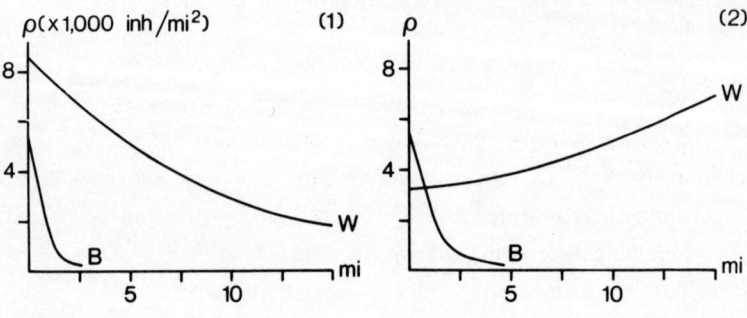

Source: Reid (1977, p.356)

Table 9.1: Net migration in US metropolitan areas 1970–1977 (in thousands)

	White	Black	Total
Central cities	−9533	−653	−10186
Suburban areas	7122	798	7920
Total	−2411	145	−2266

Source: Berry (1980, p. 9)

States industrial northeast, there were signs of revival. Although the evidence available is still fragmentary, the message it carries is intuitively clear. And although encouraging, it is not entirely free of contradictions.

"Over the past 20 years the housing of the poor and the working poor has improved primarily because they have fallen heir to what used to be called 'the grey areas'. The softening of middle-class demand for this housing stock lowered its relative price and permitted a sharp decline in overcrowding for low-income people. Whatever the troubles of the cities, this has been a fortunate outcome. But the danger appears imminent that the housing stock available to the working and welfare poor will now be sharply diminished, squeezed between reduced rates of filtering at one end and the childless multiworker household at the other. There is, in this, an incipient class conflict between the new young well-educated professional class, actively pursuing alternative living arrangements and life-styles, and the majority of the children of working-class Americans for whom marriage and the home in the suburbs remain a desirable goal."[2]

Meanwhile, what happens to the evicted poor? In the world of this book, precisely nothing. They simply vanish from the stage and into the convenient infinite sink of the alternative sector.

Types of Suburbanisation

A process of suburbanisation has already been discussed in chapter five. Namely, as technology develops, higher income and improved transportation conditions compound each other to produce a flattening of gradients in both the "transient" and the "closed" city. According to the analysis of chapter six, this conclusion will certainly be valid provided that the income elasticity of the demand for land is greater than the income elasticity of the unit cost of transportation. If this condition does not hold, (6.5) suggests the development of opposing forces which may even reverse suburbanisation. But the continuing dominance of the Property Rights view and of individualism in North America indicates that the income elasticity of the demand for land may still be greater than the income elasticity of the unit cost of transportation.[3] Is though such a process sufficient to explain the decline of central cities as described in the previous section? I believe that it is not, firstly, because this process is gradual and hence insufficient to account for the catastrophic population shifts involved, precisely as the process behind figure 8.3 was insufficient to account for sudden urban growth, and secondly, because the decline of central cities may imply feelings and interactions between members of different social classes which are clearly absent here. Is then this process a pure figment of the imagination to be discarded on the face of evidence? I believe that it is not, and I believe that there are at least two distinct processes operating at distinct time–scales. The first, discussed in chapter five, refers to long–run adjustments. The second, to be discussed here, refers to short–run adjustments. Such distinction between the short and the long run permits an analysis of each process independently of the other. This happens because the quantity of land consumed cannot be a choice variable in the short run, where the distribution of lot sizes has already been established. In consequence, by holding the quantity of land consumed constant, one may concentrate exclusively on the short–run movement of social groups within the city and on the factors that direct such movement.

A Simplified Framework

Partition the city into centre $[1,a]$ and suburb $[a + 1,b]$. The centre has a fixed total area and a fixed area allocated to production. Then there must be a fixed area allocated to residences, and, since lot sizes are fixed in the short run, the total population $\bar{N}_0$ of the centre is also fixed.[4] However, the total population N_1 of the suburb may vary, thereby varying the area of the suburb. The land converted to suburban land use is already subdivided as all urban land is. It follows that, as the suburb grows, its population grows by the number of new lots converted to suburban land use. Then the spatial extent of the suburb must be an increasing function of its population:

(9.1) $\qquad b = b[N_1] \; with \; \triangle_{N_1} b > 0.$

There are two income classes in the city, the poor and the rich, with total populations N^P and N^R respectively. Thus one may partition the total population of the city in two ways as

(9.2) $\qquad N = \bar{N}_0 + N_1 = N^P + N^R.$

The poor live only in the centre. In consequence

(9.3) $\qquad N^P = N_0^P \; and \; N_1 = N_1^R$

where N_0^P is the number of poor at the centre and N_1^R is the number of rich in the suburb.

The city is "transient". This implies that an increase in the population of the city will correspond to a significant decrease of the population outside the city which, in turn, will cause an increase of utility:

(9.4) $\qquad z^P = \bar{v}^P[N^P] \; with \; \triangle_{N^P} \bar{v}^P > 0$

and

(9.5) $\qquad z^R = \bar{v}^R[N^R] \; with \; \triangle_{N^R} \bar{v}^R > 0$

where z^P and z^R denote the equilibrium utility levels in the alternative sector for the poor and the rich respectively.

Both poor and rich may live at the centre. Since the total population of the centre is fixed, a change in the population size of one class at the centre must be related to an opposite change in the population size of the other income class. If the number of poor increases at the centre then the surplus rich will migrate either to the suburb or to the alternative sector. If, on the other hand, the number of rich increases at the centre then the only alternative available to the surplus poor is the alternative sector. Since the quantity of land consumed is fixed, the utility of the poor is simply defined over the consumption of the private good as

$$(9.6) \qquad u^P = u^P[x^P] \text{ with } \frac{\partial u^P}{\partial x^P} > 0.$$

Suppose that the quantity of land consumed per capita is one unit everywhere.[5] Also suppose that the centre is homogeneous in the sense that there is no cost of transportation within it. Since the price per unit of the private good is one unit, the income constraint of the poor is simply defined as

$$(9.7) \qquad y^P = x^P + r^P.$$

The rich at the centre are sensitive to the quality of the environment in the centre. For them, this depends on the number of poor at the centre and on the number of rich in the suburb who commute every day to the centre and who therefore congest it. Thus the utility of the rich at the centre is

$$(9.8) \qquad u_0^R = u_0^R[x_0^R, E[N^P, N_1]] \text{ with}$$

$$\frac{\partial u_0^R}{\partial x_0^R} > 0, \ \frac{\partial u_0^R}{\partial E} > 0, \ \bigtriangleup_{N^P} E < 0, \ \bigtriangleup_{N_1} E < 0$$

while the income constraint of the rich at the centre is

$$(9.9) \qquad y^R = x_0^R + r_0^R.$$

The quality of the environment in the suburb is not an issue for those who live there. Thus the utility of the rich in the suburb has a structure similar to that of the poor at the centre:

(9.10) $\quad u_i^R = u^R[x_i^R] \text{ with } \dfrac{\partial u^R}{\partial x_i^R} > 0 \text{ and } i \in [a+1, b]$.

Unlike the centre, the suburb is not homogeneous in the sense that there is a cost of transportation depending upon distance from the centre. Under these circumstances, the income constraint of the rich at the suburb may be written as

(9.11) $\quad y^R = x_i^R + r^R[i] + c[i] \text{ for } i \in [a+1, b]$.

Using (9.6) and (9.7), the equilibrium level of utility for the poor is

(9.12) $\quad z^P = u^P[y^P - \bar{r}^P]$.

Using (9.2), (9.8) and (9.9), the equilibrium level of utility for the rich at the centre is

(9.13) $\quad z^R = u_0^R[y^R - \bar{r}_0^R, E[N^P, N^P + N^R - \bar{N}_0]]$.

To write the equilibrium level of utility for the rich in the suburb in a convenient form, it is necessary to adopt an indirect approach. Since, at the border,

(9.14) $\quad r^R[b] = \check{r}$

(9.15) $\quad c[b] = c[b[N_1]] \equiv \check{c}[N_1]$,

the last equality being true by virtue of (9.1), the income of the rich at the border must be partitioned as

Decline of Central Cities

(9.16) $\quad y^R = x_b^R + \check{r} + \check{c}[N_1].$

Since, at equilibrium, utility must be invariant over the suburb and since utility in the suburb is simply defined over the consumption of the private good, the quantity of the private good consumed at equilibrium must also be invariant. In consequence, using (9.2), (9.10) and (9.16), the equilibrium level of utility for the rich at the suburb is

(9.17) $\quad z^R = u^R[y^R - \check{r} - \check{c}[N^P + N^R - \bar{N}_0]] \ for \ i \in [a+1,b]$

while the corresponding bid-rent function is

(9.18) $\quad \bar{r}_i^R = y^R - x_i^R - c[i]$

$\quad\quad\quad = \check{r} + \check{c}[N^P + N^R - \bar{N}_0] - c[i] \ for \ i \in [a+1,b]$

using (9.11) and (9.16).

Equilibrium requires that the utility level of an income class in the city be equal to the corresponding utility level in the alternative sector. For the poor, using (9.4) and (9.12), this implies

(9.19) $\quad u^P[y^P - \bar{r}^P] = \bar{v}^P[N^P]$

while for the rich, using (9.5), (9.13) and (9.17), this implies

(9.20) $\quad u_0^R[y^R - \bar{r}_0^R, E[N^P, N^P + N^R - \bar{N}_0]]$

$\quad\quad = u^R[y^R - \check{r} - \check{c}[N^P + N^R - \bar{N}_0]] = \bar{v}^R[N^R] \ for \ i \in [a+1,b].$

Equations (9.19) and (9.20) provide the background for understanding the forces that lead to the decline of central cities.

Decline of Central Cities

The Cumulative Decay Process

Suppose that incomes are fixed. Differencing (9.19) with respect to N^P yields

$$(9.21) \qquad -\frac{du^P}{dx^P} \underset{N^P}{\Delta} \bar{r}^P = \underset{N^P}{\Delta} \bar{v}^P$$

so that

$$(9.22) \qquad \underset{N^P}{\Delta} \bar{r}^P = -\underset{N^P}{\Delta} \bar{v}^P \div \frac{du^P}{dx^P} < 0$$

because of (9.4) and (9.6). That is, the bid-rent of the poor at the centre decreases as their numbers increase. Differencing (9.20) with respect to N^P yields

$$(9.23) \qquad -\frac{\partial u_0^R}{\partial x_0^R} \underset{N^P}{\Delta} \bar{r}_0^R + \frac{\partial u_0^R}{\partial E} \underset{N^P}{\delta_P E} = -\frac{du^R}{dx_i^R} \underset{N_1}{\Delta} \check{c} \, \underset{N^P}{\delta_P N_1}$$

$$= \underset{N^R}{\Delta} \bar{v}^R \underset{N^P}{\Delta} N^R$$

where

$$(9.24) \qquad \delta_P E = \underset{N^P}{\Delta} E + \underset{N_1}{\Delta} E \, \underset{N^P}{\delta_P N_1}$$

by the definition of the quality of the environment in (9.8), and where

$$(9.25) \qquad \underset{N^P}{\delta_P N_1} = 1 + \underset{N^P}{\Delta} N^R$$

by (9.2). Combining the first part of (9.23) with (9.24) and (9.25) yields

$$(9.26) \quad \bigtriangleup_{N^P} \bar{r}_0^R = \left[\frac{\partial u_0^R}{\partial E} \div \frac{\partial u_0^R}{\partial x_0^R}\right] \left[\bigtriangleup_{N^P} E + \bigtriangleup_{N_1} E \left[1 + \bigtriangleup_{N^P} N^R\right]\right]$$
$$+ \left[\frac{du^R}{dx_i^R} \div \frac{\partial u_0^R}{\partial x_0^R}\right] \bigtriangleup_{N_1} \check{c} \left[1 + \bigtriangleup_{N^P} N^R\right].$$

This last expression involves $\bigtriangleup_{N^P} N^R$, the sign of which is unknown. In order to determine this sign, use the second part of (9.23) together with (9.25) to obtain

$$(9.27) \quad \bigtriangleup_{N^P} N^R = - \bigtriangleup_{N_1} \check{c} + \left[\bigtriangleup_{N_1} \check{c} + \bigtriangleup_{N^R} \bar{v}^R + \frac{du^R}{dx_i^R}\right]$$

which, by (3.8), (9.1), (9.5), (9.10) and (9.15) implies

$$(9.28) \quad -1 < \bigtriangleup_{N^P} N^R < 0.$$

This information, together with (9.8), shows that the sign of (9.26) is ambiguous. The first term on the RHS of (9.26) is negative and the second term is positive. Hence, unlike the bid-rent of the poor, the bid-rent of the rich at the centre may either increase or decrease as the number of the poor increases. Factors that determine its behaviour include how important the quality of the environment ($\partial u_0^R \div \partial E$) is to the rich at the centre; to what extent the quality of the environment is affected by changes in the number of the poor at the centre ($\bigtriangleup_{N^P} E$) and by changes in the size of the city ($\bigtriangleup_{N_1} E$); and the state of transportation technology ($\bigtriangleup_{N_1} \check{c}$).[6] If the environmental factors are strong and the transportation technology high then there is a higher possibility that the bid-rent of the rich at the centre decreases as the number of the poor increases. If on the other hand the environmental factors are weak and the transportation technology low then there is a higher possibility that the bid-rent of the rich at the centre increases as the number of poor increases.

Figure 9.2: Stable and unstable equilibrium partitions at the centre.

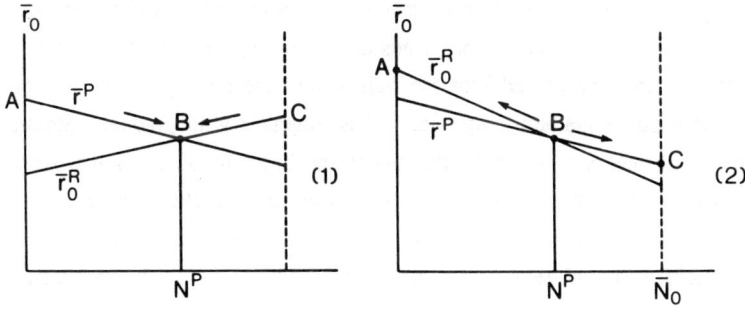

Consider figure 9.2. Based on (9.22) and (9.26), it describes the behaviour of bid–rents at the centre as functions of the number of poor. For simplicity of exposition these functions are shown as linear, although the presumption is that they must be nonlinear. The fixed population at the centre is indicated by the broken line. Between the origin and the broken line, the number of poor is measured from left to right and the number of rich from right to left as in figure 8.3. Suppose that the slope of $\bar{r}_0^R$ is greater than that of $\bar{r}_0^P$. This situation is shown in figure 9.2(1). Point B represents a stable equilibrium population partition, because if the number of poor is less (more) than that then their bid–rent is higher (lower) than the bid–rent of the rich. Consequently the number of poor will increase (decrease) toward B. In this case one observes a mixed equilibrium at the centre. Suppose now that the slope of $\bar{r}_0^R$ is smaller than that of $\bar{r}^P$. This situation is shown in figure 9.2(2). In contrast with the previous case there are three, rather than one, equilibrium population partitions. Of these, A and C are stable while B is unstable, because if the number of poor (rich) is less than that defined by B then their bid–rent is lower than the bid–rent of the rich (poor). Consequently their number will diminish toward A (C). In this case one observes complete segregation. At A there are no poor in the city. At C the entire centre is allocated to the poor while the rich are contained in the suburb.

It is interesting to note the rôle of factors such as the quality of the environment and transportation technology on the stability characteristics of equilibrium population partitions at the centre. One for example may imagine that the attitudes of the rich toward the quality of the environment become gradually stronger. This, together with gradual improvements in technology, gradually rotates the bid-rent of the rich from an initial position of stability to a final position of instability (figure 9.3).

The previous arguments were based upon the relationship between the slopes of bid-rents. But what about their levels? A fundamental assumption for what follows is that the bid-rent of the poor initially rises faster than that of the rich.

> "The level of the bid-rent depends on the income in the city and the utility level in the outside world, where a rise in the income and a fall in the utility level raise the bid-rent. Therefore, the assumption that the bid-rent of the poor rises more rapidly than that of the rich does not necessarily mean that the income of the poor rises more rapidly than that of the rich. Even if the income of the rich increases faster than that of the poor, the bid-rent of the poor may rise faster when the utility level of the poor in the rest of the world increases more slowly than that of the rich."[7]

Figure 9.3: The process toward instability.

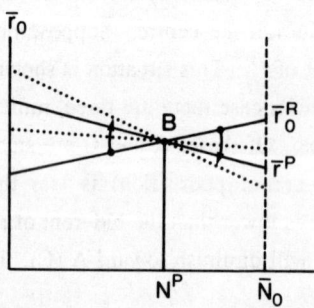

Figure 9.4: Types of population change at the centre.

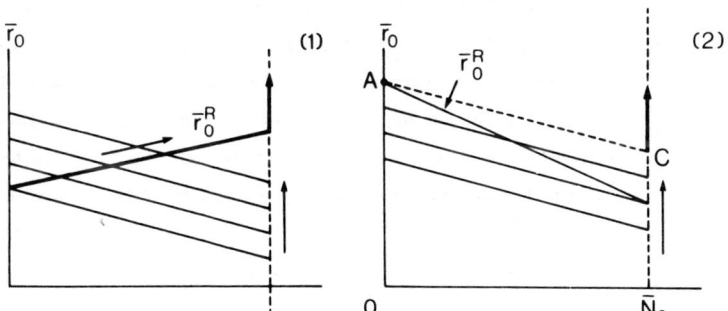

Figure 9.4 indicates shifts of $\bar{r}^P$ relative to $\bar{r}_0^R$. The slope of $\bar{r}_0^R$ in figure 9.4(1) is greater than that of $\bar{r}^P$. Under these circumstances the equilibrium population of the poor gradually rises together with the corresponding bid-rent because every possible equilibrium population partition is stable. The consequent gradual change in the equilibrium bid-rent at the centre is shown as the continuous thick line. On the other hand, the slope of $\bar{r}_0^R$ in figure 9.4(2) is smaller than that of $\bar{r}^P$. At the beginning there are no poor at the centre and OA is the equilibrium bid-rent. As long as the bid-rent of the poor is at or below A, this equilibrium population partition remains the only stable one and there is no change whatsoever either in the population mix or in the bid-rent at the centre. The moment however that the bid-rent of the poor rises above A, the stable equilibrium partition shifts from A to C. This discontinuity causes a sudden immigration of the poor to the centre and an associated emigration of the rich from the centre, which continues until C is attained, in other words, until there is no rich left in the centre. During this catastrophic process rents fall, to start gradually increasing only after the establishment of the new equilibrium.

"The catastrophic process can be viewed as the cumulative decay process analyzed by ... Oates, Howrey and Baumol (1971). A small increase in the population of the poor causes an increase in the external diseconomy, which tends to lower the bid-rent of the rich. If this effect is strong enough to ensure that a fall in the bid-rent of the rich is greater than that of the poor (this is the case if the bid-rent curve of the poor is flatter than that of the rich), the poor outbid the rich in the centre. As a result, further emigration of the rich and immigration of the poor are induced. This, in turn, aggravates deterioration in the centre and the process becomes self-feeding."[8]

Once the population of the poor in the city begins to rise, (9.25) and (9.28) lead to the conclusion that the city grows. Then the previous arguments suggest that we may distinguish two effects of such urbanisation on the bid-rent gradients at the centre: firstly, a gradual rotation of the bid-rent of the rich caused by the deterioration in the quality of the environment at the centre and by improvements in transportation technology as the city grows; secondly, a gradual rise of the bid-rent of the poor relative to that of the rich, also supported by the deterioration in the quality of the environment at the centre. This last happens because, in this model, only the rich are sensitive to the quality of the environment.[9] If urbanisation persists enough, that is, if the city becomes large enough, and if the timing between the two effects is appropriate then one may indeed witness the birth of a cumulative decay process in the centre. But the outcome need not be as extreme as figure 9.4(2) tends to suggest. The perfect polarity obtained here stems from the presumed linear form of the bid-rent gradients. There is however no special reason for such a form. Indeed, given the complexity of the phenomena under consideration, one is led to believe that the structure of bid-rents here might be closer to the structure of utility in chapter eight rather than to the linear simplicity of figure 9.4. If so, more than one integrated equilibrium population partition may exist. Of these, at least one must be stable; and if the cumulative decay process starts before the stable equilibrium partition, as in figure 9.5, then the catastrophe stops before

Figure 9.5: A more complicated case.

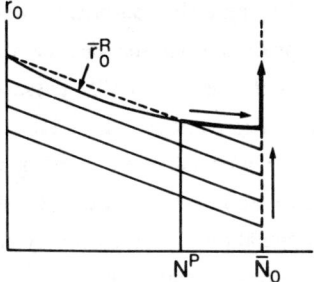

segregation becomes complete. Further complications in the structure of the bid–rents would imply a richer gamut of possible histories for the centre.

According to (9.4), the utility of the poor increases during the cumulative decay process. The utility of the rich on the other hand decreases. This happens because, according to (9.28), the number of rich in the city decreases at the same time. Then the surplus number of rich diffuses in the alternative sector, causing a decline of utility according to (9.5). It is also known by (9.22) that land values in the centre decrease during the cumulative decay process. Land values in the suburb on the other hand increase. This happens because, according to (9.25) and (9.28), the number of rich in the suburb increases at the same time. Then the increased demand for land in the suburb causes higher bid–rents according to (9.18).[10]

> "Since the rent in the suburbs rises and the rent in the centre falls during the catastrophic process, the poor prefer the centre to the suburbs more strongly after the catastrophe. Therefore, if the poor prefer the centre before the catastrophe, the rich can outbid the poor in the suburbs even if the centre becomes completely filled with the poor. This reflects the fact that the rich are willing to pay a premium for houses in the segregated suburbs while the poor are not. In such case discrimination is not necessary to keep the poor out of the suburbs at least for a while after the catastrophe."[11]

Decline of Central Cities

The somewhat surprising welfare implication of the cumulative decay process (that the decline of the central city reduces inequity) agrees with Berry's (1980) passage cited in the first section of this chapter. The demographic implications of the cumulative decay process also agree with table 9.1—as far as whites (the "rich") are concerned. But there are important differences as well. Table 9.1 shows a decline in total population. This is clearly due to the observed abandonment of central cities, a feature not allowed by the simplified framework of this chapter. Since table 9.1 pertains to metropolitan areas and since, according to what has been said in chapter eight, all cities of over one million population underwent sudden urban growth, it must be that the evidence in table 9.1 refers to a stage of urbanisation beyond sudden urban growth. A possible scenario appears in figure 9.6. The equilibrium path of urban population in this figure is analogous to that of figure 8.6(2). The observed path of urban population is represented by the dotted line. If the reaction of the city to differences from equilibrium is strong enough then oscillations in the observed path of urban population may produce periods of decline after sudden urban growth has occurred—as for example AB in figure 9.6. Table 9.1 presumably refers to such a period. A second difference between table 9.1 and the

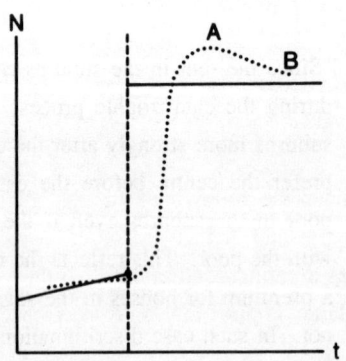

Figure 9.6: Equilibrium and observed paths of urban population.

cumulative decay process pertains to blacks. Evidence shows that during the seventies blacks also abandoned the centre for the suburbs. Allowing once more for abandonment of central cities, this can be accounted for either through the obviously imperfect assocation between the distinctions poor–rich and black–white, or through a preference for integration by the poor, or both.

For a fixed population at the centre, a preference for integration by the poor has the following consequences. Since their utility is now represented by

(9.29) $u^P = u^P[x_0^P, N_0^R]$ with $\underset{N_0^R}{\Delta} u^P > 0$,

(9.22) becomes

(9.30) $\underset{N^P}{\Delta} \bar{r}^P = -\left[\underset{N^P}{\Delta} \bar{v}^P + \underset{N_0^R}{\Delta} u^P\right] \div \frac{\partial u^P}{\partial x^P} < 0.$

Upon comparison of (9.22) with (9.30) it is seen that the bid–rent gradient of the poor is steeper when there is a preference for integration. This implies that the cumulative decay process is less likely. But if it happens then the value of land in the centre decreases more than in the previous case; and the bid–rent of the poor in the suburb increases because of the preference for integration. If this preference is strong enough, it may generate a flow of the poor toward the suburb.

Revival?

Consider the following situation after the catastrophe. Transportation costs rise and there is a change in preferences of the rich favouring the city as a public good rather than the kind of privacy offered in suburbia. The latter implies that $\Delta_{N_1} E$ now becomes positive. This, together with the higher cost of transportation, implies that the bid–rent of the rich at

Decline of Central Cities

Figure 9.7: Gradual return of the rich to the centre.

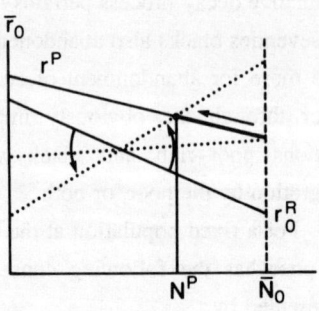

the centre as described by (9.26) flattens: a mechanism opposite to that of figure 9.3 has been set in motion. This is sufficient to account for a gradual return of the rich to the centre as in figure 9.7. The process is complicated because the change in preferences of the rich affects not only the slope of their bid–rent but also the relative shifts between the two bid–rents at the centre. In the previous case the bid–rent of the poor increased relative to that of the rich because the latter were sensitive only to the negative aspects of urbanisation. Now however the quality of the environment may either increase or decrease with urbanisation, depending upon whether N_1 affects the quality of the environment more or less than N^P does. This implies that the bid–rent of the poor may even decrease relative to that of the rich—provided that the preference of the rich for the city as a public good is strong enough.

Notes to Chapter Nine

1 This chapter is based on Kanemoto (1980A). For a more general treatment see Kanemoto (1980B, chapter six).

2 Berry (1980, p. 24).

3 Based on this line of reasoning, suburbanisation of this type in

societies where "community" is valued more than "privacy" will not be as strong as in North America.

4   For simplicity I assume single–person households.

5   One could easily recognise existing differences in the quantity of land consumed at different locations. This however would complicate notation without providing any additional insight.

6   If for example $\Delta_{N_1} \check{c}$ is small then an expansion of the city border due to an increased urban population will not add much to the costs of transportation for those at the border: transportation technology is advanced.

7   Kanemoto (1980A, p. 158).

8   Kanemoto (1980A, pp. 159–160).

9   Even if the poor were also sensitive to the quality of the environment, similar conclusions could be drawn provided that the feelings of the rich on this matter were stronger. Then the relative shifts between the bid–rents would be stronger, the greater were the differences in sensitivity toward the quality of the environment between the two income classes.

10 For any location in the suburb, the difference in the bid–rent before and after the cumulative decay process is equal to the corresponding difference in $\check{c}[N_1]$. Since N_1 increases, so does $\check{c}$.

11 Kanemoto (1980A, p. 160).

Part Two

OPTIMUM

10

Public Choice [1]

Collective Choice Rule

Since, according to what has been argued in chapter two, every individual implies a preference structure, society, being at least the collection of individuals, implies a corresponding vector of preference structures $\mathscr{H} = (..., \mathscr{H}_1, ...)$. The vector $\mathscr{H}$ is a detailed description of individual preferences in a society.

As in the case of an individual, where his preference ordering stems from his preference structure, so in the case of society a *social preference relation* O stems from the corresponding vector of preference structures, $\mathscr{H} \rightarrow O$. In contrast though to the case of an individual, the mere dependence of the social preference relation upon the vector of preference structures is not enough for understanding public choice. This asymmetry emanates from differences in the nature of choice rules. Whereas in the case of an individual the choice rule is trivial, because choice simply reflects feasible preferences, a collective choice rule c is certainly nontrivial: *what happens in the case of disagreement?* A study of society presupposes an answer to this fundamentally simple question; and a collective choice rule, being a description of how society translates individual preferences into public choice, is precisely such an answer. For this reason one may write

(10.1) $\quad c:\{\mathscr{H}\} \to \mathcal{O},$

where $\mathcal{O}$ is the set of all possible social preference relations O, that is, application of a collective choice rule over a vector of preference structures concerning states of society results in public choice.[2]

Social Choice and Individual Values

The transition from the realm of individuals to the social realm is complex because, according to (10.1), the synthesis of individuals into a society is more than the sum of its components. Difficulties begin with any investigation into the nature of the new entity c. It seems reasonable to approach this thorny problem using a process of elimination: restrict the class of collective choice rules at the outset by eliminating as many patently unreasonable alternatives as possible—for example random public choice.

What then are reasonable properties for a collective choice rule? Arrow (1963) has proposed *unrestricted domain*, the *Pareto principle*, *independence of irrelevant alternatives* and *nondictatorship* as being such properties. Unrestricted domain means that the collective choice rule should be defined over all possible sets of individual preference orderings.[3] The Pareto principle states that, for any K^1 and $K^2 \in \mathscr{H}$, if every individual is indifferent between K^1 and K^2 then society should also be indifferent between K^1 and K^2. If, on the other hand, at least one individual prefers K^1 to K^2, while the rest maintain that K^1 is at least as good as K^2, then society should prefer K^1 to K^2. Independence of irrelevant alternatives means that public choice over a set of alternatives should only depend upon the individual preference orderings over this particular set of alternatives. Finally, nondictatorship means that social choice should not coincide with the preference ordering of any individual irrespective of the preference orderings of the rest.

The list of these properties is certainly not exhaustive. Indeed much more could be demanded by many from procedures for social choice. Yet one should be extremely careful because what is reasonable for one may be unreasonable for another. Thus, reasonableness being a matter of opinion, one should be restricted to the least controversial properties—such as the above four. If this clearly defensive approach is adopted, one may even wonder whether the class of collective choice rules has been restricted to any significant extent. The stunning revelation is that, far from being a problem of dealing with too much, it now becomes a problem of dealing with too little.

10.1 *If the social preference relation is restricted to orderings then there is no collective choice rule that satisfies unrestricted domain, the Pareto principle, independence of irrelevant alternatives and nondictatorship simultaneously.*[4]

As an example of the types of contradictions that arise within this framework consider the following situation.

"There is one copy of a certain book, say *Lady Chatterley's Lover*, which is viewed differently by Mr A and Mr B. The three alternatives are that Mr A reads it (K^1), that Mr B reads it (K^2), and that no one reads it (K^3). Mr A, who is a prude, prefers most that no one reads it, but given the choice between either of the two reading it, he would prefer that he read it himself rather than exposing gullible Mr B to the influences of Lawrence. (Prudes, I am told, tend to prefer to be censors rather than being censored.) In decreasing order of preference, his rankings are K^3, K^1, K^2. Mr B however, prefers that either of them should read it rather than neither. Furthermore, he takes delight in the thought that prudish

Mr A may have to read Lawrence, and his first preference is that Mr A should read it, next best that he himself should read it, and worst that neither should. His ranking is, therefore, K^1, K^2, K^3."[5]

In this simple case, with only two individuals and three possible states of society to consider, unrestricted domain can obviously be satisfied. If the choice is between Mr A or Mr B reading the book, then there is no doubt that the former alternative must be socially preferred because of the Pareto principle. If though the choice is between Mr B reading the book and no one reading it then matters become more complicated. Since the social preference relation is restricted to orderings, it must be that either one alternative is socially preferred to the other or that society is indifferent between Mr B reading the book and no one reading it. If one alternative is socially preferred to the other then, in this particular matter, society agrees with the wishes of one individual against the wishes of the other. This violates nondictatorship.[6] Therefore society must be indifferent between Mr B reading the book and no one reading it. Since Mr A reading the book is socially preferred to Mr B reading it which, in turn, is socially indifferent to no one reading it then it must be that Mr A reading the book is socially preferred to no one reading it. But it must also be the case that Mr A reading the book is socially indifferent to no one reading it, because there is a difference of opinion between the two individuals on this matter. Therefore Mr A reading the book is both socially preferred and socially indifferent than no one reading it—a contradiction.

It is natural that this fundamental antinomy has troubled many and that many have attempted to resolve it. This is not the place to discuss the issue.[7] Nevertheless it seems fair to say that nothing yet has diminished the force of Arrow's possibility theorem. It was the first of an ever-growing string that has brought to a sharp focus some of the inherent logical difficulties involved in the transition from the realm of individuals to the social realm. Many have despaired over the truth that a harmonious synthesis of individual values, expressed as public choice reflecting some minimum requirements of rationality and justice, is logically impossible. There is however a radically different interpretation of Arrow's possibility theorem: his utopian world exists in a state of ideal anarchy because individual preferences extend over entire states of society and because there is no systematic coercion on individual preferences. Then Arrow's possibility theorem implies that anarchy as an ideal social system is, in general, impossible.[8]

The Impossibility of a Paretian Liberal

The philosophical meaning of liberty is elusive. Nevertheless one could safely distinguish a positive and a negative aspect of liberty, the former being freedom of choice while the latter, and probably more important, being freedom from coercion. Both aspects, together with the desirability of freedom itself, give rise to some "protected sphere" which is the same for everybody, over which each should be equally sovereign. This idea persists from Thucydides (−327), to von Humboldt (1792), to Mill (1859), to Rawls (1971). Although the composition and the size of this sphere is open to question, its existence is not.

Elements of the protected sphere are matters considered to be personal. For example dreaming with his eyes closed or open is a matter personal to Mr A and as such it should be the exclusive concern of Mr A. With everything else being the same, those two choices represent two distinct states of society. Similar thoughts motivate the concept of *weak libertarianism* as an index of minimum standards for personal liberty. Weak libertarianism means that every individual is decisive over at least one pair of states of society.[9] Both the Pareto principle (that, in the absence of any disagreement, expressed preferences should be accepted by society) and weak libertarianism (that individuals should enjoy at least a minimum of personal liberty) are intuitive values deeply rooted in the realm of public choice. Yet

10.2 *If the social preference relation must generate a choice function then there is no collective choice rule that satisfies unrestricted domain, the Pareto principle and weak libertarianism simultaneously.*[10]

As an example of the types of contradictions that arise within this framework consider the case of two individuals and three states of society described in the previous section.

"Now if the choice is precisely between the pair (K^1, K^3), i.e., between Mr A reading the book and no one reading it, someone with liberal values may argue that it is Mr A's preference that should count; since the prude would not like to read it, he should not be forced to. Thus, the society should prefer K^3 to K^1. Similarly, in the choice exactly between Mr B reading the book (K^2) and no one reading it (K^3), liberal values require that Mr B's preference should be decisive, and since he is clearly anxious to read the book he should be permitted to do this. Hence K^2 should be judged socially better than K^3. Thus, in terms of liberal values it is better that no one reads it rather than Mr A being forced to read it, and it is still better that Mr B is permitted to read the book rather than no one reading it. That is, the society should prefer K^2 to K^3, and K^3 to K^1. This discourse could end happily with the book being handed over to Mr B but for the fact that it is a Pareto inferior alternative, being worse than Mr B reading it, in the view of both persons, i.e., K^1 is Pareto superior to K^2."[11]

Thus, the Pareto principle and weak libertarianism represent essentially conflicting values for social choice. This may not be crucial in societies where individuals have come to respect the personal choices of others,[12] but it becomes crucial in societies where individual liberty rests on rules for social choice. In such cases, choice between two alternatives based on the Pareto principle may be in conflict with the corresponding choice based on weak libertarianism.

It is natural that this fundamental antinomy has been the object of several studies attempting to resolve it. This is not the place to discuss the issue.[13] Nevertheless it seems fair to say that a subtle change in the underlying conditions may not be the answer. The only other alternative is to adopt a "Gordian Knot" attitude: eliminate the antinomy by force. How may the antinomy be eliminated? An answer is provided by the idea of a constitution which, further to a collective choice rule, implies a partition of rights between society and individuals. A constitution constrains public choice to matters other than personal; public choice incorporates the Pareto principle, individual rights include weak libertarianism and the fundamental antinomy vanishes.[14] It may though reappear in principle whenever issues akin to the partition of rights are being examined.[15] But then no personal issues should be at stake for, instead of asking whether Mr A should dream with his eyes closed or open, the question naturally becomes one of whether the choice of dreaming mode belongs to the social or to the individual realm of rights. In consequence, no such contradiction may naturally arise and, therefore, the impossibility of a Paretian liberal underlines the necessity of a constitution as a means of resolving the inherent conflict between unanimity and freedom.

Expression of Social Preferences

There is a symmetry between the expression of social preferences and that of individual preferences. The translation of individual preferences into public choice involves extremely complex phenomena. Nevertheless, under certain conditions, the expression of social preferences becomes extremely simple. In particular, let $\mathcal{U}_1$ be the set of all possible levels of utility associated with individual 1, and $\mathcal{U} \equiv \{...,\mathcal{U}_1,...\}$. An actual distribution of utilities is denoted $U[K] \equiv (...,u_1[K],...) \in \mathcal{U}$. Then

10.3 *A social preference relation generated by a collective choice rule which is an ordering and which satisfies unrestricted domain and the Pareto principle can be represented by a function* $W : \mathcal{U} \to \mathcal{R}$ *with* $\partial W / \partial u_1 > 0$ *such that, for any* $U[K^1]$ *and* $U[K^2] \in \mathcal{U}$, $W[U[K^1]] \geq W[U[K^2]]$ *if and only if* K^1 *is socially preferred or is regarded indifferently to* K^2.[16]

The function W is called a *social welfare function* (SWF). Under W, the expression of social preferences becomes extremely simple, for, in order to determine social preference of the first state of society (hence of the first distribution of utilities) over the second, one has simply to confirm that the social welfare index associated with the first state of society is greater than the social welfare index associated with the second. In this manner, the obscure processes underlying the social evaluation of complex phenomena collapse into a single, easily comparable index. The index does not represent numerically the intensity of social preferences: the value of this index is meaningless beyond ordinal comparisons.

It is possible to establish that, within this framework, the very existence of a SWF implies the following.

1. Public choice must be based on appropriate use of relevant secondary information for each individual.[17] Such information is incompatible with independence of irrelevant alternatives. This is fine. Otherwise Arrow's possibility theorem would lead to the conclusion that every SWF reflects a dictatorial collective choice rule.

2. Public choice must be based on an established social weighting across individuals. Such weighting

"... may be derived from an ethical designation of interpersonal 'deservedness', from 'interpersonal comparisons', from the dictatorial imposition by any individual, ..., from a set of random number tables, or from wherever."[18]

That such weighting supports the very existence of a SWF, underlies Arrow's fundamental implication that any search for a value-free collective choice rule must fail. To forget this is to shy away from the fundamental truth that objective social choice and therefore objective social action are, in general, impossible.

Mathematical Representation of Choice

I now introduce a planner. *He serves as the composite of institutions in the society.* He stands completely apart from the society. This quality of absolute distinctiveness is essential. In particular, the social preference ordering that expresses his absolute power may not appear as dictatorial with respect to the individuals, in the sense that it may not coincide with the preference ordering of any individual in society irrespective of the preference orderings of the rest.

Let the behaviour of the planner be rational in the following sense. His acts are guided by his desire to use the limited resources of society in what, to him, is the best possible manner. This theory of motivation implies that the planner ranks attainable states of society according to preference and selects one at least as good as any other attainable state of society. If he is able to rank any number of alternatives (that is, if the collective choice rule upon which he bases his decisions is an ordering) and if he knows all attainable states of society then his choice behaviour will be perfectly rational in the sense that, for him, there is indeed no better choice than the one he has already taken. If, further, individual preference orderings obey transitivity, completeness and continuity, and if the collective choice rule obeys unrestricted domain and the Pareto principle (all these suitably modified where necessary to allow for differentiability), then, according to proposition 3, his preferences are represented by a continuously differentiable SWF. Now if K^* is an *optimum*, that is, if it is an attainable state of society that maximises his SWF, it must be that it is also a perfectly rational choice. In other words, there is no other attainable state of society preferred to K^*. Otherwise, according to proposition 10.3, social welfare would not be maximum, which is a contradiction. Thus to determine perfectly rational behaviour is to find a feasible maximum of some continuously differentiable function. In this manner perfectly rational behaviour is translated into a simple analytic form.

Under what circumstances is there an optimum? The following provides an answer to this fundamental question.

10.4 *If $\mathscr{S}$ is closed, connected and bounded below for every individual, and if the set of attainable states of society is compact, then there exists an optimum.*[19]

The assumptions on $\mathscr{S}$ are less restrictive than those of proposition 2.2. The very existence of a social welfare function, implied by proposition 10.4, requires that the assumptions of proposition 10.3 also hold. The very existence of a utility function implied by proposition 10.3 requires, in turn, that the assumptions of proposition 2.1 also hold. The meaning of those assumptions has already been discussed in chapter two and in this chapter. The only additional requirement, which stems from compactness, is that the set of attainable states of society be bounded, in other words, that the resources available to society be limited.

Allocation and Distribution

Two fundamental classes of issues raised in the context of theoretical planning pertain to *allocation* and to *distribution*. Allocation of resources in the most efficient manner is essentially a technical problem. Distribution of welfare amongst individuals is a philosophical and a political problem, a problem of social justice. Although conceptually distinct, both problems are in effect intertwined into one, inseparable whole.

Allocation is traditionally related to the Pareto principle. Application of this principle ensures that public choice will never result in a particular state if there is another one about which preference has been expressed without any disagreement. Therefore, whenever a state of society is characterised by the Pareto principle, there is no other such state that somebody prefers and nobody opposes. This gives rise to the concept of *Pareto efficiency*, where nobody can increase his welfare without decreasing the welfare of somebody else. In this sense, the Pareto principle is equivalent to an efficient allocation of resources. Furthermore, an optimum is Pareto efficient; for otherwise proposition 10.3 implies that social welfare is not maximised—a contradiction.

Distribution is related to the concept of equity. Analysis of equity proper is difficult and will not be attempted here. Nevertheless, it is convenient to maintain that attitudes towards the meaning of social justice are expressed by the prevailing degree of aversion to inequality.[20] Aversion to inequality implies that the SWF is strictly concave in its arguments, that is, if U^1 and U^2 are two distinct vectors of utilities then

(10.2) $\quad (1-v)W[U^1] + vW[U^2] < W[(1-v)U^1 + vU^2]$
$\quad\quad\quad$ *for* $0 < v < 1$.

In other words, when there is aversion to inequality, an "averaging" of utilities (which reduces inequality) raises social welfare.[21] Strict concavity of the SWF implies, in turn, that the corresponding indifference surfaces are strictly convex.[22] As the aversion to inequality decreases, so does the degree of convexity characterising the corresponding indifference surfaces. At the limit, where there is no concern for distribution, the SWF takes its standard sum–of–utilities form and the corresponding indifference surfaces become linear.[23] On the other hand, as the degree of aversion to inequality increases, so does the degree of convexity characterising the corresponding indifference surfaces. This continues to the point where indifference surfaces consist of the hyperplanes determined by the axes of the system translated by $(\beta,\beta,...,\beta)$. That is, the hyperplanes of the origin are parallel and equidistant with the corresponding hyperplanes of an indifference surface. It will be seen that, under these circumstances, maximising social welfare becomes equivalent to maximising the welfare of the least advantaged in society.

We thus arrive at two important cases, one where the state is indifferent as to the distribution of welfare and the other where the state is solely preoccupied with the welfare of the least advantaged. Whereas the former is ethically unfounded, a call for the latter persists from the sophist Antiphon (−400) to Rousseau (1755), and to the momentous social trends of today. Indeed the maximin principle (as maximising the welfare of the least advantaged came to be known) stems from a particular theory of justice.[24] According to this theory, participation in society is akin to participation in a game of chance with respect to assets that largely determine a way of life and, therefore, of happiness. Since the existing distribution of assets may well be unfair, enquiries on the nature of just institutions cannot depend on any particular outcome of this game. Therefore, individuals must step behind a veil of ignorance, and decide on a constitution as if they were uncertain of their actual positions in society. When this is done, two principles emerge. The first calls for a maximum protected sphere compatible with the freedom of others, an issue already discussed. The second calls for inequalities to be arranged so that they are to the greatest benefit of the least advantaged, a principle forcefully defended by Popper more than thirty years ago.[25] This last is equivalent to the maximin principle.[26]

Parametrising the Degree of Aversion to Inequality[27]

A fundamental distinction implicitly drawn already is between the *individual valuation of individual welfare* (u_1) and the corresponding *social valuation of individual welfare* (v_1). Implicit to the necessity of a social weighting across individuals, also discussed earlier in this chapter, is precisely this distinction: for the planner, the welfare of some individuals may be more important than the welfare of others. This could well depend on the identity of the individuals. Nevertheless, for us, such weights will only vary with the relative well–being of the individuals under consideration; and the roots of variation, in turn, will be found in the particular theory of distributive justice employed. In other words, the relationship between u_1 and v_1 varies with the theory of distributive justice employed.

The relationship between u_1 and v_1 under a theory of distributive justice is essential for the analysis of optima, as it provides us with an explicit link between the individual and society. The relationship adopted here is based on the following premise. As the degree of aversion to inequality increases, the social valuation of individual welfare decreases relatively faster for relatively higher utility: there is an increasing bias in favour of the less advantaged. This can be expressed as

$$(10.3) \qquad -\frac{d}{du_1}\left[\frac{dv}{du_1}\right] \div \left[\frac{1}{u_1}\frac{dv}{du_1}\right] \equiv -\eta_{dv:u} = \alpha$$

where $\eta_{dv:u}$ is the utility elasticity of the change in the social valuation of individual welfare and α is *the degree of aversion to inequality*. Social valuations consistent with this definition are represented by

$$(10.4) \qquad v_1 = \begin{cases} u_1^{1-\alpha} \div (1-\alpha) & \text{for } \alpha \neq 1 \\ \ln u_1 & \text{for } \alpha = 1 \end{cases}$$

where $u_1 > 1$ and, without loss of generality, the constants of integration have been omitted. Notice that

$$(10.5) \qquad \frac{dv}{du_1} = u_1^{-\alpha},$$

Public Choice

an expression which will be used extensively in the following chapters.

Within this framework, the SWF is simply *the sum of social valuations of utility*. For the two-person case,

(10.6) $\qquad W = v_A + v_B$

with indifference surfaces determined by

(10.7) $\qquad dW = \dfrac{dv}{du_A} du_A + \dfrac{dv}{du_B} du_B = u_A^{-\alpha} du_A + u_B^{-\alpha} du_B = 0,$

using (10.5), which implies

(10.8) $\qquad \dfrac{du_A}{du_B} = - \left[\dfrac{u_A}{u_B}\right]^\alpha.$

For $\alpha = 0$, the SWF is the sum of individual valuations of utility and, using (10.8), the social indifference curve is linear with a slope of minus one as in figure 10.1. Such a structure of the SWF implies that the social valuation of individual welfare does not depend on the position of one individual relative to the other. Namely, the social valuation of individual welfare coincides with the corresponding individual valuation,

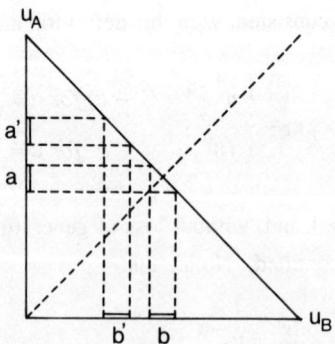

Figure 10.1: Social indifference curve under no aversion to inequality.

242

Figure 10.2: Social indifference curve under aversion to inequality.

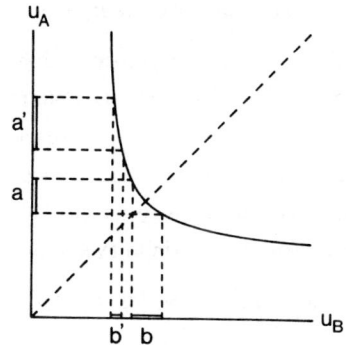

both under equality (a,b) and under inequality (a',b'). In contrast, $\alpha > 0$ implies a bias toward equality, in other words that the social valuation of individual welfare does depend on the position of the individual relative to others. This is shown in figure 10.2. Here, although the social valuation of individual welfare coincides with the corresponding individual valuation under equality (a,b), it does not coincide under inequality (a',b'). In particular, under inequality, social valuation of individual welfare favours the less advantaged: a small gain in his welfare is socially equivalent to an associated large loss in the welfare of the more advantaged (a'). Finally, for $\alpha = \infty$, $du_A \div du_B = -\infty$ for $u_A >$

Figure 10.3: Social indifference curve under infinite aversion to inequality.

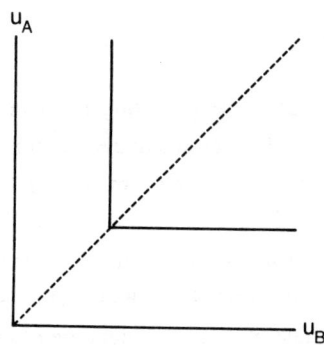

u_B and $du_A + du_B = 0$ for $u_A < u_B$. This is shown in figure 10.3, and implies an exclusive preoccupation with maximising the welfare of the least advantaged, i.e. the maximin principle.

The case of $\alpha < 0$ expresses a bias toward inequality. Under these circumstances, social indifference surfaces become strictly concave, rather than convex as in the case of a bias toward equality. At the limit, where there is an infinite aversion to equality, $du_A + du_B = 0$ for $u_A > u_B$ and $du_A + du_B = -\infty$ for $u_A < u_B$, which expresses the principle of maximising the welfare of the most advantaged.

It is argued in the appendix that $-\infty \leq \alpha \leq \infty$ contains all Pareto–efficient optima. It is also argued that this framework does not cover the entire spectrum of possible theories of distributive justice. In particular, it excludes important cases where the planner is prepared to forgo Pareto–efficiency for the sake of distribution. Since however the only type of behaviour recognised in this book is rational, and because of its simplicity, the framework of this section will provide the foundation for the entire analysis of optima. Hence the nature of an optimum will be a function of the degree of aversion to inequality, that is, of the distributive justice employed. In this manner one avoids the metaphysical dilemma of what theory of distributive justice should be employed, because one displays all possible rational (from the Pareto point of view) responses to such a dilemma.

Traditional Misconceptions

Apart from the persisting myth of an objective social engineer, which has already been mentioned, two important sources of misunderstanding relate to (1) utilitarianism and (2) the issue of equity versus efficiency.

1. Utilitarianism is the traditional name for zero aversion to inequality. It has a relatively long history starting with Bentham (1789) and an important place in the literature of public choice.

"The trouble with this approach is that maximizing the sum of individual utilities is supremely unconcerned with the interpersonal distribution of that sum. This should make it a particularly unsuitable approach to use for measuring or judging inequality. Interestingly enough, however, not only has utilitarianism been fairly widely used for distributional judgements, it has—somewhat amazingly—even developed the reputation of being an egalitarian criterion. This seems to have come about through a peculiar dialectical process whereby such adherents of utilitarianism as Marshall and Pigou were attacked by Robbins and others for their supposedly egalitarian use of the utilitarian framework. This gave utilitarianism a ready-made reputation for being equality-conscious."[28]

Misrepresenting utilitarianism as an egalitarian criterion is understandable because the idea of treating individuals in precisely the same way with respect to utility under the sum of the SWF may be blurred with the idea of treating individuals in precisely the same way. Misunderstanding has further been supported by the symmetry of the utility–possibility frontier when individuals have identical preference structures.[29] Then, in the absence of nonconvexities, the optimum for any $\alpha \geq 0$ obviously calls for individuals to be treated in precisely the same way. This is shown in figure 10.4, where the curve AB represents the symmetric utility–possibility frontier. As with utility maximisation, the optimum will belong to the highest social indifference curve that contains at least one point of the utility–possibility frontier.

2. The issue of equity versus efficiency refers to the tradeoff between the two. The measure of efficiency here is the level of aggregate welfare under zero aversion to inequality, and the presumption is that to gain in efficiency, that is, in the average level of utility, you must lose in equity and vice versa. A wrong implication, which stems from con-

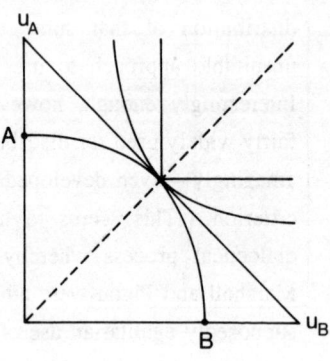

Figure 10.4: Optimal equality under a symmetric utility–possibility frontier.

fusing this measure of efficiency with Pareto efficiency, is that to deal with the latter is to be unconcerned about inequality. The source of such confusion must be found in the very nature of the Pareto principle. If for example you have ten individuals and ten loaves of bread, and if you give each individual one loaf then your decision is obviously Pareto efficient. But equally Pareto–efficient would be your decision to give all the loaves to a single individual and let the others starve. Indeed, any distribution that uses all the loaves will be Pareto efficient. Only if you throw away a loaf will Pareto inefficiency occur, because then you could increase the welfare of someone by giving him the tenth loaf without decreasing the welfare of anyone else. The obvious conclusion is that an exclusive concern with Pareto efficiency completely suppresses the distributive issues involved. This is not to say, however, that an exclusive concern with Pareto efficiency implies some particular view of distributive justice.

The tradeoff between equity and efficiency occurs when individuals differ. Then the utility–possibility frontier is asymmetric as, say, in figure 10.5(1), the consequence being that different attitudes toward distributive justice are associated with different optima.[30] As the degree

Figure 10.5: Equity versus efficiency.

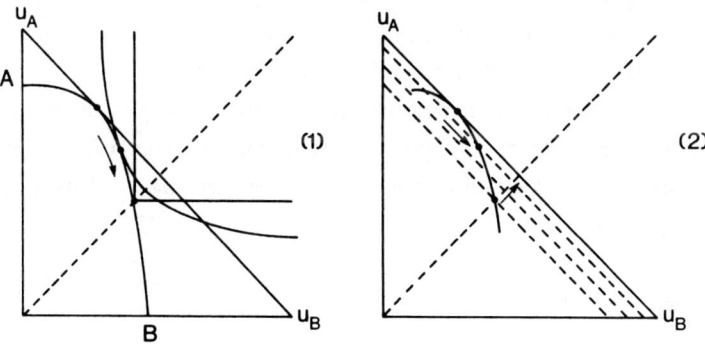

of aversion to inequality increases, inequality decreases. There is a tradeoff however between the level of average utility and the degree of equality attained. In particular, increasing the degree of equality imposes increasing limitations on how far Pareto efficiency can push the level of average utility (figure 10.5(2)). Clearly, no optimal allocation in figure 10.5 is Pareto inferior to any other optimal allocation. In other words, the planner cannot shift to another optimal allocation without a loss to someone. This implies that the dilemma here does not lie between Pareto efficiency and equality: even under infinite aversion to inequality, the optimal allocation is Pareto efficient. The dilemma actually rests between an abstract notion of efficiency (the level of average utility) as a social value by itself, and equality. Such antinomy will generate an equilibrium that reflects the relative importance the planner attaches to each. Stronger attitudes toward efficiency as a social value by itself will result in greater inequality.

Appendix to Chapter Ten

This appendix uses a simple model to display the entire spectrum of parametrised theories of distributive justice. The analysis leading to figure 10.6 is due to Dominique Peeters.

Consider the utilitarian and the maximin principles as primitive, rather than derived, concepts. I take it that a theory of distributive justice implies a position relative to these principles. This can be expressed as

$$(10.9) \qquad W = (1 - \lambda)f + \lambda g$$

where f is a measure of the SWF when there is no concern for distribution and g is a measure of the SWF at the maximin principle. Thus, when λ is equal to zero, the SWF purely reflects a state of indifference toward distribution, and when λ is equal to one, the SWF purely reflects the maximin principle. It has already been argued that λ between zero and one (minus one) corresponds to strictly convex (concave) indifference surfaces. But (10.9) suggests that there may be theories of distributive justice represented by λ beyond $[-1,1]$. It is therefore useful to examine in some detail how λ shapes indifference surfaces of the SWF in (10.9) for given f and g.

For illustrative purposes, consider the case of two individuals, A and B, and let f be the average utility and g be the minimum utility. For a given distribution of utilities $(\bar{u}_A, \bar{u}_B)$ the level of social welfare is a function of λ:

$$(10.10) \qquad \bar{W}[\lambda] = (1 - \lambda) \frac{\bar{u}_A + \bar{u}_B}{2} + \lambda \bar{u}_B \quad for \ \bar{u}_A \geq \bar{u}_B.$$

The corresponding indifference curve is given by

(10.11) $\bar{W}[\lambda] = (1 - \lambda) \dfrac{u_A + u_B}{2} + \lambda u_B \quad \text{for } u_A \geq u_B.$

Subtracting (10.10) from (10.11) yields

(10.12) $(1 - \lambda)(u_A - \bar{u}_A) = -(1 + \lambda)(u_B - \bar{u}_B),$

which represents a family of straight lines passing through $(\bar{u}_A, \bar{u}_B)$ with slope

(10.13) $m[\lambda] = -\dfrac{1 + \lambda}{1 - \lambda}.$

The graph of (10.13), a hyperbola, is shown in figure 10.6. For $\lambda < -1$, where m becomes positive, there is a pure bias toward inequality—super–inegalitarianism. Super–egalitarianism on the other hand, a pure bias toward equality, corresponds to $\lambda > 1$ where m is also positive.[31] What essentially distinguishes these two cases from the rest is the abandonment of the Pareto principle in pursuit of such pure bias.[32] Therefore, in order to admit theories of distributive justice represented by any λ beyond $[-1, 1]$, it is necessary to accept a structure of the SWF more general than that of proposition 10.3, in other words, to accept the

Figure 10.6: The graph of equation (13).

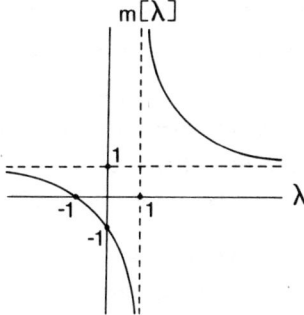

Figure 10.7: Utility–possibility
frontier with
Pareto inefficient regions.

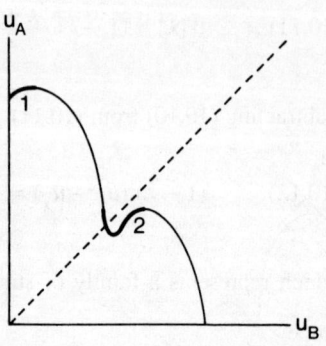

possibility of a Pareto inefficient public choice. To see this consider figure 10.7. It represents a utility–possibility frontier with Pareto inefficient regions. Region 1 has been constructed so that increasing utilities imply more equality. This will be used to illustrate how the Pareto principle may be abandoned in pursuit of a pure bias toward inequality. On the other hand, the end of region 2 has been constructed so that increasing utilities imply more inequality. This will be used to illustrate how the Pareto principle may be abandoned in pursuit of a pure bias toward equality. Over regions 1 and 2, both Mr A and Mr B would benefit from some appropriate change. In consequence, a position there could only be forced upon Mr A and Mr B. A position anywhere else, on the other hand, is Pareto efficient because neither can increase his welfare without decreasing the welfare of the other.

When a pure bias toward inequality is sufficiently strong, that is, when λ is sufficiently small, the optimum will be found at the corner of region 1. The extreme case of $\lambda = -\infty$, where the social decision rule is to maximise the difference between the two utilities, appears in figure 10.8(1) where the symmetric case $u_B \geq u_A$ is also shown in order to complete the indifference curve.[33] (Implicit in this symmetry is the assumption that social valuations are never based on the identity of individuals.) Arrows point toward higher social welfare. As the pure

Figure 10.8: Optimum under variable λ.

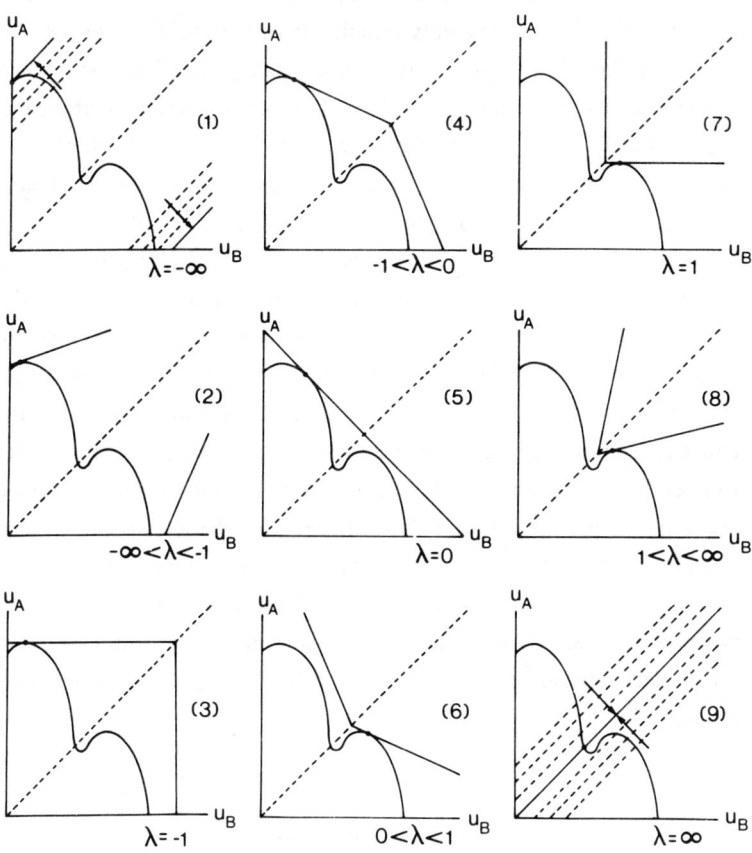

bias toward inequality decreases, the optimum begins to move along region 1 toward less unequal distributions (figure 10.8(2)). In both cases the positive slopes of the social indifference curve indicate that, for moves toward a less unequal distribution, social welfare decreases with sufficiently small increases in utility. This is in conflict with proposition

10.3, as it implies that the optimum will belong to the Pareto inefficient region 1 of the utility–possibility frontier. For $\lambda = -1$, where the social decision rule is to maximise the maximum utility, the slope of the social indifference curve is zero and the optimum enters a Pareto efficient region of the utility–possibility frontier (figure 10.8(3)). Both at this point and for $-1 < \lambda < 0$ (figure 10.8(4)), there is still a bias toward inequality, but it is not strong enough to cause Pareto inefficiency. Figure 10.8(5) marks a border for social attitudes toward distribution. It is precisely the point where distributive issues are completely ignored, the social decision rule being to maximise the sum of the two utilities. For $\lambda > 0$ there is an increasing bias toward equality (figure 10.8(6)) which, at $\lambda = 1$, generates the maximin principle (figure 10.8(7)). Under these circumstances, inequality is condoned only if it is necessary in order to maximise minimum welfare. Beyond that there is a pure bias toward equality, super–egalitarianism, strong enough to force the optimum into the Pareto–inefficient region 2 of the utility–possibility frontier (figure 10.8(8)).[34] As the pure bias toward equality increases, the angle formed by the two line segments of the social indifference curve narrows until, at the limit, social indifference curves take the form of those under $\lambda = -\infty$, but with opposite direction (figure 10.8(9)). This is the point where all that matters is equality, in other words, where the social decision rule is to minimise the difference between the two utilities.

Notes to Chapter Ten

1   Most of this chapter is taken from Papageorgiou (1977).

2   An intuitive example of a collective choice rule is the majority rule. Another one is the equivalence between a social preference relation and the preference ordering of a particular individual.

3   In other words the existence of a social preference relation should never be affected by the corresponding pattern of individual preferences: public choice should be possible under any circumstances.

4   An ordering is a relation that satisfies transitivity, completeness and reflexivity. We say that a relation is reflexive if every element over which this relation is defined is related to itself. For example, the relation "preferred or indifferent to" is reflexive because it is obviously true that every K^j is preferred or indifferent to K^j. (Thus individual preference orderings discussed in chapter two are orderings because, further to transitivity and completeness, they also satisfy reflexivity.) These comments imply that collective choice rules which generate proposition 1 are defined over orderings.

   The original proof of this famous proposition is in Arrow (1963, pp. 97–100). The proposition holds under conditions more general than those described here. Namely the Pareto principle can be replaced by the weak Pareto principle, which states that if every individual prefers K^1 to K^2 then society should also prefer K^1 to K^2. If the proposition holds under the weak Pareto principle then it certainly holds under the Pareto principle. The more restricted version has been adopted for comparability with subsequent results.

5   Sen (1970, p. 155). Here I have changed the names for consistency. The situation has been developed by Sen in the context of an example to illustrate his "impossibility of a Paretian liberal", a matter discussed in the following section of this chapter. Since the two sections are related, for comparability I use the same situation here.

6   For a proof of this implication see Arrow (1963, pp. 50–51).

Public Choice

Invoking the independence of irrelevant alternatives and the Pareto principle, Arrow shows that if society agrees with a particular ordering of one individual against the wishes of the other then society must also agree with *any* ordering of that individual irrespective of the wishes of the other. Thus one individual is a dictator.

7   See Mueller (1976) and Sen (1977).

8   These remarks are due to Walsh (1970, p. 121).

9   Being decisive over (K^1, K^2) means that if the individual prefers K^1 to K^2 so does society, and if the individual prefers K^2 to K^1 so does society.

10 The original proof of this proposition is in Sen (1970, p. 154). A choice function ascertains that in every subset of alternatives there is at least one alternative at least as good as any other alternative in that subset. This requirement is not as strong as the requirement for an ordering in Arrow's possibility theorem. Moreover, similarly to Arrow's possibility theorem, the impossibility of a Paretian liberal also holds under the weak Pareto principle, which only requires that unanimous preferences be socially acceptable. Clearly the impossibility of a Paretian liberal holds under conditions more general than those required for Arrow's possibility theorem. Indeed the antinomy is so strong that it holds under conditions of minimal libertarianism, whereby only two individuals in the entire society necessarily enjoy the privilege of being decisive over at least two states of society.

11 Sen (1970, p. 155). Here, as in the related passage cited in the previous section, I have changed names for consistency.

12 These remarks are also due to Sen (1970, p. 155). Classical Athens was in some respects an early example of such a society. Thucydides (−327, Book 2:37) for example maintains that "... ου δι ' οργης τον πελας, ει καϑ ' ηδονην τι δρα εχοντες ..." which means that "... we do not hold it against someone that he behaves as he likes... ".

13 See Sen (1976).

14 The idea of constrained public choice as a means to resolve this antinomy belongs to Nozick (1974).

15 This seems to be the view held by Sen (1976, pp. 229–231).

16 For a proof see Mayston (1976). The assumptions of this proposition, as well as the assumptions of proposition 2.1 implied here by the very existence of a utility function, are suitably modified where necessary to allow for differentiability.

17 Whereas primary preference information is exemplified by statements such as "K^1 is at least as good as K^2", secondary preference information is exemplified by statements such as "from K^1 to K^2 is at least as great an improvement as from K^3 to K^4". Both types are purely ordinal.

18 Mayston (1976, p. 18).

19 For a proof see Debreu (1959, pp. 92–93).

20 The term "social justice" is used in a sense more general than that usually ascribed to the concept. One could for example associate the intuitive meaning of the term with a proper subset of society. It should also be noted that aversion to inequality is a highly ag-

gregated concept implying, among other things, institutional structure and chance. Nothing is said of the processes that determine aversion to inequality: rather than dealing with how a particular degree of aversion to inequality came to be, one is dealing with the fundamental qualitative implications underlying *any* degree of aversion to inequality.

21 See Sen (1973, p. 20).

22 The argument is identical with that used to determine the structure of individual indifference surfaces in chapter three. Nonsatiation now corresponds to an SWF which, by proposition 10.3, is strictly increasing in its arguments. Thus figure 3.2 may be taken to represent a family of social indifference curves under some aversion to inequality, if utilities replace commodities.

23 In conjunction with (10.3), let $W = u_A + u_B$. If $U^1 = (u_A^1, u_B^1)$ and $U^2 = (u_A^2, u_B^2)$ then

$$(1-v)(u_A^1 + u_B^1) + v(u_A^2 + u_B^2) =$$

$$((1-v)u_A^1 + vu_A^2) + ((1-v)u_B^1 + vu_B^2).$$

In other words, when there is no aversion to inequality, an "averaging" of utilities (which reduces inequality) leaves social welfare unaffected.

24 Rawls (1971).

25 Popper (1977, p. 235, note 6).

26 Those principles have raised a controversy. See for example Arrow (1973). Dasgupta (1974), Rawls (1974), Harsanyi (1975) and Buchanan (1976).

27 This approach has been introduced to spatial analysis by Dixit (1971). I also draw here from Papageorgiou (1980A).

28 Sen (1973, p. 16).

29 The utility–possibility frontier gives the set of possible maxima for u_A associated with every possible u_B. More generally, for every possible combination of $n-1$ utility levels in a society of n individuals, it gives the associated set of maximum possible utility levels for the remaining individual.

30 This figure is due to Levhari, Oron and Pines (1978).

31 The term "super–egalitarianism" belongs to Nozick (1974).

32 Some comments of Jacques Thisse on this issue were very helpful.

33 Equation (10.9) generates piecewise linear social indifference curves because m depends only on λ given *any* $u_A \geq u_B$. It has been seen that the approach based on the prevailing degree of aversion to inequality, although limited in that it does not cover the entire spectrum of possible theories of distributive justice as (10.9) does, is nevertheless more general because it allows the slope of a social indifference curve to depend not only upon λ but also upon the distribution (u_A, u_B). However, anything beyond $-1 \leq \lambda \leq 1$, in the context of the prevailing degree of aversion to inequality, would require the use of correspondences, rather than functions, and this would impose considerable technical difficulties unless

a simplification such as the present one were adopted. In consequence, I accept here piecewise linear social indifference curves as a crude approximation to their well-balanced counterparts.

34 An example of such a social attitude has been provided by the Khmer Rouge in Kampuchea.

11

Simple Urban Optimum

Equilibrium and Optimality

A fundamental difference between the study of equilibrium in chapters four to nine and the study of optimality begun in this chapter is the following. *Equilibrium is characterised by an absolute dispersion of power. Optimality on the other hand is characterised by an absolute concentration of power.* Neither can be found to exist, yet comparison of these two theoretical extremes may offer some insight about what lies in between, that is, experienced human societies.

The Problem of the Planner

Suppose that an optimal city is to be created. Toward this end, the planner must determine the consumption and the location of everyone in the city.[1] Since it is unknown whether everyone should enjoy the same level of utility at the optimum, the planner must also determine the optimal pattern of land values. Thus, in addition to assuming all decision-making powers of individuals, the planner must also set aside the land-market mechanism which led to the determination of bid-rents.

The planner knows that individuals are rational in the sense of chapter three. However, since it is unknown whether everyone should enjoy the same level of utility at the optimum, problem (3.10) is now generalised to allow for possible optimal inequalities as

(11.1) $\quad \psi[i;r[i],z[i]] = min\{x_i + r[i]q_i + c[i] \,|\, z[i] \leq u_i\}.$

The solution to this problem specifies the behaviour of individuals in area i provided that the given level of utility in this area requires an expenditure above the minimum possible for sustenance. As before, $r[i]$ and $z[i]$ are parameters varying only with respect to location.

Assuming once more that solutions are interior, and following an argument exactly analogous to that of chapter three, the necessary and sufficient conditions for a unique solution to problem (11.1) are

(11.2) $\quad u_i = z[i]$

(11.3) $\quad 1 - \lambda_i \dfrac{\partial u}{\partial x_i} \Big|_{u_i = z[i]} = 0$

(11.4) $\quad \left[r[i] - \lambda_i \dfrac{\partial u}{\partial q_i}\right] \underset{n_i}{\triangle} q \Big|_{u_i = z[i]} = 0$

where the condition (11.4) about the optimal use of land has been expressed in terms of population, rather than per capita amounts as in the corresponding condition (3.19), by using (4.14); and where $\lambda_i = \partial \psi \div \partial z_i$ is the lagrangean multiplier of problem (11.1).

In the case of equilibrium analysis, study was confined to those land-value structures which eliminate advantages of location, that is, which render utility invariant throughout. Here, on the other hand, one does not know a priori whether the optimal city should be at equilibrium or not; in other words, whether utility should be invariant throughout. Generalising the concept to account for possible optimal inequalities, we confine our study to those land–value structures which support a *given* distribution of utility. The generalised condition of Muth (3.21) now includes possibly non–zero differences in utility:

$$(11.5) \qquad q_i \bigwedge_i r + \bigwedge_i c + \lambda_i \bigwedge_i z = 0$$

In order to gain some intuition about the meaning of (11.5), consider the case of two adjacent areas with a difference in the optimal utility level $\Delta_i z \neq 0$. If the income difference between the two areas were smaller than $\lambda_i \Delta_i z$, an individual in area i with fixed income ψ_i would improve his utility by moving to area $i + 1$. If, on the other hand, the difference between the two areas were greater than $\lambda_i \Delta_i z$, an individual in area $i + 1$ with fixed income ψ_{i+1} would improve his utility by moving to area i. Thus (11.5) conveys the idea that the movement between adjacent areas will stop when the established differences in locational benefits and costs between adjacent areas precisely offset the income differences necessary to attain the corresponding exogenous utility differences.

This concludes the modifications in the description of individual behaviour which are necessary for the analysis of optimal cities. Here, as well as in the next chapter, the simplest case of a city with fixed total area within a perfectly undifferentiated environment will be examined. Complications will be gradually introduced later on. The only constraint facing our planner is a technological one: the city should be self–sufficient, in other words, it should generate at least the income spent by its inhabitants. Taking into account (11.2), this income is given by

$$(11.6) \qquad x[r[i],z[i]] + r[i]q[r[i],z[i]] + c[i] \equiv$$

$$(x_i + r[i]q_i + c[i])\big|_{z[i]=v_i} = (x_i + r[i]q_i + c[i])\big|_{u_i=v_i} \equiv \bar{y}_i.$$

Simple Urban Optimum

Following chapter eight, income is obtained by working at the centre to produce the private good. Thus the technology of producing the private good imposes limits on production which, in turn, affect the income available. I now simplify the framework of chapter eight. Let production use a fixed amount of land at the centre and let no land rent (or, equivalently, a fixed land rent) be charged by the planner for production. Then production will depend only on employment and, given that $z \equiv (z[i],...,z[b])$ represents a desired distribution of utility levels experienced by the individuals,

$$(11.7) \qquad \sum_{j=1}^{b} n_j \bar{y}_j \leq X[N]$$

expresses the idea that the net value of what is produced in the city cannot be less than the total income spent by its inhabitants.[2]

Given a degree of aversion to inequality, we need to know the optimal distribution of land values, utilities and consumption. We shall proceed in two stages. Firstly, in this chapter, given any feasible distribution of land values and utilities, we shall determine consumption in a way which is consistent with the requirements for optimality. Secondly, in the next chapter, we shall adopt a procedure that specifies optimal land values and utilities corresponding to the given degree of aversion to inequality. Following chapter ten, for any degree of aversion to inequality, the optimal city must be Pareto efficient. In other words, the socially evaluated utility of individuals in any area is at a maximum, given a distribution of socially evaluated utility in the remaining areas. Otherwise someone could increase his welfare without decreasing the welfare of anyone else, which is a contradiction. These observations suggest that Pareto efficiency implies the following approach. For an arbitrary area, say area i, the planner must determine a feasible consumption mix (x_i, q_i) for everyone in the city so that the socially evaluated utility of those in area i is at a maximum, given a feasible distribution of socially evaluated utility in the remaining areas $j, j \neq i$:

(11.8) $\quad v[u_i;\alpha]\big|_{u_i=v_i} =$
$$\max\left\{v_i \,\Big|\, \bar{z}[k] \leq v_k \text{ for } k \in \mathcal{J}, k \neq i \text{ and } \sum_{j=1}^{b} n_j \bar{y}_j \leq X[N]\right\} \text{ for } i \in \mathcal{J}$$

where $\bar{z} \equiv (\bar{z}[1],...,\bar{z}[b])$ represents a desired distribution of socially evaluated utility levels. Recall however that every equilibrium argument in this book has been cast in money terms. It is useful for consistency to follow the same approach here. Similarly to the case of an individual discussed in chapter three, for $|\alpha| < \infty$, it is true that to maximise the socially evaluated utility in an arbitrary area subject to a constraint about the distribution of socially evaluated utility in the remaining areas and to an aggregate income deficit constraint is to minimise the aggregate income deficit subject to a constraint about the distribution of socially evaluated utility. The converse is also true—provided that the given distribution of socially evaluated utility requires an aggregate income above the minimum possible for sustenance.[3] Hence, under these circumstances, the problem of the planner is to determine a feasible consumption mix (x_i,q_i) for everyone in the city such that

(11.9) $\quad D[r,\bar{z};\alpha] =$
$$\min\left\{\sum_{j=1}^{b} n_j \bar{y}_j - X[N] \,\bigg|\, \bar{z}[i] \leq v[u_i;\alpha]\big|_{u_i=v_i} \text{ for } i \in \mathcal{J}\right\}$$

where D represents an aggregate income deficit and $r \equiv (r[1],...,r[b])$. As in the case of individuals, $r[i]$ and $\bar{z}[i]$ are parameters varying only with respect to location. Since (11.9) can be solved for any feasible $(r,\bar{z})$, it can also be solved for the optimal (r^*,z^*). This, in turn, will be specified using the concept of an optimal decentralisation policy in the next chapter. Problem (11.9), and its variations in subsequent chapters, will provide the foundation for the entire analysis of optimality.

Simple Urban Optimum

Optimal Conditions

The existence of a solution to problem (11.8) will depend on the nature of the associated set of attainable states which is determined by the constraints. This set may of course be empty because the existing technological conditions impose limits to attainable utility, so that one could always determine a $z[j]$ prohibitively high with respect to (11.7). But if this set is nonempty then it is also compact and, according to proposition 10.4, there exists an optimum. Translated into problem (11.9) these observations mean that the planner, in addition to solving this problem, must arrange matters so that there is no aggregate income deficit.

As with the problem of an individual in chapter three, I shall assume that any solutions to problem (11.9) are interior. From now on, I shall also assume that *sufficient conditions hold throughout*. Under these circumstances, the necessary conditions for an optimum are

(11.10) $\qquad \mu_i(\bar{z}[i] - v_i) = 0$

(11.11) $\qquad n_i \dfrac{\partial \bar{y}}{\partial x_i} - \mu_i \dfrac{dv}{du_i} \dfrac{\partial u}{\partial x_i} \Big|_{u_i = v_i} = 0 \;\; \textit{for } i \in \mathcal{J}$

(11.12) $\qquad \bar{y}_i + (n_i + 1) \bigtriangleup_{n_i} \bar{y} - \bigtriangleup_{N} X - \mu_i \dfrac{dv}{du_i} \dfrac{\partial u}{\partial q_i} \bigtriangleup_{n_i} q \Big|_{u_i = v_i} = 0$

for $i \in \mathcal{J}$

where all utilities are evaluated at their respective optimisation levels because the planner assumes individuals to behave as in chapter three; and where μ_i is the lagrangean multiplier associated with the utility constraint of area i. Finally, as in the case of individuals, analysis is confined to spatial structures which support a given distribution of utility. In other words, for every area *i*, it is required that $D[r,\bar{z};\alpha]$ is a local minimum with respect to location:

(11.13) $\quad n_i \bigwedge_i \bar{y} + \mu_i \bigwedge_i \bar{z} = 0 \ for \ i \in \mathcal{J}.$[4]

Using (3.13) and (11.6),

(11.14) $\quad \psi[i;r[i],z[i]] = \bar{y}_i \ for \ i \in \mathcal{J}$

holds as an identity. Therefore, applying the envelope theorem to problem (11.9),

(11.15) $\quad \mu_i = \dfrac{\partial D}{\partial \bar{z}[i]} = n_i \dfrac{\partial \psi}{\partial z[i]} \dfrac{dz[i]}{d\bar{z}[i]} > 0 \ for \ i \in \mathcal{J}.$

Thus μ_i represents the additional funds necessary to raise the level of socially evaluated utility in area i by one unit. Using (11.10) and (11.15)

(11.16) $\quad \bar{z}[i] = v_i \ for \ i \in \mathcal{J}.$

The remaining conditions (11.12)–(11.13) are different manifestations of the marginal principle. The first term in (11.11) represents the marginal social cost (MSC) of the aggregate change in income required to increase the consumption of the private good in area i by one unit. The second term represents the corresponding marginal social benefit (MSB). With respect to condition (11.12), when the planner decides to add another individual in area i, the consequences are as follows. Firstly the newcomer must be provided with income. This appears in the first term of (11.12). However, the reduction in the land consumed per capita will also cause a corresponding reduction in the expenditure required per capita. This appears in the second term of (11.12) and, unlike the first, it represents an MSB. Secondly the newcomer works at the centre and produces as does everyone else. This is another MSB associated with the addition of another individual in area i, represented by the third term in (11.12). Thirdly congestion increases and results in a corresponding loss of social welfare. This appears in the last term of (11.12). The

Simple Urban Optimum

quantity $\Delta_{ni}q$ represents the loss of land per capita because of the addition of someone in area i. The quantity $-(\partial u + \partial q_i)\Delta_{ni}q$ represents the value of this loss to someone in area i. The quantity $-(dv + du_i) \cdot (\partial u + \partial q_i)\Delta_{ni}q$ represents the social evaluation of this loss. Hence the last term of (11.12) represents the loss in social welfare due to the congestion imposed by the newcomer. Finally, with respect to condition (11.13), when the planner decides to change the location of those in area i to area $i + 1$, the consequences are as follows. Social welfare changes by the aggregate change in the socially evaluated utility between areas i and $i + 1$. At the same time there is also a corresponding change in the aggregate income necessary to support the migrants which stems from changes in locational costs. Depending on whether utility increases or decreases away from the centre, one of those effects is an MSB and the other is an MSC. If for example utility increases away from the centre then the first term in (11.13) represents an MSC necessary to attain this increased utility level and the second term represents an MSB. In general, conditions (11.11)–(11.13) require a balance between corresponding MSB and MSC at the optimum.

Appendix to Chapter Eleven

This appendix contains a proof of the statement that, for $|\alpha| < \infty$, to maximise the socially evaluated utility in an arbitrary area subject to a constraint about the distribution of socially evaluated utility in the remaining areas and to an aggregate income deficit constraint is to minimise the aggregate income deficit subject to a constraint about the distribution of socially evaluated utility; and that the converse is also true—provided that the given level of utility requires an expenditure above the minimum possible for sustenance. The proof for both parts of the statement is a modification of Arrow and Hahn (1971, p. 81).

According to the discussion preceding (11.10)–(11.13), a solution to the planning problem is a vector $m(x,n)$, where r and $\bar{z}$ are given and where $x = (x_1,...,x_b)$, $n \equiv (n_1,...,n_b)$. Both propositions use the continuity of m. In particular, proposition 11.2 treats n explicitly as continuous. Denote $v[u_i;\alpha]|_m \equiv v_i[m]$ and $\Sigma_{j=1}^{b} n_j \bar{y}_j - X[N] \equiv \bar{D}$. Then

11.1   *For $|\alpha| < \infty$, if m^* maximises v_i subject to $\bar{z}[k] - v_k \leq 0$ for $k \neq i$, $k = 1,...,b$ and to $\bar{D} \leq 0$ then m^* minimises $\bar{D}$ subject to $\bar{v}[k] - v_k \leq 0$ for $k \neq i$, $k = 1,...,b$ and to $v_i[m^*] - v_i[m] \leq 0$.*

Suppose that the conclusion is false. Then there exists m^1 such that $\bar{z}[k] - v_k[m^1] \leq 0$, $v_i[m^*] - v_i[m^1] \leq 0$ and $\bar{D}^* > \bar{D}^1$. It is always possible to determine m^2 arbitrarily close to m^1 for which $v_i[m^2] > v_i[m^1]$ and, therefore, $v_i[m^2] > v_i[m^*]$. For example, with everything else remaining fixed, increase x_i^1 slightly by the same amount so that $u_i|_{m^2} > u_i|_{m^1}$ and, since α is finite, $v_i[m^2] > v_i[m^1]$. We now may select m^2 close enough to m^1 to guarantee $\bar{D}^2 \leq \bar{D}^* \leq 0$ which contradicts the hypothesis that m^* maximizes v_i subject to $\bar{z}[k] - v_k \leq 0$ and to $\bar{D} \leq 0$. ∎

11.2   *If m^* minimises $\bar{D}$ subject to $\bar{z}[j] - v_j \leq 0$ for $j = 1,...,b$ and if $\bar{D}^* > \bar{D}^1$ for some feasible m^1 such that $\bar{z}[k] - v_k[m^1] \leq 0$ for $k \neq i$, $k = 1,...,b$, then m^* maximises v_i subject to $\bar{z}[k] - v_k \leq 0$ and to $\bar{D} \leq \bar{D}^*$.*

Consider any m^2 for which $\bar{z}[k] - v_k[m^2] \leq 0$ and $\bar{D}^2 \leq \bar{D}^*$. Let

(11.17) $m[v] \equiv v[m^1] + (1-v)m^2.$

Then

(11.18) $\bar{D}|_{m[v]} \equiv \tilde{D}[m[v]] < \bar{D}^*$

Simple Urban Optimum

and $\bar{z}[k] - v_k[m[v]] \leq 0$ for $0 < v \leq 1$. If $v_i[m[v]] \geq \bar{z}[i]$ then by hypothesis $\bar{D}^* \leq \tilde{D}[m[v]]$. This, by (11.18), is a contradiction. Therefore $\bar{z}[i] > v_i[m[v]]$ and

(11.19) $\quad m[v] \in \{m \mid \bar{z}[i] \geq v_i[m] \text{ and } \bar{z}[k] - v_k[m] \leq 0\}$.

Since this last set is closed, it contains $\lim_{v \to 0} m[v] = m^2$. Since $v_j[m^*] \geq \bar{z}[j]$ it follows that $v_i[m^*] \geq v_i[m^2]$ for any m^2 for which $\bar{z}[k] - v_k[m^2] \leq 0$ and $\bar{D}^2 \leq \bar{D}^*$. ∎

Notes to Chapter Eleven

1. According to (4.14)–(4.16), the consumption of land per capita in an area determines the population of that area and vice versa. Thus to say that the planner must determine, among other things, the consumption of land for everyone is to say that he must determine the spatial distribution of population over the city. From now on, we emphasise the latter by taking n_i instead of q_i as a decision variable throughout.

2. As it is unknown whether everyone should enjoy the same level of utility at the optimum, so it is unknown whether everyone should be given the same income. This is why per capita expenditure in (11.6) has been indexed by location.

3. See appendix.

4. Condition (11.10) is the Kuhn–Tucker condition for inequality constraints. The lagrangean function of the problem of the planner is

Simple Urban Optimum

$$L \equiv \sum_j n_j \bar{y}_j - X + \sum_j \mu_j (z[j] - v_j).$$

Conditions (11.11) are obtained upon partial differentiation of the lagrangean function in terms of x_i. Conditions (11.12) and (11.13) are obtained upon partial differencing of the lagrangean function in terms of n_i and i, respectively. Conditions (11.12) use the rule

$$\Delta_{n_i} X = \Delta_N X \quad \Delta_{n_i} X = \Delta_N X$$

because $\Delta_{n_i} N = 1$ by (5.4).

12

Decentralisation

A solution to the problem of the planner must prescribe exactly how the optimal city should be. In particular, for everyone in the city, it should prescribe income; consumption of the private good; consumption of land (hence the optimal city size) together with the price for the use of land everywhere in the city; and the location of everyone in the city. Now a question about how the optimal city should be does not necessarily imply a definite commitment toward its realisation: such knowledge may simply be used as a yardstick to measure reality and to facilitate planning decisions. Yet if the acts of the planner are guided by his desire to use the limited resources of society in what to him is the best possible manner, the question of how to achieve an optimum becomes unavoidable. How is an optimum to be achieved? One way is of course by fiat. Then the contrast between an equilibrium and an optimum becomes complete: whereas the former represents a perfectly decentralised system of authority, the latter is perfectly centralised. But is such an extreme approach necessary to achieve an optimum? In other words, is it true that all private decisions necessarily differ from the corresponding public decisions at the optimum? If not then the planner should concentrate only where private decisions and the corresponding public decisions deviate. This would not only save him some effort but would also, to some extent, resolve the problem of individual freedom which is bound to be acute in a highly centralised system.

The previous remarks lead to the fundamental issue of decentralisation. Invoking the principle of a maximum protected sphere already discussed in chapter ten, the gist of the issue pertains to the minimum of public controls sufficient to support an optimum.[1] This is an old question. Traditionally, it extends well beyond the problem of what is a good public policy and into the very nature of a best constitution.

A.C. Pigou and the Correction Principle

An optimal decentralisation policy is a way to maintain a solution to the problem of the planner under a maximum possible protected sphere. To enquire into the nature of an optimal decentralisation policy is to understand the nature of deviations between private decisions and the corresponding public decisions at the optimum. Such decisions are guided by the marginal principle: the optimal scale of an activity is where the marginal benefits associated with a change of scale in the activity are balanced by the corresponding marginal costs. Thus the private point of view stems as a balance between MPB and MPC, while the public point of view stems as a balance between MSB and MSC. If there is no deviation between corresponding private and public decisions then there is no need to intervene because, according to the principle of decentralisation, such decisions should be left within the realm of the protected sphere. No such deviation implies either coincidences between MPB and MSB and between MPC and MSC (figure 12.1(1)); or differences between MPB and MSB and between MPC and MSC somehow balanced at precisely the same point (figure 12.1(2)).

Consider now the case where there is such a deviation. To fix ideas, planting a flower creates beauty that pleases someone and using a machine creates noise that displeases someone. If I am not aware of the

Figure 12.1: The activity z belongs to the protected sphere.

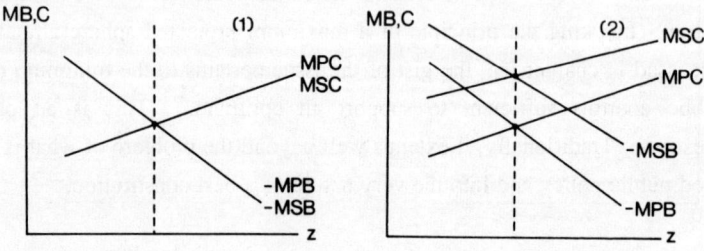

additional pleasure (displeasure) I create, or if I do not care about it, then MPB (MPC) differ from the corresponding MSB (MSC). In the former case, where MSB exceed MPB, the optimal scale of the activity under consideration should be larger from society's point of view (figure 12.2(1)). In the latter case, where MSC exceed MPC, the optimal scale of the activity under consideration should be smaller from society's point of view (figure 12.2(2)).

It is precisely on these observations that the *correction principle* of Pigou (1920) rests. As most great concepts it is extremely simple.

Figure 12.2: The activity z does not belong to the protected sphere.

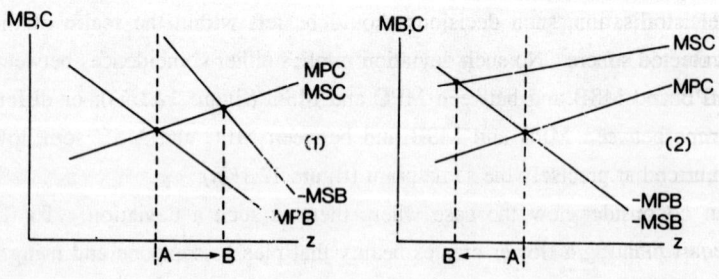

Figure 12.3: The correction principle.

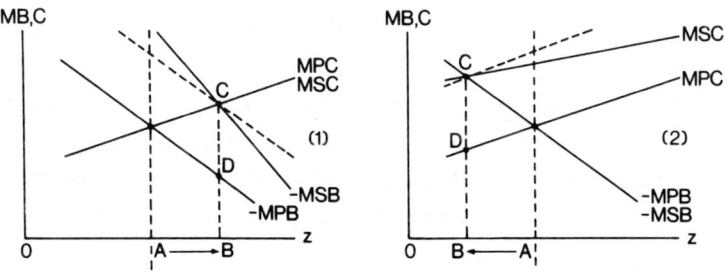

Consider figure 12.3(1). If the planner raises MPB by the difference CD = − MSB + MPB evaluated at the optimum then the deviation between MPB and MSB at the optimum disappears. This is sufficient in order to attain the optimum. Hence, by definition, the optimal decentralisation policy in this case is a subsidy to the individual at a marginal rate equal to the net marginal social benefit (NMSB) of his decision evaluated at the optimum. This would force him to raise the value of z from OA to the socially desirable OB. Consider figure 12.3(2). If the planner raises MPC by the difference CD = MSC − MPC evaluated at the optimum then the deviation between MPC and MSC at the optimum disappears. As before this is sufficient in order to attain an optimum. Hence the optimal decentralisation policy in this case is a tax to the individual at a marginal rate equal to the net marginal social cost (NMSC) of his decision evaluated at the optimum. This would force him to lower the value of z from OA to the socially desirable OB. If there is a difference in both marginal benefits and marginal costs then the planner should impose a sum equal to − NMSB + NMSC, both evaluated at the optimum, corresponding to a subsidy (tax) if this sum is negative (positive). In consequence, *the concept of an optimal decentralisation policy is equivalent to facing everybody with the social consequences of his acts at the optimum.* This is a completely general principle in the sense that it transcends socioeconomic systems. It is a matter of efficiency—not of distribution which remains a separate issue. Contrary to traditional liberalist thought which would limit society's role to discouraging evil, an optimal decentralisation policy would extend it to encouraging good as well.[2]

It is important to remember that the correction principle must be applied comprehensively. It may for example be impossible to achieve everything at once. One could hope however that gradual application of conditions for optimal decentralisation policy may circumvent the problem so that, eventually, all conditions for optimal decentralisation policy could be achieved in spite of the original difficulties. Such an approach, pertaining to the application of only a subset of conditions for optimal decentralisation policy, is named a *piecemeal policy*. Intuitively, even if the gradual attainment of all conditions for an optimal decentralisation policy is deemed impossible, one could hope that the application of piecemeal policy over a part of the state of society would improve social welfare. Nevertheless the *application of piecemeal policy may even reduce social welfare*.[3] This happens because, once a condition for optimal decentralisation policy is violated, the remaining conditions are no longer desirable in general.[4] Thus current social ideals cannot be used as blueprints for social action; and the correction principle becomes irrelevant unless it is applied all at once.

Optimal Decentralisation Policy

We have thus arrived at the following situation. In order to determine the minimum of public controls sufficient to support an optimal city we must compare the decisions of individuals, as expressed in the related first-order conditions, with the corresponding public decisions. If the two coincide then there is no need for public interference. If they differ then we must seek conditions that will render them equivalent, in other words we must seek to determine the NMSB or NMSC at the optimum. These then will represent the optimal decentralisation policy sought.

Individual decisions concerning the private good, land and location are represented by (11.3), (11.4) and (11.5) respectively. Corresponding public decisions are represented by (11.11), (11.12) and (11.13). Thus, in order to define an optimal decentralisation policy, one must compare (11.3) with (11.11), (11.4) with (11.12), and (11.5) with (11.13). *Comparability dictates that parameters which appear in both problems (11.1) and (11.9) must be the same*, that is, for comparison purposes, individuals and the planner must be faced by the same parameter set (r,z) in the contexts of problems (11.1) and (11.9) respectively. Using (11.15), this implies

$$(12.1) \qquad \mu_i = \frac{\partial D}{\partial z[i]} = n_i \frac{\partial \psi}{\partial z[i]}.$$

Using (11.2), (11.6) and (12.1),

$$(12.2) \qquad \frac{\partial D}{\partial z[i]} \frac{\partial v}{\partial u_i} \Big|_{z[i]=v[i]} = n_i \frac{\partial \psi}{\partial z[i]} \frac{\partial v}{\partial u_i} \Big|_{z[i]=v[i]} = n_i \frac{\partial \psi}{\partial u_i}$$

by the chain rule. Since u_i is evaluated at v_i in the solution of problem (11.9), $\partial \psi / \partial u_i = \lambda_i$. This, together with (10.5), implies

$$(12.3) \qquad \mu_i = n_i \lambda_i z^\alpha[i]$$

which is a relation used extensively from now on in comparisons between private and corresponding public decisions to determine optimal decentralisation policy.

Table 12.1 displays the various optimality conditions which are relevant to optimal decentralisation policy in the context of chapter eleven. Since this type of table will be used repeatedly in subsequent chapters whenever optimal decentralisation policy is involved, it seems useful to describe it here in more detail. The conditions to be compared, as well as the associated main implications for optimal decentralisation

Decentralisation

policy, are organised across the rows of the table. The variable to which a row pertains appears on the extreme LHS. For example, the second row of table 12.1 pertains to decisions about the consumption of land. Furthermore, the part of the row associated with the optimality conditions of the planner contains two entries, the upper being the condition as first derived from the constrained optimisation problem and the lower being the equivalent condition as transformed for direct comparison with the corresponding optimality condition of individuals. The equation numbers for all conditions are also included.

Applying (12.3) in (11.11), (11.12) and (11.13) respectively, and recalling the arguments used in the derivation of (12.3), we obtain

$$(12.4) \quad n_i \left[1 - \lambda_i \frac{\partial u}{\partial x_i} \right] \Big|_{u_i = z[i]} = 0$$

$$(12.5) \quad n_i \left[r_i - \lambda_i \frac{\partial u}{\partial q_i} \right] \bigtriangleup_{n_i} q \Big|_{u_i = z[i]} + \left[\left[\bar{y}_i + \bigtriangleup_{n_i} \bar{y} \right] - \bigtriangleup_N X \right] = 0$$

$$(12.6) \quad n_i \left[\left[q_i \bigtriangleup_i r + \bigtriangleup_i c + \lambda_i \bigtriangleup_i z \right] + \left[\frac{\mu_i}{n_i} - \lambda_i \right] \bigtriangleup_i z \right] = 0.$$

Notice once more that, because of (11.2) and (11.16), *both individual and public decisions are evaluated at $u = z$ during comparisons*. From now on, for simplicity, we shall avoid the explicit notation $|u_i = z_i$.

Individual decisions concerning the consumption of the private good are based on (11.3). Corresponding public decisions are based on (12.4). Comparison between these two indicates that the choice of individuals regarding the consumption of the private good coincides with that of the planner, provided that $n \gg 0$. Thus there is no need to interfere in that type of decision.

Individual decisions concerning the consumption of land are based on (11.4). Corresponding public decisions are based on (12.5). From (11.6) and (4.14), the quantity

$$(12.7) \quad \bar{y}_i + \bigwedge_{n_i} \bar{y} = x_i + r[i]q_i + c[i] + r[i]\bigwedge_{n_i} q$$

$$= x_i + r[i]q_i \big|_{n_i+1} + c[i]$$

represents the per capita income in area i, adjusted for the presence of the marginal individual. Suppose that the planner distributes an income equal to the value of the marginal product of individuals, that is, suppose

$$(12.8) \quad \bar{y}_i + \bigwedge_{n_i} \bar{y} \equiv y = \bigwedge_N X.$$

Then (12.5) becomes equivalent to (11.4) provided that $n \gg 0$.

Individual decisions concerning location are based on (11.5). Corresponding public decisions are based on (12.6). It becomes clear that individual decisions concerning location deviate from the corresponding public decisions by the second of the two terms in (12.6). If the planner sets a marginal rate on location equal to

$$(12.9) \quad \phi_i^i = \left[\frac{\mu_i}{n_i} - \lambda_i\right] \bigwedge_i z$$

and if this rate is treated parametrically by the individuals, then (11.5) would be augmented by ϕ_i^i and would become equivalent to (12.6) at the optimum.[5] According to the correction principle this term must represent the NMSB or NMSC of someone in area i who moves to the adjacent area $i+1$. This is precisely the case. An individual who moves from zone i to zone $i+1$ experiences a change in utility valued as $\lambda_i \Delta_i z$. For the planner, however, this change is valued as $(\mu_i + n_i)\Delta_i z$.[6] Since all other consequences of a move are properly taken into account by individuals, the difference in (12.9) represents the NMSB or NMSC of location in area i.

It will now be argued that ϕ_i^i in (12.9) can be taken as approximately equal to zero, in other words that (11.5) and (12.6) are approximately equivalent. Using (12.8),

Table 12.1: Decision rules.

		Optimality Conditions
		Planner
x_i	(11.11):	$n_i \dfrac{\partial y}{\partial x_i} - \mu_i \dfrac{dv}{du_i} \dfrac{\partial u}{\partial x_i} \big|_{u_i = v_i} =$
	(12.4):	$n_i \left[1 - \lambda_i \dfrac{\partial u}{\partial x_i} \right] \big|_{u_i = z[i]} = 0$
n_i	(11.12):	$\bar{y}_i + (n_i + 1) \bigwedge\limits_{n_i} \bar{y} - \bigwedge\limits_{N} X - \mu_i \dfrac{dv}{du_i} \dfrac{\partial u}{\partial q_i} \bigwedge\limits_{n_i} q \big|_{u_i = v_i} =$
	(12.5):	$n_i \left[\bar{r}_i - \lambda_i \dfrac{\partial u}{\partial q_i} \right] \bigwedge\limits_{n_i} q \big|_{u_i = z[i]} + \left[\left(\bar{y}_i + \bigwedge\limits_{n_i} \bar{y} \right) - \bigwedge\limits_{N} X \right] = 0$
i	(11.13):	$n_i \bigwedge\limits_{i} \bar{y} + \mu_i \bigwedge\limits_{i} \bar{z} =$
	(12.6):	$n_i \left[\left(q_i \bigwedge\limits_{i} r + \bigwedge\limits_{i} c + \lambda_i \bigwedge\limits_{i} z \right) + \left(\dfrac{\mu_i}{n_i} - \lambda_i \right) \bigwedge\limits_{i} z \right] = 0$

Decentralisation

	Individuals	Decentralisation
(11.3):	$1 - \lambda_i \frac{\partial u}{\partial x_i}\big|_{u_i = z[i]} = 0$	No correction
(11.4):	$\left[r_i - \lambda_i \frac{\partial u}{\partial q_i} \right] \bigtriangleup_{n_i} q \big|_{u_i = z[i]} = 0$	$\bar{y}_i + \bigtriangleup_{n_i} \bar{y} = \bigtriangleup_N X$
(11.5):	$q_i \bigtriangleup_i r + \bigtriangleup_i c + \lambda_i \bigtriangleup_i z = 0$	No correction because $\left[\frac{\mu_j}{n_i} - \lambda_i \right] \bigtriangleup_i z \approx 0$

279

Decentralisation

(12.10) $$\triangle_i \left[\bar{y}_i + \triangle_{n_i} \bar{y} \right] = \triangle_i \left[x_i + r[i]q_i + c[i] + r[i]\triangle_{n_i} q \right]$$

$$= \triangle_i \left[x_i + r[i]q_i \big|_{n_i+1} + c[i] \right]$$

$$= q_i \big|_{n_i+1} \triangle_i r + \triangle_i c \approx q_i \triangle_i r + \triangle_i c = \triangle_i \bar{y} = 0$$

provided that the number of individuals in area i is large enough.[7] *From now on, we shall adopt this approximation* because it considerably facilitates our arguments and it helps concentrate the analysis on the impact of major urban externalities. Introducing the approximation in (11.13) and (12.9) respectively,

(12.11) $\triangle_i z \approx 0$

(12.12) $\phi_i^i \approx 0$

Suppose that the planner aims for self-sufficiency at the optimum, that is, $D = 0$. This, in conjunction with (12.8) implies

(12.13) $Ny = N \triangle_N X = X[N]$,

in other words, that the planner must determine the urban population size in such a way that the marginal product of labour equals the corresponding average product at the optimum. A geometric interpretation of (12.13) appears in figure 12.4. Returns to scale in production first increase and then decrease. The optimal population size will be found at N^*, where (12.13) is satisfied and where the average product of labour is maximised. The corresponding optimal income level is determined at y. Given any feasible z, the structure of bid-rents is determined through (4.5). Therefore, once the planner has determined an optimal level of utility z^*, optimal bid-rents will be given by $r^*[i] = \sigma[i;y,z^*]$. Conversely, setting an optimal land value for a particular area will also determine the corresponding z^*—hence everything else. In general,

Figure 12.4: Efficient production of the private good.

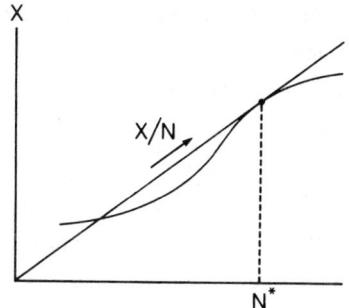

different levels of z^* will correspond to different fractions of the aggregate urban product given away to the absentee landowners. Taking this into account, since efficient production, which is suggested by the equality between the marginal and average products of labour, may be achieved though competition rather than through planning, the optimal decentralisation policy is to do precisely nothing other than setting an optimal land value for a particular area. Competition will ensure that all other socially desirable conditions will obtain: *the optimum is a Casetti equilibrium under any theory of distributive justice employed.*

Theory and Reality

One of the main conclusions in general equilibrium analysis is that if there are no externalities and if initial resources are properly redistributed then any Pareto–efficient allocation can be achieved as a competitive equilibrium.[8] A special case of this famous statement is represented by the simple urban optimum of chapter eleven. In this case, since a competitive market may support the necessary conditions for an optimum, individual aspirations expressed within the confines of a market mechanism are bound to preserve the socially desired status quo: we have actually described conditions for pure laissez–faire. It is a strange world where anarchy and absolute authoritarianism meet to produce the same outcome.

The world however is not like this. A pretty woman passing by gives me the pleasure of her presence without being aware of it; and when you decide to use the highway during the rush hour, you have of course taken into account the expected discomfort to you, but not the additional discomfort that your decision imposes on me who happens to drive alongside. Clearly, in such a world of externalities, the social conditions for optimal resource allocation are violated under a state of competitive equilibrium and laissez-faire becomes socially undesirable. What then is the appropriate optimal decentralisation policy? In the case of the pretty woman, she should be compensated for the pleasure that her unexpected presence gave to me. One for example could imagine a shadow observer who immediately calculates the money equivalent that an additional unit of effort toward her beauty contributes to my happiness at the optimum, multiplies it by the index value of her effort and hands her the estimated, say, 4.7 cents. In the case of the highway driver, a similar procedure would generate a tax to be collected by the shadow observer. This tax should vary according to the additional congestion imposed by the driver which, in turn, varies according to the length of trip, the hour of the day and the route. Pretty women however rarely, if at all, get compensated in this direct manner just for their good looks; and drivers are taxed according to their consumption of gasoline which, although it accounts for the length of trip, remains insensitive to the other determinants of congestion. One reason for such discrepancy is the staggering information requirements that the correction principle implies: the planner should know, for example, the preferences of every individual involved. Even if available, no government possesses yet the technology to use such information in the comprehensive way that the principle dictates. Furthermore, there are reasons which lead me to believe that the adoption of the correction principle could be undesirable, even when its proper application becomes feasible. Consider for example the issue of traffic congestion. It is not difficult to imagine the possibility of some automated system that registers the passage of every car by licence number from every intersection at any time. These data are processed by a central computer and the appropriate monthly bill is sent to every car owner. But then of course our privacy would have vanished and Orwell's (1949) prediction would be fulfilled.

Does all this imply that the correction principle is absurd? Far from it. The correction principle simply brings into sharp focus the unimaginable complexity of the issues involved in attaining any optimum when the market mechanism somehow fails. It clarifies the limits of the possible and it demonstrates that the dream of perfection is rather empty—indeed unwanted even if the information technology required could develop far enough. Then why worry about optimal decentralisation policies? Why seek a way to maintain a solution to the problem of the planner under a maximum possible protected sphere when we know that the resulting guidelines will either be nonexistent or inapplicable? A little reflection will convince you that determining the optimal decentralisation policy helps to clarify the very nature of the optimum under consideration. For example only after the related arguments in this chapter were complete was it clear that the optimal conditions of chapter twelve were indeed approximately equivalent to a Casetti equilibrium. Only then were we able to determine r^* and z^* compatible with the requirement $D = 0$. Furthermore it was also revealed that such equivalence would necessitate efficient production. Thus a convenient way to analyse an optimum is to contrast it with the related equilibrium outcome. The emerging differences, which determine an optimal decentralisation policy, will offer further insight about the very nature of the optimum.

Decentralisation

Aggregate Relationships at the Optimum [9]

Recalling (12.3), (11.12) may be written as

$$(12.14) \qquad -n_i \left[\lambda_i \frac{\partial u}{\partial q_i}\right] \bigtriangleup_{n_i} q = \bigtriangleup_N X - \left[\bar{y}_i + (n_i + 1) \bigtriangleup_{n_i} \bar{y}\right]$$

which, from (4.14), (12.5) and (12.8), becomes

$$(12.15) \qquad -n_i r[i] \bigtriangleup_{i-1} Q \left[\frac{1}{n_i + 1} - \frac{1}{n_i}\right]$$
$$= \bigtriangleup_N X - \left[\bar{y}_i + (n_i + 1) \bigtriangleup_{n_i} \bar{y}\right]$$

or

$$(12.16) \qquad r[i] \bigtriangleup_{i-1} Q = (n_i + 1)\left[\bigtriangleup_N X - \left[\bar{y}_i + (n_i + 1) \bigtriangleup_{n_i} \bar{y}\right]\right].$$

Upon aggregation over the city

$$(12.17) \qquad \sum_i r[i] \bigtriangleup_{i-1} Q = \sum_i (n_i + 1)\left[\bigtriangleup_N X - \left[\bar{y}_i + (n_i + 1) \bigtriangleup_{n_i} \bar{y}\right]\right].$$

The LHS of (12.17) denotes the total value of urban land at the optimum. Since $\Delta_N X - (\bar{y}_i + (n_i + 1)\Delta_{n_i}\bar{y})$ is the net contribution of someone in area i to production then $(n_i + 1)(\Delta_N X - (y_i + (n_i + 1)\Delta_{n_i}\bar{y}))$ is the total net contribution of those in area i to production. Thus the RHS of (12.17) denotes the total surplus value S of urban production. Summarising

12.1 *The total value of urban land equals the total surplus value of urban production at the optimum.*

The validity of proposition 4.2 rests entirely upon the spatial equilibrium condition of Muth which, according to (12.10), holds in the case of the simple urban optimum. Therefore proposition 4.2 also holds in the case of the simple urban optimum. It follows immediately that

12.2 *If the elasticity of the urban area with respect to distance is constant over distance then*

$$R = S >(=,<) \check{R} + \frac{1}{\eta_{Q:i}} C$$

according to whether the elasticity of transportation costs with respect to distance is greater than (equal to, smaller than) unity.

As with proposition 4.2, the simplicity of relationships described by propositions 12.1 and 12.2 is indeed striking. Here the total surplus value of urban production represents the benefits of urbanisation. Costs of urbanisation on the other hand pertain to the total value of land removed from the alternative use of land and to the total cost of urban transportation. The simple urban optimum exists as a balance between these costs and benefits. As with proposition 4.2, the nature of this balance depends on the shape of the city and on the technology of transportation. Under constant returns to scale in transportation, a linear city at the optimum would be characterised by

(12.18) $S = \check{R} + C$

because of (4.16).[10] Over the continuum of urban shapes between the linear and the circular, as the measure of radians gradually increases from zero to 2π, the share of transportation gradually decreases to attain

(12.19) $S = \check{R} + \frac{1}{2} C$

for the case of a circular city. In other words, for city-shapes of higher efficiency, the share of transportation in the balance between the benefits and costs of urbanisation is smaller. These conclusions can be readily extended to cases where the elasticity of transportation costs with respect to distance is other than unity.

It is interesting to note that propositions 12.1 and 12.2 are independent of the underlying theory of justice employed. In other words, the optimal population size remains insensitive to the degree of aversion to inequality. It will be seen that this holds in more general situations. It will also be seen however that the spatial arrangement of this optimal population is affected by the degree of aversion to inequality, provided that the quality of the environment varies over the landscape at the optimum as, for example, in the next chapter.

Theory and Reality

If you asked Plato what should be the population size of an optimal agglomeration he would provide you with a definite answer: 5,040 citizens (Plato (−350)). This does not include optimal support personnel (women and slaves) who, together with the children, would bring the size of his ideal to somewhere between thirty and fifty thousand. Of course, you may or may not agree with Plato's ethic (probably depending upon whether you do or do not possess a valid citizenship of the Republic) but this is not at issue here. The issue is, do you believe in a city of 5,040 citizens? (or of half a million?, or of any particular size whatsoever?) I sincerely do not. (After all, a *distribution* of city sizes is to be found almost everywhere.) Yet I maintain that the problem of an optimal agglomeration is not meaningless. It simply is not necessarily identical with that of an optimal size for cities. If one accepts to aggregate all reasons for cities in a single factor, as in this chapter, then the two problems are identical, and one has to concede that there is an optimal size for cities. If though one takes a disaggregated approach then those two problems become quite distinct.

In order to develop the argument a little further, notice that the logic behind an optimal size is tied with a particular activity (in this chapter with the production technology of a particular urban good). Each activity generates a distinct optimum and, if we accept the view that activities combine to form a hierarchy (Christaller (1933)), then we are faced with a hierarchy of optimal market sizes surrounding a hierarchy of centres. If, further, we accept the view that the city itself is a spatially limited, dense hierarchy of centres, then we realise that our object of analysis is the optimal size of elements that constitute the city–system, rather than the optimal size of the city–system itself. Such optimal elements may combine to form different syntheses of different total size. Contemporary urban design uses this concept extensively, as the typically modular structure of new towns clearly tends to suggest.

Notes to Chapter Twelve

1   A classic example of the traditional liberalist preoccupation with limited sovereignty and the minimal state is given by von Humboldt (1792).

2   For example, von Humboldt (1792) argues that the function of the state is not to do good but to ward off the evil which springs from one's disregard for the rights of others. Similarly Mill (1859) states that the only purpose for which power should be exercised over any individual, against his will, is to prevent harm to others.

3   The original demonstration of this statement is in Lipsey and Lancaster (1956).

4   There are limited circumstances where, except for the deviants, this claim does not hold. See for example Dusansky and Walsh (1976).

Decentralisation

5 A marginal rate on location ϕ_i^i implies that the planner will impose a tax

$$\phi_i \equiv i\, \phi_i^i$$

Since ϕ_i appears as a new cost in the expenditure function and since ϕ_i^i is parametric, the RHS of (5) will be augmented by $\Delta_i \phi = \phi_i^i$, thus becoming equivalent to (9).

6 Since $\mu_i \Delta_i z$ is the aggregate evaluation of the difference in utility from the planner's point of view, $\mu_i \Delta_i z \div n$ is the corresponding evaluation for a single individual.

7 Since $q_i |_{n_i + 1} < q_i$, it follows immediately from (10) that $\Delta_i \bar{y} < 0$. This, in turn, implies $\Delta_i \bar{z} > 0$ at the optimum. However, the difference between the two expressions in (10) is only $\Delta_{ni} q\, \Delta_i r$, and as the partitioning of areas and of population becomes finer, this quantity tends to zero.

8 Appropriate convexity conditions must hold, but all these are satisfied within our framework under any degree of aversion to inequality. For a proof see Debreu (1959, section 6.4). An externality, according to Buchanan and Stubblebine (1962), occurs when the social conditions for optimal resource allocation are violated under a state of competitive equilibrium. Thus if there are no externalities then there is no deviation between corresponding MPB,C and MSB,C.

9 This section is based on some ideas in Arnott (1979). See also Starret (1974) and Hartwick (1979).

10 Since different shapes of city exhibit different degrees of ef-

ficiency and since the linear is the least efficient shape from the viewpoint of transportation, it follows that (12.18) holds only if an optimum is defined given a particular shape of city.

13

Unequal Treatment of Equals [1]

The Case of Environmental Variations

When the quality of the environment varies over the urban area, utility is expressed by (7.1). Since the new factor, quality of the environment, depends on location only, the only decisions affected must be the location decisions. Thus (11.5) and (11.13) now become

(13.1) $$\bigtriangleup_i \bar{y} + \lambda_i \left[\bigtriangleup_i z - \frac{\partial u}{\partial E_i} \bigtriangleup_i E \right] = 0$$

(13.2) $$n_i \bigtriangleup_i \bar{y} + \mu_i \left[\bigtriangleup_i z - \frac{dv}{du_i}\frac{\partial u}{\partial E_i} \bigtriangleup_i E \right]\Big|_{u_i = v_i} = 0$$

respectively. Conditions (13.1) and (13.2) guide the public and individual location decisions when the quality of the environment varies over the urban area. All other individual and public conditions remain precisely as in chapters eleven and twelve. The interpretation of conditions (13.1) and (13.2) is straightforward. The only difference between those and the corresponding conditions (11.5) and (11.13) refers to marginal changes of the new factor, quality of the environment, as location changes. Such environmental changes will become another marginal benefit (cost) whenever the quality of the environment increases (decreases) because of the location change.

As in chapter twelve, table 13.1 displays the various optimality conditions in order to facilitate direct comparison. Everything concerning the consumption of the private good and land remains as in table 12.1. In view of (12.10), conditions (13.1) and (13.2) are simplified to yield

(13.3) $\quad \lambda_i \left[\Delta_i z - \frac{\partial u}{\partial E_i} \Delta_i E \right] = 0$

(13.4) $\quad \mu_i \left[\Delta_i \bar{z} - \frac{dv}{du_i} \frac{\partial u}{\partial E_i} \Delta_i E \right]\Big|_{u_i = v_i} = 0$

respectively. Comparison of these indicates that they are not equivalent. However, taking into account (11.2), (11.16) and the requirement $\bar{z} = z$ for comparisons to define an optimal decentralisation policy, (13.4) may be written as

(13.5) $\quad n_i \left[\lambda_i \left[\Delta_i z - \frac{\partial u}{\partial E_i} \Delta_i E \right]\Big|_{u_i = z[i]} + \left[\frac{\mu_i}{n_i} - \lambda_i \right] \Delta_i z \right] = 0$

because of (12.3). We thus obtain (12.9) once more as the marginal rate suggested by the correction principle for individual decisions concerning location.

Using (10.5) and (11.15), condition (13.4) is equivalent to

(13.6) $\quad \Delta_i v = u_i^{-\alpha} \frac{\partial u}{\partial E_i} \Delta_i E \Big|_{u_i = z[i]}$

which prescribes optimal inequalities associated with a given degree of aversion to inequality. At zero aversion, optimal utility differences should precisely equal the value of the corresponding environmental differences. A bias toward inequality exaggerates such differences. On the other hand increasing aversion to inequality suppresses such differences until, at infinite aversion to inequality, utility is constant over the city.

Table 13.1: Decision rules.

		Optimality Conditions
		Planner
x_i	(11.11):	$n_i \dfrac{\partial y}{\partial x_i} - \mu_i \dfrac{dv}{du_i}\dfrac{\partial u}{\partial x_i}\big|_{u_i = v_i}$
	(12.4):	$n_i\left[1 - \lambda_i \dfrac{\partial u}{\partial x_i}\right]\big|_{u_i = z[i]} = 0$
n_i	(11.12):	$\bar{y}_i + (n_i + 1)\bigtriangleup_{n_i} \bar{y} - \bigtriangleup_N X - \mu_i \dfrac{dv}{du_i}\dfrac{\partial u}{\partial q_i} \bigtriangleup_{n_i} q\big|_{u_i = v_i} =$
	(12.5):	$n_i\left[r_i - \lambda_i \dfrac{\partial u}{\partial q_i}\right] \bigtriangleup_{n_i} q\big|_{u_i = z[i]} + \left[\left[\bar{y}_i + \bigtriangleup_{n_i} \bar{y}\right] - \bigtriangleup_N X\right] = 0$
i	(13.2):	$n_i \bigtriangleup_i \bar{y} + \mu_i\left[\bigtriangleup_i \bar{z} - \dfrac{dv}{du_i}\dfrac{\partial u}{\partial E_i}\bigtriangleup_i E\right]\big|_{u_i = v_i} =$
	(13.5):	$n_i\left[\lambda_i\left[\bigtriangleup_i z - \dfrac{\partial u}{\partial E_i}\bigtriangleup_i E\right]\big|_{u_i = z[i]} + \left[\dfrac{\mu_i}{n_i} - \lambda_i\right]\bigtriangleup_i z\right] = 0$

	Decentralisation
Individuals	
(11.3): $\quad 1 - \lambda_i \frac{\partial u}{\partial x_i}\big|_{u_i = z[i]} = 0$	No correction
(11.4): $\quad \left[r_i[i] - \lambda_i \frac{\partial u}{\partial q_i} \right] \underset{n_i}{\triangle} q \big|_{u_i = z[i]} = 0$	$\bar{y}_i + \underset{n_i}{\triangle} \bar{y} = \underset{N}{\triangle} X$
(13.3): $\quad \lambda_i \left[\underset{i}{\triangle} \bar{z} - \frac{\partial u}{\partial E_i} \underset{i}{\triangle} E \right] \big|_{u_i = z[i]} = 0$	$\phi_i^i = \left[\frac{\mu_j}{n_i} - \lambda_i \right] \underset{i}{\triangle} z$ $= (1 - u_i^{-\alpha}) \lambda_i \frac{\partial u}{\partial E_i} \underset{i}{\triangle} E \big|_{u_i = z[i]}$

Using (12.3) and (13.6) in (12.9), the marginal location rate may be written as

$$(13.7) \quad \phi_i^i = (1 - z^{-\alpha}[i])\lambda_i z^\alpha [i] \bigtriangleup_i z$$

$$= (1 - u_i^{-\alpha})\lambda_i \frac{\partial u}{\partial E_i} \bigtriangleup_i E \Big|_{u_i = z[i]}$$

which, in a manner analogous to that of equation (13.6), prescribes optimal marginal rates associated with a given degree of aversion to inequality. If the planner sets a marginal rate on location equal to (13.7), and if this marginal rate is taken parametrically by the individuals, then (13.1) would be augmented by ϕ_i^i and would become equivalent to (13.5) at the optimum.

The perfect asymmetry between (13.6) and (13.7) is noteworthy. Considering (13.6), at zero aversion, optimal utility differences should precisely equal the value of the corresponding environmental differences. Increasing aversion to inequality suppresses such differences until, at infinite aversion, optimal utility is constant over the city. The instrument for obtaining optimal inequalities is provided by (13.7). At zero aversion, there is no need to intervene. This happens because, at zero aversion, individual and social valuations of utility coincide. Increasing aversion to inequality generates increasingly differentiated marginal tax or subsidy rates which reduce, in turn, every optimal location advantage.

Explanation of Optimal Inequality [2]

Suppose that individuals are characterised according to ability and tastes. Individuals are "equal" if they have the same ability and tastes. Otherwise they are "unequal". Then the following represents a classification of alternative treatments of individuals within a society:

$$\begin{bmatrix} \text{Equal treatment} & \text{Equal treatment} \\ \text{of equals} & \text{of unequals} \\ \\ \text{Unequal treatment} & \text{Unequal treatment} \\ \text{of equals} & \text{of unequals} \end{bmatrix}$$

Of these, equal treatment of equals is manifestly just while unequal treatment of equals is manifestly unjust. In consequence there is no ethical doubt left by the elements of the first column. The elements of the second column, however, mark the presence of a fundamental dilemma. For individuals of the same tastes, equal treatment of unequals expresses a principle of social justice according to need whereas unequal treatment of unequals reflects a principle according to merit—hence one that may avoid exploitation altogether.[3]

The assumption of identical individuals clearly suggests that the optimal inequality derived in the previous section constitutes unequal treatment of equals—the single manifestly unjust type of treatment within a society. Further, a comparison with the analysis of chapter twelve clearly suggests that unequal treatment of equals stems from variations in the quality of the environment: when there is no difference in the quality of the environment between areas, the RHSs of (13.6) and (13.7) become zero and the model reduces to the simple urban optimum of chapter twelve.

To explain the reasons behind this rather startling association, consider the case of the simplest possible town with two locations and two individuals. Location one has an intrinsic advantage over location two, say, a superior quality of the environment. Both individuals are identical in ability and tastes. Our planner is to decide where to locate whom and how to distribute the single loaf of bread available. The possibilities of action open to him are reflected in figure 13.1. Suppose that he decides to place Mr A at location one and Mr B at location two

Figure 13.1: Alternative utility–possibility frontiers.

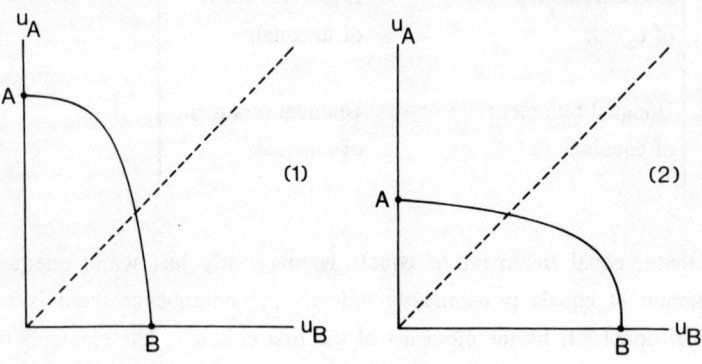

(figure 13.1(1)). He now has to decide on the allocation of bread. He may give the entire loaf to Mr A. Then Mr A is very happy, Mr B dies from starvation, and the distribution of welfare corresponds to point A on the graph. He may give the entire loaf to Mr B. Then Mr B is happy (but not as happy as Mr A was when he possessed the entire loaf because the location of Mr B is inferior to that of Mr A), Mr A dies from starvation and the distribution of welfare corresponds to point B on the graph. Or he may partition the bread otherwise between Mr A and Mr B. Then all possible partitions generate the curve AB, the utility–possibility frontier when Mr A occupies location one and Mr B occupies location two. The only other possible spatial pattern, where Mr B occupies location one and Mr A occupies location two, is represented in figure 13.1(2). Since Mr A and Mr B are identical, the new utility–possibility frontier is the reflection of the old one about the 45°-angle line.

The significant point in the example is that the quality of the environment, or indeed any other indivisible resource, creates asymmetries in the utility–possibility frontier precisely as differences amongst individuals do. Then, taking into account figure 10.5, the reasons behind optimal inequality become transparent. There, it is seen how optimal inequality reflects the balance between efficiency and equity dictated by a particular theory of justice. Of course, when there is no difference between the quality of the environment in locations one and two, the utility–possibility frontier is symmetric as in figure 10.4 and the theory of justice becomes immaterial—except if there is a sufficiently strong bias toward inequality.

Optimal Decentralisation Policy

The obvious conclusion to be drawn from what has been said in the first section of this chapter is that the planner must impose a tax or subsidy on the residents of area $i \in \mathcal{J}$ at a marginal rate ϕ_i^i as in (13.7). There is an infinite number of such taxes or subsidies represented by the family $\phi_i - A$, where $\phi_i \equiv i\phi_i^i$ and A is any constant which allows an expenditure above the minimum possible for sustenance.[4] This provides considerable flexibility to the planner because it permits transfers of money, hence of welfare, between the city and the rest of the world. In consequence, different values of A imply different utility levels for the city. Since ϕ_i^i in (13.7) is estimated at the optimum, it also follows that different values of A imply different tax or subsidy rates.[5]

In general, the new aggregate income $Ny + \Sigma_j n_j \phi_j - NA$ will not balance the total value of the urban product because of condition (12.13). Consider the case $A = 0$. If the quality of the environment increases (decreases) away from the centre then, for positive aversion to inequality, (13.7) implies that the aggregate income required to balance condition (12.13) will be larger (smaller) than the total value of the urban product. If such transfers are unacceptable then A must be chosen to equal $\bar{\phi}$, the average of optimal taxes and subsidies. Since

(13.8) $$\sum_j n_j \phi_j - N\bar{\phi} = 0,$$

$\phi_i - \bar{\phi}$ serves to redistribute the original aggregate income Ny in the way required to attain an optimum.

We are now ready to sketch a solution procedure for the problem (11.9) of the planner. Let $\mathcal{A} \equiv \{x_i, q_i; i = 1,...b\}$. For any feasible $\mathcal{A}$, we can define $\phi[i,\alpha;\mathcal{A}] \equiv \phi_i - \bar{\phi}$ using (13.7), and $\Delta z[i,\alpha;\mathcal{A}] = \Delta_i \upsilon$ using (13.6). The former, together with $y = \Delta_N X$, gives $y[i,\alpha;\mathcal{A}]$; the latter, together with $D = 0$, gives $z[i,\alpha;\mathcal{A}]$. Solving the equation $\psi[i;r[i],z[i,\alpha;\mathcal{A}]] = y[i,\alpha;\mathcal{A}]$ establishes $r[i,\alpha;\mathcal{A}]$. Now, the distribution of optimal individual allocations $\mathcal{A}^*$ is determined as a solution to either $\upsilon[i;r[i,\alpha;\mathcal{A}],y[i,\alpha;\mathcal{A}]] = max\{u_i \,|\, x_i + r[i,\alpha;\mathcal{A}]q_i + c[i] \leq y[i,\alpha;\mathcal{A}]\}$, or to $\psi[i;r[i,\alpha;\mathcal{A}],z[i,\alpha;\mathcal{A}]] = min\{x_i + r[i,\alpha;\mathcal{A}]q_i + c[i] \,|\, z[i,\alpha;\mathcal{A}] \leq u_i\}$. Once $\mathcal{A}^*$ has been established, the optimal distributions of income, land values and utilities can be computed as $y^*[i,\alpha] = y[i,\alpha;\mathcal{A}^*]$, $r^*[i,\alpha] = r[i,\alpha;\mathcal{A}^*]$, and $z^*[i,\alpha] = z[i,\alpha;\mathcal{A}^*]$. In contrast with chapter eleven, where there was an infinite number of optimal solutions, this solution procedure suggests that an optimum here is unique.

To summarise, guidelines for planning an optimal city within the context of this chapter are as follows. The planner organises production efficiently and requires that the aggregate income be equal to the total value of the urban product, thereby determining the optimal size N^*. Although individuals should receive the marginal product of their labour, the planner should, excepting zero aversion to inequality, redistribute income as $y^*[i,\alpha]$. This, together with the optimal distribution of land values imposed by the planner, generates an optimal distribution of utilities $z^*[i,\alpha]$ which, excepting infinite aversion to inequality, is structured according to environmental differences between areas. Therefore, excepting infinite aversion to inequality, some areas in the city will become more attractive than others at the optimum. In consequence the planner will find it necessary to allocate individuals to areas, thereby determining their place into the chosen scheme of optimal inequality.[6] This could be based on a lottery, a first-come first-served principle, or whatever. Since he must predetermine how many to allow in high-utility areas, how many to force into low-utility areas, and so on, he essentially partitions areas into lot sizes. In consequence, the planner will find it necessary to control everything that has to do with the use of land under a finite aversion to inequality. According to (13.5), once income and location (hence utility) have been determined for everyone, under the optimal distribution of land values, the established differences in locational benefits and costs between adjacent areas precisely offset the income differences necessary to attain the corresponding exogenous utility differences.[7] Finally, since everything else is determined, the consumption of the private good is also determined here. Nevertheless, since there is no need to correct for the consumption of the private good and since the same holds even if the single composite good is decomposed into many then, in general, decisions of this nature are always left free of interference—contrary to any decisions about the use of land under a finite aversion to inequality.

Under an infinite aversion to inequality, according to (13.7), the redistribution of income is such that every inherent location advantage is eliminated. Then it is sufficient for the planner to announce the spatial distribution of optimal tax and subsidy rates, and to keep the urban population size at N^*. Competition between those admitted will ensure (12.10) together with a uniform distribution of utility. The difference between this optimum and the corresponding equilibrium of chapter seven is the following. Whereas in chapter seven environmental differences were absorbed by bid-rents through competition, here they are absorbed through appropriate income differences imposed before competition.

Finally, since the optimal conditions (11.12) for the consumption of land still hold, the *aggregate relationships described by propositions 12.1 and 12.2 obtain under any degree of aversion to inequality and under any spatial distribution of environmental quality.*

Urban Morphologies

When the quality of the environment changes, in general, allocation of resources at the optimum also changes because allocation is estimated for a particular level of the quality of the environment. Hence the interactions between changes in the quality of the environment, the degree of aversion to inequality and spatial structure are complex. In this section, for illustrative purposes, I examine these interactions in the special case where changes in the quality of the environment have a small (negligible) impact on consumption.[8]

The arguments related to figure 7.1, describing location equilibrium under variable quality of the environment, referred to a single individual. In order to extend these arguments to the aggregate level consider figure 13.2. It describes conditions for locational indifference, where the reflection of MPB about the abscissa coincides with MPC.[9] The solid lines represent the spatial equilibrium condition of Muth (4.4) in the context of a Casetti equilibrium. In this case the quality of the

Figure 13.2: Casetti equilibrium adjustments
under variable quality of the environment.

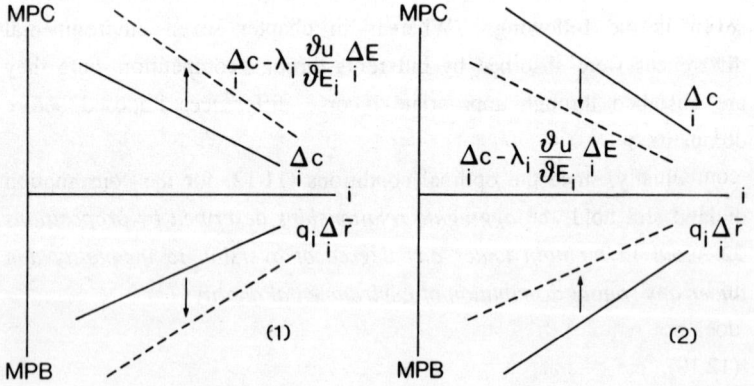

environment is invariant over the landscape. The broken lines represent the generalised spatial equilibrium condition of Muth (7.4), also in the context of a Casetti equilibrium. In this case the quality of the environment varies over the landscape. If the quality of the environment decreases away from the centre then

(13.9) $\quad -\lambda_i \frac{\partial u}{\partial E_i} \bigtriangleup_i E > 0.$

Under these circumstances a change in the quality of the environment becomes another MPC which raises the original solid MPC line (figure 13.2(1)). Then the Casetti equilibrium dictates that MPB will also be raised to match the rise in MPC everywhere. In other words the slope of the bid-rent function will generally become steeper, resulting in a more compact equilibrium. If, on the other hand, the quality of the environment increases away from the centre then

(13.10) $\quad -\lambda_i \frac{\partial u}{\partial E_i} \bigtriangleup_i E < 0.$

Under these circumstances a change in the quality of the environment becomes another MPB which lowers the original solid MPC line (figure 13.2(2)). Then the Casetti equilibrium dictates that the remaining MPB will also be lowered to match the decline of MPC everywhere. In other words the slope of the bid-rent will become generally flatter resulting in a more dispersed equilibrium.

These simple observations provide the basis for the comparison of urban morphologies created under competitive conditions and under the continuum of degrees of aversion to inequality. The instrument for such analysis is the correspondence between a Casetti equilibrium with invariant quality of the environment and an optimum under zero aversion to inequality with variable quality of the environment. Such an optimum does not require a redistribution of income by (13.7). Furthermore, by (12.10), the planner arranges land values as if the optimum were a Casetti equilibrium with invariant quality of the environment. (In this way, according to (13.6), the planner establishes welfare differences between areas equal to the corresponding differences in the value of the quality of the environment.) Thus, although the equilibrium and the optimum are generated under completely different premises, their spatial structure is essentially the same for the same level of income. Taking into account the spatial relationships between equilibria with and without differences in the quality of the environment discussed in the previous paragraph,

13.1   *If the quality of the environment increases (decreases) away from the centre then the optimum under zero aversion to inequality is more compact (dispersed) than the corresponding Casetti equilibrium.*

I complete the study of spatial adjustments in the special case of this section with a comparison of optimal urban morphologies under different degrees of aversion to inequality. Under positive aversion to inequality, income is redistributed to compensate for differences in the quality of the environment. Thus, according to (13.7), income is higher where the quality of the environment is lower. Such differences gradually increase as the degree of aversion to inequality increases. It follows that the consumption of land gradually increases (decreases) in areas of low (high) environmental quality as the degree of aversion to inequality increases. In consequence

13.2   *If the quality of the environment increases (decreases) away from the centre then the optimum becomes more dispersed (compact) as the degree of aversion to inequality increases.*

Figure 13.3(1) summarises the two propositions when the quality of the environment increases away from the centre and figure 13.3(2) when it decreases. These can easily be extended to include the case of aversion to equality: if the quality of the environment increases (de–

Figure 13.3: Urban morphologies under variable degree of aversion to inequality.

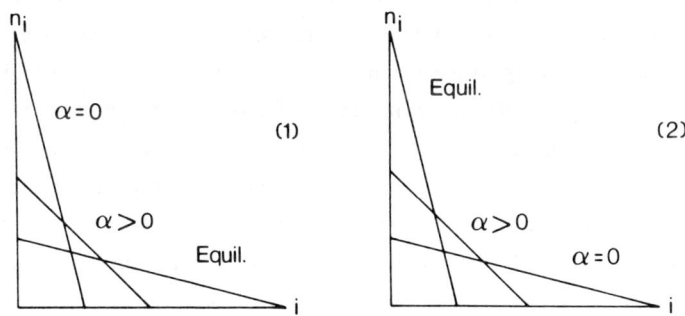

creases) away from the centre then the optimum becomes more compact (dispersed) as the degree of aversion to equality increases provided that such bias is sufficiently strong and utility sufficiently high. Finally, if variations in the quality of the environment are nonmonotonic, the spatial adjustments become more complex but the principles remain.

Theory and Reality

A standard practice in theory is to associate policy with the solution of some constrained optimisation problem which represents the planner's viewpoint.[10] Such use of the word may, in the context of this book, mislead on two counts: firstly because it narrows down the feasible spectrum of political institutions to absolute authoritarianism; and secondly because it pertains to an ideal, long-run point of view—as if policy referred to the creation of an abstract new town. In this manner the heuristic flair of day-to-day policy decisions, constraining and being constrained by the shifting realities of our life, has somehow been lost. Yet this dependence of urban policy upon short-run considerations is important since well-defined land holdings cannot stretch or shrink, existing housing stock is reasonably durable and, for now, you can do only so much in order to alleviate social injustice.

A solution to problem (11.9), with (r^*, z^*) determined by the optimal decentralisation principle, completely describes how the city should be according to the planner. There is nothing more implied by such a description. However, naming a solution "policy" implies that the planner is omnipotent in the sense that he may decide on the life of individuals in the city to the last detail. Even an optimal decentralisation policy, by definition, implies the same. Surrounding this concept, there is a strong aura of "inevitability cum freedom": the protected sphere becomes an illusion as it contains only those decisions which are identical with the decisions of the planner.[11] Clearly such "policies" exclude the entire spectrum of circumstances under which there is a nontrivial partition of rights between individuals and the state. In other words, they eliminate almost every meaningful connection betwen theory and reality.[12]

Suppose now that such a type of difficulty has been resolved through consideration of problems that incorporate a nontrivial partition of rights between individuals and the state. Can solutions to these problems be named "policies"? In the context of this book I believe they cannot because, instead of being blueprints on how to *achieve* a goal, they are blueprints of how to *maintain* a goal—once this goal has somehow been achieved.[13] Furthermore, under any circumstances, such policies would imply that the planner has a clear conception of the optimum, in other words that he can grasp states of society in all their unimaginable complexity, compare them and select the best from his point of view. This of course is our assumption throughout. *But it is put to use only in order to explore the nature of an optimum.* To assume that planners have best choices, in order to explore the nature of these choices, is not to say that they have a clear conception of how to achieve them. Since urban policy pertains to the latter, one should admit a more realistic public choice behaviour when one seeks to understand it. Given that urban policy is an allocation of public resources over the city, it seems that the allocation adjustments discussed in the section "theory and reality" of chapter two are relevant to the problem at hand. According to this view, urban policy is the outcome of heuristic adjustments determined by the theory of justice held by the planner, the pressures applied by various social groups, and the ability of the planner to handle and direct such social pressures towards what he believes to be proper.

Notes to Chapter Thirteen

1   This issue was first raised by Mirrlees (1972).

2   The diagrammatic exposition of optimal inequality belongs to Levhari, Oron and Pines (1978). The discussion draws from Papageorgiou (1980A).

3   For a discussion of these issues see Sen (1973, chapter four). To grasp the magnitude of this dilemma consider some of the recent events in China. There the choice between equal treatment of unequals and unequal treatment of unequals expressed itself as the political struggle between the so-called "gang of four" and the present government respectively. It appears that Marx himself would stand with the gang of four on that issue (see Marx (1875), especially his passage quoted in Sen (1973, pp. 88–89)).

4   The lagrangean function of the problem of the individual now becomes

$y + \phi_i - A + \lambda_i (z[i] - u_i)$.

Differencing with respect to location

$$\phi_i^i + \lambda_i \left[\bigtriangleup_i z - \frac{\partial u}{\partial E_i} \bigtriangleup_i E \right]$$

$$= \left[\frac{\mu_i}{n_i} - \lambda_i \right] \bigtriangleup_i z + \lambda_i \left[\bigtriangleup_i z - \frac{\partial u}{\partial E_i} \bigtriangleup_i E \right]$$

by (12.9) and (12.10), which is equivalent to the desired (13.5) given that $n \gg 0$.

5   There are other kinds of flexibility allowed by this tax or subsidy structure (Holtermann (1976)). Consider for example only negative externalities whereby MPC < MSC at the optimum. Then $\phi_i - A$ may be interpreted to imply that the tax is imposed only above a specified level A, hence only on output of the externality above a correspondingly specified level. On the other hand the equivalent form $-(A - \phi_i)$ may be interpreted to imply a subsidy, rather than a tax, paid for output of the externality below a specified level.

> "An example is provided by subsidies paid to low-income owners of slum housing for external improvements. The dilapidated appearance of a house is an external diseconomy which would, under the normal tax on output of externalities, require a tax on the owners. This would make them worse off, an outcome that is hardly likely to be acceptable on distributional grounds. A subsidy paid for house improvements can achieve Pareto optimality and the desired reduction in the externality without making the owners worse off." (Holtermann (1976, p. 11))

6   "One may feel that inequality is not necessary for optimality in our model, since no harm is done by frequently changing the treatment of individuals while keeping the

overall distribution of incomes constant. After all, it does not matter who receives a high income, only that some people should receive relatively high incomes. But there is no consideration in the model to show that such a constant permutation of incomes would yield an improvement in social welfare. If, therefore, there is any cost—as there surely is—to changing a man's place in the world, the 'optimum with equality' that is obtained by changing positions of individuals within the income distribution is actually inferior to the more straightforward solution." (Mirrlees (1972, pp. 123–124))

7   Clearly, once the spatial pattern of occupancy has been established, subletting of properties or any other (direct or indirect) land-market mechanism should be forbidden. For otherwise the city will become suboptimal.

8   The argument holds exactly in the case of utility functions exhibiting constant elasticities of substitution, such as the Cobb–Douglas utility function.

9   Figure 13.2 is to figure 7.1 what figure 4.1 is to figure 3.2. The second pair, in turn, is a special case of the first as it corresponds to a uniform quality of the environment.

10   See for example Arrow and Kurz (1969).

11   Inevitability cum freedom extends to equilibria as well. Indeed one of the main conclusions in general equilibrium analysis is that the core, that is, the set of all possible bargaining positions in an economy, is equivalent to the corresponding set of equilibria. Thus a perfectly competitive market drags individuals toward

some, essentially predetermined, subset of collective outcomes. One cannot help but compare all this to the insights provided by Marx (1867) in his theory of alienation.

12 One way to resolve this particular type of difficulty is through analysis of second–best problems. To fix ideas, partition the elements of a state of society $K \in \mathcal{K}$ into endogenous and exogenous elements. Further, partition the endogenous elements into controls and everything else. Any feasible value of everything else is derivable from the application of controls upon the state of society. A constitution partitions controls into public controls P and private controls $\setminus P$. The latter, manifestations of the protected sphere, are further partitioned between individuals, so that $\setminus P \equiv (...,\setminus P_1,...)$. In our simple world of theory, problem (3.10) tacitly admits a constitution of only private controls, while problem (11.9) admits a constitution of only public controls. Anywhere between these two extremes, such problems reflect a fundamental symbiotic relationship which, in maximisation form, may be written as

$$\text{maximise } u_1[\setminus P, P] \qquad \text{maximise } W[U]$$
$$\setminus P_1 \qquad\qquad\qquad\qquad P$$
$$\text{subject to } f_1[\setminus P, P] \leq 0 \qquad \text{subject to } g[\setminus P, P] \leq 0$$

for $l = 1,...,N$, where f_1 and g are vectors of private and social constraints respectively. Variations in the partition $(\setminus P, P)$ result in a plethora of second–best models of city. Take for example the quantity of land consumed as a control. If it belongs to private controls, it describes conditions similar to those prevailing in market economies. If it belongs to public controls, it describes conditions similar to those prevailing in planned economies. Examples of second–best models include Kanemoto (1976, 1977).

13 Optimisation through time does not suffer from this conceptual shortcoming.

Part Three

EXTERNALITIES

14

Conceptual Framework [1]

Until now the quality of the urban environment has been treated as strictly exogenous with respect to individuals. In contrast, from now on, our concern will be about the interaction between individuals and their environment. Such interdependence, recognised throughout history as pervasive in all aspects of humanity, is fundamental to the study of cities.[2]

An important aspect of the environment refers to its spatial dimensions. The environment of an individual at a particular location depends not only on attributes related to that location, but also upon attributes related to other locations. In consequence, the choice behaviour of an individual is determined both by preferences and by spatial distributions which contribute to the environment of that individual. Economic analysis explicitly recognises the impact of external effects on choice behaviour. However, traditional economic analysis has suppressed the ways external effects arise within a spatial context. Therefore traditional economic analysis has neglected to take into account how choice behaviour depends on the spatial aspects of the environment. Geographical analysis, on the other hand, has explicitly recognised the ways external effects arise within a spatial context. However, geo–

Conceptual Framework

graphical analysis often confines itself to phenomena exhibiting a trivial choice behaviour in response to environmental stimuli.[3] Therefore geographical analysis has traditionally neglected to take into account how choice behaviour depends on preferences.[4] One way of dealing with this problem is through the idea of a *spatial externality*: the mere concept of an externality implies preferences; and the word "spatial" embodies the truth that the environment at a particular location is a set- rather than a point-determined process.[5]

A spatial externality may be understood as follows. Consider a distribution of individuals over some landscape $\mathcal{J}$. Every individual emits an externality which somehow diffuses its impact to other individuals in $\mathcal{J}$. Thus every individual experiences a composite of externalities emitted by individuals over $\mathcal{J}$. We name this composite a spatial externality. If the externality diffusion process is nontrivial (in the sense that the level of a contribution to the externality changes with distance and/or direction from the source) then the level of the spatial externality anywhere in the landscape (and hence the entire distribution of the spatial externality in $\mathcal{J}$) depends on the distribution of individuals in $\mathcal{J}$. Further, a distribution of the spatial externality in $\mathcal{J}$ prompts adjustments which alter the associated distribution of individuals. In this manner one obtains two interacting surfaces unfolding over the landscape—a population surface and an externality surface. The nature of such interaction depends on the nature of the externality diffusion process, in other words on the structure of the spatial externality.

It is conceptually straightforward to generalise these ideas to the case of several interacting classes of agents—in other words to several land uses. Understanding such complex interdependence is the key to developing any sensible theory of land-use planning. Indeed land-use planning is nothing much more than an appropriate arrangement of interacting land uses; and the loaded word "appropriate" implies, among many other things, a knowledge of how land uses react to a complex of spatial externalities.

The idea of a spatial externality covers many phenomena. It

Conceptual Framework

transcends diverse fields of enquiry dealing with the same, fundamental issue of interdependences.[6] Given that various types of externality are conceptually similar, my objective will be to develop an analysis of common structure underlying such phenomena.[7] The main purpose will be to understand (in a general, qualitative manner) how cities respond to different spatial externalities. Toward this end, I first describe an accounting system that allocates externality flows to agents, thus endowing externalities with an explicit spatial distribution. I then examine the possibility of equilibrium in such cities, and close the chapter by discussing a more general equilibrium concept which comes closer to experience. Chapter fifteen analyses a simple model with externalities, while subsequent chapters are devoted to some characteristic spatial externalities.

Composition

In general, the externality received by someone depends on distance from the source, on intensity at the source and, perhaps, on local conditions at the receiving end. Thus, in general, one may write the externality received by someone in area j from those in area i as $E_{ij} = f_{ij}[\rho_i, \rho_j]$. For example, this may describe the time delay to an individual in area j from the traffic congestion contributed by those in area i. It is convenient, however, to adopt a simpler structure that is adequate for our purposes, namely

$$(14.1) \qquad E_{ij} = \zeta_{ij}\, \xi[\rho_i, \rho_j],$$

where ζ is a *distance-response* function which subsumes the externality diffusion process and ξ is a *density-response* function which equals zero if $\rho_i = 0$. In the specification of the distance–response function rests the complex definitional aspect of a spatial externality. In one direction $(i \rightarrow j)$ it introduces the degree of "localness" of the externality

Conceptual Framework

imposed on an individual in area j. In the other direction $(j \to i)$ it introduces the spatial dimensions of the concept of property rights—dimensions related to the mode of economic organisation.[8]

The sign of ζ_{ij} reflects whether the externality received is positive or negative. Normally, the distance–response function will attenuate with distance. If however this function arises as a composite of externality effects, i.e. $\zeta_{ij} = \Sigma_k \zeta_{ij}^k$, then distance response may become more complicated. Consider for example a highway. It generates a positive effect (ζ^1) due to accessibility, and a spatially compact, yet intense, negative effect (ζ^2) due to pollution (figure 14.1(1)). Although both effects attenuate with distance, their composition does not (figure 14.1(2)): to those in its immediate vicinity, the highway acts as a nuisance—a feeling reversed further away where advantages outweigh the corresponding disadvantages.

For analytical simplicity, we shall assume throughout that spatial externality effects are only transmitted along the diameters of our circular city, thereby underlining once more the essentially unidimensional character of our constructs. We shall describe any diagonal as $(-b,...,-1,0,1,...,b)$ and let it represent $\mathcal{J}$, with the understanding that area zero is empty of residences. Thus the spatial externality experienced by someone in area j will be

$$(14.2) \qquad E_j = \sum_{i=-b}^{b} E_{ij}.$$

Using the previous definitions, we may classify the main types of spatial externality as follows.

1. *Urban contact fields.* This is a spatial externality such that the density–response function associated with the externality received by someone in area j depends only on the density in area i. In other words, the density at j is irrelevant to the composition of an urban contact field:

Conceptual Framework

Figure 14.1: A distance–response function.

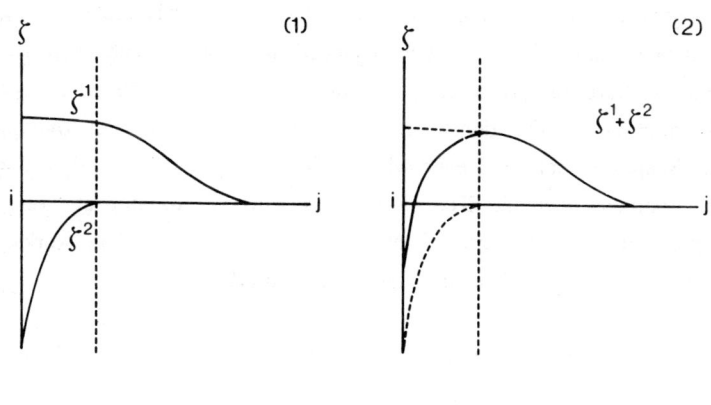

(14.3) $E_{ij} = \zeta_{ij}\, \xi[\rho_i]$.

The concept was introduced by Moore (1970) and elaborated by Dacey (1971). It represents the most widely used model of a spatial externality with applications ranging from interaction to traffic pollution and congestion.[9]

2. *Density models.* A density model of a spatial externality implies that the distance–response function is trivial. We recognise two polar cases. First is the case where there are no spillover effects, so that $|\zeta_{ij}| = 1$ for $i,j \in \mathcal{J}$ and zero otherwise. Applications are to be found in works by Mirrlees (1972) and Yinger (1976). Second is the case where there is no distance response, so that $|\zeta_{ij}| = 1$ for $i,j \in \mathcal{J}$. If, further, the externality is an urban contact field, it represents the usual spaceless situation in economic analysis.[10]

3. *Distance models.* A distance model of a spatial externality implies that the density–response function has a trivial spatial distribution. Once more we recognise two polar cases. First is the case where the extern-

317

Conceptual Framework

ality is generated from a single location: the spatial distribution of the density–response function is a "spike" over the landscape, so that $E_j = E_{ij}$. If, further, the externality is an urban contact field then, for exogenous levels of emission, E_{ij} depends entirely upon a single distance. Hence the term "border model" has become established within the literature on prejudice.[11] Second is the case where the spatial distribution of the density–response function is uniform over the landscape, so that $\xi = 1$ everywhere. The locally uniform quality of the environment, through distance–response, diffuses its impact over $\mathcal{J}$. Applications, in the case of interaction, are to be found in works by Capozza (1973) and Boruchov and Hochman (1977).

When there is a number of interacting land uses, such as housing, commercial, industrial, recreational and other,

$$(14.4) \qquad E_{ij}^{kl} = \zeta_{ij}^{kl} \xi^{kl} [\rho_i^k, \rho_j^l]$$

would represent the externality received by an agent of class l in area j from the agents of class k in area i; the spatial externality experienced by an agent of class l in area j from the agents of class k would be

$$(14.5) \qquad E_j^{kl} = \sum_{i=-b}^{b} E_{ij}^{kl};$$

and the quality of the environment experienced by an agent of class l in area j would be

$$(14.6) \qquad E_j^l = \sum_{k=1}^{m} E_j^{kl}$$

where m is the total number of distinct classes of land use. In this case the city is represented by m density surfaces and by $m \times m$ externality surfaces of the type shown in (5), all, in principle, interdependent.

Conceptual Framework

The essence of city is to be found precisely in this complex interdependence.

Equilibrium

In the absence of externalities, the Casetti equilibrium for individuals described by (4.4) involves a balance between the marginal location effects (MLE) $q_i \Delta_i r$ and $\Delta_i c$ over $\mathcal{J}$, which may be simply expressed as MLE = 0. When the quality of the environment is introduced, the Casetti equilibrium for individuals described by (7.4) involves a balance between MLE and the new marginal externality effect (MEE) $-\lambda_i \cdot (\partial u/\partial E_i)\Delta_i E$ over $\mathcal{J}$, which may now be expressed as MLE + MEE = 0. The distinction between MLE and MEE applies to any type of land use. Indeed, the *spatial equilibrium* for a particular land use (i.e. a state in which all agents of that class enjoy a particular level of well-being over $\mathcal{J}$) implies that, in every area $j \in \mathcal{J}$, there is a balance between the MLE characterising this land use and the corresponding MEE, which describes the interaction between the land use under consideration with itself and with the other land uses. In consequence, the spatial equilibrium of a city composed by several land-uses implies the system

$$(14.7) \qquad (\text{MLE})^l + \sum_{k=1}^{m} (\text{MEE})^{kl} = 0 \; for \; l = 1,...,m$$

which holds for every area of the city. Given that it is possible to express the quantities in (14.7) as functions of density and location, a solution to this system would consist of a set of density functions specifying the spatial distribution of each land use under a state of spatial equilibrium.[12]

All this bears remarkable similarity with the pioneering work of Amson (1972, 1973, 1974 and 1976). Although his origins are to be found in the realm of social physics, thus being alien, or even discredited, to many, the principles of his intuition appear close to those

Conceptual Framework

underlying properly constructed behavioural models. Amson is perhaps the only one who addresses himself explicitly to the problem of solving (14.7) for various types of interacting land use. His externality structure (for continuous space and *two* dimensions)

$$(14.8) \qquad \vec{E}_{ij}^{kl} = \zeta_{ij}^{kl} \rho_i^k \rho_j^l \frac{j-i}{\|j-i\|}$$

is a vector with norm $\|\vec{E}_{ij}^{kl}\|$ obviously corresponding to E_{ij}^{kl} of the present, behavioural framework. If, further, $\zeta_{ij}^{kl} = \|j-i\|^{-1}$ then, for cities possessing locational symmetry, Newton's theorems [13] may be invoked to provide explicit estimates of $\vec{E}_{j}^{kl}$. This constitutes the basis of Amson's work. The emerging series of simple integrated equilibria crucially depend on the form of his "coercion matrix" ([MEE] of note 12).

The aura of complexity and richness surrounding Amson's point of view fascinates me. The special, even conceptually problematic, nature of his endeavours does not affect the promise and the power of his principles. I like to think that he has opened a door to provide us with a fleeting view of the marvels inside; and that the key to this door is the key to a more complete theory of urban land use. Yet problems remain: in the two–dimensional equivalent of system (14.7)

> "it is tacitly postulated that the civic 'forces' (of coercion, relocation inducement, and so on) are vectorial, not only in that they have a unique 'magnitude' and a unique 'spatial direction' but also in that they obey the laws of vector addition and scalar multiplication. This postulate, however convenient for the purposes of analysis, is nevertheless drawn from a questionable analogy between urban systems and mechanical systems, and is an extremely dubious one from an urban studies viewpoint. For example, it seems very unlikely that a citizen, say, exposed to two simultaneous coercions to relocate in two different directions, will

in fact relocate in a direction determined by an application of the 'parallelogram law of resultant forces' from mechanics. From probabilistic considerations alone, such a citizen is much more likely to accept relocation in the direction of the stronger of the two competing coercions." (Amson (1972, p. 434))

Hence until a new, appropriate calculus is developed, system (14.7) must be limited to cities possessing rotational symmetry, where the conceptual reservations about vector additivity disappear. This however is not the end of the difficulties. More often than not, system (14.7) represents an intractable system of differential equations. How fast analytical complications rise with ambition is to be found in Amson (1973), Yellin (1974) and Smith (1976). Issues of existence (McCalden (1975), Fisch (1976) and Smith (1976)) and stability of spatial equilibria have remained obscure. For the second question, Yinger (1976) demonstrates an instability for a spatial equilibrium in the case of an externality arising as a point–determined process, while Yellin (1974) and Smith (1976) demonstrate a possible stability in the case of an externality arising as a set–determined process. How suggestive these early insights are, concerning a relation between stability and the structure of spatial externalities, remains to be seen.

Given the unimaginable complexity of cities, as reflected in system (14.7), it is necessary to establish conditions under which (14.7) has a solution, in other words conditions under which the concept of equilibrium is meaningful for cities. Consider a city of m land uses, each one dispersed throughout the homogeneous urban landscape. For every land use k, there is a continuum of agents $[O,N^k]$ belonging to this class, where N^k is fixed.[14] The spatial distribution of land use k is

(14.9) $\quad n^k \equiv (n_{-b}^k,...,n_b^k) \in \{n^k; \sum_{i=-b}^{b} n_i^k = N^k \text{ and } n_i^k \geq 0\}$

and the spatial distribution of all land uses is $n \equiv (n^1,...,n^m)$. Denote by

Conceptual Framework

u_i^k the level of well-being enjoyed by an agent of class k in area i. For example, u_i^k could represent the utility experienced by an individual in area i or the profit enjoyed by a firm in the same area. Utilities, in general, are continuous functions of the spatial distribution n. Under these circumstances, spatial equilibrium is a distribution n^* in which all agents of class k, $k = 1,...,m$ enjoy the same level of utility, i.e.

$$(14.10) \qquad u_i^k [n^*] \leq u^k [n^*] \text{ for } i \in \mathcal{J}$$

where $u^k \equiv \Sigma_i n_i^k u_i^k / N^k$ is the average level of utility in class k. Notice that $u_i^k < u^k$ in (14.10) implies $n_i^{k*} = 0$. Indeed, by definition of u^k, we have $\Sigma_i n_i^{k*} (u_i^k [n^*] - u^k [n^*]) = 0$. Furthermore, from (14.10), $n_i^{k*} \cdot (u_i^k [n^*] - u^k [n^*]) \leq 0$ for $i \in \mathcal{J}$. Hence, if $n_i^{k*} > 0$ for some i such that $u_i^k [n^*] < u^k [n^*]$, it must be that $\Sigma_i n_i^{k*} (u_i^k [n^*] - u^k [n^*]) < 0$, a contradiction to $\Sigma_i n_i^{k*} (u_i^k [n^*] - u^k [n^*]) = 0$.

We may now maintain that

14.1 *If, for all i and k, u_i^k becomes arbitrarily large when n_i^k becomes arbitrarily small then there exists a symmetric spatial equilibrium with $n \gg 0$.*

It is important to understand what is intuitively implied by the assumptions supporting proposition 14.1. Assuming N^k fixed for all land uses means that we examine the possibility for equilibrium at a particular instant. Given the premises of proposition 14.1, at every instant there is a spatial structure for the city which corresponds to spatial equilibrium, irrespectively of how numerous and complex are the interdependences between the urban elements. Thus, over time, we can envisage a series of spatial equilibria which may form a continuous, evidently unobservable, trajectory. Assuming every u_i^k to be a continuous function of the entire n is a manifestation of complete urban interdependence. Such generality allows for any continuous structure of spatial externalities. Notice that the impact of an externality is not necessarily global: u_i^k could be represented by a constant function over part of n. Hence proposition 14.1 is not restrictive for spatial externalities. Furthermore, one could maintain that demand, supply and prices also depend on spatial distributions. Consider for example two classes of agents: households and firms. Households are attracted to places where the density of firms is high because there the price of the good sold by firms is low owing to a higher degree of competition; and they are repulsed by places where the density of households is high because they dislike congestion. Firms are attracted to places where the density of consumers is high because there the expected volume of business is large; and they are repulsed by places where the density of sellers is high because of the stronger competition prevailing there. It follows that the spatial distribution of both classes concerns everyone in this simple economy. Since this can be generalised to urban systems of any complexity, u_i^k may be taken to subsume not only spatial externalities but also endogenous prices, demands and the like—provided that all these do not violate the continuity of functions u_i^k.

Although the proof of proposition 14.1, to be consistent with the framework of this book, is constructed for cities obeying circular symmetry, it can be modified to allow for any irregularity in spatial distributions.[15] Furthermore, in general, there is no need to demand that utilities become arbitrarily large when consumption of a good becomes arbitrarily large—unless one wants to ascertain that all areas are populated at equilibrium. Thus the concept of spatial equilibrium is meaningful for general patterns of integrated, interacting land uses. The stability of spatial equilibria, on the other hand, appears elusive. In order to examine stability, it is necessary to specify first an adjustment process for our spatial system. A simple adjustment process, consistent with the idea of spatial equilibrium, is given by

Conceptual Framework

$$(14.11) \quad \frac{d}{dt} n_i^k = \begin{cases} u_i^k - \frac{1}{2b} \sum_j u_j^k & \text{for } n_i^k > 0 \\ \max\{0, u_i^k - \frac{1}{2b} \sum_j u_j^k\} & \text{for } n_i^k = 0 \end{cases}$$

for $i \in \mathcal{J}$ and $k = 1,...,m$, where all speeds of adjustment have been normalised to unity. According to this adjustment process, agents are attracted (repulsed) by locations associated with high (low) utility levels. Furthermore, an equilibrium for (14.11) is a spatial equilibrium and vice versa, that is,

$$(14.12) \quad \frac{d}{dt} n_i^k = 0 \text{ if and only if } u_i^k \leq \frac{1}{2b} \sum_j u_j^k$$

$$= \sum_j n_i^k \left[\frac{1}{2b} \sum_j u_j^k \right] \div N^k = u^k.$$

In consequence, flows will stop only under spatial equilibrium. Obviously, a spatial equilibrium need not be stable. For example, it is not difficult to imagine a number of land uses which, overreacting to current differences in the distribution of well-being, never settle down to some invariant spatial pattern. Yet one expects that conditions for stability will hold for at least some spatial equilibria. It is argued in the appendix that, although possible, sufficient conditions for stability are very restrictive: the concept of spatial equilibrium is demanding in the presence of spatial externalities. In their absence, sufficient conditions for stability become less demanding. At the limit, when there is a single class of locally interdependent individuals, the adjustment process (14.12) becomes globally stable. Thus the process toward a Casetti equilibrium described in figure 4.2 is globally stable.

Conceptual Framework

A More General Point of View

Since the concept of spatial equilibrium is central to this book, proposition 14.1 is necessary in order to ascertain the logical foundations of our approach. However, to ask for spatial equilibrium in reality is to ask for too much. The question then would arise of whether spatial equilibrium could be viewed as an extreme case of a more general concept which comes closer to observation. This would be intuitively satisfying and would remove what are, to some extent, legitimate objections about the extensive use of spatial equilibrium in the field: studying the extreme case of some reasonable model is preferable to studying what, for some, appears to be unreasonable.

Consider a city of m interacting, interdependent land uses as in the previous section. Abandon rotational symmetry and let the city extend over a large number b of distinct locations, so that the spatial distribution of land use k now becomes

$$(14.13) \qquad n^k \equiv (n_1^k, ..., n_b^k) \in \{n^k; \sum_{i=1}^{b} n_i^k = N^k \text{ and } n_i^k \geq 0\}.$$

Agents belonging to any particular land use continuously reassess the advantages of their location relative to others, using information available about the spatial distribution of well-being. Since information is imperfect, there is a distinction to be drawn between the actual distribution of well-being and the corresponding perceived distribution. The latter arises within the context of a cognitive model possessed by agents. Assuming that information flows depend on the spatial distribution of agents, so does their judgement concerning the distribution of well-being. Thus although an agent adjusts toward highest perceived opportunities, his behaviour from the viewpoint of an observer can only be described by a set of relocation probabilities which depend upon the spatial distribution of welfare opportunities and, perhaps, directly upon the spatial distribution of agents. These may be expressed as continuous functions of n obeying

$$(14.14) \qquad \sum_j p_{ij}^k = 1 \quad and \quad p_{ij}^k \geq 0$$

for $k = 1,...,m$ and $i,j = 1,...,b$; where p_{ij}^k denotes the probability that an agent of class k will move from location i to j during some short time period.

The city's adjustment process follows a simple conservation principle, namely, that the expected change in the number of agents at i is the expected inflow net of the expected outflow at i:

$$(14.15) \qquad \frac{d}{dt} n_i^k = \sum_j n_j^k p_{ji}^k - \sum_j n_j^k p_{ij}^k = \sum_j n_j^k p_{ji}^k - n_i^k.$$

Here, as in the adjustment process (14.11), all speeds of adjustment have been normalised to unity. A *steady-state* $\bar{n}$ of the city corresponds to no expected change, that is, to $dn_i^k/dt = 0$ for all i and k.[17] The difference between a steady-state and a spatial equilibrium is the following. Whereas a steady-state is characterised by a global balance between corresponding aggregate inflows and outflows, a spatial equilibrium is characterised by a global balance between corresponding marginal costs and marginal benefits arising from changes in location. Since, for every class of agent, such global balance implies that well-being is the same everywhere, a spatial equilibrium of the system is characterised by a global equality of well-being within classes. If, further, agents are rational in all respects then well-being is also maximised, and there is no incentive to relocate. Clearly a spatial equilibrium is a steady-state, but a steady-state may not be a spatial equilibrium: a steady-state is more general and less demanding than the concept of spatial equilibrium.

We have thus arrived at a description of a city closer to observation. Besides the complexity allowed and the generality of spatial form, the description admits an adjustment process founded on behavioural principles which appear intuitively plausible.[18] The outcome of this

Conceptual Framework

adjustment process may be a steady–state which now replaces spatial equilibrium. The question then arises as to whether such steady–states exist and, if so, under what circumstances they are stable, in other words whether a city of various interacting, interdependent land uses may have preferred states. Now

14.2 A steady–state exists.

In order to establish conditions for stability, it is necessary first to describe in some detail how local agglomerations may affect the adjustment process. Clearly, at every moment of adjustment, different locations in the city attract or repulse agents of a particular land use to different degrees. Such differential attractivity is bound to depend on, among other things, the local density of the land use under consideration. For example, a high density of households at i may discourage other households entering. In contrast, a high density of firms at j may encourage other firms to enter. Now the degree of *self-attractivity* associated with a particular area i and land–use k can be represented as $\partial(\Sigma_h n_h^k p_{hi}^k)/\partial n_i^k$. It describes the impact of an increase in the observed size n_i^k on the corresponding expected size $\Sigma_h n_i^k p_{hi}^k$. If a marginal increase in the observed size causes an increase (decrease) in the corresponding expected size then there is increasing (decreasing) self–attractivity for land use k in area i. The next proposition establishes that the stability of an interior steady–state holds for a wide variety of adjustment types, including those that generate moderately increasing self–attractivity. This is somewhat surprising because, in general, increasing returns vitiate equilibrium.

14.3   *If all functions p_{ij}^k are differentiable in $n[t]$ then, for every land use k and area i under increasing (decreasing) self-attractivity, there is a number $v_i^k \leq -1\ (\geq 1)$ such that if self-attractivity is smaller (larger) than $1/(1 - v_i^k)$ for every feasible spatial distribution then the steady-state*

Conceptual Framework

$\bar{n} \gg 0$ *is globally stable. If these restrictions hold in the neighbourhood of a steady-state then* $\bar{n} \gg 0$ *is locally stable.*

The two stability bounds placed on self-attractivity by proposition 14.3 are not symmetric with respect to constant self-attractivity. For decreasing self-attractivity, it can be seen that the bound belongs to $]-\infty,0[$. The extreme case is obtained when an increase in the observed n_i^k, $i = 1,...,b$, does not cause a decrease in any other expected amount. Then the steady-state is globally stable for any corresponding degree of decreasing self-attractivity.[19] On the other hand, the bound for increasing self-attractivity is confined to $]0,1/2[$, with the upper limit corresponding to the case where an increase in the observed n_i^k, $i = 1,...,b$, does not cause an increase in any other expected amount. Since these are sufficient conditions, stability of the steady-state may persist for a wider range of self-attractivity than that established in each case by proposition 14.3.

Appendix to Chapter Fourteen

1

This section of the appendix contains a proof of the proposition that if, for $i \in \mathcal{I}$ and $k = 1,...,m$, u_i^k is continuous in n, then there exists a symmetric spatial equilibrium. The proof is taken from Papageorgiou and Thisse (1985), and follows the lines of Arrow and Hahn (1971, chapter two, theorem 3).

Define the set of symmetric spatial distributions by

(14.16) $\mathcal{S} \equiv \{n;\ n_i^k = n_{-i}^k\ for\ i = 1,...,b\ and\ k = 1,...,m\}.$

Since the urban landscape is homogeneous and since we consider only

Conceptual Framework

symmetric spatial distributions, areas i and $-i$ are interchangeable, so that $u_i^k[n] = u_{-i}^k[n]$ for any $n \in \mathscr{S}$ and $i = 1,\ldots,b$. Denote by $F[s]$ a continuous function from $\mathscr{R}$ in $[0,1]$ such that $F[s] = 0$ for $s \leq 0$ and $F[s] = 1$ for $s \geq \bar{s}$, where $\bar{s}$ is a positive number. Define

$$(14.17) \qquad \psi_i^k[n] \equiv \begin{cases} (1 - F^k[n])\, max\{0, u_i^k[n] - u^k\} + F^k[n] & \text{for } n \gg 0 \\ 1 & \text{otherwise} \end{cases}$$

where $F^k[n] \equiv F[\Sigma_j (u_j^k[n] - u^k)]$. Using the premises of the proposition, it is easy to verify that the functions $n_i^k + \psi_i^k[n]$ are continuous and positive for all i and k. Then

$$(14.18) \qquad H^k[n] \equiv (n^k + \psi^k[n])\, N^k \div \sum_j (n_j^k + \psi_j^k[n]),$$

where $\psi^k[n]$ is the vector with elements $\psi_i^k[n]$ and represents a continuous function from $\mathscr{S}$ into itself. By the theorem of Brouwer it has a fixed point n^* so that

$$(14.19) \qquad \psi^k[n^*] = g^k n^{k*}$$

where $g^k \equiv \Sigma_j (n_j^{k*} + \psi_j^k[n^*])/N^k - 1 \geq 0$. It then follows that $n^* \gg 0$. Indeed, if $n_i^{k*} = 0$ for some i, we would obtain $\psi^k[n^*] = 1$, a contradiction to (14.19).

We now show that n^* is a spatial equilibrium. Multiplying (14.19) by the vector with components $u_i^k[n^*] - u^k[n^*]$, $i = 1,\ldots,b$,

$$(14.20) \qquad \sum_i \psi_i^k[n^*](u_i^k[n^*] - u^k[n^*])$$
$$= g^k \sum_i u_i^{k*}(u_i^k[n^*] - u^k[n^*]).$$

As the RHS of (14.20) is equal to zero, we have

Conceptual Framework

(14.21) $\quad (1 - F^k[n^*]) \sum_i max\{0, u_i^k[n^*] - u^k[n^*]\} \cdot$

$\cdot (u_i^k[n^*] - u^k[n^*]) + F^k[n^*] \sum_i (u_i^k[n^*] - u^k[n^*]) = 0.$

Since the first summation in (14.21) is nonnegative

(14.22) $\quad F^k[n^*] \sum_i (u_i^k[n^*] - u^k[n^*]) \leq 0.$

By definition of $F[s]$, (14.22) holds only if $F^k[n^*] = 0$. Hence, from (14.21), $\Sigma_i max\{0, u_i^k[n^*] - u^k[n^*]\}(u_i^k[n^*] - u^k[n^*]) = 0$ so that $u_i^k[n^*] - u^k[n^*] \leq 0$ for all i which, in turn, implies $u_i^k[n^*] = u^k[n^*]$ for all i. ∎

2

This section of the appendix expounds on difficulties in obtaining sufficient conditions for stability of spatial equilibria. It is based on Ginsburgh, Papageorgiou and Thisse (1985).

In what follows, we assume $n[t] \gg 0$ always. Under these circumstances, the adjustment process (14.13) reduces to

(14.23) $\quad \dfrac{d}{dt} n_j^k = u_j^k - \dfrac{1}{2b} \sum_{h=1}^{b} u_h^k$

for $j = 1,...,b$ and $k = 1,...,m$. Motivated by this adjustment process, construct a mapping $\psi: \mathcal{N} \to \mathcal{R}^{bm}$, where $\mathcal{N}$ is the closed rectangular region $\{n \mid 0 \leq n_i^k \leq N^k\}$ and ψ is a vector of vectors with elements

(14.24) $\quad \psi_j^k = u_j^k - \dfrac{1}{b} \sum_{h=1}^{b} u_h^k$

for $j = 1,...,b$ and $k = 1,...,m$. Suppose that ψ is differentiable in $\mathcal{N}$. The

Jacobian of ψ may be organised as a matrix of matrices ψ^{kl} with elements

$$(14.25) \quad \psi_{ji}^{kl} \equiv \frac{\partial u_j^k}{\partial n_i^l} - \frac{1}{b} \sum_h \frac{\partial u_h^k}{\partial n_i^l}.$$

There are two main types of sufficient condition for the stability of spatial equilibrium associated with the elements of this matrix. The first is based on diagonal dominance of the matrix and the second on substitutability of the elements of the matrix.

1. *Diagonal dominance.* If the Jacobian of ψ has a dominant diagonal with negative elements, i.e. if either

$$(14.26) \quad -\psi_{ii}^{kk} > \sum_{j \neq i} |\psi_{ji}^{kk}| + \sum_{l \neq k} \sum_j |\psi_{ji}^{lk}|$$

(column-wise diagonal dominance) or

$$(14.27) \quad -\psi_{ii}^{kk} > \sum_{j \neq i} |\psi_{ij}^{kk}| + \sum_{l \neq k} \sum_j |\psi_{ij}^{kl}|$$

(row-wise diagonal dominance) then according to a theorem due to Arrow, Block and Hurwicz (1959) the spatial equilibrium is stable. Global stability is obtained if diagonal dominance holds for any feasible spatial distribution. Local stability, on the other hand, is ascertained if diagonal dominance holds only in the neighbourhood of an equilibrium for $i = 1,...,b$ and $k = 1,...,m$. Now

$$(14.28) \quad \psi_{ii}^{kk} + \sum_{j \neq i} \psi_{ji}^{kk}$$

$$= \frac{\partial u_i^k}{\partial n_i^k} - \frac{1}{b} \sum_h \frac{\partial u_h^k}{\partial n_i^k} + \sum_{j \neq i} \frac{\partial u_j^k}{\partial n_i^k} - \frac{1}{b} \sum_{j \neq i} \sum_h \frac{\partial u_h^k}{\partial n_i^k}$$

$$= \sum_j \frac{\partial u_j^k}{\partial n_i^k} - \frac{1}{b} \sum_j \sum_h \frac{\partial u_h^k}{\partial n_i^k}$$

Conceptual Framework

$$= \sum_j \frac{\partial u_j^k}{\partial n_i^k} - \frac{b}{b} \sum_h \frac{\partial u_h^k}{\partial n_i^k} = 0.$$

Therefore

$$(14.29) \quad 0 = \psi_{ii}^{kk} + \sum_{j \neq 1} \psi_{ji}^{kk} \leq \psi_{ii}^{kk} + \sum_{j \neq 1} |\psi_{ji}^{kk}| + \sum_{l \neq k} \sum_j |\psi_{ji}^{lk}|,$$

which rules out column-wise diagonal dominance. Furthermore, notice that either $\psi_{ii}^{kk} + \Sigma_{j \neq i} \psi_{ij}^{kk} = 0$ for all i and k, or there exists i and k such that

$$(14.30) \quad 0 < \psi_{ii}^{kk} + \sum_{j \neq 1} \psi_{ij}^{kk} \leq \psi_{ii}^{kk} + \sum_{j \neq 1} |\psi_{ij}^{kk}| + \sum_{l \neq k} \sum_j |\psi_{ji}^{lk}|,$$

which rules out row-wise diagonal dominance.

When there are no externalities, (14.25) reduces to

$$(14.31) \quad \psi_{ii}^{kk} + \sum_{l \neq k} |\psi_{ii}^{kk}| = \left(1 - \frac{1}{b}\right) \left[\frac{\partial u_i^k}{\partial n_i^k} + \sum_{l \neq k} \left|\frac{\partial u_i^l}{\partial n_i^k}\right|\right] < 0.$$

Since $1 - 1/b$ is positive,

$$(14.32) \quad \frac{\partial u_i^k}{\partial n_i^k} + \sum_{l \neq k} \left|\frac{\partial u_i^l}{\partial n_i^k}\right| < 0$$

for all i and k is sufficient for stability. When there is only one class, global stability requires $\partial u_i / \partial n_i < 0$ for all i. Thus the process toward a Casetti equilibrium of chapter four is globally stable.

2. *Substitutability.* If the Jacobian of ψ is such that $\psi_{ii}^{kk} < 0$ and $\psi_{ij}^{kl} > 0$ for all i, j, k and l and if some other conditions discussed by Arrow, Block and Hurwicz (1959) hold then the spatial equilibrium is stable. In order to examine this possibility, notice first that (14.25)

represents a deviation from the average. The condition $\psi_{ii}^{kk} < 0$ and $\psi_{ij}^{kk} > 0$ for $j \neq i$ is possible because it requires that the local effect on the utility of class k is below average, while all other effects on the utility of the same class are above average. On the other hand, the condition $\psi_{ij}^{kl} > 0$ for $i \neq j$ and $k \neq l$ is impossible because it requires that all effects on the utility of a class are above average. Therefore these sufficient conditions for stability apply only in the case of a single class with externalities. For *gross substitutability*, i.e. $\psi_{ii}^{kk} < 0$ and $\psi_{ij}^{kl} \geq 0$ for all i, j, k and l, sufficient conditions are possible only with $\psi_{ij}^{kl} = 0$ for $i \neq j$ and $k \neq l$. Additional requirements are discussed by Arrow, Block and Hurwicz (1959).

Since the above are only sufficient conditions for the stability of spatial equilibrium, stability may hold under less demanding circumstances. However, it seems from the previous discussion that stability of spatial equilibria is not easy to obtain in the general case.

3

This section of the appendix contains a proof of the proposition that if all functions p_{ij}^k are continuous in $n[t]$ then a steady-state exists. The proof is based on Grunberg and Modigliani (1954).

A steady-state is defined as

(14.33) $$\sum_j n_j^k p_{ji}^k = n_i^k.$$

Using (14.13) and (14.14)

(14.34) $$\sum_i \sum_j n_j^k p_{ji}^k = \sum_j n_j^k \sum_i p_{ji}^k = N^k.$$

Therefore

Conceptual Framework

(14.35) $$\sum_j n_j^k p_{ji}^k \leq N^k$$

because n_j^k and p_{ji}^k cannot be negative, also by (14.13) and (14.14). Define a vector function F with components $\Sigma_j n_j^k p_{ji}^k$ for $i = 1,...,b$ and $k = 1,...,m$. In view of (14.34) and (14.35), F maps from a product of simplices with nonnegative elements to itself. It is also continuous in n. Therefore, according to the theorem of Brouwer, there exists $\bar{n} > 0$ such that $F|_{\bar{n}} = \bar{n}$. This, together with (14.33), ensures that $\bar{n}$ is indeed a steady-state. ∎

4

This section of the appendix contains a proof of the proposition that if all functions p_{ij}^k are differentiable in $n[t]$ then, for every land use k and area i under increasing (decreasing) self-attractivity, there is a number $v_i^k \leq -1$ (≥ 1) such that if self-attractivity is smaller (larger) than $1/(1 - v_i^k)$ for every feasible spatial distribution then the steady-state $\bar{n} \gg 0$ is globally stable; and that if these restrictions hold in the neighbourhood of a steady-state then $\bar{n} \gg 0$ is locally stable. This is based on Ginsburgh, Papageorgiou and Thisse (1985).

Construct a mapping $\psi : \mathcal{N} \to \mathcal{R}^{bm}$, where ψ is a vector of vectors with elements

(14.36) $$\psi_j^k = \sum_{h=1}^{b} n_h^k p_{hj}^k - n_j^k$$

for $j = 1,...,b$ and $k = 1,...,m$. By assumption, ψ is differentiable in $\mathcal{N}$. The Jacobian of ψ may be organised as a matrix of matrices ψ^{kl} with elements ψ_{ji}^{kl}, where

$$(14.37) \quad \psi_{ji}^{kl} \equiv \frac{\partial \psi_j^k}{\partial n_i^l} = \frac{\partial}{\partial n_i^l} \sum_h n_h^k p_{hj}^k$$

for $i \neq j$ or $k \neq l$ or both, and

$$(14.38) \quad \psi_{ii}^{kk} \equiv \frac{\partial \psi_i^k}{\partial n_i^k} = \frac{\partial}{\partial n_i^l} \sum_h n_h^k p_{hi}^k - 1$$

for the diagonal elements. Taking into account (14.34), (14.37) and (14.38)

$$(14.39) \quad \frac{\partial}{\partial n_i^l} \sum_j \sum_h n_h^k p_{hj}^k = \sum_j \frac{\partial}{\partial n_i^l} \sum_h n_h^k p_{hi}^k = \sum_j \psi_{ji}^{kl} = 0$$

$$(14.40) \quad \frac{\partial}{\partial n_i^k} \sum_j \sum_h n_h^k p_{hj}^k = \psi_{ii}^{kk} + 1 + \sum_{j \neq 1} \psi_{ji}^{kk} = 0.$$

Therefore

$$(14.41) \quad \psi_{ii}^{kk} + 1 + \sum_{j \neq i} \psi_{ji}^{kk} + \sum_{l \neq k} \sum_j \psi_{ji}^{kl} = 0.$$

Now let v_i^k be defined by

$$(14.42) \quad v_i^k(\psi_{ii}^{kk} + 1) + \sum_{j \neq i} |\psi_{ji}^{kk}| + \sum_{l \neq k} \sum_j |\psi_{ji}^{kl}| = 0.$$

Comparison between (14.41) and (14.42) leads immediately to $|v_i^k| \geq 1$. Furthermore

$$(14.43) \quad (1 - v_i^k)(\psi_{ii}^{kk} + 1) < 1$$

implies

$$(14.44) \quad -\psi_{ii}^{kk} > \sum_{j \neq i} |\psi_{ji}^{kk}| + \sum_{l \neq k} \sum_j |\psi_{ji}^{kl}|,$$

that is, the Jacobian of ψ has a dominant diagonal with negative elements.

Conceptual Framework

When there is increasing self–attractivity, i.e. $\psi_{ii}^{kk} + 1 > 0$, (14.40) implies $\Sigma_{j \neq i} \psi_{ji}^{kk} < 0$ which, in turn, implies $v_i^k \leq -1$ or, equivalently, $1 - v_i^k \geq 2$. When there is decreasing self–attractivity, $v_i^k \geq 1$ or, equivalently, $1 - v_i^k \leq 0$. Thus, in general, condition (14.43) places an upper bound $1/(1 - v_i^k)$ on the degree of self–attractivity for a land use under increasing self–attractivity and, if $v_i^k \neq 1$, a corresponding lower bound for a land use under decreasing self–attractivity. ∎

Suppose that an increase in the observed size n_i^k does not cause a decrease in any other expected size, that is,

$$(14.45) \quad \sum_{j \neq i} |\psi_{ji}^{kk}| + \sum_{l \neq k} \sum_{j} |\psi_{ji}^{kl}| = \sum_{j \neq i} \psi_{ji}^{kk} + \sum_{l \neq k} \sum_{j} \psi_{ji}^{kl}.$$

Then land use k in area i must be under decreasing self–attractivity, and $v_i^k = 1$ upon comparison between (14.41) and (14.42). In this case (14.43) is satisfied for any degree of self–attractivity so that the characteristics of land use k in area i do not impose any restrictions on the stability of a steady–state. On the other hand, suppose that an increase in the observed size n_i^k does not cause an increase in any other expected size, that is,

$$(14.46) \sum_{j \neq i} |\psi_{ji}^{kk}| + \sum_{l \neq k} \sum_{j} |\psi_{ji}^{kl}| = -\sum_{j \neq i} \psi_{ji}^{kk} - \sum_{l \neq k} \sum_{j} \psi_{ji}^{kl}.$$

Then land use k in area i must be under increasing self–attractivity and $v_i^k = -1$. In this case the stability condition is satisfied for self–attractivity smaller than one–half. Notice that the two extreme bounds on stability obtain when an increase in some observed size has the same qualitative impact upon all other expected sizes. As this impact becomes progressively mixed, that is, as $|\Sigma_{j \neq i} \psi_{ji}^{kk} + \Sigma_{l \neq k} \Sigma_j \psi_{ji}^{kl}|$ becomes smaller, the stability condition places more stringent demands on self–attractivity.

Notes to Chapter Fourteen

1. This chapter draws from Papageorgiou (1978A, 1978B). Most of the analysis on existence and stability is based on Ginsburgh, Papageorgiou and Thisse (1985). Papageorgiou and Thisse (1985) is also used.

2. Marcus Aurelius (175, Book 7.9) for example maintains that "παντα αλληλοις επιπλεκεται και η συνδεσις ιερα και σχεδον τι ουδεν αλλοτριον αλλο αλλω" which means that "everything is interwoven with everything else and the bond is holy, and there is hardly anything that is alien to any other thing".

3. The classic case is diffusion of innovations, exemplified by the work of Hägerstrand (1967).

4. This is why behavioural geography emerged. Nevertheless, to this day, behavioural geography, confined within the limits of *ad hoc* conceptualisation and detailed empiricism, has not been endowed with a substantive deductive foundation.

5. For a detailed definition and classification of externalities see the introductory chapters in Baumol and Oates (1975).

6. See for example Haken (1974).

7. The effect of smoke on my welfare decreases with distance from the source. So does the effect of a black (white) presence on the welfare of a white (black) racist.

8. In commenting on the specification of the distance–response function, I could do no better than to paraphrase Fisch (1976). The affinity of the spatial externality structure with the established

Conceptual Framework

concept of the potential in macrogeography is obvious (see Carrothers (1956) and Wilson (1967)).

9   Studies of urban contact fields as models of interaction include those by Solow and Vickrey (1971), Kraus (1974), Vaughan (1975) and Beckmann (1976). Models of pollution from stationary sources are represented by Robson (1976B). Models of pollution from moving sources relevant to urban contact fields include those by Rydell and Stevens (1968), Oron, Pines and Sheshinski (1974) and Riley (1974). Models of congestion from moving sources relevant to urban contact fields include those by Lave (1970), Solow (1972, 1973), Legey, Ripper and Varaiya (1973), Oron, Pines and Sheshinski (1973), Hochman (1975), Kanemoto (1975, 1976), and Barr (1976). Models of prejudice are represented by Yellin (1974).

10 See for example Seskin (1973), Henderson (1974A) and Tolley (1974).

11 See Courant (1974), Rose–Ackermann (1975, 1977), White (1977), and Courant and Yinger (1977). Border models of pollution include those by Stull (1974), Helpman and Pines (1975B), Oron and Pines (1975) and Strotz and Wright (1975).

12 The $m \times m$ matrix [MEE] with elements $(MEE)^{kl}$ is the key descriptor of the interactions between different land uses. For example, in the case of two land uses,

$$[MEE] = \begin{bmatrix} + & - \\ - & + \end{bmatrix}$$

means that both land uses are self–averted and attracted by each other, and

$$[\text{MEE}] = \begin{bmatrix} 0 & - \\ 0 & + \end{bmatrix}$$

means that the first land use is self–indifferent and attracted by the other, while the second land use is indifferent to the other and self–averted.

13   Newton's theorems in two dimensions state that, if $\vec{E}^{kl}$ is a Newtonian attraction and for cities possessing rotational symmetry: (1) the spatial externality to an agent of class l at j from class k outside the central circle drawn through j has a net value of zero; and (2) the spatial externality to an agent of class l at j from class k inside the central circle drawn through j is the same as that obtained if the entire class k inside the central circle drawn through j were located at zero.

14   In order to prove existence we must deal with continuous population distributions, contrary to the standard practice of this book.

15   See Ginsburgh, Papageorgiou and Thisse (1985).

16   Although u_i^k in (14.10) is compared with average utility within class k, in (14.11) it is compared with average utility across locations. This happens because, at spatial equilibrium, all agents must reach the same utility level while, out of spatial equilibrium, every agent is concerned with the utility level that he can reach at different locations.

17   This concept is essentially that of Miyao (1978).

18   These principles are general enough to allow for any continuous pattern of relocation costs through a proper specification of how actual and perceived levels of well–being, as viewed from a

particular location by an agent belonging to a particular class, are distributed over the city.

19   See end of section 4 of the appendix.

15

Spatial Externalities and the City

Following the ideas of chapter fourteen, utility in this chapter is written as

(15.1) $\quad u_i = u[x_i, q_i, E_i[n]]$

thus taking explicitly into account that the quality of the environment depends on spatial distributions. The problems for the individuals and the planner remain (11.1) and (11.9) respectively. Clearly, conditions (11.3) and (11.11), associated with the consumption of the private good, still hold. The same is true for conditions (13.1) and (13.2) associated with the decision where to locate. Therefore the only difference arising between this model and the model of chapter thirteen concerns decisions associated with the consumption of land. When the quality of the environment is exogenous, decisions associated with the consumption of land are determined by (11.4) and (11.12) for the individuals and the planner respectively. Now that the quality of the environment depends on spatial distributions, (11.12) becomes

Spatial Externalities

(15.2) $$\bar{y}_i + (n_i + 1)\underset{n_i}{\triangle} \bar{y} - \underset{N}{\triangle} X$$
$$- \left[\mu_i \frac{dv}{du_i}\frac{\partial u}{\partial q_i}\underset{n_i}{\triangle} q + \sum_j \mu_j \frac{dv}{du_j}\frac{\partial u}{\partial E_j}\underset{n_i}{\triangle} E_j\right]\bigg|_{u=v} = 0$$

where $u \equiv (u_1,...,u_b)$ and $v \equiv (v_1,...,v_b)$. The difference, arising here because of the endogenous quality of the environment, is represented by the last term in (15.2) which describes the effect of someone as being diffused through the spatial externality on others. The quantity $\Delta_{n_i} E_j$ represents the change of environmental quality in area j because of the addition of someone in area i. The quantity $-(\partial u/\partial E_j)\Delta_{n_i} E_j$ represents the value of this change to someone in area j. The quantity $-(dv/du_j)(\partial u/\partial E_j)\Delta_{n_i} E_j$ represents the social evaluation of this change. Thus the last term in (15.2) represents the total change in social welfare stemming from changes in the quality of the environment which are caused by the addition of someone in area i. This is further to the other effects already discussed in conjuction with (11.12).

In principle, analogous modifications would be expected in the case of individual decisions.[1] However, it is very unlikely that an individual would take into account the effect of his presence on the overall quality of the environment. The argument is similar to the one used for substantiating the parametric treatment of land rents and tax rates, namely, that the effect of any particular individual on the quality of his environment is negligible, especially in the case of large metropolitan areas. Thus individuals, when deciding whether or not to locate in some area, take into account the existing average, rather than marginal, levels of pollution, congestion and other determinants of environmental quality: individuals treat the environment parametrically. In consequence, (11.4) is taken to represent individual decisions associated with the consumption of land even when the quality of the environment becomes endogenous.

Optimal Decentralisation Policy

The conditions relevant to optimal decentralisation policy are collected in table 15.1. Applying (12.3) in (15.2) and taking into account (12.8) we obtain

$$(15.3) \quad \left[n_i \left[r[i] - \lambda_i \right] \frac{\partial u}{\partial q_i} \underset{n_i}{\Delta} q - \sum_j n_j \lambda_j \frac{\partial u}{\partial E_j} \underset{n_i}{\Delta} E_j \right] \Big|_{u=z} = 0$$

because $\upsilon = z$ at the optimum. Comparison between (11.4) and (15.3) indicates that individual decisions concerning the consumption of land deviate from the corresponding public decisions by the second of the two terms in (15.3). Indeed, if the planner sets a marginal rate on the consumption of land equal to

$$(15.4) \quad \phi_i^n = -\frac{1}{n_i} \sum_j n_j \lambda_j \frac{\partial u}{\partial E_j} \underset{n_i}{\Delta} E_j \Big|_{u=z}$$

and if this marginal rate is taken parametrically by the individuals then (11.4) would be augmented by ϕ_i^n and would become equivalent to (15.3) at the optimum.

It has already been shown that the expression under the sum on the RHS of (15.4) is associated with the total change in social welfare stemming from changes in the quality of the environment which are caused by the addition of someone in area i. Since individuals do not take into account the effect of their presence upon the quality of the environment experienced over the city, the expression under the sum on the RHS of (15.4) must represent the NMSC (or NMSB) of those in area i associated with their consumption of land, in other words, with the land-use intensity found in area i. Since there is no distinction between individuals in area i, this marginal effect must be equally borne by everyone there—hence the division by n_i. The minus sign ascertains that if $\Delta_{n_i} E_j$ is negative (that is, if further congestion is a cost) then ϕ_i^n will be positive (a tax), and if $\Delta_{n_i} E_j$ is positive then ϕ_i^n will be negative (a subsidy). Thus (15.4) represents another instance of the correction

Table 15.1: Decision rules.

	Optimality conditions
	Planner
x_i	(11.11): $n_i \dfrac{\partial y}{\partial x_i} - \mu_i \dfrac{dv}{du_i}\dfrac{\partial u}{\partial x_i}\big|_{u_i = v_i} =$ (12.4): $n_i\left[1 - \lambda_i \dfrac{\partial u}{\partial x_i}\right]\big|_{u_i = z[i]} = 0$
n_i	(15.2): $\bar{y}_i + (n_i + 1)\bigtriangleup_{n_i}\bar{y} - \bigtriangleup_N X - \left[\mu_i \dfrac{dv}{du_i}\dfrac{\partial u}{\partial q_i}\bigtriangleup_{n_i} q + \sum_j \mu_j \dfrac{dv}{du_j}\dfrac{\partial u}{\partial E_j}\bigtriangleup_{n_i} E_j\right]\big|_{u=v} =$ $\left[n_i\left[r[i] - \lambda_i \dfrac{\partial u}{\partial q_i}\right]\bigtriangleup_{n_i} q + \right.$ $\left.\left[\left[\bar{y}_i + \bigtriangleup_n \bar{y}\right] - \bigtriangleup_N X\right] - \sum_j n_j \lambda_j \dfrac{\partial u}{\partial E_j}\bigtriangleup_{n_i} E_j\right]\big|_{u=z} = 0$
i	(13.2): $n_i \bigtriangleup_i \bar{y} + \mu_i\left[\bigtriangleup_i \bar{z} - \dfrac{dv}{du_i}\dfrac{\partial u}{\partial E_i}\bigtriangleup_i E\right]\big|_{u_i = v_i} =$ (13.5): $n_i\left[\lambda_i\left[\bigtriangleup_i z - \dfrac{\partial u}{\partial E_i}\bigtriangleup_i E\right]\big|_{u_i = z[i]} + \left[\dfrac{\mu_i}{n_i} - \lambda_i\right]\bigtriangleup_i z\right] = 0$

	Individuals	Decentralisation
(11.3):	$1 - \lambda_i \frac{\partial u}{\partial x_i}\big|_{u_i = z[i]} = 0$	No correction
(11.4):	$\left[r[i] - \lambda_i \frac{\partial u}{\partial q_i}\right] \underset{n_i}{\triangle} q \big|_{u_i = z[i]} = 0$	$\bar{y}_i + \underset{n_i}{\triangle} \bar{y} = \underset{N}{\triangle} X$ and $\phi_i^n = -\frac{1}{n_i} \sum_j n_j \lambda_j \frac{\partial u}{\partial E_i} \underset{n_i}{\triangle} E_j \big|_{u = z}$
(13.3):	$\lambda_i \left[\underset{i}{\triangle} z - \frac{\partial u}{\partial E_i} \underset{i}{\triangle} E\right]\big|_{u_i = z[i]} = 0$	$\phi_i^i = \left[\frac{\mu_j}{n_i} - \lambda_i\right] \underset{i}{\triangle} z$ $= (1 - \bar{u}_i^{-\alpha}) \lambda_i \frac{\partial u}{\partial E_i} \underset{i}{\triangle} E \big|_{u_i = z[i]}$

Spatial Externalities

principle. Finally, since the only difference between the optimal city with an endogenous and an exogenous quality of the environment is to be found in the additional planning requirement (15.4), the only change occurs in the optimal tax which now takes the form

$$(15.5) \qquad \phi_i = n_i \phi_i^n + i\phi_i^i - \bar{\phi}.$$

In all other respects, *the optimal decentralisation policy of chapter fourteen remains*. In consequence, the solution procedure of that chapter also remains, except that $\phi[i, \alpha, \mathscr{N}] = \phi_i - \bar{\phi}$ is now determined using (13.7), (15.4) and (15.5).

Comparison Between Private Goods and Spatial Externalities [2]

The condition (12.4) for the consumption of the private good may be written as

$$(15.6) \qquad 1 = \lambda_i \frac{\partial u}{\partial x_i}.$$

On the other hand, using (15.4) and (15.5) and assuming no redistribution, the optimal tax to be paid by someone in area i for his contribution to the spatial externality is

$$(15.7) \qquad n_i \phi_i^n = -\sum_j n_j \lambda_j \frac{\partial u}{\partial E_j} \underset{n_i}{\triangle} E_j \equiv -\sum_j n_j \phi_{ij}^n$$

where

$$(15.8) \qquad \phi_{ij}^n = \lambda_j \frac{\partial u}{\partial E_j} \underset{n_i}{\triangle} E_j.$$

Now the LHS of (15.6) denotes the amount of money an individual in area i is prepared to pay at the optimum for increasing his consumption of the private good by one unit with utility held constant. On the other hand, ϕ_{ij}^n in (15.8) denotes the amount of money an individual in area j is prepared to pay at the optimum for increasing the number of individuals in area i by one, thereby altering the experienced level of spatial externality, with utility held constant. Given that the quantities ϕ_{ij}^n may be thought of as "prices", an individual in area i, as externality generator, may be thought of as being "compensated" by the aggregate sum that these "prices" generate at the optimum.

A crucial difference between private goods and spatial externalities is the following. Under optimal conditions, whereas in the case of a private good individuals consume different quantities at the same marginal cost (one dollar), in the case of a positive (negative) spatial externality individuals "consume" the same quantity (n_i) at different levels of marginal cost (benefit) represented by ϕ_{ij}^n. This is essentially the distinction between (15.6) and (15.7), illustrated in figure 15.1. Consider two individuals, each in a different area. The demands of these individuals for the private good appear in figure 15.1(1) as lines D_1 and

Figure 15.1: Aggregation of individual demands.

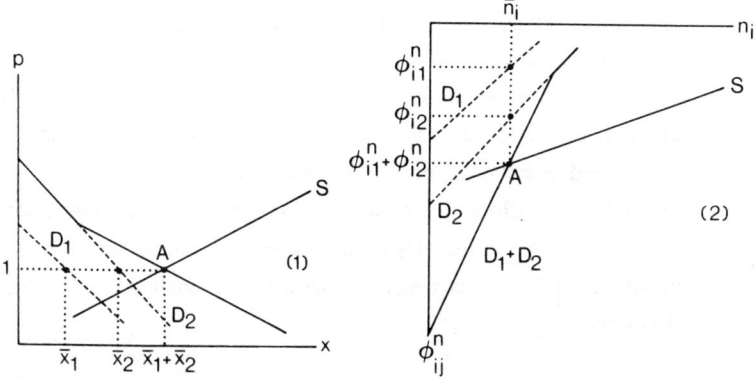

Spatial Externalities

D_2. Aggregate demand, $D_1 + D_2$, is obtained by *horizontal* addition of individual demands because the total amount consumed is the sum of individual amounts. Equality of supply S and demand at A determines a common price, 1 (which in this book is treated as exogenous throughout), individual consumptions $\bar{x}_1$ and $\bar{x}_2$ and therefore total consumption. Notice that the vertical distance under each individual's demand curve reflects the social valuation of the marginal benefit which he gains from consumption, i.e. $\lambda_i \partial u/\partial x_i$ for $i = 1,2$, and this equals the corresponding marginal cost, 1, as in (15.6). Thus efficiency is ascertained without any need for further correction—as it has already been established by the optimal decentralisation rules. Indeed

> "... perfect competition among productive enterprises would ensure that goods are produced at minimum costs and are sold at proper marginal costs, with all factors receiving their proper marginal productivities; and ... each individual, in seeking as a competitive buyer to get to the highest level of indifference subject to given prices and tax, would be led as if by an Invisible Hand to the grand solution of the social maximum position. Of course the institutional framework of competition would have to be maintained, and political decision-making would still be necessary, but of a computationally minimum type: namely, algebraic taxes and transfers ... would have to be varied until society is swung to the ethical observer's optimum. The servant of the ethical observer would not have to make explicit decisions about each person's detailed consumption and work; he need only decide about generalized purchasing power, knowing that each person can be counted on to allocate it optimally. In terms of communication theory and game terminology, each person is motivated to do the signalling of his tastes needed to define and reach the attainable bliss point."[3]

Similarly to the case of the private good, the individual "demands" for a negative spatial externality are represented in figure 15.1(2) by lines D_1 and D_2. (A positive spatial externality would be represented by the reflection of figure 15.1(2) about the abscissa.) Aggregate "demand", $D_1 + D_2$, is obtained by *vertical* addition of individual demands because each "consumes" the same amount. "Demand" here is a schedule of potential compensations necessary to maintain utility at different levels of land-use intensity in area i. "Supply" S, on the other hand, is a schedule of optimal land-use intensity in area i at different levels of externality damage. Equality of "supply" and "demand" at A determines a "consumption" $\bar{n}_i$, individual "prices" ϕ_{i1}^n and ϕ_{i2}^n and therefore total "revenue". This last is used to "compensate" the externality generator at i, that is, individuals at i must pay a total amount equal to $-(\phi_{i1}^n + \phi_{i2}^n)$ in order to account for their damage on the two others. Notice that the vertical distance above each individual's "demand" curve reflects the social valuation of the marginal cost which he incurs from "consumption", that is, $\lambda_j (\partial u/\partial E_j) \Delta_{ni} E_j$ for $j = 1,2$, and this equals the corresponding potential marginal benefit ϕ_{ij}^n as in (15.8). Thus efficiency is ascertained. At this point, the sum of social valuations of net marginal costs of individuals equals the total potential compensation to be paid, one for which the individual at i must be accountable irrespectively of whether the others are compensated or not.[4]

Contrary to the case of the private good, where every individual exposes the relevant part of his tastes by seeking to satisfy (15.6), individual tastes in the case of the spatial externality are hidden under the summation symbol of (15.7). The staggering information requirements for optimality, and other implications of this mathematical structure, have already been discussed in one of the "theory and reality" sections of chapter fourteen. What compounds the difficulty even further is the incentive for wrong signalling by the individuals under the summation symbol. For example, suppose that the recipients of the externality are not compensated. Then they must have an incentive to *overstate* the effects of the spatial externality. In this manner each hopes that he will cause an increase (decrease) in the output of the positive

Spatial Externalities

(negative) externality, thereby increasing his welfare. False signalling here produces an output more (less) than the optimal.[5] Of course

> "one could imagine every person in the community being indoctrinated to behave like a "parametric decentralized bureaucrat" who *reveals* his preferences by signalling in response to price parameters or Lagrangian multipliers, to questionnaires, or to other devices. But there is still this fundamental technical difference going to the heart of the whole problem of *social* economy: by departing from his indoctrinated rules, any one person can hope to snatch some selfish benefit in a way not possible under the self-policing competitive pricing of private goods; and the "external economies" or "jointness of demand" intrinsic to the very concept of collective goods and governmental activities makes it impossible for the grand ensemble of optimizing equations to have that special pattern of zeros which makes *laissez-faire* competition even *theoretically* possible as an analogue computer."[6]

In consequence, the optimal city under externalities remains surrounded by invisible barriers: although we see its abstract form, we cannot touch it.[7]

Aggregate Relationships at the Optimum [8]

Recalling (12.3), (15.2) may be written

$$(15.9) \quad -n_i \lambda_i \frac{\partial u}{\partial q_i} \bigtriangleup_{n_i} q - \sum_j n_j \lambda_j \frac{\partial u}{\partial E_j} \bigtriangleup_{n_i} E_j$$

$$= \bigtriangleup_N X - \left[\bar{y}_i + \left[n_i + 1 \right] \bigtriangleup_{n_i} \bar{y} \right].$$

Following the same procedure as in the corresponding section of chapter twelve and aggregating over the city

(15.10) $\sum_i \lambda_i \frac{\partial u}{\partial q_i} \underset{i-1}{\Delta} Q - \sum_i (n_i + 1) \sum_j n_j \lambda_j \frac{\partial u}{\partial E_j} \underset{n_i}{\Delta} E_j$

$= \sum_i (n_i + 1) \left[\underset{N}{\Delta} X - \left[\bar{y}_i + (n_i + 1) \underset{n_i}{\Delta} \bar{y} \right] \right].$

Comparing this with (12.17), we see that the two equations differ with respect to their LHSs. Firstly, the shadow value of urban land $\lambda_i (\partial u/\partial q_i)$ remains in (15.10) because it does not equal the corresponding rent as in (12.17). Therefore the first term on the LHS of (15.10) can be interpreted as the total shadow value of urban land $\tilde{R}$. Secondly, since $\Sigma_j n_j \lambda_j (\partial u/\partial E_j) \cdot \Delta_{n_i} E_j$ denotes the total change in social welfare stemming from changes in the quality of the environment caused by an individual in area i, the new term in (15.10) represents the total effect E on social welfare of the spatial externality at the optimum. Therefore

15.1 *The difference between the total shadow value of urban land and the total externality effect equals the total surplus value of urban production at the optimum.*

When the spatial externality is positive (negative), proposition 15.1 implies that the total shadow value of urban land is larger (smaller) than the total surplus value of urban production at the optimum. Thus urban shadow values compensate for the presence of the spatial externality in a way dictated by intuition: a negative spatial externality lowers shadow values, and vice versa.

It is possible to relate market and shadow land values through the externality. Taking into account (12.8), (15.2) can be written as

(15.11) $\left[r[i] - \lambda_i \frac{\partial u}{\partial q_i} \right] \underset{i-1}{\Delta} Q = (n_i + 1) \sum_j n_j \lambda_j \frac{\partial u}{\partial E_j} \underset{n_i}{\Delta} E_j$

which, upon aggregation, implies that

15.2 *The difference between total market and shadow land values equals the total externality effect at the optimum.*

Spatial Externalities

Since (12.10) holds, proposition 4.2 also holds. Combining it with propositions 15.1 and 15.2, we obtain

15.3   *If the elasticity of the urban area with respect to distance is constant over distance then*

$$R = S + 2E >(=,<) \check{R} + \frac{1}{n_{Q:i}} C$$

according to whether the elasticity of transportation costs with respect to distance is greater than (equal to, smaller than) unity.[9]

As in chapter twelve, the total surplus value of production represents benefits of urbanisation, while the total value of urban land removed from production in the alternative sector and the total cost of urban transportation represent costs of urbanisation. On the other hand, the spatial externality enters this balance as a benefit or cost of urbanisation according to whether it is positive or negative. Finally, as in chapter twelve, it is worth noticing that propositions 15.1–15.3 are independent of the underlying theory of justice employed.

Adjustment to Spatial Externalities[10]

The way individuals respond to a spatial externality when both optimal land values and bid-rents equal the shadow value of land has been described by proposition 13.1—given that consumption remains insensitive to variations in the spatial externality. This proposition implies that (1) the optimum under zero aversion becomes more (less) compact relative to the corresponding equilibrium with externality if $\Delta_i E >(<) 0$; (2) the optimum under zero aversion becomes less (more) compact relative to the corresponding equilibrium with externality if $\Delta_i E <(>) 0$.

When the quality of the environment is endogenous, further to the *spatial externality effect* just described, spatial adjustments are also influenced by a *land-value effect*. This happens because, although bid–rents still equal the shadow value of land, optimal rents do not. In particular, (11.4) and (15.11) imply

(15.12) $r_i - \bar{r}_i >(=,<) 0$ *if and only if* $\bigwedge\limits_{n_i} E >(=,<) 0$

which, in turn, implies that (3) the optimum under zero aversion becomes more (less) compact relative to the corresponding equilibrium with externality if $\Delta_{n_i} E_j >(<) 0$. Combining statements (1) and (3), the spatial externality and land–value effects work in the same direction for a positive (negative) externality increasing (decreasing) away from the centre. On the other hand, combining statements (2) and (3), the spatial externality and land–value effects work in the opposite direction for a positive (negative) externality decreasing (increasing) away from the centre. In this case it is not possible to determine whether the optimum under zero aversion is more or less compact relative to the corresponding equilibrium. However, *proposition 13.2 still holds.*

I now employ these remarks to determine how cities adjust to a number of major spatial externalities. In order to save some notation, the examples are structured as the simplest possible urban contact fields and applied to a linear city, where $\rho_i = n_i$. However, the same procedure could be used for externality diffusion patterns of any complexity— given that consumption remains insensitive to variations in the spatial externality.

1. *Pollution from stationary sources.* Consider a city where industry and residences are integrated. Robson (1976B) maintains that pollution in such a city would exhibit a definite, radial, outward bias. Following his view assume, in the simplest case, that pollution from stationary

Spatial Externalities

sources diffuses without distance decay. Someone in area j is polluted by those closer to the centre:

(15.13) $\quad E_{ij} = \zeta_{ij} n_i \text{ with } \zeta_{ij} = \begin{cases} -1 \text{ for } i \leq j \\ 0 \text{ for } i > j. \end{cases}$

Therefore

(15.14) $\quad E_j = -\sum_{i=1}^{j} n_i$

(15.15) $\quad \underset{j}{\Delta} E = -\left[\sum_{i=1}^{j+1} - \sum_{i=1}^{j} \right] n_i = -n_{j+1} < 0.$

It follows that the competitive adjustment to pollution from stationary sources will result in a city more compact than the corresponding optimum under zero aversion to inequality. Also, using (13.6) and under finite aversion to inequality, optimal utility decreases with distance from the centre. Further, as the aversion to inequality increases, the corresponding optimal city contracts and the level of social welfare decreases together with social inequality.

2. *Pollution from moving sources.* Pollution from moving sources is proportional to the corresponding congestion. Suppose that travel is only toward the centre. Along a given dense, radial transportation network, additional congestion at j is generated by those further away. Thus pollution from moving sources exhibits a direction bias opposite to that of pollution from stationary sources:

(15.16) $\quad E_{ij} = \zeta_{ij} n_i \text{ with } \zeta_{ij} = \begin{cases} -1 \text{ for } i \geq j \\ 0 \text{ for } i < j. \end{cases}$

Therefore

(15.17) $$E_j = -\sum_{i=j}^{b} n_i$$

(15.18) $$\triangle_j E = -\left[\sum_{i=j+1}^{b} - \sum_{i=j}^{b}\right] n_i = n_j > 0.$$

It follows that, under finite aversion to inequality, optimal utility increases with distance from the centre. Further, as the aversion to inequality increases, the corresponding optimal city disperses and the level of social welfare decreases together with social inequality.

3. *Congestion from stationary sources.* Congestion from stationary sources arises from closeness: if the average distance from everyone in $\mathcal{J}$ decreases, congestion increases. Hence we may study a distance weighted by the inverse of density at the source as a positive externality:

(15.19) $$E_{ij} = |i-j| n_i^{-1}.$$

Therefore

(15.20) $$E_j = \sum_{i \neq j} |i-j| n_i^{-1}$$

(15.21) $$\triangle_j E = \sum_{i=-b}^{j-1} \triangle_j (j-i) n_i^{-1} + \sum_{i=j+1}^{b} \triangle_j (i-j) n_i^{-1}$$
$$= \left[\sum_{i=-b}^{j-1} - \sum_{i=j+1}^{b}\right] n_i^{-1} > 0$$

for $i > 0$ because the spatial distribution n is symmetric about zero. Thus the adjustment to congestion from stationary sources will be qualitatively the same as that caused by pollution from moving sources.[11]

4. *Congestion from moving sources.* Suppose again that travel is

Spatial Externalities

only toward the centre. Along a given dense, radial transportation network, additional congestion at j is generated by those further away:

(15.22) $\quad E_{ij} = \zeta_{ij} n_i \text{ with } \zeta_{ij} = \begin{cases} -1 \text{ for } i \geq j \\ 0 \text{ for } i < 0. \end{cases}$

The total congestion at j is created by commuters at and beyond j:

(15.23) $\quad e_j = -\sum_{i=j}^{b} n_i.$

Someone at j experiences congestion over the entire ray between j and the centre. Therefore

(15.24) $\quad E_j = \sum_{k=1}^{j} e_k = -\sum_{k=1}^{j} \sum_{i=k}^{b} n_i$

(15.25) $\quad \underset{j}{\Delta} E = -\left[\sum_{k=1}^{j+1} \sum_{i=k}^{b} - \sum_{k=1}^{j} \sum_{i=k}^{b} \right] n_i = -\sum_{i=j+1}^{b} n_i < 0.$

Thus the adjustment to congestion from moving sources will be qualitatively the same to that caused by pollution from stationary sources.

Discussion

The examples of the previous section brought into focus some issues concerning major urban externalities. Spatial adjustments to pollution from moving sources and congestion from stationary sources are summarised, in part, by figure 13.3(1). Spatial adjustments to pollution from stationary sources and congestion from moving sources are summarised in figure 13.3(2).

The private costs of pollution from moving sources and congestion from stationary sources decrease with distance from the centre. For pollution, a longer distance means being exposed to the cumulative effect of a smaller number of sources, those located further away. For congestion it means a lower potential to interact which, in conjunction with distance decay, accounts for this phenomenon. Under these circumstances individuals will move away from the centre to lower the effect of the spatial externality through dispersion. Individuals will find that their reaction to pollution has been futile as everyone else did the same, while congestion from moving sources has increased because they now encounter the same cumulative traffic flow over a longer distance. In contrast, congestion from stationary sources will actually decrease. On the other hand, the private costs of pollution from stationary sources and congestion from moving sources increase with distance from the centre. For pollution, a longer distance means being exposed to the cumulative effect of a larger number of sources, a phenomenon that crucially depends on the assumption of outward direction bias. For congestion it means encountering more sources on the road. Under these circumstances individuals will be attracted toward the centre to lower the effect of the spatial externality through concentration. In consequence the average distance over which the effects of a source are experienced will decrease. Individuals will find once more that their reaction to pollution has been futile as everyone else did the same, while congestion from stationary sources has increased. In contrast, congestion from moving sources will actually decrease. It is interesting to note that individual reactions will succeed in both types of congestion, and will fail in both types of pollution. This provides another example of Schelling's (1971) ecology of micromotives.

In spite of the correct direction of some individual reactions, the planner will have to intervene in every case. The social costs of pollution from moving sources and congestion from stationary sources decrease with distance from the centre. For pollution, this is explained as follows. The effect of others on someone decreases with distance from the centre. Conversely, his effect on others increases because a longer distance means he encounters more victims along the road.

Hence decreasing social costs imply that, as he moves away from the centre, his effect on others does not increase as fast as the effect of others on him decreases. For congestion, there is a symmetry between reception and emission of the externality. Hence decreasing private costs imply decreasing social costs. In both cases, under a finite aversion to inequality, the public interest will dictate a redistribution of wealth such that utility increases with distance from the centre. Consequently, as the aversion to inequality increases, the optimal city disperses and the level of social welfare decreases together with social inequality. Since, for pollution from moving sources and congestion from stationary sources, the spatial externality effect and the land-value effect work in opposite directions, it is not possible to determine how optima must be spatially adjusted relative to the equilibrium. In contrast, for pollution from stationary sources and congestion from moving sources, it is known that the deviation between private and social costs is of a nature that consistently generates individual overreactions from the viewpoint of the planner. Social costs increase with distance from the centre for both types of externality. For pollution, the effect of others on someone increases with distance from the centre. Conversely, his effect on others decreases because a longer distance means that fewer individuals are exposed to the spatial externality, those further away. Hence increasing social costs imply that, as he moves away from the centre, his effect on others does not decrease as fast as the effect of others on him increases. For congestion, there is a symmetry between reception and emission of the externality. Hence increasing private costs imply increasing social costs. In both cases, under a finite aversion to inequality, the public interest will dictate a redistribution of wealth such that utility decreases with distance from the centre. Consequently, as the aversion to inequality increases, the optimal city contracts and the level of social welfare decreases together with social inequality.

It is easy, within this framework, to examine how robust these conclusions are for different specifications of a spatial externality. It is also possible to compare the effects of different spatial externalities.

Spatial Externalities

Here, such comparisons have revealed a realm full of conflicts: facing particular issues of the urban environment in isolation appears to be inefficient. This, in turn, calls for an ability to deal with various spatial externalities simultaneously. It is easy to extend this framework in this direction. Spatial adjustments would then appear to be the resultant of various centripetal and centrifugal forces.

Notes to Chapter Fifteen

1. Introducing (15.1) in problem (11.1), the condition associated with the consumption of land in area i becomes

$$\left[\left[r[i] - \lambda_i \frac{\partial u}{\partial q_i}\right] \underset{n_i}{\triangle} q - \lambda_i \frac{\partial u}{\partial E_i} \underset{n_i}{\triangle} E\right]\Big|_{u_i = z[i]} = 0.$$

   This differs from (11.4) by the last, additional term which represents the change in individual welfare due to the change in the quality of the local environment stemming from the very decision of the individual to locate in area i.

2. In this section some standard ideas concerning public goods are modified and extended to the more general realm of spatial externalities. See for example Musgrave (1959).

3. Samuelson (1954, p. 388).

4. It should be remembered that the correction principle pertains *only* to those who generate the externality. Whether the recipients of the externality should or should not be compensated is irrelevant to the correction principle. Compensation is only relevant to distributive issues, and is therefore implicitly subsumed in the structure of the marginal rate (13.7) which determines the degree of optimal

inequality corresponding to the theory of justice professed by the planner.

At a more naive level, suppose that the planner wishes to compensate the recipients of the externality without any further distributive considerations. Obviously, the total amount received (given) for the correction of the negative (positive) externality equals the total amount to be given (received) as compensation. In this sense there is no difficulty in implementing the scheme. The only question remaining is whether compensation can preserve efficiency. Now if individuals take compensation as parametric, their necessary and sufficient condition for optimality will be the same before and after compensation. Therefore, under these circumstances, compensation is Pareto efficient. On the other hand, a nonparametric view of compensation by the individuals would violate Pareto efficiency.

5   When the recipients of an externality are compensated, they have an incentive to *understate* (*overstate*) the effects of a positive (negative) spatial externality. In this manner each individual hopes that he will decrease his taxes (increase compensation) thereby increasing his welfare because the effect of his false signalling will be negligible on the level of the spatial externality. This corresponds to the famous "free rider" problem in the literature on public goods. False signalling here produces in both cases an output less than the optimal.

6   Samuelson (1954, p. 388). This admirable passage was written for public goods. Since however public goods are nothing more than intentionally created spatial externalities, the passage can be used in the context of this chapter without any conceptual difficulty.

7   In the context of public goods, there are ingenious and complicated rules in existence called "optimal planning procedures" that aim

to bypass the fundamental problem of false signalling. These have originated with Drèze and de la Vallée Poussin (1971), and Malinvaud (1972B). Although, in principle, such rules may be applicable to the more general realm of spatial externalities, we shall not discuss them any further. For a good review see Tulkens (1978).

8   This section is based on some ideas in Arnott (1979).

9   For cities other than linear or circular, I take it that the spatial externality diffuses over radii, rather than diameters, of the city.

10   This section draws upon Papageorgiou (1978B).

11   The propensity to interact with others is a fundamental human attribute. As a spatial externality, it could obviously be represented by the negative of (15.18). Even if the centre were not predetermined, the propensity to interact would produce a symmetric, bell-shaped distribution of population over $\mathcal{J}$. This result persists across different specifications of one-dimensional (Beckmann (1976)) and two-dimensional (Boruchov and Hochman (1977)) constructs. Hence the propensity to interact appears to be a pure reason for cities.

16

Prejudice

For lack of better terminology, I shall name the groups associated with problems of prejudice "whites" and "blacks". Nevertheless, I believe that prejudice is far more general than this choice of words tends to suggest.

Density–Response Specification [1]

The simplest way to treat prejudice is through a density model without spillovers. According to this view, individuals are sensitive only to the composition of their own neighbourhood, and remain indifferent to the character of other neighbourhoods nearby. Let the composition of an area i be described by the proportion of blacks in that area, i.e. by $n_i^B/(n_i^W + n_i^B) \equiv A_i$, where n_i^W and n_i^B represent the number of blacks and whites respectively in area i respectively, and $A_i \in [0,1]$. Thus the spatial externality felt by individuals can be expressed as

(16.1) $\quad E_i^j = \xi^j [A_i]\ for\ j = B,W.$

For whites, $d\xi^W/dA_i > (=,<) 0$ would imply preference (indifference, prejudice) for blacks. For blacks, $d\xi^B/dA_i > (=,<) 0$ would imply prejudice (indifference, preference) for whites.

As in chapter nine, I simplify the problem at hand by holding lot size constant. Therefore utility is determined by the consumption of the private good and by the spatial externality:

(16.2) $\quad u_i^j = u^j [x_i^j, E_i^j].$

Given that individuals differ only by race, their income constraint is

(16.3) $\quad y = x_i^j + r^j [i] + c[i].$

Substituting (16.3) in (16.2),

(16.4) $\quad u_i^j = u^j [y - (r^j [i] + c[i]), E_i^j].$

Spatial equilibrium implies $\delta_i u^j = 0$ for both groups at every location, that is,

(16.5) $\quad -\frac{\partial u^j}{\partial x_i^j} \left[\bigtriangleup_i \bar{r}^j + \bigtriangleup_i c \right] + \frac{\partial u^j}{\partial E_i^j} \bigtriangleup_i E^j = 0$

for $i = 1,...,b$ and $j = B,W$.

Integration

Suppose that racist feelings are mutual, in other words, $d\xi^W/dA_i < 0$ and $d\xi^B/dA_i > 0$. Consider a completely integrated spatial equilibrium, one where $n_i^W > 0$ and $n_i^B > 0$ for $i = 1,...,b$. Then this spatial equilibrium must be characterised by *absolute integration*, where the proportion of blacks *in situ* is the same for all areas, that is, the spatial distribution of the externality is uniform with respect to each group. To see this, notice that complete integration necessarily implies $\bar{r}^B[i] = \bar{r}^W[i]$ for $i = 1,...,b$. In conjunction with (16.5), this leads to

$$(16.6) \quad \left[\frac{\partial u^W}{\partial E_i^W} + \frac{\partial u^W}{\partial x_i^W}\right] \Delta_i E^W = \left[\frac{\partial u^B}{\partial E_i^B} + \frac{\partial u^B}{\partial x_i^B}\right] \Delta_i E^B \text{ for } i = 1,...,b.$$

Since, by assumption, feelings are mutual and since both terms in parentheses are strictly positive, the only way in which (16.6) can be satisfied is when $\Delta_i E^W = \Delta_i E^B = 0$ for $i = 1,...,b$. That is, the only possible integrated spatial equilibrium when racist feelings are mutual must reflect the same unhappy state of affairs for everybody.

The same is true under more general circumstances. Indeed, it suffices to impose simply that the preference of whites for white neighbours is stronger than that of blacks (or that the preference of blacks for black neighbours is stronger than that of whites) in the following sense:

$$(16.7) \quad \left[\frac{\partial u^W}{\partial E_i^W} + \frac{\partial u^W}{\partial x_i^W}\right] \frac{d\xi^W}{dA_i} < \left[\frac{\partial u^B}{\partial E_i^B} + \frac{\partial u^B}{\partial x_i^B}\right] \frac{d\xi^B}{dA_i}.$$

Then, multiplying both sides by $\Delta_i A$, we also conclude that (16.6) cannot hold unless $\Delta_i A = 0$ for $i = 1,...,b$. Under these circumstances, it is also true that the integrated spatial equilibrium is unstable: the decision of a white to move into area i would cause an increase of E_i^W stronger than the corresponding E_i^B. This would produce bid–rent adjustments such that whites outbid blacks in that area. As displaced blacks move to other areas, they, in turn, will outbid whites, and so on. Clearly, the process is not self–limiting.[2] This happens because

> "any completely segregated pattern of location ... will have the same price–distance function as the model without prejudice and will be an equilibrium. Furthermore, completely segregated patterns of location clearly represent a gain in utility for both

blacks and whites; the trade–off between housing costs and transportation costs is the same for the completely integrated and any completely segregated pattern of location but in the case of segregated patterns no household has any disutility from living with members of the other race ... In other words, ... complete segregation is Pareto–superior to integration."[3]

Thus any state of complete segregation is a stable equilibrium.[4]

The important characteristic leading to segregation here is not that feelings are racist. For example, $d\xi^W/dA_i < 0$ and $d\xi^B/dA_i > 0$ does not only imply feelings against the other group. It may also imply a wish to be near one's own group. According to this point of view, ghettos are formed not only because of mutual aversion between groups, but also because of mutual attraction within groups. This seems to be the case for many ethnic communities around the world.

Segregation

Suppose that, in the context of the previous discussion, there is a deviant black with a propensity to integrate. For everyone else, absolute integration is an unstable equilibrium. However, complete segregation is also unstable because the deviant black will always bid higher in segregated, prejudiced white areas. To see this, assume that blacks occupy the central areas $1,...,a$ and whites occupy the peripheral areas $a+1,...,b$. Now, using (16.4),

$$(16.8) \qquad \delta_a u^B = -\frac{\partial u^B}{\partial x_a^B}\left[\underset{a}{\Delta}\bar{r}^B + \underset{a}{\Delta} c\right] + \frac{\partial u^B}{\partial E_a^B}\underset{a}{\Delta} E^B.$$

Notice that finer partitioning of $\mathcal{J}$ into areas brings both $\Delta_a \bar{r}^B + \Delta_a c$ and $\bar{r}^B[a] - \bar{r}^W[a+1]$ closer to zero. Thus the difference in location costs for a black who moves from area a to area $a+1$ and competes for land

Prejudice

there can approach zero by an appropriate partitioning of the city into areas. On the other hand, for the deviant black, the increase in the quality of the environment as expressed by $\Delta_a E^B$ will necessarily be of a discrete magnitude. Therefore the deviant black can always increase utility by crossing the border. In this manner any such asymmetry of feelings renders a completely segregated market equilibrium unstable; and there is no stable racial equilibrium whatsoever under the institution of competitive markets. Uncertainty ensues.

> "To the degree that this uncertainty involves disutility for whites, whites have an incentive to discriminate against blacks by restricting them to certain areas ... Another way of stating this result is that stability is a public good for the white community that can be purchased with discrimination."[5]

This strong conclusion, that, in a competitive market with prejudiced whites and with some blacks seeking to integrate, there cannot be a stable equilibrium without discrimination, depends upon the assumptions (1) that equilibrium bid-rents at the border are equal, and (2) that the preference for white neighbours is stronger for whites than for blacks. If the first assumption is violated then the stability of a segregated equilibrium is possible. If, on the other hand, the second assumption is violated then absolute integration is a stable equilibrium.[6]

1. If the border between whites and blacks is not taken to be perfectly responsive to changes in bid-rent functions then it is possible that bid-rent differences develop that are sufficient to contain the deviant black. More precisely, using (16.8), if

$$(16.9) \quad \Delta_a \bar{r} \geq \left[\frac{\partial u^B}{\partial E_a^B} \div \frac{\partial u^B}{\partial x_a^B} \right] \Delta_a E^B - \Delta_a c$$

then there is no incentive for the deviant black to cross the border. This stability condition imposes that the difference in bid–rents as one crosses the border should not be smaller than the associated externality advantage discounted by the disadvantage of longer commuting distance. It is straightforward to discuss also white bid–rents sufficiently high to induce whites entering the ghetto. Then conditions similar to (16.9) for the opposite migration flow become relevant. Under these circumstances, it is not necessary for the stability of a segregated equilibrium that all whites and all blacks be prejudiced. It remains to specify at least a way in which a segregated equilibrium can actually support bid–rent differences at the border. Consider a difference $\Delta_a \bar{r}$ smaller than necessary to satisfy (16.9). It follows that blacks who seek integration will outbid whites. If profit maximisation is consistent with nondiscriminating behaviour then suppliers in the white area will transfer land to blacks and, in the process, the difference $\Delta_a \bar{r}$ will increase until (16.9) is satisfied and integration stops. The border still exists between the completely black ghetto and the now mixed white–black area: in place of complete segregation, there is only partial segregation. The argument is true if profit maximisation is consistent with nondiscriminating behaviour by suppliers of land (housing). To examine this assumption,

> "it is useful to distinguish between homeowners selling single–family houses and landlords supplying rental housing. Since his financial stake in the neighbourhood typically ends once his home has been sold, a seller in the owner market who is motivated solely by financial gain will always sell to the highest bidder, irrespective of race. Non–discriminatory behaviour is clearly consistent with profit maximization. In the renter market, each landlord must concern himself not only with current returns but with the stream of rents over the entire life of his structure. This stream will depend in part upon the race of tenants selected in the future by neighbouring landlords. If his current tenant decision could be expected to influence the future decisions of his neighbours, he would have to take account of this influence. In a competitive

Prejudice

market, however, each landlord controls so small a part of his neighbourhood that his actions have no impact on incentives faced by others and none, therefore, on their decisions. Like the home-owner, the profit-maximizing landlord can rent to the highest current bidder, secure in the knowledge that the future course of neighbourhood racial composition will be independent of his actions."[7]

2. Consider now the case where positive feelings toward the other groups are mutual, in other words $d\xi^W/dA_i > 0$ and $d\xi^B/dA_i < 0$. Then the only way in which (16.6) can be satisfied is when $\Delta_i E^W = \Delta_i E^B = 0$ for $i = 1,...,b$. The same is true even with the weaker requirement that the preference of blacks for white neighbours is stronger than that of whites (or that the preferences of whites for black neighbours is stronger than that of blacks) in a sense analogous to (16.7):

$$(16.10) \quad \left[\frac{\partial u^W}{\partial E^W} + \frac{\partial u^W}{\partial x_i^W}\right] \frac{d\xi^W}{dA_i} > \left[\frac{\partial u^B}{\partial E^B} + \frac{\partial u^B}{\partial x_i^B}\right] \frac{d\xi^B}{dA_i}.$$

Under these circumstances it is also true that absolute integration is a stable equilibrium: the decision of a white to move into area i will cause an increase in E_i^B stronger than the corresponding increase in E_i^W. This will produce bid-rent adjustments such that blacks outbid whites in that area so that integration is restored. The process will cease only when equilibrium is attained, i.e. when integration becomes absolute.

In terms of the matrix of marginal externality effects discussed in chapter fourteen, some of the above results can be summarised as follows. If

$$(16.11) \quad [MEE] = \begin{bmatrix} - & + \\ + & - \end{bmatrix}$$

then absolute integration is an unstable equilibrium and absolute segregation is a stable equilibrium. If, on the other hand,

$$(16.12) \qquad [MEE] = \begin{bmatrix} + & - \\ - & + \end{bmatrix}$$

then absolute integration is a stable equilibrium and absolute segregation is an unstable equilibrium. Conditions (16.11) and (16.12) may be relaxed through (16.7) and (16.10) as already discussed.

Distance–Response Specification [8]

The previous sections treated prejudice as a point–determined process. It is clear however that prejudice is characterised by a nontrivial spatial diffusion pattern which has interesting implications for urban structure. For this reason, I now examine prejudice as a set–determined process. A full treatment of this case is technically difficult.[9] In consequence, I limit myself to the study of complete segregation in two areas. Then one is able to employ the simplest specification of prejudice as a set–determined process, a specification in which the density response function is trivial, so that only distance from the source matters. Now since how the externality is composed as it passes through the border to affect surrounding individuals is irrelevant, the impact of the externality can be characterised through a single distance—the distance from the border.

Suppose that land is a decision variable as usual. In the case of two income groups without externalities, there is segregation by income. Moreover, as was argued in chapter six, if the income elasticity of the demand for land is higher than the income elasticity of the unit cost of transportation then the poor generate bid–rent gradients steeper than those of the rich. Hence, if the poor can afford a place to live, it will be close to the centre. Let the border between the two groups be at a.

Prejudice

Figure 16.1: Effects of prejudice on the bid–rent gradient.

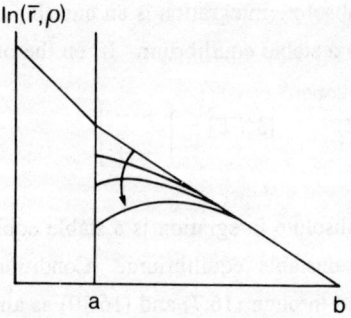

Suppose now that blacks are poor and unprejudiced and whites are rich and prejudiced. This situation can be described by a border model where the inner group generates a negative spatial externality affecting the outer group. In consequence, the black bid–rents obey (4.4) and the white bid–rents obey (7.8). If the spatial externality felt by whites decreases away from the border with blacks, that is, if $\Delta_i E > 0$ for $i > a$, then the analysis concerning "density craters" of chapter seven becomes relevant: to a racist, the effect of a black presence dissipates with distance precisely as the effect of industrial pollution does. Clearly, if the externality is strong enough, positive bid–rent and density gradients may be observed in the white area close to the ghetto. Nevertheless, because of distance decay, the gradient will eventually become negative at some distance from the centre as in figure 16.1, where the arrow points in the direction of increasing prejudice. It follows immediately that the segregated land–use pattern, established in the absence of prejudice, will persist because prejudice further disperses whites.[10] Competitive adjustments however will vary according to whether the city is "open", "transient" or "closed". The following discussion pertains only to "open" and "closed" cities. "Transient" cities will behave as a combination of the two polar types.

The competitive adjustments for an "open" city are shown in figure 16.2.[11] The initial situation is described by line A2. If some exogenous advantage for blacks is established, so that black bid–rents increase from

370

Figure 16.2: Competitive adjustments for an "open" city.

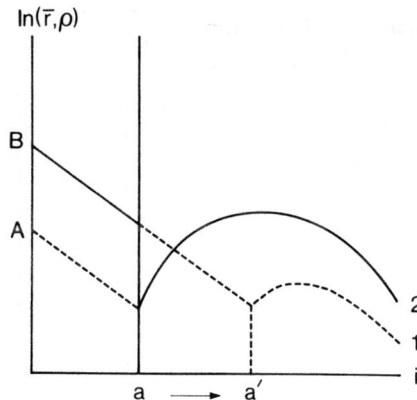

line A to line B, then the ghetto expands to a' and the black population increases. Consider a location in the white area which has not been taken by the expanded ghetto. If it is sufficiently close to the border, the spatial externality there must be stronger than before because the border is closer and the black population has increased. Thus, in order to maintain the exogenous level of utility, density has to decrease: even all–white areas will suffer a net loss of population as the ghetto expands. In consequence the white population decreases and the final situation could be described by line B1. If the spatial diffusion pattern of the externality is long enough, in the sense that the presence of the new ghetto border is felt by all remaining whites, then it must be that the city has actually contracted. Otherwise an individual at the outer border has lost utility, a contradiction. If, on the other hand, the spatial diffusion pattern of the externality is not long enough then the existing white bid–rent and density pattern in areas far enough from the ghetto will remain unaffected, so that the outer border of the city will also remain unaffected. Finally, consider the initial situation being described by line B2. If there is an increase in white prejudice, white bid–rents and densities "slide" down along the steady black bid–rents and, once more, line B1 obtains.

The competitive adjustments for a "closed" city are shown in

Prejudice

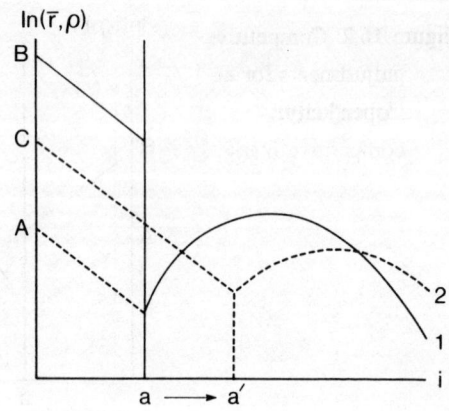

Figure 16.3: Competitive adjustments for a "closed" city.

figure 16.3. The initial situation is described by line A1. If some exogenous factor, such as an increase in black population, occurs then black bid-rents increase from line A to line B causing disequilibrium. As in the case of an "open" city, the ghetto expands. In the process, black bid-rents and densities fall because the black population remains fixed. On the other hand, as in the case of an "open" city, white bid-rents and densities in areas sufficiently close to the new border of the ghetto decrease. Since however the white population also remains fixed, white bid-rents and densities are bound to increase in peripheral areas. In consequence, the city expands and the final situation is described by line C2.

What are the welfare implications of such prejudice under the institution of competitive markets? In the "open" case, none, by definition. In the "closed" case such prejudice should offer an advantage to blacks and a disadvantage to whites. The argument is illustrated in figure 16.4. Line A1 represents the initial situation without prejudice. With prejudice, the tendency of whites to disperse away from the ghetto border is reflected in line 2. The subsequent adjustments to restore equilibrium at line B3 must be such that, for a linear city, the shaded areas are equal *in terms of population*.[12] Since the black per capita consumption of land increases, so does the black utility level. In

372

Figure 16.4: The impact of prejudice under the institution of competitive markets.

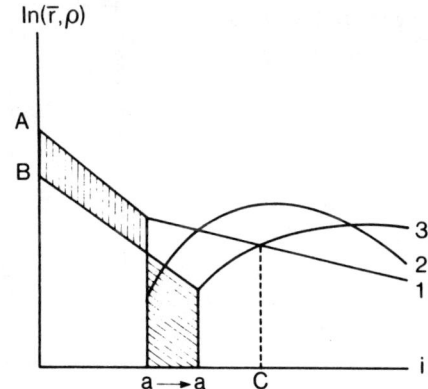

contrast, the white per capita consumption of land decreases beyond C. Since the only other new factor, prejudice, works against white welfare, the white utility level decreases at the new equilibrium.

If one ponders reality, one may, at least in some cases, brand the theory absurd. Or it may be that, in these cases, under white prejudice, the institution of competitive markets is not allowed to operate. Thus one is led to the study of market segmentation. Toward this end, for a "closed" city, we shall examine two types of organised interests which may restrict the operation of a free market, namely, a private cartel and a local government.

Money Counts

Suppose that places near the border belong to absentee landowners: for a linear city, decisions are determined by profit alone as in figure 16.5. The initial situation is again described by line A1. If there is no resistance, any exogenous factor that shifts black bid-rents from line A to line B will cause line C2. Such realisation depends entirely on the spatial extent of the cartel. If it does not extend to E, the cartel favours competitive markets: gains over aD are greater than losses beyond D. If

Prejudice

Figure 16.5: The case of a cartel.

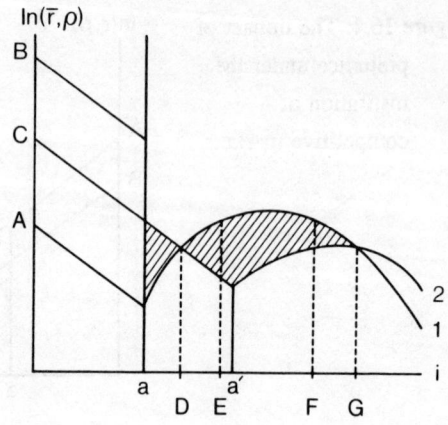

it extends just to E, the cartel is indifferent about the issue of market segmentation: gains over aD from increased black bid-rents precisely equal the losses over DE from decreased white bid-rents. If however the cartel extends beyond E, say to F, the cartel favours market segmentation: gains over aD are smaller than losses over DF. Those over FG, being outside the cartel, would enjoy the advantages of market segmentation without having to compensate those over aD or those beyond G for the losses they incur. It follows that, in this case, the most successful cartel against integration would end at G.[13] Finally, for any cartel, an increase of prejudice may either increase or decrease the net difference between the two areas.[14] Thus higher levels of prejudice do not necessarily imply a higher propensity of the cartel to discriminate.

Votes Count

Suppose now that the border marks a change in political jurisdiction and that every white is a resident owner: decisions here are determined by votes alone as in figure 6. There is once more an initial situation A1, an exogenous shift from line A to line B and, in the absence of resistance, a final solution C2. We have already argued that if line C2 obtains then

Figure 16.6: The case of a political jurisdiction.

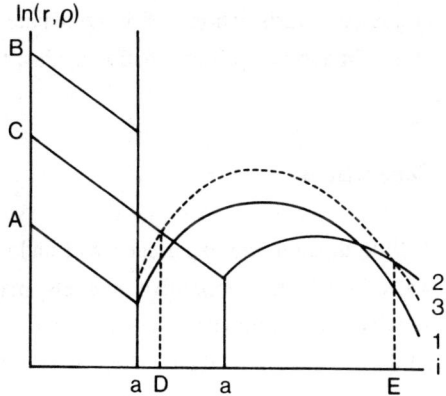

the equilibrium utility of whites decreases. In consequence, a white will oppose market segmentation only if the black bid–price exceeds the combined present value of his property adjusted for the expected decrease in his welfare:

(16.13) $\bar{r}^B[i]q_i^W > \bar{r}^W[i]q_i^W - \lambda_i \Delta \bar{u}^W$ for $i > a$

or

(16.14) $\bar{r}^B[i] > \bar{r}^W[i] - \lambda_i \dfrac{\Delta \bar{u}^W}{q_i^W}$

where $\bar{r}^B$ and $\bar{r}^W$ refer to bid–rents along lines C and 1 respectively. Since the quantity of land is inversely related to its price, $\Delta \bar{u}^W/q_i^W$ is proportionately related to $\bar{r}^W[i]$. Thus the RHS of the last inequality is represented on figure 16.6 by line 3. Whites over aD and beyond E favour competitive markets because, there, line 3 is below line C2 so that (16.14) obtains. Those over DE favour market segmentation. Once more, everything depends on the spatial extent of the jurisdiction. Very small and large jurisdictions alike may yield to black pressure in spite of

Prejudice

prejudice. Jurisdictions of intermediate size on the other hand may persist in applying discrimination against blacks.

Comparisons

A little thought and experience will undoubtedly produce several simple ways in which competitive markets may be restricted by organised activity. For example a green belt over the areas beyond the ghetto border, where black bid-rents exceed white bid-rents, would accomplish the objective—neatly and legally. The various regressive policies adopted by some local governments, the minimum lot size requirements for new housing and the maximum density ordinances for old housing, to name just a few, may also represent such instruments. A study of all this however is beyond our scope. Instead, I shall close chapter eighteen with a comparison of the previous two alternatives, illustrated in figure 7. The profits of the cartel and the net votes of the political jurisdiction in favour of discrimination are represented by lines 1 and 2 respectively.[15] With an outer boundary between A and B the cartel favours competitive markets while the political jurisdiction favours market segmentation.

> "These differences can in the end be traced to two basic structural features of political as opposed to economic organization. First, in the political process, each household counts equally regardless of the amount of land it owns, while in a cartel every dollar counts equally regardless of household density. Second, voters care about changes in utility as well as capital gains and losses, while the cartel of absentee landlords is only concerned with revenues."[16]

Since line 1 is based on bid-rents while line 2 is based on density, one may construct examples where the relative position of the two indifference points and of the two maxima are reversed: intuitively, it is a

Figure 16.7: Advantages and disadvantages of discrimination for a continuum of spatial entities.

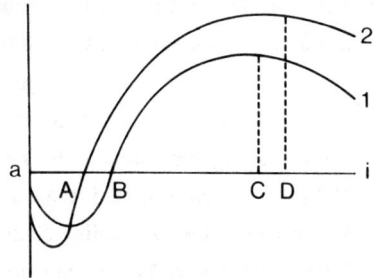

matter of the difference between bid–rent and density slopes. There is however a clear bias in favour of the situation as already described.[17] Therefore, at least for strong racist feelings where $\Delta \bar{u}^W$ is sizeable, discrimination seems more likely under political rather than under economic institutions.

Notes to Chapter Sixteen

1 The first three sections are based on the ideas of Yinger (1976).

2 For a careful discussion of such processes see Schelling (1971).

3 Yinger (1976, p. 391).

4 These results crucially depend on the decision to treat the externality as a point–determined process. Consider now the externality as an urban contact field over a linear city which is further congested by traffic. Yellin (1974) has demonstrated that, in the case of multiple, mutually prejudiced groups, a spatial equilibrium corresponding to complete integration does exist and is Pareto efficient. Within every group, such equilibrium reflects the same unhappy state of affairs for everybody. This however does not necessarily imply absolute integration in the sense of Yinger.

Also, unlike Yinger, such an equilibrium may be either stable or unstable. In the latter case Pareto efficiency obtains as long as all groups keep their relative prejudices at a certain balance. Any small deviation will direct the city toward one of its innumerable, stable, segregated states as in Yinger. Moreover, for two groups, Yellin has demonstrated that a segregated city corresponds to lower aggregate externality costs than its integrated counterpart. This is similar to Yinger, but notice that externality costs do not vanish because they are described by a set- rather than a point- determined process.

5   Yinger (1976, pp. 394–395).

6   Both these arguments are due to Kern (1981).

7   Kern (1981, p. 168). The situation described is essentially an n-person prisoner's dilemma game. The outcomes of such games are discussed in Luce and Raiffa (1957, pp. 94–97).

8   This and the remaining sections are based on the ideas of Rose-Ackermann (1975, 1977).

9   An intuition about the difficulties involved can be obtained from Yellin (1974) and Smith (1976).

10 If there is some mix of incomes among groups then multiple zones may arise (Courant and Yinger (1977, pp. 272–291)). Since prejudice will reinforce these zones, one possible way to deal with the problem is to consider multiple endogenous border effects.

11 This case has been investigated by White (1977).

12 For other city-shapes, figure 4 must be modified to account for the

increase $\Delta_{i-1} Q$ away from the centre. The same is true for all subsequent figures which, like figure 4, refer to a linear city with $\Delta_{i-1} Q = 1$.

13 Figure 5 suggests that there may be cartels extending far enough beyond G to restore the institution of competitive markets as more profitable. However, from empirical considerations alone, such a size of cartel is very improbable.

14 This is based on the assumption that the marginal utility of land relative to the marginal utility of income is independent of the white household's distance from the ghetto. For the details of the argument see Rose–Ackermann (1977, p. 158).

15 The relative position of the two indifference points A and B, where decisions are reversed, and of the two maxima C and D, where decisions to discriminate are the strongest, reflect the relative positions of lines 1 and 3 in figure 16.6.

16 Rose–Ackermann (1977, p. 163).

17 This bias stems from the relative positions of lines 1 and 3 in figure 16.6.

17

Industrial Pollution

As in chapter eight, I consider here a city partitioned in two concentric zones $[1,a]$ and $[a+1,b]$, occupied by industry and residences respectively. However, unlike chapter eight where no environmental issues were recognised, I assume here explicitly that the inner land use pollutes the outer and that pollution exhibits distance–decay. Without any conceptual sacrifice one could restrict attention to the volume of pollution crossing the border between the industrial and residential zones of the city.

There are now three, rather than two, types of agent involved, that is, individuals, the industry and the planner. Decisions of individuals are based on problem (11.1) with the utility being written as

(17.1) $\quad u_i = u[x_i, q_i, E_i[a,X]],$

thus taking explicitly into account how the quality of the environment is affected by industrial production. Clearly, $\Delta_i E > 0$ for $a < i \le b$, $\Delta_a E_i < 0$ and $\partial E_i / \partial X < 0$, that is, the quality of the environment improves away from the industrial area, and deteriorates as production expands either spatially or in volume. Decisions of the industry are based on problem (8.1). Finally, decisions of the planner are now based on the problem

(17.2) $\quad D[r^0,r,\bar{z};a] =$

$$\min\left\{ \sum_{j=1}^{a} r_j^0 \bigtriangleup Q + \sum_{j=a+1}^{b} n_j \bar{y}_j - X[N,N[\bar{a}],a] \Big| \right.$$
$$\left. \bar{z}[i] \leq v[u_i;\alpha]\Big|_{u_i = v_i} \textit{ for } i \in \mathcal{J} \right\}.$$

As in chapter eleven, the distribution of land values and utilities is exogenous for the time being. Upon comparison of problems (8.1) and (17.2), it is seen that the planner aims to constrain the objectives of the industry through the requirement of a publicly desirable distribution of welfare. Further to the planning decisions of problem (11.9), the planner must now decide on the optimal partitioning of the urban area into industrial and residential zones.

Equilibrium

Since residential bid-rents obey (7.8), the analysis concerning "density craters" of chapter seven holds. Indeed the cause of "density craters" in chapter seven could well be industrial pollution, the only difference being that pollution there was treated as exogenous while here it is treated as endogenous. How increasing levels of pollution affect the shape of residential bid-rent and density gradients is indicated by the arrow in figure 16.1. Furthermore, were production, hence per capita income, exogenous then the qualitative analysis of competitive adjustments to industrial pollution would be identical with that of prejudice.[1] Endogeneity however complicates matters to a considerable degree.

Given that the decisions of the industry are those of chapter eight, per capita income is determined by the marginal productivity of labour

$\Delta_N X[N,N[a],a]$ according to (8.2), while the level of industrial bid–rents is determined by the marginal productivity of land $\Delta_a X[N,N[a],a]$ according to (8.3). Furthermore, notice that the indirect utility function can still be written as in (7.16). Consider first the case of an "open" city. If some exogenous advantage for the use of land in production is established then industrial bid–rents will increase because $\Delta_a X$ has increased. In consequence, for the same population size, production volume and the emission of industrial pollutants would increase; hence the quality of the environment at locations experiencing pollution would decrease. If the marginal productivity of labour were independent of the amount of land used in production then, for the same population size and using the indirect utility function (7.16), decreasing quality of the urban environment would require decreasing residential bid–rents in order to keep utility constant. This implies a decreasing demand for residential land, and hence decreasing urban population. Decreasing urban population, in turn, would imply changes in the marginal productivity of labour which, together with the associated bid–rent changes, would generate the second round of adjustments and so on. The final outcome could still be described by figure 16.2. Using the indirect utility function, this would remain true even if the marginal productivity of labour decreases with an increasing amount of industrial land, the only difference being a stronger outmigration because now, for the same population size, both income and the quality of the environment decrease as the industrial area expands. If however the marginal productivity of labour increases with an increasing amount of industrial land then it is not clear how urban population changes. This happens because, for the same population size, increasing per capita income and decreasing quality of the environment have opposing effects on the indirect utility function. If the environmental effect dominates then the urban population will decrease in order that utility is kept constant. If, on the other hand, the income effect dominates then the urban population will increase. Where the income effect is weak enough relative to the environmental effect, figure 16.2 still applies. Otherwise the competitive adjustments for an "open" city are described by figure 16.3, even if there is some loss in urban population to compensate for the corresponding loss in the quality of the environment. A further complication in the case of an "open" city stems from the shape of urban equilibrium utility curves $\bar{u}[N]$ discussed in chapter eight. There, it was argued how slight parameter changes could cause unexpectedly catastrophic population shifts. Therefore, in some cases, the transition from one equilibrium to another may be far stronger than figures 16.3 and 16.4 are meant to suggest. Consider now the case of a "closed" city. Since urban population remains fixed, the marginal productivity of labour, and hence per capita income, can only be affected by the amount of land used for production. If per capita income does not increase as industrial land and production expand then the equilibrium level of utility will decrease. If however per capita income increases then the equilibrium level of utility may either increase or decrease, depending upon how strong the income effect is relative to the environmental effect. In any case, figure 16.3 applies.

With regard to market segmentation, for a given border, the behaviour of a cartel formed by landowners will be similar to that under prejudice. Given that the effects of pollution are felt over a wider area than the effects of the ghetto, the segment aE in figure 16.5 will be longer under industrial pollution than under prejudice. For this reason, the likelihood of a cartel favouring market segmentation seems to be higher under prejudice than under industrial pollution. On the other hand, the behaviour of a political jurisdiction will be somewhat different to that under prejudice. This happens because the equilibrium level of utility may now either increase or decrease. In the former case, line 3 of figure 16.6 will be found under, rather than over, line 1. If, further, there exist additional positive implications from allowing the industry to expand into the jurisdiction, such as new tax revenues that somehow benefit the voters, then line 3 of figure 16.6 will slide even lower relative to line 1. Therefore, as in the case of a cartel, the likelihood of

Industrial Pollution

a political jurisdiction favouring market segmentation seems to be higher under prejudice than under industrial pollution.

Optimum

Table 17.1 displays the conditions relevant to optimal decentralisation policy. For individuals, the conditions are still those of table 15.1 provided that they take environmental quality parametrically.[2] For the industry, employment decisions are based on (8.2). On the other hand assumptions supporting the condition (8.3), associated with the amount of land used for production, could be relaxed.[3] Nevertheless, as long as such complications are taken into account both by the industry and the planner, the optimal decentralisation policy remains unaffected. With this understanding, I adopt the simpler condition (8.3). For the planner, the conditions associated with the consumption of the private good and the decision where to locate remain those of table 15.1. On the other hand, (15.2) now becomes

$$(17.3) \quad \bar{y}_i + (n_i + 1)\bigtriangleup_{n_i} \bar{y} - \bigtriangleup_N X - (\mu_i \frac{dv}{du_i}\frac{\partial u}{\partial q_i} \bigtriangleup_{n_i} q$$

$$+ \sum_{j=a+1}^{b} \mu_j \frac{dv}{du_j}\frac{\partial u}{\partial E_j}\frac{\partial E_j}{\partial X} \bigtriangleup_N X)|_{u=v} = 0$$

because the composition of environmental quality differs from that of chapter fifteen. Finally, the condition associated with the publicly optimal amount of land used for production is

$$(17.4) \quad \overset{0}{r}_{a+1} \bigtriangleup_a Q + n_{a+1}\left[\bigtriangleup_N X - \bar{y}_{a+1}\right]$$

$$- \bigtriangleup_a X - \sum_{j=a+2}^{b} \mu_j \frac{dv}{du_j}\frac{\partial u}{\partial E_j} \delta_a E_j|_{u=v} = 0.[4]$$

Applying (12.3) to (17.3) and (17.4), and taking into account (12.8), we obtain

$$(17.5) \quad \left[n_i \left[r[i] - \lambda_i \frac{\partial u}{\partial q_i} \right] \underset{n_i}{\Delta} q - \sum_{j=a+1}^{b} n_j \lambda_j \frac{\partial u}{\partial E_j} \frac{\partial E_j}{\partial X} \underset{N}{\Delta} X \right]\bigg|_{u=z}$$
$$= 0$$

$$(17.6) \quad \overset{0}{r}_{a+1} \underset{a}{\Delta} Q - \underset{a}{\Delta} X + n_{a+1} \underset{n_{a+1}}{\Delta} \bar{y} - \sum_{j=a+2}^{b} n_j \lambda_j \frac{\partial u}{\partial E_j} \underset{a}{\delta} E_j \bigg|_{u=z}$$
$$= 0$$

respectively, taking into account that $v = z$ at the optimum.

Decisions associated with the consumption of the private good and the choice of location, which refer to individuals and the planner, remain as before. In contrast, decisions associated with the consumption of land now refer to all three types of agent. Nevertheless, the optimal decentralisation policy of chapter fifteen also holds essentially unaltered. The decision of the industry to set wages equal to the marginal product of labour is in complete agreement with the aims of the planner; and comparison between (11.4) and (17.3) leads to the conclusion that, similarly to chapter fifteen, the planner must set a marginal rate on the consumption of land by individuals equal to

$$(17.7) \quad \phi_i^n = -\frac{1}{n_i} \sum_{j=a+1}^{b} n_j \lambda_j \frac{\partial u}{\partial E_j} \frac{\partial E_j}{\partial X} \underset{N}{\Delta} X \bigg|_{u=z} .$$

Whereas the marginal rate (15.4) referred to a spatial externality in general, (17.7) is far more explicit. Since unemployment is not recognised here, the size of the urban labour force strictly depends on how many individuals prefer the city to the alternative sector. Thus an individual, by his mere decision to enter the city, causes an increase $\Delta_N X$ in production. The consequent decrease in the quality of the environment for area j, due to increased pollution, is $(\partial E_j / \partial X) \Delta_N X$.

Table 17.1: Decision rules.

	\multicolumn{2}{c}{Optimality Conditions}	
	Industry	Planner
x_i		(11.11): $n_i \frac{\partial y}{\partial x_i} - \mu_i \frac{dv}{du_i}\frac{\partial u}{\partial x_i}\big|_{u_i = v_i}$
		(12.4): $n_i\left[1 - \lambda_i \frac{\partial u}{\partial x_i}\right]\big|_{u_i = z[i]} = 0$
n_i	(8.2): $y = \bigtriangleup_N X$	(17.3): $\bar{y}_i + (n_i + 1)\bigtriangleup_{n_i} \bar{y} - \bigtriangleup_N X -$
		$\left[\mu_i \frac{dv}{du_i}\frac{\partial u}{\partial q_i}\bigtriangleup_{n_i} + \sum_{j=a+1}^{b} u_j \frac{dv}{du}\frac{\partial y}{\partial E}\frac{\partial E^j}{\partial X^j}\bigtriangleup_N X\right]\big|_{u = v} =$
		$\left[n_i(r_i[i] - \lambda_i \frac{\partial u}{\partial q_i})\bigtriangleup_{n_i} q + \left[\left[\bar{y}_i + \bigtriangleup_{n_i}\bar{y}\right] - \bigtriangleup_N X\right] -\right.$
		$\left.\sum_{j=a+1}^{b} n_j \lambda_j \frac{\partial u}{\partial E_j}\frac{\partial E_j}{\partial X^j}\bigtriangleup_N X\right]\big|_{u = z} = 0$
i		(13.2): $n_i \bigtriangleup_i \bar{y} + \mu_i\left[\bigtriangleup_i \bar{z} - \frac{dv}{du_i}\frac{\partial u}{\partial E_i}\bigtriangleup_i E\right]\big|_{u_i = z_i} =$
		(13.5): $n_i\left[\lambda_i\left[\bigtriangleup_i \bar{z} - \frac{\partial u}{\partial E_i}\bigtriangleup_i E\right]\big|_{u_i = z[i]} + \left[\frac{\mu_i}{n_i} - \lambda_i\right]\bigtriangleup_i z\right] = 0$
a	(8.3): $\overset{0}{r}_{a+1}\bigtriangleup_a Q$	(17.6): $\overset{0}{r}_{a+1}\bigtriangleup_a Q - \bigtriangleup_a X + n_{a+1}\bigtriangleup_{n_{a+1}} \bar{y} -$
	$-\bigtriangleup_a X = 0$	$\sum_{j=a+2}^{b} n_j \lambda_j \frac{\partial u}{\partial E_j}\delta_a E_j\big|_{u = z} = 0$

	Individuals	Decentralisation
(11.3):	$1 - \lambda_i \frac{\partial u}{\partial x_i}\big|_{u_i = z[i]} = 0$	No correction
(11.4):	$\left[r[i] - \lambda_i \frac{\partial u}{\partial q_i} \right] \bigtriangleup_{n_i} q \big|_{u_i = z[i]} = 0$	$\bar{y}_i + \bigtriangleup_{n_i} \bar{y} = \bigtriangleup_N X$ and $\phi_i^n = -\frac{1}{n_i} \sum_{j=a+1}^{b} n_j \lambda_j \frac{\partial u}{\partial E_j} \frac{\partial E_j}{\partial X} \bigtriangleup_N X \big|_{u = z}$
(13.3):	$\lambda_i \left[\bigtriangleup_i \bar{z} - \frac{\partial u}{\partial E_i} \bigtriangleup_i E \right] \big|_{u_i = z[i]} = 0$	$\phi_i^i = \left[\frac{\mu_j}{n_i} - \lambda_i \right] \bigtriangleup_i z =$ $(1 - \bar{u}_i^{-\alpha}) \lambda_i \frac{\partial u}{\partial x_i} \bigtriangleup_i E \big|_{u_i = z[i]}$
		$\phi^a = n_{a+1} \bigtriangleup_{n_{a+1}} \bar{y} -$ $\sum_{j=a+2}^{b} n_j \lambda_j \frac{\partial u}{\partial E_j} \delta_a E_j \big|_{u = z}$

Hence the expression under the sum on the RHS of (17.7) represents the NMSC of individuals, being the total decrease in social welfare which stems from the increase of industrial pollution caused by the addition of someone to the labour force. As before, the division by n_i means that there is no distinction between individuals of the same area, and the minus sign ascertains that ϕ_i^n is indeed a tax.

Deterioration in the quality of the environment is not only caused by an increasing workforce, but also by an expansion of the industrial zone. Decisions about the size of the industrial zone, which pertain to the industry and the planner, are represented by (8.3) and (17.6) respectively. Comparison indicates that industrial and public decisions concerning the use of areas for production differ by the last two terms of (17.6). If the planner sets a marginal rate on the use of areas for production equal to

$$(17.8) \qquad \phi^a = n_{a+1} \bigtriangleup_{n_{a+1}} \bar{y} - \sum_{j=a+2}^{b} n_j \lambda_j \frac{\partial u}{\partial E_j} \delta_a E_j \big|_{u=z}$$

and if this rate is taken parametrically by the industry then (8.3) would be augmented by (17.8) and would become equivalent to (17.6) at the optimum.[5] The first term on the RHS of (17.8) can be interpreted as follows. If the optimal per capita expenditure of those in zone $a+1$ is greater (smaller) than the corresponding value of their marginal product then expanding the industrial zone decreases (increases) the aggregate income deficit. In consequence, industry should be encouraged (discouraged) to expand spatially. Now, per capita expenditure greater (smaller) than the corresponding value of marginal product implies $\Delta_{n_{a+1}} \bar{y} < (>) 0$. Therefore ϕ^a decreases (increases) according to whether an expansion of the industrial zone results in a smaller (larger) aggregate income deficit. With respect to the second term on the RHS of (17.8), since $\delta_a X = \Delta_N X \Delta_a N + \Delta_a X$, its sign also remains undetermined because the first term refers to the decrease in industrial production caused by the displacement of n_{a+1} workers and the second term refers to the corresponding increase caused by the availability of additional land $\Delta_a Q$ for production. However, if expanding the industrial area does not decrease the total volume of production, that is, $\delta_a X \geq 0$,

(17.9) $$\delta_a E_j = \bigwedge_a E_j + \frac{\partial E_j}{\partial X} \delta_a X < 0$$

in (17.8) represents the deterioration in the quality of the environment in the residential area j caused by an expansion of the industrial zone. The quantity $\lambda_j (\partial u/\partial E_j) \delta_a E_j$ represents the corresponding loss of utility for someone in area j expressed in money terms. Thus the expression under the sum on the RHS of (17.8) represents the total decrease in social welfare which stems from the increase of industrial pollution caused by the expansion of the industrial zone. Since the industry is sensitive to profit only, ϕ^a represents the NMSC of industrial pollution modified to account for the effect on the aggregate income deficit of the associated emigration; and since, in comparison with chapter fifteen, this is the only new element relevant to an optimal decentralisation policy, *the prescriptions of chapter fifteen are simply augmented here by the requirement that the industry be taxed for the use of land in production according to the marginal rate* (17.8). Of course, *propositions 15.1–15.3 also hold*.

Regarding the issue of a solution procedure for the problem (17.2), everything said in chapter thirteen, as modified in chapter fifteen, applies. This procedure determines all unknowns sought by the planner, except the optimal land values for the industrial zone. Toward this end notice that, for any feasible $\mathscr{A}$, we can define $\phi^a[\alpha; \mathscr{A}] \equiv a\phi^a$. Therefore $\phi^{a*}[\alpha] = \phi^a[\alpha; \mathscr{A}^*]$ is also determined. Taking into account the principle of self–sufficiency $D = 0$, we are now able to evaluate the total amount paid by the industry for land, $\sum_{j=1}^{a} r_j^0 \Delta_{j-1} Q$, at the optimum. In order to go further than that, we need to propose some mechanism of rent determination in the industrial zone which can provide us with an explicit estimate of $\Delta_i r^0$ for $i = 1,...,a$.

Industrial Pollution

In summary, externality control applies both to the volume of the polluting activity and to the inner border. The NMSC of the former, represented by the expression under the sum on the RHS of (17.7), equals the total amount individuals would be prepared to forgo in order to reduce the volume of the polluting activity by one unit, for given levels of utility. The NMSC of the latter, represented by the expression on the RHS of (17.8), equals the total amount individuals would be prepared to forgo in order to push the border one area away, for given levels of utility.[6] Finally, since pollution decreases away from the centre, optimal utility increases away from the centre under finite aversion to inequality because of (13.6). Nevertheless propositions 13.1 and 13.2 (concerning the adjustment to spatial externalities) cannot be applied, even with the modifications discussed in the section "Adjustment to Spatial Externalities" of chapter fifteen, because income is now affected by the spatial structure itself. Recall that the comparisons of spatial structure in chapters thirteen and fifteen were based on cities of the same size, and hence of the same per capita income. This happened because production depended on N only and because $y = \Delta_N X$, so that efficient city size and per capita income remained invariant over the entire range of equilibrium and optimal arrangements. Now that production also depends on the inner border a, city size and per capita income differ between equilibrium and optimum. This happens because optimality requires correction of the inner border which, in turn, affects the marginal productivity of labour.

Zoning [7]

Consider figure 17.1. In the absence of land-use controls the inner border is at a', where $r_a^{0'} = r_a'$. Such an equilibrium would produce a spatially overexpanded industry because the externality involved is negative. In order to see how the desired border a can be achieved through application of the marginal rate (17.8), recall that this marginal

Figure 17.1: Land–value patterns in the case of a negative externality.

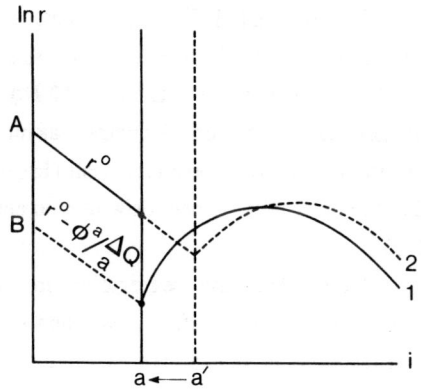

rate refers to the entire area $\Delta_a Q$. Thus, per unit of land, the marginal burden on industry would equal $\phi^a/\Delta_a Q$. Suppose $\phi^a > 0$. Under these circumstances, the marginal rate (17.8) would operate as if the land-rent-paying ability of the industry was reduced from r^0 to $r^0 - \phi^a/\Delta_a Q$, that is, as if line A in figure 17.1 were lowered to line B. Equality of the modified rents at the border would result in the optimal partitioning of land between the industrial and residential sectors. Of course, the same results could be achieved by simply zoning the areas $[1,a]$ industrial and the areas $[a+1,b]$ residential. In both cases there would be an observed difference of rents at the border between industry and residences equal to

$$(17.10) \quad r^0_{a+1} - r[a+1] = \frac{1}{\Delta_a Q}\left[n_{a+1} \underset{n_{a+1}}{\Delta} \bar{y} - \sum_{j=a+2}^{b} n_j \lambda_j \frac{\partial u}{\partial E_j} \underset{a}{\delta} E_j \big|_{u=z} \right],$$

that is, a difference that reflects the adjusted aggregate marginal value of the loss in utility due to increased pollution when an additional unit of land is converted to industrial use.[8] In the case of zoning, this would indicate disequilibrium because the industry would be prepared to pay a higher price for land at $a + 1$ were it allowed to do so.

Industrial Pollution

The optimal difference of rents at the inner border represents a general principle of segregated land-uses. Since the spatial externality involved is negative, the LHS of (17.10) is positive so that the externality generator is forced to contract as in figure 17.1. Were the spatial externality involved positive, the LHS of (17.10) would be negative so that the externality generator would be encouraged to expand as in figure 17.2.[9]

Often, land-use segregation in the case of a positive spatial externality can be justified only when it is necessary for the functioning of a land-use involved. For example, introducing residences into a park would eventually destroy it. Otherwise zoning may be abandoned in favour of integration. Under these circumstances, entry should be regulated by corrective taxation based as always on the impact which an additional unit of the externality generator has on others.[10] Notice that all this can be easily generalised for the case of mutually interacting land-uses. Then every rent shift in figures 17.1 and 17.2 would be caused by the application of a Pigouvian tax; and, in general, the resulting (integrated or segregated) pattern would reflect the net impact of both externalities.[11]

The previous analysis implies that, under some optimal policy, an observer could obtain considerable information about the types of spatial

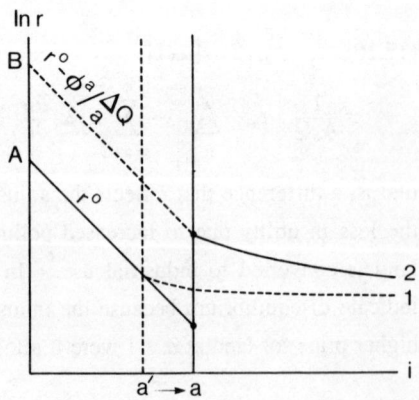

Figure 17.2: Land-value patterns in the case of a positive externality.

392

interdependence between segregated land uses from the established land–value differences at the corresponding borders. In particular, he would know that every land use associated with the higher rent at the border either emits a negative spatial externality to the other or receives a positive spatial externality from the other. Furthermore, he would know that the differences in land values reflect the corresponding NMSC (NMSB) scaled down by the length of the border between the land uses and, finally, that if there is no difference in land values then either no net externality effect is involved and segregation is caused by differently sloped rents or a negative externality must be involved and it is purely local, that is, one which can be represented by a density model without spillovers. Pure localness is ensured by the equality of rents at the border. On the other hand, if the purely local externality were positive then integration would be Pareto superior to segregation, which contradicts optimality.[12]

Whenever applicable, optimal zoning and optimal taxation are identical from the allocative point of view in the sense that they can both be used to produce the same optimum. However, from the distributive point of view they differ. Taxing the industry against pollution means lowering its rent–paying ability at the inner border area $a + 1$, that is, preventing the owners of land there from allowing the development of an obnoxious facility on it. Even if the optimal policy for individuals is arranged simply to redistribute income, as in section "Optimal Decentralisation Policy" of chapter thirteen ($A = \bar{\phi}$), taxing the industry against pollution would leave the planner with a surplus which he may either distribute equally among individuals ($A > \bar{\phi}$), or use for other purposes.[13] Therefore optimal taxation of industry could be seen as a distributive instrument. In contrast, since zoning does not involve transfers of money between the industry and the planner, it remains neutral with respect to distribution. Of course, both the information requirements discussed in chapter thirteen and the incentive for wrong signalling discussed in chapter fifteen hinder optimal zoning and taxation in precisely the same manner.

Industrial Pollution

Zoning need not be confined to inner boundaries. Where the consequences of urban sprawl are significant, the outer boundary b of the city becomes a decision variable. Sprawl here implies a degradation of the surrounding nonurban landscape, and this lowers the quality of the urban environment. Hence the decision to create new residences on the fringe, further to the other consequences that any location decision entails, is associated with an entirely new negative spatial externality which modifies environmental quality as $E_i[a,b,X]$ with $\Delta_b E_i < 0$. Moreover, production must also be generalised as $X[a,N[a,b],N]$, where $N[a,b]$ is such that $\Delta_b N = n_{b+1}$, in order to account for the gain in manpower due to the expansion of the fringe. Under these circumstances, decisions of the planner concerning the optimal extent of the city are directed by

$$(17.11) \quad n_b \underset{b}{\Delta} \bar{y} + \left[\mu_b \left[\underset{b}{\Delta} \bar{z} - \frac{\partial v}{\partial E_b} \underset{b}{\delta} E \right] - n_{b+1} \underset{n_{b+1}}{\Delta} \bar{y} \right.$$

$$\left. - \sum_{j=a+1}^{b} \mu_j \frac{dv}{du_j} \frac{\partial u}{\partial E_j} \underset{b}{\delta} E_j \right] \bigg|_{u=v} = 0.^{14}$$

Comparison between (13.2) and (17.11) reveals that the decision of the planner to locate individuals on the fringe differs from his decision to locate them anywhere else in the city by the last two terms in (17.11). On the other hand, since individuals take the quality of the environment parametrically, their decision to locate on the fringe is still described by (13.3) with $i = b$. Therefore, in addition to the optimal decentralisation policy measures generated from the comparison between (13.3) and (13.5) and discussed in chapter thirteen, the planner must also impose on the individuals on the fringe a new marginal rate

$$(17.12) \quad \phi^b = -\left[\underset{n_{b+1}}{\Delta} \bar{y} + \frac{1}{n_{b+1}} \sum_{j=a+1}^{b} n_j \lambda_j \frac{\partial u}{\partial E_j} \underset{b}{\delta} E_j \bigg|_{u=z} \right]$$

which has an interpretation entirely analogous to the marginal rate on the inner border, the only difference being that ϕ^b is equally partitioned between the individuals on the fringe and that, unlike ϕ^a which might become a subsidy since the sign of both its components remains undetermined, ϕ^b is more likely to be a tax here because

$$(17.13) \qquad \underset{b}{\delta} E_j = \underset{b}{\triangle} E_j + \frac{\partial E_j}{\partial X} \underset{N}{\triangle} X \underset{b}{\triangle} N < 0.$$

Notice that, in contrast with the standard location rate, the fringe rate does not depend on the degree of aversion to inequality.

The fringe rate affects the outer border as ϕ^a does the inner. Per unit of land, the marginal burden on individuals can be found as follows. Before the new externality is introduced, $\Delta_b \bar{y}$ in (13.2) equals zero according to (12.10). This may be written as

$$(17.14) \qquad n_{b+1} \underset{b+1}{\triangle} c = \underset{b}{\triangle} Q(r[b+1] - \check{r})$$

by (11.6) and (4.14), and taking into account that $r[b+2] = \check{r}$. Holding the optimal location policy unaltered, that is, setting the first term in parentheses of (17.11) equal to zero as in (13.2), implies

$$(17.15) \qquad n_{b+1} \underset{b+1}{\triangle} c$$

$$= \underset{b}{\triangle} Q \left[\left[r[b+1] + \frac{1}{\Delta_b Q} \left[n_{b+1} \underset{n_{b+1}}{\triangle} \bar{y} + \sum_{j=a+1}^{b} n_j \lambda_j \frac{\partial u}{\partial E_j} \underset{b}{\delta} E_j \right] \right] - \check{r} \right]$$

after the new externality has been introduced. Comparison between (17.14) and (17.15) indicates that the marginal rate (17.12) reduces the rent-paying ability of individuals on the fringe from $r[b+1]$ to $r[b+1] - \phi^b/\Delta_b Q$, that is, it acts as if line A in figure 17.3 were lowered to line B. Consequently, when the adverse effects of urban sprawl are taken into account, the spatial extent of the city is reduced from b' to b. If an optimal policy is adopted, the difference between rents at the fringe

Industrial Pollution

Figure 17.3: Land–value patterns at the urban fringe.

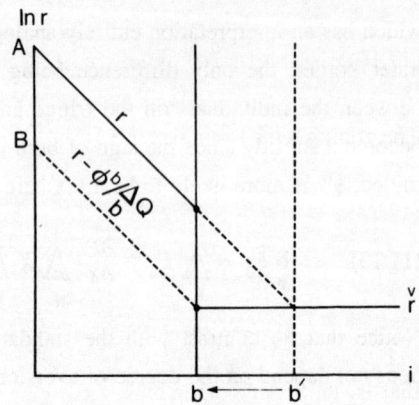

area b will reflect, in addition to marginal transportation costs, the adjusted aggregate marginal value of the loss in utility due to the degradation of the surrounding nonurban landscape when an additional unit of land at the fringe is converted to residential land use.

Land–Development Projects [15]

Chapter sixteen examined the case of a cartel owning land on one side of the inner border. In general, however, if the cartel owns both sides, the inner border itself may become a decision variable. This is a problem in land development which cannot be proposed reasonably (or overtly) as an issue in the case of prejudice.

Consider a cartel extending over $[1,b]$. The cartel wants to allocate land between industry and households so as to maximise the aggregate value of land it owns. Given that land use is determined in a competitive manner and that industrial bid–rents are steeper than residential bid–rents, the total area must be partitioned in two and the industry must be located around the centre. Thus the cartel aims to

(17.16) $\quad\text{maximise}_a \left[\sum_{j=1}^{a} r_j^0 \mathop{\triangle}_{j-1} Q + \sum_{j=a+1}^{b} \bar{r}[j] \mathop{\triangle}_{j-1} Q \right].$

The zoning which satisfies (17.16) is such that

(17.17) $\quad (r_{a+1}^0 - \bar{r}[a+1]) \mathop{\triangle}_a Q$

$= - \left[\sum_{j=1}^{a} \mathop{\triangle}_a r_j^0 \mathop{\triangle}_{j=1} Q + \sum_{j=a+2}^{b} \mathop{\triangle}_a \bar{r}[a] \mathop{\triangle}_{j-1} Q \right],$

that is, the inner border must be located where the aggregate difference of bid–rents at the inner border is precisely balanced by the total change in bid–-rents which would come about if the inner border were moved slightly outwards.[16]

Which of the bid–rents will be higher at the border, given that the inner land use generates a negative externality for the outer, and given that this externality becomes stronger as the inner land use expands? According to (17.17) the answer depends on the signs of $\Delta_a r_j^0$ and $\Delta_a \bar{r}[a]$. If there are increasing (constant, decreasing) returns to scale for land used in production then $\Delta_a r_j^0 >(=,<) 0$ for $1 \leq j \leq a$. On the other hand, if the city is "open", $\Delta_a \bar{r}[j] < 0$ for $a+1 \leq j \leq b$ necessarily holds to compensate for the increased nuisance. However, if the city is "closed", $\Delta_a \bar{r}[j]$ will be negative near a and positive near b so that the sign of the second term on the RHS of (17.17) will depend on the spatial extent of the cartel. A small cartel extending, say, to F in figure 16.5 would generate a negative sign for the second term on the RHS of (17.17). As the cartel becomes larger and reaches beyond G in the same figure, the second term on the RHS (17.17) begins to increase until, eventually, it may even become positive. Based on these remarks, an answer to the question at the beginning of this paragraph is now possible. If returns to scale for land used in production are nonincreasing and if the city is "open" then the bid–rent difference on the LHS of (17.17) will be positive: the cartel will constrain the industry in order to exploit

Industrial Pollution

the increased bid–rents over both the industrial and residential zones. At the other extreme, if returns to scale for land used in production are nondecreasing, if the city is "closed" and if the cartel is long enough for the second term on the RHS of (17.17) to be positive then the bid–rent difference on the LHS of (17.17) will be negative: the cartel will encourage the industry to expand in order to exploit the increased bid–rents over the industrial zone and over the periphery of the residential zone. Between these two extremes the difference of bid–rents at the inner border remains undetermined.

Under what circumstances does the zoning proposed by the cartel satisfy the public interest? It will be argued below that this happens if (1) the planner has an infinite aversion to inequality; (2) there are constant returns to scale in production; and (3) the city is "open". Under any other circumstances agreement between the two will be coincidental. Therefore, in general, decisions of land developers should be corrected by the planner.

1. Bid–rents ensure $u_i = z$ over a landscape of variable environmental quality. Using (13.6), it follows that the planner must have an infinite aversion to inequality.

2. If there are constant returns to scale for land used in production then (17.17) is reduced to

$$(17.18) \quad r^0_{a+1} - \bar{r}[a+1] = -\frac{1}{\Delta_a Q} \sum_{j=a+2}^{b} \bigtriangleup_a \bar{r}[j] \bigtriangleup_{j-1} Q,$$

which is equal to the total amount per unit of land that individuals would be prepared to forgo in order to push the inner border one area away, for given levels of welfare. If, on the other hand, there are constant returns to scale for labour then (17.10) is reduced to

(17.19) $\quad \overset{0}{r_{a+1}} - r[a+1] = -\frac{1}{\Delta_a Q} \sum_{j=a+2}^{b} n_j \lambda_j \frac{\partial u}{\partial E_j} \underset{a}{\delta} E_j.$

It remains to determine conditions under which the RHSs of (17.18) and (17.19) are equal.

3. Given that the total land revenue is maximised, if the city is "open" then the individual expenditures on land must also be maximised subject to a fixed level of utility. In other words $\bar{r}[j]q_j$ at the maximum cartel profit must correspond to the solution of

(17.20) $\quad \bar{r}[j]q_j = max\{y - (x_j - c[j]) | z \leq u_j\}.$

Applying the envelope theorem on (20), one concludes that

(17.21) $\quad \underset{a}{\triangle} r[j] \underset{j-1}{\triangle} Q = n_j \lambda_j \frac{\partial u}{\partial E_j} \underset{a}{\delta} E_j$

as required.[17]

A More General Point of View

Prejudice in chapter sixteen and industrial pollution in this chapter exhibit many similarities from a mathematical point of view. Both belong to the broad class of phenomena called "incompatible land uses" (steel mill and tourism, high-rise and airport, throughway and neighbourhood; and so on). Incompatible land uses, in turn, belong to the more general class of interdependent land uses discussed in chapter fourteen.

Because of the underlying common structure, the results in chapters sixteen and seventeen can be readily extended to the more general setting. Consider, for example, residential and commercial land uses in the equilibrium context of Yinger (1976). Since residences

Industrial Pollution

are averted by commerce and since commerce is attracted by residences, there can be no stable equilibrium. Stability will be attained through discrimination—in this case zoning regulations. On the other hand, examples about how optimality results can be extended have already been given in the section "Zoning" of this chapter. Furthermore, it has been argued in the previous section that there are cases where optimality can be achieved without public intervention. In general however public intervention is necessary for optimality. Then the optimal rules of chapters fifteen and seventeen may be modified to fit any case of interdependent land uses. There is no conceptual difficulty in creating new rules. The difficulty stems from jurisdictional fragmentation which often renders the application of such rules practically impossible.[18] Finally, prejudice shows that optimality cannot be applied everywhere. This is because to accept optimality in this context is to accept a particular state of prejudice, which is ethically unfounded. It seems to me that planning decisions on such issues should be of a teleological rather than a Pareto efficiency character. School busing, which appears to address itself to the roots of the problem in spite of Pareto efficiency, is an appropriate example.

Notes to Chapter Seventeen

1   For example, in the case of an "open" city, figure 16.2 would apply. Suppose that the initial situation is described by line A2. If some exogenous advantage for the use of land in production is established, so that industrial bid–rents increase, then the industrial area expands, production volume and the emission of industrial pollutants increase, population decreases and the final situation could be described by line B2.

2   See the discussion in the first full paragraph following (15.2).

3   For example, using note 8.4, if land values were not treated parametrically then condition (8.3) would become

$$\sum_{j=1}^{a} \Delta_a r_j^0 \Delta_{j-1} Q + r_{a+1}^0 \Delta_a Q - \Delta_a X = 0.$$

4   The lagrangean function of problem (17.2) is

$$L = \sum_{j=1}^{a} r_j^0 \Delta_{j-1} Q + \sum_{j=a+1}^{b} n_j \bar{y}_j - X + \sum_{j=a+1}^{b} \mu_j (\bar{z}[j] - v_j).$$

Partially differencing L with respect to a, we have

$$\sum_{j=1}^{a} \Delta_a r_j^0 \Delta_{j-1} Q + r_{a+1}^0 \Delta_a Q + \sum_{j=a+2}^{b} n_j \Delta_a y_j - n_{a+1} y_{a+1}$$

$$- \Delta_N X \Delta_a N - \Delta_a X + \sum_{j=a+2}^{b} \mu_j \left[\Delta_a \bar{z}[j] - \Delta_a v_j \right]$$

$$- \mu_{a+1} (\bar{z}[a+1] - v_{a+1}) = 0.$$

Following the discussion of note 8.4, the first and third terms vanish. Then (17.4) is obtained by noting that $\Delta_a \bar{z}[j] = 0$ and $\bar{z}[a+1] = v_{a+1}$ by (11.16).

5   The optimal tax for the industry should be of the form

$$\phi = a\phi^a$$

and should be added to problem (8.1) as a new term.

6   Similar conclusions have been reached by Helpman and Pines (1975), Oron and Pines (1975), and Strotz and Wright (1975).

7   The term "zoning" usually refers to any type of direct control on land use. In this sense it is more general than the meaning attached here: for us, zoning will be associated specifically with regulations about the spatial extent of *segregated* economic activities within the urban area.

There have been many criticisms of zoning, especially in the law literature (see for example Delafons (1969), Mandelker (1971) and Siegan (1972)). These however seem to refer to the abuses of zoning regulations as currently practised, rather than to the principle itself. Theoretical work in economics about zoning issues is represented by Davis (1963), Ohls, Weisberg and White (1974), Stull (1974), Helpman and Pines (1975B), White (1975), Courant (1976), Moss (1977), Rubinfeld (1978) and Mills (1979).

8   Further to Pigouvian taxation and zoning, the optimum could also be achieved through abatement. The optimal policy associated with this alternative is a subsidy per additional unit of the abatement device equal to the total amount individuals are prepared to forgo in order to reduce the polluting activity to the level that the additional unit of the abatement device actually has, for given levels of welfare (Strotz and Wright (1975)).

9   As indicated in both figures, optimal control of externalities causes land-value adjustments. For example, in figure 17.1, the original pattern of land values A1 becomes A2 after zoning has been introduced. It follows that zoning generally affects the aggregate value of residential land. Consider now the second-best case where residential land use is determined in a competitive manner. Changes in bid-rents are caused by improvements in the quality of the environment after zoning has been introduced. For reasons analogous to those discussed in chapter seven, such changes cannot measure the effectiveness of zoning. Indeed, zoning (or any other type of optimal policy) may either increase or decrease the

aggregate value of residential land. See for example Ohls, Weisberg and White (1974), and Courant (1976).

10 For a good discussion of optimal policies in the case of integrated land uses see Mills (1979).

11 For example, suppose that land use one generates a positive externality on land–use two resulting in a given land use proportion at the optimum. Now introduce an externality generated by land use two on land use one. If it is negative, the optimal proportion will change in favour of land use one. If on the other hand it is positive, the optimal proportion will change in favour of land use two.

12 The analysis in the section "Density–Response Specification" of chapter sixteen could be applied here for any pair of locally interacting land–uses which replace "black" and "whites". An earlier discussion on zoning of such land uses is to be found in Davis (1963).

13 In the case of a positive spatial externality, subsidising will, in the same manner, also be addressed to the absentee landowners of industrial land. Subsidising can always be achieved by passing the burden to the individuals $(A < \bar{\phi})$.

14 Partially differencing the lagrangean function of note 4 with respect to b,

$$\sum_{j=a+1}^{b} n_j \triangle_b \bar{y}_j + n_{b+1} \bar{y}_{b+1} - \triangle_N X \triangle_b N + \sum_{j=a+1}^{b} \mu_j \triangle_b (\bar{z}[j] - v_j)$$
$$+ \mu_{b+1} (\bar{z}[b+1] - v_{b+1}) = 0.$$

Industrial Pollution

Condition (17.11) then follows noting that $\bar{y}_j$ and $\bar{z}[j]$ depend on b in the sense of location if $j = b$; that v_j depends on b both in the sense of location if $j = b$ and through the externality for $a + 1 \leq j \leq b$; and that $\bar{z}[b+1] = v_{b+1}$ by (11.16).

15 This section is based on the ideas of Stull (1974), and Helpman and Pines (1977).

16 Partially differencing (17.16) with respect to a, we have

$$\sum_{j=1}^{a} \underset{a}{\Delta} \overset{0}{r_j} \underset{j-1}{\Delta} Q + \overset{0}{r_{a+1}} \underset{a}{\Delta} Q$$

$$+ \sum_{j=a+2}^{b} \underset{a}{\Delta} \bar{r}[j] \underset{j-1}{\Delta} Q - \bar{r}[a+1] \underset{a}{\Delta} Q = 0$$

using the discrete rule of Leibnitz. Then (17.17) follows immediately.

17 The lagrangean function of problem (17.19) is

$$L_j = \bar{r}[j] q_j + \lambda_j (z - u_j).$$

Partially differencing L_j with respect to a, we obtain

$$\underset{a}{\Delta} L_j = q_j \underset{a}{\Delta} \bar{r}[j] - \lambda_j \frac{\partial u}{\partial E_j} \underset{a}{\delta} E_j.$$

A necessary condition for maximum $\bar{r}[j] q_j$ is $\Delta_a L_j = 0$. Then the result follows by (4.14).

18 Think, for example, about the issue of acid rain between Canada and the USA.

18

Spatial Public Goods[1]

Conceptual Framework [2]

In 1954 Samuelson published his famous paper introducing the concept of a pure public good. Such a good, once available, obeys (1) *non-excludability*, that is, it cannot be withheld from anyone who wishes to consume it; (2) *joint supply*, that is, it can be made available to any number of individuals at the same level of service and at no additional cost; and (3) *non-rejectability*, that is, it has to be consumed by everyone. In these terms, a pure public good stands at one extreme of the continuum bordered by a pure private good at the other extreme. For the latter, exclusion is perfectly feasible, marginal costs of consumption precisely reflect the corresponding marginal costs of production, and the decision of whether or not to consume is entirely left with the individual.

Most goods in reality are to be found between the two extremes. Within this more general context, one may reasonably hold that any

> "theory of public goods is a theory of market failure. The closer a good is to the public good pole, the less likely is that private firms will provide the good at all ... . (The principal reason for the

non-provision by private firms relates to the non-exclusion attribute: if firms are not able to effectively exclude consumers, they cannot extract a price and will collect no revenues.) ... If a good is not provided by private firms, but is desirable, chances are that a reasonably efficient collective provision process ... could provide (it) at levels which would cause a net welfare gain to society ... . This is a most compelling rationale for the existence of government.[3]

Under these circumstances the planner is bound to provide public goods and to raise, somehow, funds necessary for their provision. The related urban policy is a particular distribution of public expenditure and taxation over the social and spatial realms of the city. Here, instead of combining the two dimensions of urban policy, I shall first consider only the problem of provision. Some issues of finance will be discussed toward the end of the chapter.

Public goods contribute to the quality of the environment over the city. The relationship between a particular distribution ω of public expenditure and the associated environmental quality is extremely complex. Since the latter is a composite index there are, in principle, many ways in which ω could arise. Expenditures to alleviate congestion or to improve health and education facilities are examples of partitioning ω. Such partitioning is in itself an optimisation problem, depending upon the needs of the urban society and upon the priorities as perceived by the planner. Instead of further discussing this thorny issue, I hasten to assume that the planner, in his wisdom, decides efficiently on the allocation of public funds between various public goods and that such efficiency is precisely reflected in a composite public good. Thus ω implies a particular infrastructure over the city. Indeed ω may be taken to represent the operating costs necessary for that particular infrastructure: the relationship between infrastructure and operating costs is known. That is, given an infrastructure, the corresponding spatial distribution of public expenditure can be determined; and given a spatial distribution of public expenditure, the precise physical characteristics of the corresponding infrastructure can also be determined. The relationship, on the other hand, between infrastructure and the level of the composite public good experienced by someone living at a particular location is far more complicated. This happens because individuals may visit public facilities beyond their immediate neighbourhood, thereby using significant parts of the entire infrastructure and, at the same time, congesting it. Therefore the level of the composite public good experienced at any particular location, and hence the quality of the urban environment, must depend on both the spatial distribution of public expenditure and the spatial distribution of population.

Distance determines an explicitly spatial type of exclusion for the public good in one direction, and a corresponding type of rejection in the other. If spatial interaction remains uninhibited by distance, that is, if the friction of distance is zero then there is no spatial exclusion or rejection. If, on the other hand, the friction of distance is infinite then one deals in effect with a local public good. Between these two extremes there is a continuum of public goods ranked according to the degree of spatial exclusion or rejection. A primary school for example exhibits a higher degree of spatial exclusion than a secondary school and this, in turn, exhibits a higher degree of spatial exclusion than a university. In other words, the impact of different public goods diffuses differently over space. Such spatial diffusion, in turn, operates in two directions. Firstly, for every residential location, it generates a composite of public goods accessible to the individual in the sense that they are close enough for some interaction. Secondly, for every public good location, it generates congestion by those individuals who are close enough for some interaction. In this manner spatial interaction becomes a pervasive source of impurities, not only because it violates non-excludability and non-rejectability, but also because it violates joint supply through congestion.

As a model of this system, consider a distribution of individuals and a distribution of public expenditure over some landscape $\mathcal{J}$. Every unit of public expenditure emits an externality which somehow diffuses its impact to individuals in $\mathcal{J}$. The externality, in turn, is affected by the very distribution of individuals over $\mathcal{J}$. In this sense every individual also emits an externality to other individuals in $\mathcal{J}$. Thus every individual experiences a composite of externalities emitted by individuals and by public expenditure over $\mathcal{J}$. We name this composite a *spatial public good*. If the externality diffusion processes involved are nontrivial (in the sense that the level of a contribution to each externality changes with distance and/or direction from the source) then the level of the spatial public good anywhere in the landscape (hence the entire distribution of the spatial public good in $\mathcal{J}$) depends on the distribution of individuals and of public expenditure in $\mathcal{J}$. In this manner one obtains three interacting surfaces unfolding over the landscape—a population surface, a public expenditure surface and a consequent public good surface. The planner seeks to determine the optimal form of these surfaces. The nature of his solution depends on the nature of the externality diffusion processes involved, in other words on the structure of the spatial public good.

We have thus arrived at the point where externalities and public goods appear to be different faces of the same coin. Indeed there is every reason to relax the definition of an externality and perceive spatial public goods as *intentional* spatial externalities. In particular cases, this may hold true only over a subset of the population.[4] In general, however, it is fair to say that the quality of the urban environment is structured from a large number of comprehensively interdependent, intentional and unintentional, spatial externality effects. This intricate pattern of spatial interdependence is the essence of our problem; and the problem of the planner, in these terms, is nothing more than to manipulate the elements that compose the quality of the urban environment in some optimal way.

The Model

In the simplest case, there is a fixed total amount Ω of public funds to be distributed over the city. Thus a feasible optimal distribution of public expenditure is

$$(18.1) \qquad \omega \equiv (\omega_1,...,\omega_b) \in \{\omega | \sum_{i=1}^{b} \omega_i \leq \Omega \text{ and } \omega_i \geq 0, i = 1,...,b\}.$$

The level of the public good experienced by someone in area i stems from potential interaction with all areas. The contribution of public expenditure in area i to the level of the public good experienced by someone in area j is

$$(18.2) \qquad E_{ij} = f_{ij}[n, \omega_i]$$

where, for convenience, the externality is expressed here directly in terms of population and investment size, rather than density as in chapter sixteen. Equation (18.2) reflects the idea that E_{ij} depends on the distance between the two areas (through the spatial diffusion of the public good), on the spatial distribution of population (which, together with the relative position of area i, determines the level of congestion of the public good in that area) and on the public expenditure realised in area i.[5] Then the level of the public good experienced by someone in area j is

$$(18.3) \qquad E_j[n,\omega] = \sum_{i=-b}^{b} E_{ij}$$

with $\Delta_{ni} E_j < 0$ and $\partial E_j / \partial \omega_i > 0$.

This more general structure of environmental quality now enters the utility function of individuals. Nevertheless, as ω is not a decision

Spatial Public Goods

variable for individuals, their problem is still represented by (11.1). The problem (11.9) of the planner, on the other hand, must be modified as

(18.4) $\quad D[r,\bar{z};\alpha,\Omega]$

$$= min\left\{ \sum_{j=1}^{b} n_j \bar{y}_j - X[N] \middle| \right.$$

$$\left. \bar{z}[i] \leq v[u_i;\alpha]\big|_{u_i = v_i} \text{ for } i \in \mathcal{J} \text{ and } \sum_{j=1}^{b} \omega_j \leq \Omega \right\}$$

in order to take into account the new control vector ω. Clearly, all the conditions of chapter fifteen still hold. The only additional requirements, which distinguish a spatial public good from a spatial externality, refer to the conditions associated with public expenditure. These are written as

(18.5) $\quad v\left[\sum_j \omega_j - \Omega\right] = 0$

(18.6) $\quad -\left[\sum_j \mu_j \dfrac{dv}{du_j}\dfrac{\partial u}{\partial E_j}\dfrac{\partial E_j}{\partial \omega_i} + v\right]\bigg|_{u=v} = 0 \text{ for } i = 1,...,b.$[6]

Using the envelope theorem on problem (18.4)

(18.7) $\quad v = -\dfrac{dD}{d\Omega} > 0,$

the negative sign occurring because the aggregate income necessary to support a given distribution of utility decreases as funds available for the public good increase. Using (18.5) and (18.7)

(18.8) $\quad \sum_j \omega_j = \Omega,$

that is, all public funds available are spent at the optimum. On the other hand, with respect to conditions (18.6), the quantity $\partial E_j/\partial \omega_i$ represents the gain in the level of the public good experienced in area j because the public expenditure in area i has been raised by one dollar. The quantity $(\partial u/\partial E_j)(\partial E/\partial \omega_i)$ represents the value of this gain to someone in area j. The quantity $(dv/du_j)(\partial u/\partial E_j)(\partial E_j/\partial \omega_i)$ represents the social evaluation of this gain. Hence the first term in (18.6) represents the MSB of public expenditure in area i. The second term, which is the marginal social value of a dollar spent, represents MSC. These conditions say that the MSB of public expenditure should be the same in all areas at the optimum.

The conditions relevant to optimal decentralisation policy are collected in table 18.1. Since the only difference between the optimal city under spatial externalities and spatial public goods is to be found in the new conditions (18.5) and (18.6), *the prescriptions of chapter fifteen are simply augmented here by the requirement that the planner spends the entire amount of funds available and that he distributes them in such a way that the associated MSB is the same in all areas at the optimum.*

A solution procedure for the problem (18.4) of the planner follows. According to (18.6) and (18.8), the planner must spend the entire amount of public funds available, and distribute them over the city in such a way that the marginal social benefit of public investment is the same in all zones at the optimum. For any feasible $\mathcal{A} \equiv \{x_i, q_i; i = 1,...,b\}$, (18.6) gives $\omega[i,\alpha,\Omega; \mathcal{A}]$. This, in conjunction with (18.3), determines $E[i,\alpha,\Omega; \mathcal{A}]$. By comparing first-order conditions, we have $\phi[i,\alpha,\Omega; \mathcal{A}] \equiv \phi_i - \bar{\phi}$ (using (13.7), (15.4) and (15.5)), and $\Delta_i z[i,\alpha,\Omega; \mathcal{A}] = \Delta_i \upsilon$ using (13.6). From then on, the solution procedure exactly parallels that of chapter thirteen with $\omega^*[i,\alpha,\Omega] = \omega[i,\alpha,\Omega; \mathcal{A}^*]$.

Since the optimal decentralisation policy concerning the private good and land remains that of chapter fifteen, the analysis in the section entitled "Comparison Between Private Goods and Spatial Externalities" of that chapter continues to apply here. Notice that there, where the spatial externality was written as $E_i[n]$, the analysis was based on (15.7) only. Here, however, where the spatial public good is written as $E_i[n,\omega]$, the analysis should involve both (15.7) and (18.6). In particular, the discussion concerning (15.7) may be adjusted for (18.6) as

Table 18.1: Decision rules.

	Optimality Conditions
	Planner
x_i	(11.11): $n_i \dfrac{\partial y}{\partial x_i} - \mu_i \dfrac{dv}{du_i}\dfrac{\partial u}{\partial x_i} \big|_{u_i = v_i} =$ (12.4): $n_i \left[1 - \lambda_i \dfrac{\partial u}{\partial x_i} \right] \big|_{u_i = z[i]} = 0$
n_i	(15.2): $\bar{y}_i + (n_i + 1) \bigtriangleup_{n_i} \bar{y} - \bigtriangleup_N X - \left[\mu_i \dfrac{dv}{du_i}\dfrac{\partial u}{\partial q_i} \bigtriangleup_{n_i} q + \sum_j \mu_j \dfrac{dv}{du_j}\dfrac{\partial u}{\partial E_j} \bigtriangleup_{n_i} E_j \right] \big|_{u = v} =$ $\left[n_i \left[r[i] - \lambda_i \dfrac{\partial u}{\partial q_i} \right] \bigtriangleup_{n_i} q + \left[\left[\bar{y}_i + \bigtriangleup_n \bar{y} \right] \bigtriangleup_N X \right] \right.$ $\left. - \sum_j n_j \lambda_j \dfrac{\partial u}{\partial E_i} \bigtriangleup_{n_i} E_j \right] \big|_{u = z} = 0$
i	(13.2): $n_i \bigtriangleup_i \bar{y} + \mu_i \left[\bigtriangleup_i \bar{z} - \dfrac{dv}{du_i}\dfrac{\partial u}{\partial E_i} \bigtriangleup_i E \right] \big|_{u_i = v_i} =$ (13.5): $n_i \left[\lambda_i \left[\bigtriangleup_i - \dfrac{\partial u}{\partial E_i} \bigtriangleup_i E \right] \big|_{u_i = z[i]} + \left[\dfrac{\mu_i}{n_i} - \lambda_i \right] \bigtriangleup_i z \right] = 0$
ω_i	(18.6): $\left[\sum_j \mu_j \dfrac{dv}{du_j}\dfrac{\partial u}{\partial E_j}\dfrac{\partial E_j}{\partial \omega_i} + v \right] \big|_{u = v} =$ $- \sum_j n_j \lambda_j \dfrac{\partial u}{\partial E_j}\dfrac{\partial E_j}{\partial \omega_i} + \dfrac{dD}{d\Omega} \big|_{u = z} = 0$

		Decentralisation
	Individuals	
(11.3):	$1 - \lambda_i \frac{\partial u}{\partial x_i}\big|_{u_i = z[i]} = 0$	No correction
(11.4):	$\left[r_i - \lambda_i \frac{\partial u}{\partial q_i}\right] \underset{n_i}{\triangle} q \big|_{u_i = z[i]} = 0$	$\bar{y}_i + \underset{n_i}{\triangle} \bar{y} = \underset{N}{\triangle} X$ and $\phi_i^n = -\frac{1}{n_i} \sum_j n_j \lambda_j \frac{\partial u}{\partial E_j} \underset{n_i}{\triangle} E_j \big|_{u = z}$
(13.3):	$\lambda_i \left[\underset{i}{\triangle} z - \frac{\partial u}{\partial E_i} \underset{i}{\triangle} E\right]\big|_{u_i = z[i]} = 0$	$\phi_i^i = \left[\frac{\mu_i}{n_i} - \lambda_i\right] \underset{i}{\triangle} z$ $= \left[1 - \bar{u}_i^{-\alpha}\right] \lambda_i \frac{\partial u}{\partial E_i} \underset{i}{\triangle} E \big|_{u_i = z[i]}$

well: using (12.3) and (18.7) on (18.6),

$$(18.9) \quad -\frac{dD}{d\Omega} = \sum_j n_j \lambda_j \frac{\partial u}{\partial E_j} \frac{\partial E_j}{\partial \omega_i} \equiv \sum_j n_j \phi^{\omega}_{ij},$$

where

$$(18.10) \quad \phi^{\omega}_{ij} = \lambda_j \frac{\partial u}{\partial E_j} \frac{\partial E_j}{\partial \omega_i}$$

is called a *Lindahl price* and denotes the amount of money an individual in area j is prepared to pay for increasing public investment in area i by one dollar, thereby increasing the experienced level of the spatial public good, with utility held constant.[7] Given that the quantities ϕ^{ω}_{ij} may be thought of as "prices", the planner, as externality generator, may be thought of as being "compensated" (for slightly increasing public investment) on the basis of these "prices" at the optimum, in the sense that he can now reduce the aggregate income deficit by an amount equal to the marginal social value of a dollar spent in area i.

Consider two individuals, each in a different area. The "demands" of these individuals for public expenditure in area i are represented in

Figure 18.1: Aggregation of individual demands.

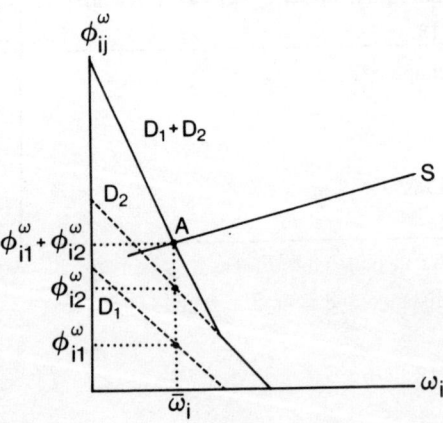

figure 18.1 by lines D_1 and D_2. Aggregate "demand", $D_1 + D_2$, is obtained by *vertical* addition of individual demands because each consumes the same amount. This is precisely analogous to figure 15.1(2). "Demand" here is a schedule of potential marginal changes necessary to maintain utility at different levels of public expenditure in area i. Supply S, on the other hand, is a schedule of optimal public expenditure at different levels of externality benefit. Equality of supply and "demand" at A determines a level of public expenditure $\bar{\omega}_i$, Lindahl prices ϕ^ω_{i1} and ϕ^ω_{i2} and therefore total revenue. This last may be used as a basis in order to "compensate" the externality generator at i, that is, individuals at 1 and 2 would be prepared to pay a total amount equal to $\bar{\omega}_i(\phi^\omega_{i1} + \phi^\omega_{i2})$ in order to enjoy the effects of public expenditure at i. Notice that the vertical distance below each individual's demand curve reflects the social valuation of the marginal benefit which he incurs from consumption, that is, $\lambda_j (\partial u/\partial E_j)(\partial E_j/\partial \omega_i)$ for $j = 1, 2$, and this equals the corresponding marginal cost ϕ^ω_{ij} as in (18.10). Thus efficiency is ascertained. At this point, the sum of social valuations of marginal benefits of individuals equals the total reduction in the aggregate income deficit necessary to maintain utility. Although, in principle, Lindahl prices could be used to charge individuals for their consumption of the public good at i, implementation of the scher·· is difficult because individual tastes are once more hidden under the summation symbol of (18.9): this is the celebrated "free rider" problem already discussed in chapter fifteen.[8]

Classification

As in chapter fourteen, it is convenient to distinguish explicitly between distance and density effects. Thus (18.2) is now written as

(18.11) $\quad E_{ij} = \zeta_{ij}\xi_{ij}[n,\omega_i],$

Spatial Public Goods

where the explicit dependence of ξ on both i and j reflects the truth that public goods in areas differing with respect to relative location and size are congested differently by the same population. Using the definitions of chapter fourteen, we may classify the main types of a spatial public good as follows.

1. *Clubs*. The origin of clubs here is to be found in a density model with no distance–response, that is, one where exclusion over $\mathcal{J}$ is impossible. Since $\zeta_{ij} = 1$ for $i,j \in \mathcal{J}$, it must also be true that $\xi_{ij}[n,\omega_i] = g_i[N,\omega_i]$, that is, that the spatial distribution of population is immaterial. Thus the quality of the environment experienced everywhere within the city is

$$(18.12) \qquad E_j = \sum_{k=-b}^{b} g_k[N,\omega_k] = 2\sum_{k=1}^{b} g_k[N,\omega_k] \equiv \bar{E}$$

using (18.3). That is, in the absence of distance–response, the quality of the environment is invariant over the landscape. Since both the optimal utility differences and the marginal location rates are proportional to environmental quality differences (13.6) and (13.7), we conclude that $\Delta_i z = 0$ and $\overset{i}{\phi}_i = 0$ for $i = 1,\ldots,b$ irrespective of the degree of aversion to inequality. On the other hand, from (15.4) and (18.2),

$$(18.13) \qquad \overset{n}{\phi}_i = -\frac{1}{n_j} \sum_j n_j \lambda_j \frac{\partial u}{\partial E_j} \underset{n_i}{\Delta} 2 \sum_k g_k$$

$$= -\frac{2}{n_i} \sum_k \underset{N}{\Delta} g_k \sum_j n_j \lambda_j \frac{\partial u}{\partial E_j}.$$

Taking into account that the total value of the urban product is distributed to the inhabitants of the optimal city, the planner must impose a tax or subsidy on the residents of zone i equal to

$$(18.14) \qquad \phi_i - \bar{\phi} = n_i \overset{n}{\phi}_i + i\overset{i}{\phi}_i - \bar{\phi}$$

$$= -\left[2\sum_k \triangle_N g_k \sum_j n_j \lambda_j \frac{\partial u}{\partial E_j} + \bar{\phi}\right] = 0$$

because $n_i \phi_i^n$ is invariant over the landscape. Hence there is no need for income redistribution under any degree of aversion to inequality. It follows that, in this case, the theory of justice espoused by the planner is immaterial. Absence of the friction of distance, a fundamental geographical characteristic, equalises the quality of the environment which, in turn, dictates equal treatment of equals in any case. Therefore, the optimal decentralisation policy reduces to the problem of producing the private and public goods efficiently. Efficient production of the private good implies that the planner must impose an optimal population size N^*. Efficient production of the public good, on the other hand, hinges upon returns to scale in its production: if under decreasing returns, Ω should be uniformly distributed over $\mathcal{J}$; if under increasing returns, it should be concentrated somewhere; and if increasing returns are exhausted at a size smaller than Ω, another multitude of solutions will emerge. It seems that this context trivialises such spatial issues. Once efficient production and optimal population size are ascertained, competition for land between those admitted will lead to the optimum. In consequence, absence of the friction of distance eliminates the need for any land controls.

When space is completely abstracted, $\bar{E} = g[N,\Omega]$ and the model acquires the standard form of a club. Then the marginal rate on the use of land is simply

(18.15) $\quad \phi_i^n = -\lambda \frac{\partial u}{\partial E} \triangle_N g.$

Following Buchanan's (1965) original contribution, a growing literature has focused on the interaction between the size of a club and the corresponding level of public investment.[9] In this context, the optimal size reflects a balance between the economies of increasing population size and the diseconomies of congestion.

Spatial Public Goods

2. *Urban contact fields.* Whereas the impurity in the case of clubs rests with joint supply, in the case of urban contact fields it rests with non–excludability or non–rejectability. Since ζ_{ij} is nontrivial, the quality of the environment varies over the landscape. In consequence, contrary to the case of clubs, both the optimal utility differences and the marginal location rates vary, in general, with the degree of aversion to inequality as in (13.6) and (13.7). On the other hand, since $\xi_{ij} = g_i[\omega_i]$, it is true that $\Delta_n E_j = 0$. Consequently, $\overset{n}{\phi}_i = 0$ according to (15.4). In other words, since congestion does not affect the quality of the environment, there is no reason to correct for it. This is the only simplification to be made. Everything else, including the need to control everything that has to do with the use of land under a finite aversion to inequality, still holds. Models in this area include those of Williams (1966) and Wright (1977).

3. *Pure public goods.* A good that has the distance–response of a club and the density response of an urban contact field is a pure public good. Then, following (18.12),

$$(18.16) \qquad \bar{E} = 2 \sum_{k=1}^{b} g_k[\omega_k].$$

Clearly, $\Delta_i u = 0$ and $\overset{i}{\phi}_i = 0$ as for clubs; and $\overset{n}{\phi}_i = 0$ as for urban contact fields. Therefore, once more, the optimal decentralisation policy reduces to the problem of producing the private and public goods efficiently. Since, as for clubs, issues of distributing Ω over $\mathcal{J}$ become rather trivial, space is typically abstracted from such models. Thus $\bar{E} = g[\Omega]$ simply. Of course, the tradeoff between population size and the corresponding level of public investment, which is the central issue in the theory of clubs, also disappears. Spatial models in this area include those of Barr (1972), Helpman and Pines (1975A) and Thrall (1982).

4. *Local public goods.* These are represented by a density model

with no spillover effects, that is, one where spatial exclusion is perfect. Under these circumstances, $\zeta_{ij} = 1$ for $i = j$ and zero otherwise leads immediately to $\xi_{ij}[n,\omega_i] = g_i[n_i,\omega_i]$, and hence to

(18.17) $\quad E_j = g_j[n_j,\omega_j]$.

Under these circumstances, the marginal rate on the use of land in (15.4) is simplified as

(18.18) $\quad \phi_i^n = \lambda_i \dfrac{\partial u}{\partial E_i} \underset{n_i}{\triangle} g.$

On the other hand, the variation in optimal utilities and marginal location rates, as described in (13.6) and (13.7), remains: here, as in the case of urban contact fields, the question of an optimal distribution of public expenditure over $\mathcal{J}$ becomes central. Such optimal policy, together with the corresponding distribution of population, would determine the optimal distribution of environmental quality over $\mathcal{J}$. Papers dealing with these questions include those of Boruchov (1972), Schuler (1974), Wile (1975), Helpman, Pines and Boruchov (1977) and Schuler (1977). In particular, Helpman, Pines and Boruchov (1977) provide the analysis of a case where policy variables are the price system, the production and distribution of public services, and taxation. They examine the case where the resulting allocation is a competitive equilibrium with equal incomes and equal utilities: in our terms, there is an infinite aversion to inequality. It is seen that the spatial distribution of population and land values adheres to the standard pattern, that is, $\triangle_i \rho < 0$ and $\triangle_i r < 0$. Furthermore, if q_i and E_i are net substitutes (complements) then the quality of the environment decreases (increases) away from the centre. In the former case, the density of public investment, $\omega_i/\triangle_{i-1} Q$, also decreases. In the latter, it remains ambiguous.[10]

5. *Agora models.* Suppose that all public investment is concentrated

Spatial Public Goods

at the centre. The centre now becomes a public good, an agora, enjoyed by all; and it can be described by a distance model such that

(18.19) $E_j = \zeta_j g[n,\Omega]$.

This situation bears a strong resemblance to the one discussed in the second half of chapter sixteen. Since the centre now attracts, rather than repulses, surrounding individuals, spatial adjustments will be opposite to those caused by prejudice. In the "open" city case, increasing the level of the spatial public good will increase densities everywhere. Consequently, the city will become larger in terms both of population and spatial extent. In the "closed" city case, on the other hand, densities will increase around the centre and will decrease at the periphery. Although the city will probably contract, utility must increase.

Turning now to issues of agora optimality, notice that here ζ is a function of distance between the centre and zone j. Since this function decreases with increasing distance from the centre, the quality of the environment for more distant zones also decreases. Thus, in the case of finite aversion to inequality, optimal utilities decrease away from the centre according to (13.6). As the aversion to inequality increases, following (13.7), subsidisation of more distant zones increases relatively in order to reduce optimal inequalities. Finally, the marginal rate on the use of land in (15.4) becomes

(18.20) $\phi_i^n = -\dfrac{1}{n_i} \bigtriangleup_{n_i} g \sum_j n_j \lambda_j \dfrac{\partial u}{\partial E_j} \zeta_j$.

It is perhaps useful at this point to clarify the explicit dependence of g in (18.19) on the spatial distribution of population, rather than on the total population. A distance model of this kind suggests that individuals in more distant zones enjoy the agora relatively less because distance is an impediment to interaction. At the same time, for the same reason, individuals in more distant zones impose relatively less congestion. The former is captured by ζ_j; the latter, by the explicit dependence of g on n: for more distant zones, $\Delta_{ni}g$ is expected to become less strongly negative. Since the value of the summation on the RHS of (18.20) is the same for all i (once at the centre you congest everybody there irrespective of the zone from which you originate), the portion of the optimal tax attributed to the use of land, $n_i\phi_i^n$, is proportional to $-\Delta_{ni}g$. In particular, individuals in zones closer to the centre pay more because, by using the agora often, they congest more. Clearly, this framework requires a distinction between time spent at the centre for work and time spent for enjoyment. If both are combined then the frequency of interaction with the centre, and hence the levels of enjoyment and congestion, are the same for everyone. Under these circumstances, $E = \zeta\,g[N,\Omega]$ and the model can be treated as a club.

Public Goods that Occupy Land

Until now the analysis has been simplified by assuming that only investment was necessary for the production of the public good. When the need for land is recognised, (18.2) may be modified as

$$(18.21) \qquad E_{ij} = f_{ij}[n,G[H_i,\omega_i]]$$

where G is a production function for the public good which, for area i, depends on the amount of land allocated to the public good in this area, H_i, and on the corresponding public investment. Clearly, $\partial f/\partial G > 0$, $\partial G/\partial H_i > 0$, $\partial G/\partial \omega > 0$ and $0 \leq H_i \leq \Delta_{i-1}Q$. That is, the spatial externality emitted from area i to those in area j increases when the level of the public good in area i increases; the level of the public good, in turn, increases when land and/or investment allocated to its production increase; and the (nonnegative) amount of land allocated to the production of a public good in area i cannot be larger than the total available in that area. Aggregating over i, we obtain

Spatial Public Goods

(18.22) $$E_j[n,G[H,\omega]] = \sum_{i=-b}^{b} E_{ij}$$

where $G[H,\omega] \equiv (G[H_{-b},\omega_{-b}],...,G[H_b,\omega_b])$.

Every residential area in $\mathcal{J}$ may now contain two land uses, rather than a single land use. Consequently, (4.14) becomes

(18.23) $$q_i = \left[\bigwedge_{i-1} Q - H_i \right] \div n_i.$$

Furthermore, since land occupied by the public good over $\mathcal{J}$ is costly, the problem of the planner (18.4) is modified to

(18.24) $$D[r^0,r,\bar{z};\alpha,\Omega] = min\left\{ \sum_{j=1}^{b} (\overset{0}{r}_j H_j + n_j \bar{y}_j) - X[N] \right|$$

$$z[i] \leq v[u_i;\alpha]\big|_{u_i=v_i} \text{ for } i \in \mathcal{J} \text{ and } \sum_{j=1}^{b} \omega_j \leq \Omega \bigg\}$$

where $\overset{0}{r}_j$ is the land rent associated with the production of the public good at j. Clearly, in addition to the control variables of problem (18.4), the aggregate income deficit must now be minimised with respect to $H \equiv (H_1,...,H_b)$. The new conditions regulating the allocation of land between residential and public land use read

(18.25) $$\overset{0}{r}_i + n_i r[i] \frac{\partial q}{\partial H_i} - n_i \lambda_i \frac{\partial u}{\partial q_i}\frac{\partial q}{\partial H_i} - \sum_j n_j \lambda_j \frac{\partial u}{\partial E_j}\frac{\partial E_j}{\partial H_i} = 0.^{11}$$

When a unit of land in area i is taken from residential land use and given to public land use, there is a marginal cost from payment for the use of this additional unit by the public sector (first term in (18.25)); a corresponding marginal benefit from savings in the residential sector (now that the per capita consumption of land there has been reduced by $\partial q/\partial H_i$ and hence that the saving in residential rent per capita is $r_i \partial q/\partial H_i$) (second term); a marginal cost of reducing utility for everyone in area i because of increased congestion generated by the residential land–use contraction there (third term); and a corresponding marginal benefit of increasing utility for everyone in $\mathcal{J}$ because of the improvements in the quality of the environment generated by the public land–use expansion in area i (fourth term).

At the optimum, the marginal social cost of reducing utility for everyone in area i because of increased congestion should equal the corresponding marginal social benefit of increasing utility for everyone in $\mathcal{J}$ because of improved quality of the environment. Otherwise, the socially evaluated sum of utilities would not be maximised at the optimum—a contradiction. Therefore, at the optimum, it must be that

$$(18.26) \quad -n_i \lambda_i \frac{\partial u}{\partial q_j} \frac{\partial q}{\partial H_i} - \sum_j n_j \lambda_j \frac{\partial u}{\partial E_j} \frac{\partial E_j}{\partial H_i} = 0.$$

Moreover, using (18.23), notice that

$$(18.27) \quad n_i \frac{\partial q}{\partial H_i} = -1$$

that is, the loss of land in the residential sector as a result of transferring one unit to the public sector is precisely one unit. Taking into account (18.26) and (18.27), (18.25) implies

$$(18.28) \quad \overset{0}{r}_i = r[i],$$

in other words, the two types of land use should be charged the same land rents everywhere in $\mathcal{J}$. For arbitrary degree of aversion to inequality, we know that such rents must be imposed by the planner. In the special case of infinite aversion to inequality however, where $z[i] = z$, it is sufficient for the planner to fix the urban population at the optimal size and to announce the spatial distribution of optimal tax and subsidy rates ϕ_i^n and ϕ_i^i. Since the optimal redistribution of income created by these rates is such that every inherent location advantage is eliminated, competition between those admitted will ensure bid–rents that satisfy

Spatial Public Goods

both (15.2) and the spatial equilibrium condition of Muth (12.10)—as required for optimality. These bid–rents, in turn, will guide the public land–use as well because of (18.28). That is, in the case of infinite aversion to inequality, the optimal urban form is established by competition for land between the residential and public sectors everywhere over $\mathcal{J}$.

Transportation as a public good is a special case of what has already been said. Following chapter fifteen, suppose that travel occurs along a given dense, radial transportation network. Additional congestion at i is generated by those further away from the centre:

$$(18.29) \quad E_{ki} = \zeta_{ki}\xi[n_k, G[H_i, \omega_i]] \; with \; \zeta_{ki} = \begin{cases} -1 \; for \; i \leq k \\ 0 \; for \; i > k. \end{cases}$$

The total congestion at i is created by commuters at and beyond i:

$$(18.30) \quad e_i = \sum_{k=i}^{b} \xi[n_k, G[H_i, \omega_i]] \equiv -g_i[(n_i,...,n_b), H_i, \omega_i]$$

with $\Delta_{nk} e_i < 0$, $\partial e/\partial H_i > 0$ and $\partial e/\partial \omega_i > 0$. Someone at j experiences congestion over the entire ray between j and the centre. Therefore

$$(18.31) \quad E_j = \sum_{i=1}^{j} e_i.$$

Since

$$(18.32) \quad \bigtriangleup_j E = -\left[\sum_{i=1}^{j+1} - \sum_{i=1}^{j}\right] g_i[n, H_i, \omega_i]$$

$$= -g_{j+1}[n, H_{j+1}, \omega_{j+1}] = -\sum_{k=j+1}^{b} \xi_{k,j+1}[n, G[H_{j+1}, \omega_{j+1}]] < 0,$$

optimal utilities decrease away from the centre under finite aversion to inequality according to (13.6). This happens because more distant locations imply longer congested trips, and hence lower quality of the environment there from that particular point of view. Finally, in order to determine the marginal rate on the use of land, notice that

$$(18.33) \quad \mathop{\Delta}_{n_i} E_j = \begin{cases} \sum_{l=1}^{J} \mathop{\Delta}_{n_i} g_l \ for \ i \geq j \\ \sum_{l=1}^{i} \mathop{\Delta}_{n_i} g_l \ for \ i < j \end{cases}$$

because someone added in zone i congests others only between this zone and the centre. Therefore, using (15.4), the marginal rate on the use of land becomes

$$(18.34) \quad \phi_i^n = \frac{1}{n_i} \left[\sum_{j=1}^{i} \sum_{l=1}^{j} + \sum_{j=i+1}^{b} \sum_{l=1}^{i} \right] n_j \lambda_j \frac{\partial u}{\partial E_j} \mathop{\Delta}_{n_i} g_l .$$

The literature on transportation is extensive.[12] Within this, Strotz (1965) remains a classic reference which includes most of the fundamental intuitions now available on optimal transportation policy. Taking into account what has been said since chapter twelve, the optimal transportation policy can be summarised here as follows. Suppose that there is a fixed amount of public funds available for transportation and that the recovery of these funds is not an issue.[13] Furthermore, suppose that the aggregate income of urban residents is required to equal the total value of the urban product. The planner must organise the production of the urban good efficiently. However, although individuals should receive the marginal product of their labour, the planner must redistribute income through congestion tolls and location taxes charged to individuals according to (15.5). The congestion toll $n_i \phi_i$, based on the marginal congestion rate (15.4), equals the total damage someone imposes on the other drivers as he travels to and from work in the centre. The location tax $i\phi_i^i$, based on the marginal location rate (13.7), reflects environmental differences weighted by the theory of justice adopted by

425

the planner. Given that individuals take these rates parametrically, excepting infinite aversion to inequality, the resulting optimum will be such that some areas in the city will become more attractive than others —utility differences between areas being associated with corresponding spatial externality differences. In consequence the planner will find it necessary to control everything that has to do with the use of land under a finite aversion to inequality. Firstly he must determine a price for the use of land compatible with (12.10) and (15.2). Secondly, based on this price, he must partition land in each area between residential land use and transportation. The principle of partitioning dictates that the marginal product of land should be the same for the two uses as in (18.26).[14] Thirdly, he must allocate individuals to areas thereby determining their place in the chosen scheme of optimal inequality. In doing this, he essentially partitions residential areas into lot sizes compatible with (12.10) and (15.2) by determining the optimal number of individuals for every area. Once income and location (hence utility) have been determined for everyone, under the optimal distribution of land values, the established differences in locational benefits and costs between adjacent areas precisely offset the income differences necessary to attain the corresponding optimal utility differences. Finally, as in the case of optimal land allocation between residential and transportation uses, public expenditure on roads should be distributed between areas so that its marginal product is everywhere the same according to (18.6). It appears therefore that optimal controls in the case of finite aversion to inequality are very strong. In contrast, when there is an infinite aversion to inequality, it is sufficient for the planner to fix the urban population at the optimal size and to announce the spatial distribution of optimal tax and subsidy rates ϕ_i^n and ϕ_i^i. It seems worth pointing out that

> "(t)he burden of congestion on motorists is dimensionally a product of two factors: congestion as a characteristic of driving conditions at a point and distance travelled. The burden of congestion may be reduced either by reducing congestion along the route or by

reducing the length of the route. It is worse to drive ten miles in congested traffic than one mile. Suppose a man occupies an estate near the center of the city and that all those who live farther out and who commute to work to the city center must every day drive past this estate in congested traffic. Their burden is greater, the greater the front footage the estate occupies because they must drive farther in congestion.

It would appear that the occupancy of space along a route imposes, in measure with its front footage, an external real diseconomy on those who travel past. Optimal pricing therefore suggests that not only should there (a) be a toll to discourage motorists from making too many trips and imposing external diseconomies of congestion (at every point at which they travel) on other motorists, but that (b) there should be a land rent (based on front footage or area) to discourage excessive space occupancy and thereby to reduce the mileage of congested driving for any given traffic flow. We might expect this to be in addition to the rent that, in the absence of anybody wanting to travel, would still be paid for the use of the limited desired space itself." (Strotz (1965, p. 151)).

Surprisingly enough, we know that there is no need to impose such a tax under any circumstances. That is, for arbitrary degree of aversion to inequality, the previous analysis suggests that there is no need to apply policies which specifically encourage or discourage any particular pattern of land occupancy at the optimum.[15]

I close this section with some remarks on agora models. When land is introduced into an agora model, the model becomes closely similar to the model of chapter seventeen. In order to isolate the public good character of the centre, assume that the production of the private good does not pollute, and that it is produced only with labour. Therefore both land in the centre and public funds are explictly related to the production of the public good. Under these circumstances we may write

427

Spatial Public Goods

the spatial externality as $E[n, G[a, \Omega]]$. Given once more that Ω is fixed, the problem of the planner is now written as

$$(18.35) \quad D[\mathbf{r}^0, \mathbf{r}, \bar{\mathbf{z}}; \alpha, \Omega] = min\left\{ \sum_{j=1}^{a} r_j^0 \bigtriangleup_{j-1} Q + \sum_{j=a+1}^{b} n_j y_j - X[N, N[a]] \right|$$
$$z[i] \le v[u_i, \alpha]\Big|_{u_i = v_i} \text{ for } i = a+1, \ldots b \Big\}$$

where the first term of the RHS represents public expenditure on land, and the production function of the private good depends on the spatial extent of the centre only inasmuch as it affects the workforce. Following a procedure exactly similar to the one that led to (17.6), we obtain the interior border condition

$$(18.36) \quad r_{a+1}^0 = \frac{1}{\Delta_a Q}\left[-n_{a+1}\bigtriangleup_{n_{a+1}} \bar{y} + \sum_{j=a+2}^{b} n_j \lambda_j \frac{\partial u}{\partial E_j} \bigtriangleup_a E_j \right]$$

which helps to determine the publicly optimal amount of land used to construct the agora. In a manner analogous to chapter seventeen, the first term on the RHS represents the effect of expanding the agora on the aggregate income deficit generated by the displacement of individuals in the marginal zone. On the other hand, the expression under the sum equals the total amount individuals would be prepared to forgo in order to bring the border of the agora one area closer, for given levels of utility. Rent at the border must equal the value of the two components distributed per unit of land. Clearly, since the planner takes into account all spatial externality effects, land values at the border between the two sectors are equal, that is, $r_{a+1}^0 = r[a+1]$. This contrasts with (17.10) where there was a difference between the two rents at the inner border reflecting the change in the aggregate value of the externality effect when an additional unit of land was converted to production.

The Mohring Paradox

Throughout this chapter, the total amount of public investment was treated as given exogenously. In this section I consider Ω endogenous. As a consequence, the issue of public finance is bound to surface: although one could still maintain that public funds somehow appear from the outside, it is far more convincing to admit that what benefits those in the city should be supported at the optimum by the same. Suppose that the location tax $i\phi_i^i$ still serves to redistribute income, while the congestion toll $n_i\phi_i^n$ is now collected to help finance the provision of the public good. The fundamental question is, *will this revenue be sufficient at the optimum* or will it be necessary to further apply lump–sum taxes or subsidies, as those represented by A in the section "Optimal Decentralisation Policy" of chapter thirteen, in order to balance the budget? An answer to this question is provided by the Mohring paradox.[16] I consider first the case where the public good is produced only with capital.

Since what has been said in previous sections holds for any feasible value of Ω, it must also hold for the optimal level of public expenditure. What is a reasonable principle to determine the optimal level of public expenditure? In the context of the Mohring paradox, it is that *the public sector should pay competitive prices*. When there is a competitive equilibrium between sectors for the use of resource services, the value of the marginal product of a resource service unit must equal its price. Since for public expenditure the price is simply one dollar, we obtain using (18.9)

$$(18.37) \qquad \sum_j n_j \lambda_j \frac{\partial u}{\partial E_j} \frac{\partial E_j}{\partial \omega_i} = -\frac{dD}{d\Omega} = 1$$

as a condition which determines the level of public expenditure when the public sector pays competitive prices. This is a reasonable principle to admit. If, for example, $-dD/d\Omega > 1$ then spending an additional dollar on the public good would save more than one dollar at the optimum, for given levels of utility. Therefore it would seem proper that public expenditure be augmented at the expense of something else. If, on the other hand, $-dD/d\Omega < 1$ then public expenditure should be reduced to provide individuals with higher disposable income. In this sense, the principle of competitive pricing seems to be perfectly compatible with the aim to optimise. It can however break down where optimality itself requires noncompetitive pricing—as will be seen later on when land is introduced in the production of the public good.

Further to competitive pricing, the Mohring paradox requires (1) that the spatial diffusion pattern of the public good be trivial, in the sense of ζ_{ij} being either zero or one everywhere in $\mathcal{J}$; and (2) that the components of environmental quality g_i be homogeneous functions with respect to their arguments. The second requirement implies that the functions $e_i = g_i[N,\omega_i]$ obey

(18.38) $\qquad \lambda^\beta e_i = g_i[\lambda N, \lambda \omega_i] \ for \ \lambda > 0.$

When the parameter β is zero, doubling population and public expenditure everywhere ($\lambda = 2$) implies no change in the quality of the environment. On the other hand, when $\beta >(<) 0$, doubling population and public expenditure everywhere implies an improved (deteriorated) quality of the environment. It follows that $\beta >(=,<) 0$ signifies increasing (constant, decreasing) returns to scale in the maintenance of a given environmental quality. Under these circumstances, the Mohring paradox states that

18.1 *If there are increasing (constant, decreasing) returns to scale in the maintenance of a given environmental quality then there is a deficit (balance, surplus) in the budget allocated for the production of the public good at the optimum.*

As already mentioned, proposition 18.1 applies where the spatial diffusion pattern of the public good is trivial, that is, to clubs, local public goods, spaceless transportation and agora models without distance–response.[17]

I now consider the case where land enters as a factor of production. In this case, when areas are partitioned between residential and public land use, one cannot impose a priori a condition on land analogous to (18.37). This happens because (18.28) fixes the value of public land at the same level as the value of residential land which, in turn, is also determined at the optimum. To calculate this value, notice that (18.26) and (18.27) imply

$$(18.39) \qquad \lambda_i \frac{\partial u}{\partial g_i} = \sum_j n_j \lambda_j \frac{\partial u}{\partial E_j} \frac{\partial E_j}{\partial H_i}.$$

This, in conjunction with (12.3), (12.8), (15.2) and (15.4), leads to

$$(18.40) \qquad \sum_j n_j \lambda_i \frac{\partial u}{\partial E_j} \frac{\partial E_j}{\partial H_i} - \frac{\phi_i^n}{\Delta_{n_i} q} = r[i].$$

It follows immediately that only when there is no population externality, i.e. $\phi_i^n = 0$ for $i \in \mathcal{J}$, will competitive pricing in the market for land represent an optimal policy. *When there is a negative (positive) population externality, the public sector is bound to pay a price for land greater (smaller) than the value of its marginal product.* In particular, since from (15.4) and (18.23)

$$(18.41) \qquad -\frac{\phi_i^n}{\Delta_{n_i} q} = -\frac{1}{\Delta_{i-1} Q - H_i}(n_i + 1) \sum_j n_j \lambda_j \frac{\partial u}{\partial E_j} \mathop{\Delta}_{n_i} E_j,$$

the competitive price of land should be adjusted at the optimum by the externality effect of those in area i distributed per unit of public land. When this is taken into account, proposition 18.1 is modified as

18.2   *If returns to scale in the maintenance of a given environmental quality are larger (equal, smaller) than*

$$\frac{1}{\bar{E}} \sum_i \frac{H_i}{\Delta_{i-1}Q - H_i} \left[\underset{n_i}{\Delta} \bar{E} \right] (n_i + 1)$$

then there is a deficit (balance, surplus) in the budget allocated for the production of the public good at the optimum.

Thus when areas are partitioned between residential and public land use, in the presence of a congestion externality, the Mohring paradox is deformed by a negative quantity. Therefore a balanced budget will occur at decreasing returns to scale in the maintenance of a given environmental quality: when land enters as a factor of production, the likelihood of a deficit increases.

The previous conclusions hold for any integrated land–use pattern associated with trivial distance–response, such as local public goods and transportation. When though the land–use pattern is segregated, as in agora models, the Mohring paradox can be restored. This happens because now it is possible to require that the value of the marginal product of land be equal to its price at the optimum. However, the Mohring paradox further requires constant returns to scale for land in the production of the public good.[18] It seems that the Mohring paradox in its pure form is quite restrictive in matters concerning land; and that the same observation holds for the spatial diffusion of the externality in both the Mohring paradox and its variations.

It is worth noting that our conclusions hold for any degree of aversion to inequality. Further, the principal virtue of the Mohring paradox rests with the intuition that, in general, the budget allocated for the production of the public good does not balance at the optimum with the associated congestion tax receipts. In general, therefore, it will be necessary to further apply lump–sum taxes or subsidies, such as those represented by A in the section "Optimal Decentralisation Policy" of chapter thirteen, in order to balance the budget. As long as a particular A applies to everyone, and everyone takes it parametrically, the optimum can be retained at a balanced budget. But the optimum requires, in addition to lump–sum taxes or subsidies, the detailed tax or subsidy schemes based on ϕ_i^n and ϕ_i^n. Indeed, in the context of this book, lump–sum taxes or subsidies are meaningless when independent of Pigouvian taxation. We know already the nature of difficulties associated with the application of such schemes. Thus, in general, reality forces the imposition of taxes or subsidies which distort optimality. The tax on drivers, for example, follows their consumption of gasoline and remains insensitive to the spatial distribution of other drivers; and homeowners pay a tax which reflects the spatial distribution of property values, rather than the spatial distribution of externality damages as required for optimality.

Aggregate Relationships at the Optimum[19]

Since (15.2) holds, propositions 15.1–15.3 also hold. Notice that the total externality effect E in these propositions equals $-\Phi^n$, where Φ^n is the total public revenue from congestion taxes. This, together with proposition 15.3, implies

(18.42) $\quad \Phi^n <(=,>) \frac{1}{2}\left[S - \left[\check{R} + \frac{1}{\eta_{Q:i}}C\right]\right] \text{ if } \eta_{c:i} >(=,<) 1.$

Suppose that the public good is produced only with capital. Then, combining proposition 18.1 with (18.42),

(18.43) $\quad \beta <(=,>) 0$ *implies*

$\Omega <(=,>) \Phi^n <(=,>) \frac{1}{2}\left[S - \left[\check{R} + \frac{1}{\eta_{Q:i}}C\right]\right] \text{ if } \eta_{c:i} >(=,<) 1.$

It follows immediately that if returns to scale in both the maintenance of a given environmental quality and transportation are decreasing (constant, increasing) then

Spatial Public Goods

(18.44) $\quad S >(=,<) 2\Omega + \check{R} + \dfrac{1}{\eta_{Q:i}} C$

provided that the elasticity of the urban area with respect to distance is constant over distance. Therefore, under decreasing (constant, increasing) returns to scale, the total surplus value of production, which represents the benefits of urbanisation, should be greater (equal, smaller) than the corresponding costs of urbanisation. Returns to scale refer here to the two main components of urban infrastructure, that is, the production of public goods and the nature of transportation costs. In this sense, (18.44) implies that weaker returns to scale associated with an urban infrastructure require stronger benefits of urbanisation at the optimal size of city.

When the public good occupies land, the extreme LHS of (18.43) should be modified according to proposition 18.2. Finally, all our conclusions in this section are independent of the theory of justice employed by the planner.

Appendix to Chapter Eighteen

This appendix gives the details of the Mohring paradox and its variations. The first part is associated with proposition 1, the second with proposition 2 and the third with the application of the Mohring paradox in the case of agora models with land as a factor of production.

1

Taking into account (15.4) and (15.5), the tax someone in area k pays for his damage to those in area j is given by $-n_j \lambda_j (\partial u/\partial E_j) \Delta_{nk} E_j$. The distribution of this damage between the various areas that those in j interact with is, using (18.3), $-n_j \lambda_j (\partial u/\partial E_j) \Sigma_i \Delta_{nk} E_{ij}$. Hence, the portion of the tax someone in k pays for his damage to those in j as they visit area i together is $-n_j \lambda_j (\partial u/\partial E_j) \Delta_{nk} E_{ij}$. Aggregating over all his victims, $-\Sigma_j n_j \lambda_j (\partial u/\partial E_j) \Delta_{nk} E_{ij}$ is the portion of the tax someone in k pays for his damage to those over $\mathcal{J}$ as he visits area i. The total portion of the tax paid by those in k for their damage related to area i is $-(n_k+1) \Sigma_j n_j \lambda_j (\partial u/\partial E_j) \Delta_{nk} E_{ij}$. It follows immediately that

$$(18.45) \quad \Phi_i^n \equiv -\sum_k (n_k+1) \sum_j n_j \lambda_j \frac{\partial u}{\partial E_j} \underset{n_k}{\Delta} E_{ij}$$

$$= -\sum_j n_j \lambda_j \frac{\partial u}{\partial E_j} \sum_k \left[\underset{n_k}{\Delta} E_{ij} \right] (n_k+1)$$

is the total tax raised for area i.

The net revenues of the public sector associated with area i are

$$(18.46) \quad \Phi_i^n - \omega_i =$$

$$-\sum_j n_j \lambda_j \frac{\partial u}{\partial E_j} \sum_k \left[\underset{n_k}{\Delta} E_{ij} \right] (n_k+1) - \sum_j n_j \lambda_j \frac{\partial u}{\partial E_j} \frac{\partial E_j}{\partial \omega_i} \omega_i$$

using (18.37) and (18.38). Suppose now that the public good is a club, so that $E_{ij} = g_i[N, \omega_i] \equiv e_i$ and $E_j = \bar{E}$ for $j \in \mathcal{J}$. Let $\Phi^n \equiv \Sigma_i \phi_i^n$ be the total revenue of the public sector from congestion taxes. Aggregating (18.46), we have

$$(18.47) \quad \Phi^n - \Omega$$

$$= -\sum_i \sum_j n_j \lambda_j \frac{\partial u}{\partial \bar{E}} \left[\sum_k \left[\underset{n_k}{\Delta} g_i \right] (n_k+1) + \frac{\partial g_i}{\partial \omega_i} \omega_i \right]$$

$$= -\sum_i \sum_j n_j \lambda_j \frac{\partial u}{\partial \bar{E}} (\beta e_i)$$

provided that the functions g_i are β–homogeneous with respect to their arguments. (A β–homogeneous function $y = f[x_1,...,x_n]$ obeys $\beta y = \Sigma_i (\partial f/\partial x_i) x_i$.) Notice that the step from (18.46) to (18.47) uses $\partial \bar{E}/\partial \omega_i = \Sigma_j \partial g_j/\partial \omega_i = \partial g_i/\partial \omega_i$ and $\Delta_{n_k} g_i = \Delta_N g_i \Delta_{n_k} N = \Delta_N g_i$.

The Mohring paradox holds only if ζ_{ij} can be either zero or one everywhere in $\mathcal{J}$. Then it is possible to reorder (18.46) as in (18.47). On the other hand, if distance–response is nontrivial, the transition from (18.46) to (18.47), becomes impossible and the Mohring paradox collapses.

In the case of local public goods where $E_i = g_i[n_i, \omega_i]$, the tax paid by someone in i for his damage to those over $\mathcal{J}$ is simply $-n_i \lambda_i \cdot (\partial u/\partial E_i)\Delta_{n_i} E_i$. Thus the net revenues of the public sector become

$$(18.48) \quad \Phi^n - \Omega = -\sum_i n_i \lambda_i \frac{\partial u}{\partial E_i} \left[\left[\underset{n_k}{\Delta} g_i \right](n_k + 1) + \frac{\partial g_i}{\partial \omega_i} \omega_i \right]$$

$$= -\sum_i n_i \lambda_i \frac{\partial u}{\partial E_i} (\beta E_i),$$

using (18.37) in a form obviously simplified. For transportation, observe from (18.30) that those who damage others in area i must be located at or beyond i. In consequence (18.45) is now written as

$$(18.49) \quad \Phi_i^n \equiv \sum_{k=i}^{b}(n_k + 1) \sum_{j=1}^{b} n_j \lambda_j \frac{\partial u}{\partial E_j} \underset{n_k}{\Delta} g_i$$

$$= \sum_{j=i}^{b} n_j \lambda_j \frac{\partial u}{\partial E_j} \sum_{k=i}^{b} \left[\underset{n_k}{\Delta} g_i \right](n_k + 1).$$

Given that (18.37) also holds and that transportation is spaceless, we have

$$(18.50) \quad \Phi^n - \Omega = \sum_{i=1}^{b} \sum_{j=i}^{b} n_j \lambda_j \frac{\partial u}{\partial E_j} \left[\sum_{k=i}^{b} \left[\underset{n_k}{\Delta} g_i \right](n_k + 1) + \frac{\partial g_i}{\partial \omega_i} \omega_i \right]$$

$$= \sum_{i=1}^{b} \sum_{j=i}^{b} n_j \lambda_j \frac{\partial u}{\partial E_j} (\beta e_i)$$

where the negative signs in (18.49) and (18.50) disappear because e_i is negative. Finally, in the case of agora models

$$(18.51) \qquad \Phi_i^n = -\sum_{k=a+1}^{b} (n_k + 1) n_i \lambda_i \frac{\partial u}{\partial E_i} \underset{n_k}{\triangle} E_i$$

$$= -n_i \lambda_i \frac{\partial u}{\partial E_i} \sum_{k=a+1}^{b} (\underset{n_k}{\triangle} E_i)(n_k + 1).$$

If the public good is also a club, so that $E_i = g[N,\Omega] \equiv \bar{E}$, then

$$(18.52) \qquad \Phi^n - \Omega = -\sum_{i=a+1}^{b} n_i \lambda_i \frac{\partial u}{\partial \bar{E}} \left[\sum_{k=a+1}^{b} \left[\underset{n_k}{\triangle} g \right] (n_k + 1) + \frac{\partial g}{\partial \Omega} \Omega \right]$$

$$= -\sum_{i=a+1}^{b} n_i \lambda_i \frac{\partial u}{\partial \bar{E}} (\beta \bar{E}).$$

2

When land is a factor of production, the net revenues of the public sector become

$$(18.53) \qquad \Phi_i^n - (r_i H_i + \omega_i) = -\sum_j n_j \lambda_j \frac{\partial u}{\partial E_j} \sum_k \left[\underset{n_k}{\triangle} E_{ij} \right] (n_k + 1)$$

$$-\sum_j n_j \lambda_j \frac{\partial u}{\partial E_j} \frac{\partial E_j}{\partial H_i} H_i + \frac{H_j}{\Delta_{i-1} Q - H_i} (n_i + 1) \sum_j n_j \lambda_j \frac{\partial u}{\partial E_j} \underset{n_i}{\triangle} E_j$$

$$-\sum_j n_j \lambda_j \frac{\partial u}{\partial E_j} \frac{\partial E_j}{\partial \omega_i} \omega_i,$$

using (18.40) and (18.41). If, further, the public good is a club, so that

$E_{ij} = g_i[N,H_i,\omega_i] \equiv e_i$ and $E_j = \bar{E}$ for $j \in \mathcal{J}$, the total net revenue is

$$
(18.54) \quad \Phi^n - \left[\sum_i r_i H_i + \Omega\right] = -\sum_i \sum_j n_j \lambda_j \frac{\partial u}{\partial \bar{E}}(\beta e_i)
$$
$$
+ \sum_i \frac{H_j}{\Delta_{i-1}Q - H_i}(n_i + 1) \sum_j n_j \lambda_j \frac{\partial u}{\partial \bar{E}} \underset{n_i}{\Delta} \bar{E}
$$
$$
= -\sum_j n_j \lambda_j \frac{\partial u}{\partial \bar{E}} \left[\beta \bar{E}_i - \sum_i \frac{H_j}{\Delta_{i-1}Q - H_i} \left[\underset{n_i}{\Delta} \bar{E}\right](n_i + 1)\right].
$$

The remaining cases are similar.

3

Competitive pricing of public land in an agora model implies

$$
(18.55) \quad \frac{1}{\Delta_{j-1}Q} \sum_{i=a+1}^{b} n_i \lambda_i \frac{\partial u}{\partial \bar{E}} \underset{j-1}{\Delta} g = r_j^0 \text{ for } 1 \le j \le a,
$$

provided that the public good is also a club, so that $E_i = g[N,a,\Omega] \equiv \bar{E}$. Notice that (18.55) is entirely compatible with (18.36): for zones in the interior of the agora, the first term on the RHS of (18.21) vanishes because there is no displacement of individuals. Under these circumstances, the total net revenues of the public sector are

$$
(18.56) \quad \Phi^n - \left[\sum_{j=1}^{a} r_j^0 \underset{j-1}{\Delta} Q + \Omega\right]
$$
$$
= -\sum_{i=a+1}^{b} n_i \lambda_i \frac{\partial u}{\partial \bar{E}} \sum_{k=a+1}^{b} \left[\underset{n_k}{\Delta} g\right](n_k + 1)
$$
$$
- \left[\sum_{j=1}^{a} \sum_{i=a+1}^{b} n_i \lambda_i \frac{\partial u}{\partial \bar{E}} \underset{j-1}{\Delta} g + \sum_{i=a+1}^{b} n_i \lambda_i \frac{\partial u}{\partial \bar{E}} \frac{\partial g}{\partial \Omega} \Omega\right].
$$

Suppose that there are constant returns to scale in land used for the production of the public good. Then

$$(18.57) \qquad \bigtriangleup_{j-1} g = \frac{\partial g}{\partial Q_{j-1}} \bigtriangleup_{j-1} \frac{\partial g}{\partial Q} \bigtriangleup_{j-1} Q.$$

Replacing (18.57) in (18.56),

$$(18.58) \qquad \Phi^n - \left[\sum_{j=1}^{a} r_j^0 \bigtriangleup_{j-1} Q + \Omega \right]$$

$$= - \sum_{i=a+1}^{b} n_i \lambda_i \frac{\partial u}{\partial \bar{E}} \left[\sum_{k=a+1}^{b} \left[\bigtriangleup_{n_k} g \right] (n_k + 1) + \frac{\partial g}{\partial Q} \sum_{j=1}^{a} \bigtriangleup_{j=1} Q + \frac{\partial g}{\partial \Omega} \Omega \right]$$

$$= - \sum_{i=a+1}^{b} n_i \lambda_i \frac{\partial u}{\partial \bar{E}} - (\beta \bar{E})$$

because $\Sigma_{j=1}^{a} \Delta_{j-1} Q = Q_a$.

Notes to Chapter Eighteen

1 This chapter is based on Papageorgiou (1987A,B).

2 This section draws on some ideas of Lea (1981).

3 Lea (1981, pp. 353–354). I have taken the liberty of moving the full sentence in parenthesis to a new place.

4 A particular public good may be addressed to a particular class of individuals and may, for another class, be a purely external (unintentional) effect. For example, building a primary school next to the home of a childless couple may, in their view, generate a negative spatial externality.

5   It is also possible to define E_{ij} as depending upon ω rather than merely upon ω_i, in other words to recognise the rôle of the other potential opportunities on how important public investment is in area i. Since however no further intuition emerges, the simpler (18.2) is chosen for convenience.

6   Condition (18.5) is the Kuhn–Tucker condition for inequality constraints. The lagrangean function of problem (18.4) is

$$L = D + \sum_j \mu_j (\bar{z}[j] - v_j) + v \left[\sum_j \omega_j - \Omega \right].$$

Conditions (18.6) are obtained upon partial differentiation of the lagrangean function with respect to ω_i.

7   See Lindahl (1919).

8   Another, explicitly spatial, type of difficulty appears because such taxes differ between areas. There is, therefore, a new marginal cost or benefit associated with the decision of an individual where to locate. This must be taken into account by the planner, that is, ϕ_i^i, and hence the redistribution of income, must be modified accordingly. Thus, in a spatial context, it is not optimal simply to charge in a way that the marginal tax price is equal to the marginal benefit of individuals, that is, to use (18.10) directly. When though space is abstracted, optimality remains under the taxation scheme. This is well-known in the literature, and is associated with the so-called "Lindahl solution" (Lindahl (1919)) which arises in a pure voluntary exchange setting.

9   See for example Pauly (1970), Oakland (1972), Ellickson (1973), Ng (1973), Chamberlin (1974), McGuire (1974), Fisch (1975), Berglas (1976), Lancaster (1976) and Henderson (1979).

10 Contrary to equilibrium studies where the spatial structure of the city is established in some detail, little is known about the ways optimal public controls are distributed over the city. In this sense the study of Helpman, Pines and Boruchov (1977) is significant. (The only other analogous example, to my knowledge, is provided by the literature on the optimal allocation of land to streets.) The same questions, in the context of a general model, remain unanswered. Also unanswered remain questions about comparative statics, including how the spatial distribution of public controls is affected by the theory of justice employed.

11 These conditions are obtained upon partial differentiation of the lagrangean function in note 6, modified by (18.24), with respect to H_i and taking into account (12.3).

12 See for example Walters (1961), Strotz (1965), Vickrey (1969), Lave (1970), Boruchov (1971), Mills and de Ferranti (1971), Solow and Vickrey (1971), Solow (1972), Averous and Lee (1973), Dixit (1973), Legey, Ripper and Varaiya (1973), Livesey (1973), Riley (1973), Sheshinski (1973), Solow (1973), Henderson (1974B), Kraus (1974), Riley (1974), Boruchov (1975), Henderson (1975), Hochman (1975), Barr (1976), Robson (1976A), Arnott and Mackinnon (1977A,B), Boardman and Lave (1977), Kanemoto (1977), and Wheaton (1978).

13 These assumptions will be relaxed in the following sections.

14 Since fewer people cross the road in areas further away from the centre, the marginal benefit of land used for streets falls with distance from the centre. To the extent that per capita consumption of land increases away from the centre, (18.26) implies that the corresponding marginal cost of land used for streets also falls with distance from the centre. Thus it is not generally

Spatial Public Goods

possible to determine how the proportion of land allocated to streets behaves with distance from the centre. However, under specific conditions which include that G depends only on land, one may conclude the following. The *proportion* of land allocated to streets decreases at an increasing rate away from the centre. In absolute terms, the same is true for small cities, that is, the *amount* of land allocated to streets also decreases at an increasing rate away from the centre. For larger cities, we observe an initial increase followed by a decrease. There may also be some very large cities where there is an area around the centre which is completely allocated to transportation. In any case, the amount of land allocated to streets appears to be a concave function of distance which becomes zero at the outer city border. The original contributions dealing with this problem are those of Mills and de Ferranti (1971), and Solow and Vickrey (1971). Dixit (1973) placed the Mills and de Ferranti results within a properly optimal framework. Subsequent generalisations include Legey, Ripper and Varaiya (1973) and Sheshinski (1973).

15 This conclusion holds in the more general case of public goods that occupy land.

16 The original source is Mohring and Harwitz (1962), chapter two. Although Strotz (1965) mentions this explicitly, it is frequently referred to as the "Strotz result". Other contributions include Forsund (1973), Kolm (1975), Greenwald (1976) and Helpman, Pines and Boruchov (1977).

17 For the details see the appendix. It is perhaps worth mentioning at this point that agora models could be easily reinterpreted to fit the case of chapter seventeen, with Ω now representing a pollution abatement device so that the quality of the environment is expressed as $E_i[\Omega,X]$. In this context, (18.37) implies that the optimal

policy associated with this alternative is a subsidy per additional unit of the abatement device equal to the total amount individuals are prepared to forgo in order to reduce the polluting activity to the level that the additional unit of the abatement device actually has, for given levels of welfare (see note 17.8). Furthermore, in the extreme case where pollution diffuses perfectly well, the Mohring paradox implies that if there are increasing (constant, decreasing) returns to scale in the maintenance of a given environmental quality through pollution abatement then there is a deficit (balance, surplus) in the budget allocated for the abatement device at the optimum.

18 For details see the appendix. Also notice that note 17 applies with $E_i[a,\Omega,X[N,N[a],a]]$.

19 This section is based on some ideas in Arnott (1979).

References

W. Alonso, 1964, **Location and Land Use.** Harvard University Press, Cambridge, Mass.

J. C. Amson, 1972, Equilibrium Models of Cities: 1. An Axiomatic Theory. **Environment and Planning** 4, 429–444.

J. C. Amson, 1973, Equilibrium Models of Cities: 2. Single–Species Cities. **Environment and Planning** 5, 295–338.

J. C. Amson, 1974, Equilibrium and Catastrophic Modes of Urban Growth. In E. L. Cripps (ed.) London Papers in Regional Science 4. **Space–Time Concepts in Urban and Regional Models**, Pion, London, 108–128.

J. C. Amson, 1976, A Regional Plasma Theory of Land Use. In Y.Y. Papageorgiou (ed.) **Mathematical Land Use Theory**, Lexington Books, Lexington Mass., 99–116.

A. Anas, 1978, Dynamics of Urban Residential Growth. **Journal of Urban Economics** 5, 66–87.

Antiphon, circa − 400, **On Truth.**

R. J. Arnott, 1979, Optimal City Size in a Spatial Economy. **Journal of Urban Economics** 6, 65–89.

References

R. J. Arnott, 1980, A Simple Urban Growth Model with Durable Housing. **Regional Science and Urban Economics** 10, 53–76.

R. J. Arnott, J. G. MacKinnon, 1977A, Market and Shadow Land Rents with Congestion. **American Economic Review** 67, 588–600.

R. J. Arnott, J. G. McKinnon, 1977B, The Effects of Urban Transportation Changes: A General Equilibrium Simulation. **Journal of Public Economics** 8, 19–36.

R. J. Arnott, J. G. MacKinnon, W. C. Wheaton, 1978, The Welfare Implications of Spatial Interdependence. **Journal of Urban Economics** 5, 131–136.

R. J. Arnott, J. E. Stiglitz, 1979, Aggregate Land Rents, Expenditure on Public Goods, and Optimal City Size. **Quarterly Journal of Economics** 93, 471–500.

K. J. Arrow, 1963, **Social Choice and Individual Values.** Yale University Press, New Haven, Conn.

K. J. Arrow, 1973, Some Ordinalist–Utilitarian Notes on Rawls's Theory of Justice. **Journal of Philosophy** 70, 245–263.

K. J. Arrow, H. D. Block, L. Hurwicz, 1959, The Stability of Competitive Equilibrium II. **Econometrica** 27, 82–109.

K. J. Arrow, F. H. Hahn, 1971, **General Competitive Analysis.** Holden-Day, San Francisco, Calif.

K. J. Arrow, M. Kurz, 1969, Optimal Public Investment Policy and Controllability with Fixed Private Savings Ratio. **Journal of Economic Theory** 1, 141–177.

C. P. Averous, D. B. Lee Jr., 1973, Land Allocation and Transportation Pricing in a Mixed Urban Economy. **Journal of Regional Science** 13, 173–185.

R. C. Baesemann, 1977, The Formation of Small Market Places in a Competitive Economic Process — The Dynamics of Agglomeration. **Econometrica** 45, 361–374.

J. L. Barr, 1972, City Size, Land Rent, and the Supply of Public Goods. **Regional and Urban Economics** 2, 67–103.

References

J. L. Barr, 1976, Decentralized Urban Resource Allocation. **Journal of Regional Science** 16, 35–43.

W. J. Baumol, W. E. Oates, 1975, **The Theory of Environmental Policy.** Prentice–Hall, Englewood Cliffs, N. J.

M. J. Beckmann, 1957, On the Distribution of Urban Rent and Residential Density in Cities. Paper presented at the interdepartmental seminar on Mathematical Applications in the Social Sciences, Yale University.

M. J. Beckmann, 1969, On the Distribution of Urban Rent and Residential Density. **Journal of Economic Theory** 1, 60–68.

M. J. Beckmann, 1976, Spatial Equilibrium in the Dispersed City. In Y.Y. Papageorgiou (ed.), **Mathematical Land Use Theory,** Lexington Books, Lexington, Mass., 117–125.

J. Bentham, 1789, **An Introduction to the Principles of Morals and Legislation.**

L. van den Berg, R. Drewett, L. H. Klaasen, A. Rossi, C. H. T. Vijverberg, 1982, **Urban Europe: A Study of Growth and Decline.** Pergamon, Oxford.

E. Berglas, 1976, On the Theory of Clubs. **American Economic Review, Papers and Proceedings** 66, 116–121.

B. J. L. Berry, 1980, Inner City Futures: An American Dilemma Revisited. **Transactions, Institute of British Geographers,** New Series 5, 1–28.

B. J. L. Berry, J. W. Simmons, R. J. Tennant, 1963, Urban Population Densities: Structure and Change. **Geographical Review** 53, 389–405.

J. R. Bettman, 1979, **An Information Processing Theory of Consumer Choice.** Addison–Wesley, Reading, Mass.

H. Bleicher, 1892, **Statistiche Beschreibung Der Stadt Frankfurt Am Main Und Ihrer Bevolkerung.**

H. D. Block, J. Marschak, 1960, Random Ordering and Stochastic Theories of Response. In I. Oklin et al. (eds.), **Contributions to Probability and Statistics,** Stanford University Press, 97–132.

References

A. E. Boardman, L. B. Lave, 1977, Highway Congestion and Congestion Tolls. **Journal of Urban Economics** 4, 340–359.

E. Boruchov, 1971, Diseconomies of Scale in Urban Transportation. **Southern Economic Journal** 38, 79–82.

E. Boruchov, 1972, Optimal Provision and Financing of Local Public Goods. **Public Finance,** 27, 267–281.

E. Boruchov, 1975, The Effects of Public Provision of Roads on the Structure and Size of Cities. **Environment and Planning A** 7, 349–355.

E. Boruchov, O. Hochman, 1977, Optimum and Market Equilibrium in a Model of a City without a Predetermined Center. **Environment and Planning A** 9, 849–856.

J. M. Buchanan, 1965, An Economic Theory of Clubs. **Economica** 32, 1–14.

J. M. Buchanan, 1976, A Hobbesian Interpretation of the Rawlsian Difference Principle. **Kyclos** 29, 5–25.

J. M. Buchanan, W. C. Stubblebine, 1962, Externality. **Economica** 29, 371–384.

L.S. Burns, 1982, Review of L. van den Berg, R. Drewett, L. H. Klaassen, A. Rossi, C. H. T. Vijverberg, 1982, Urban Europe: A Study of Growth and Decline. **Journal of Economic Literature** 20, 1617–1619.

D. R. Capozza, 1973, Subways and Land Use. **Environment and Planning** 5, 555–576.

G. A. P. Carrothers, 1956, An Historical Review of the Gravity and Potential Concepts of Human Interaction. **Journal of the American Institute of Planners** 22, 94–102.

H. Carter, 1977, Urban Origins: A Review. **Progress in Human Geography** 1, 12–32.

E. Casetti, 1969, Alternate Urban Population Density Models: An Analytical Comparison of Their Validity Range. In A. J. Scott (ed.) **Studies in Regional Science**, Pion, London.

References

E. Casetti, 1971, Equilibrium Values and Population Densities in an Urban Setting. **Economic Geography** 47, 16–20.

E. Casetti, 1973, Urban Land Value Functions: Equilibrium Versus Optimum. **Economic Geography** 49, 357–365.

E. Casetti, 1980, Equilibrium Population Partitions Between Urban and Agricultural Occupations. **Geographical Analysis** 12, 47–54. (Originally published in 1970 in mimeographed form by the Department of Geography, The Ohio State University, Columbus, Ohio).

J. R. Chamberlin, 1974, Provision of Collective Goods as a Function of Group Size. **American Political Science Review** 68, 707–716.

A. C. Chiang, 1974, **Fundamental Methods in Mathematical Economics**. McGraw-Hill, New York.

W. Christaller, 1933, **Die Zentralen Orte in Süddeutschland**. Gustav Fischer Verlag, Berlin.

C. Clark, 1951, Urban Population Densities. **Journal of the Royal Statistical Society**, Series A 114, 490–496.

P. N. Courant, 1974, Urban Residential Structure and Racial Prejudice. **Discussion Paper 62**, Institute of Public Policy Studies, University of Michigan.

P. N. Courant, 1976, On the Effect of Fiscal Zoning on Land and Housing Values. **Journal of Urban Economics** 3, 88–94.

P. N. Courant, D. L. Rubinfeld, 1978, On the Measurement of Benefits in an Urban Context: Some General Equilibrium Issues. **Journal of Urban Economics** 5, 346–356.

P. N. Courant, J. Yinger, 1977, On Models of Racial Prejudice and Urban Residential Structure. **Journal of Urban Economics** 4, 272–291.

M. F. Dacey, 1971, Two–Dimensional Urban Contract Fields. **Geographical Analysis** 3, 109–120.

P. Dasgupta, 1974, On Some Problems Arising from Professor Rawls' Conception of Distributive Justice. **Theory and Decision** 4, 325–344.

References

O. Davis, 1963, Economic Elements in Municipal Zoning Decisions. **Land Economics** 39, 375–387.

G. Debreu, 1959, **Theory of Value.** Yale University Press, New Haven, Conn.

J. Delafons, 1969, **Land Use Controls in the United States.** MIT Press, Cambridge, Mass.

D. B. Diamond, Jr., 1980, The Relationships Between Amenities and Urban Land Prices. **Land Economics** 56, 21–32.

A. Dixit, 1973, The Optimum Factory Town. **Bell Journal of Economics and Management Science** 4, 637–651.

A. K. Dixit, 1976, **Optimization in Economic Theory.** Oxford University Press, Oxford.

C. A. Doxiadis, 1967, Ecumenopolis: The Coming City. In A. Toynbee (ed.), **Cities of Destiny,** Thames and Hudson, London, 336–358.

C. A. Doxiadis, 1968, **Ekistics.** Hutchinson, London.

J. Drèze, and D. de la Vallée Poussin, 1971, A Tatonnement Process for Public Goods. **Review of Economic Studies** 38, 133–150.

R. Dusansky, J. Walsh, 1976, Separability, Welfare Economics and the Theory of Second-Best. **Review of Economic Studies** 43, 49–51.

B. Ellickson, 1973, A Generalization of the Pure Theory of Public Goods. **American Economic Review** 63, 417–432.

O. Fisch, 1975, Optimal City Size: The Economic Theory of Clubs and Exclusionary Zoning. **Public Choice** 24, 59–70.

O. Fisch, 1976, Spatial Equilibrium with Local Public Goods: Urban Land Rent, Optimal City Size and the Tiebout Hypothesis. In Y.Y. Papageorgiou (ed.), **Mathematical Land Use Theory,** Lexington Books, Lexington, Mass., 177–197.

F. R. Försund, 1973, Externalities, Environmental Pollution and Allocation in Space: A General Equilibrium Approach. **Regional and Urban Economics** 3, 3–32.

M. Fujita, 1976, Spatial Patterns of Urban Growth: Optimum and Market. **Journal of Urban Economics** 3, 209–241.

References

D. Gale, H. Nikaidô, 1965, The Jacobian Matrix and Global Univalence of Mappings. **Mathematische Annalen** 159, 81–93.

M. Getz, 1975, A Model of the Impact of Transportation Investment on Land Rents. **Journal of Public Economics**, 4, 57–74.

V. Ginsburgh, Y. Y. Papageorgiou, J.– F. Thisse, 1985, On Existence and Stability of Spatial Equilibria and Steady–States. **Regional Science and Urban Economics** 15, 149–158.

B. Greenwald, 1976, Conventional Returns to Scale and Financing Pollution Control. **Econometrica** 44, 811–814.

F. Grunberg, F. Modigliani, 1954, The Predictability of Social Events. **Journal of Political Economy** 62, 456–478.

G. Haag, W. Weidlich, 1984, A Stochastic Theory of Interregional Migration. **Geographical Analysis** 16, 331–357.

T. Hägerstrand, 1967, **Innovation Diffusion as a Spatial Process**. The University of Chicago Press, Chicago, Ill.

H. Haken, 1974, Synergetics: Basic Concepts and Mathematical Tools. In H. Haken (ed.), **Cooperative Phenomena**, North–Holland, Amsterdam, 1–32.

J. C. Harsanyi, 1975, Can the Maximin Principle Serve as a Basis for Morality? A Critique to John Rawls' Theory. **American Political Science Review** 69, 594–606.

J. Hartwick, 1979, Optimal Scale in a Large, Homogeneous Area. **Journal of Urban Economics** 6, 12–24.

J. Hartwick, U. Schweizer, P. Varaiya, 1976, Comparative Statics of a Residential Economy with Several Classes. In Y. Y. Papageorgiou (ed.), **Mathematical Land Use Theory**, Lexington Books, Lexington, Mass.

E. Helpman, D. Pines, 1975A, Optimal Public Investment and Dispersion Policy in a System of Open Cities. **Working Paper 97**, The Foerder Institute for Economic Research, Tel–Aviv University.

E. Helpman, D. Pines, 1975B, Optimal Zoning and Corrective Taxation in a System of Open Cities. **Working Paper 90**, Foerder Institute for Economic Research, Tel–Aviv University.

References

E. Helpman, D. Pines, 1977, Land and Zoning in an Urban Economy: Further Results. **American Economic Review** 67, 982–986.

E. Helpman, D. Pines, E. Boruchov, 1977, The Interaction Between Local Government and Urban Residential Location: Comment. **American Economic Review** 66, 961–967.

J. M. Henderson, R. E. Quandt, 1980, **Microeconomic Theory**. McGraw–Hill, New York.

J. V. Henderson, 1974A, Optimum City Size: The External Diseconomy Question. **Journal of Political Economy** 82, 373–388.

J. V. Henderson, 1974B, Road Congestion: A Reconsideration of Pricing Theory. **Journal of Urban Economics** 1, 346–365.

J. V. Henderson, 1975, Congestion and Optimum City Size. **Journal of Urban Economics** 2, 48–62.

J. V. Henderson, 1977, **Economic Theory and the Cities**. Academic Press, New York.

J. V. Henderson, 1979, Theories of Groups, Jurisdictions and City Size. In P. Mieszkowski, M. Straszheim (eds.), **Current Issues in Urban Economics**, Johns Hopkins University Press, Baltimore, Md.

W. Hildebrand, 1974, **Core and Equilibria of a Large Economy**. Princeton University Press, Princeton, N. J.

O. Hochman, 1975, Market Equilibrium Versus Optimum in a Model with Congestion: Note. **American Economic Review** 65, 992–996.

S. Holtermann, 1976, Alternative Tax Systems to Correct for Externalities and the Efficiency of Paying Compensation. **Economica** 43, 1–16.

W. von Humboldt, 1792, **Ideas Toward an Investigation to Determine the Proper Limits of the Activity of the State**.

G. K. Ingram, A. Carrol, 1981, The Spatial Structure of Latin American Cities. **Journal of Urban Economics** 9, 257–273.

W. Isard, 1956, **Location and Space Economy**. MIT Press, Cambridge, Mass.

References

Y. Kanemoto, 1975, Congestion and Cost–Benefit Analysis in Cities. **Journal of Urban Economics** 2, 246–264.

Y. Kanemoto, 1976, Optimum, Market and Second–Best Land–Use Patterns in a von Thünen City with Congestion. **Regional Science and Urban Economics** 6, 23–32.

Y. Kanemoto, 1977, Cost–Benefit Analysis and the Second–Best Land–Use for Transportation. **Journal of Urban Economics** 4, 483–503.

Y. Kanemoto, 1980A, Externality, Migration, and Urban Crises. **Journal of Urban Economics** 8, 150–164.

Y. Kanemoto, 1980B, **Theories of Urban Externalities.** North–Holland, Amsterdam.

C. R. Kern, 1981, Racial Prejudice and Residential Segregation: The Yinger Model Revisited. **Journal of Urban Economics** 10, 164–172.

S. C. Kolm, 1975, Rendement Qualitatif et Financement Optimal des Politiques d'Environnement. **Econometrica** 43, 93–115.

M. Kraus, 1974, Land Use in a Circular City. **Journal of Economic Theory** 8, 440–457.

H. W. Kuhn, A. W. Tucker, 1950, Nonlinear Programming. **Proceedings of the Second Berkeley Symposium on Mathematical Statistics and Probability.** University of California Press, Berkeley, 481–492.

K. Lancaster, 1962, The Scope of Qualitative Economics. **Review of Economic Studies** 29, 99–133.

K. Lancaster, 1976, The Pure Theory of Impure Public Goods. In R. E. Grieson (ed.), **Public and Urban Economics**, Lexington Books, Lexington, Mass.

L. B. Lave, 1970, Congestion and Urban Location. **Papers of the Regional Science Association** 25, 133–150.

A. C. Lea, 1981, Public Facility Location Models and the Theory of Impure Public Goods. **Sistemi Urbani** 3, 345–390.

L. Legey, M. Ripper, P. Varaiya, 1973, Effects of Congestion on the Shape of a City. **Journal of Economic Theory** 6, 162–179.

References

D. Levhari, Y. Oron, D. Pines, 1978, A Note on Unequal Treatment of Equals in an Urban Setting. **Journal of Urban Economics** 5, 278–284.

R. C. Lind, 1973, Spatial Equilibrium, the Theory of Rents and Public Program Benefits. **Quarterly Journal of Economics** 87, 188–207.

E. Lindhal, 1919, Just Taxation: A Positive Solution. In R. A. Musgrave, T.A.Peacock (eds), **Classics in the Theory of Public Finance**, Macmillan, London, 1958.

R. G. Lipsey, K. Lancaster, 1956, The General Theory of the Second Best. **Review of Economic Studies** 24, 11–32.

D. A. Livesey, 1973, Optimum City Size: A Minimum Congestion Cost Approach. **Journal of Economic Theory** 6, 144–161.

W. H. Long, 1971, Demand in Space: Some Neglected Aspects. **Papers of the Regional Science Association** 27, 54–60.

R. D. Luce, H. Raiffa, 1957, **Games and Decisions**. Wiley, New York.

E. Malinvaud, 1972A, **Lectures on Microeconomic Theory**. North-Holland/American Elsevier, Amsterdam/New York.

E. Malinvaud, 1972B, Prices for Individual Consumption, Quality Indicators for Collective Consumption. **Review of Economic Studies** 39, 385–405.

R. D. Mandelker, 1971, **The Zoning Dilemma**. Bobbs-Merrill, Indianapolis, Ind.

Marcus Aurelius, circa 175, **Meditations**.

J. Marschak, 1950, Rational Behaviour, Uncertain Prospects, and Measurable Utility. **Econometrica** 18, 111–141.

K. Marx, 1867, **Capital**.

K. Marx, 1875, **Critique of the Gotha Programme**.

D. J. Mayston, 1976, Ordinalism and Quasi-Ordinalism in the Theory of Social Choice. **Discussion Paper 76–24**, Department of Economics, University of British Columbia and University of Essex.

G. McCalden, 1975, Microgeographic Functions: A Review and Extension. **Geographical Analysis** 7, 411–419.

M. McGuire, 1974, Group Segregation and Optimal Jurisdiction. **Journal of Political Economy** 80, 112–132.

J. S. Mill, 1859, **On Liberty**.

D. E. Mills, 1979, Interdependencies and the Urban Land Market. **Journal of Urban Economics** 6, 1–11.

E. S. Mills, 1972, **Studies in the Structure of the Urban Economy**. Johns Hopkins University Press, Baltimore, Md.

E. S. Mills, D. M. de Ferranti, 1971, Market Choices and Optimum City Size. **American Economic Review, Papers and Proceedings** 61, 340–345.

J. A. Mirrlees, 1972, The Optimum Town. **Swedish Journal of Economics** 74, 114–135.

T. Miyao, 1978, A Probabilistic Model of Location Choice with Neighbourhood Effects. **Journal of Economic Theory** 19, 347–358.

H. D Mohring, 1961, Land Value and the Measurement of Highway Benefits. Journal of Political Economy 69, 236–249.

H. D. Mohring, M. Harwitz, 1962, **Highway Benefits**. Northwestern University Press, Evanston, Ill.

E. G. Moore, 1970, Some Spatial Properties of Urban Contact Fields. Geographical Analysis 2, 376–386.

W. G. Moss, 1977, Large Lot Zoning, Property Taxes, and Metropolitan Area. **Journal of Urban Economics** 4, 408–427.

D. C. Mueller, 1976, Public Choice: A Survey. **Journal of Economic Literature** 14, 395–433.

R. A. Musgrave, 1959, **Theory of Public Finance: a Study in Public Economy**. McGraw-Hill, New York.

R. F. Muth, 1969, **Cities and Housing**. The University of Chicago Press, Chicago, Ill.

Y.- K. Ng, 1973, The Economic Theory of Clubs: Pareto Optimality Conditions. Economica 40, 291–298.

R. Nozick, 1974, **Anarchy, State and Utopia**. Basic Books, New York.

References

W. H. Oakland, 1972, Congestion, Public Goods and Welfare. **Journal of Public Economics** 1, 339–357.

W. E. Oates, E. P. Howrey, W. J. Baumol, 1971, The Analysis of Public Policy in Urban Dynamic Models. **Journal of Political Economy** 79, 142–153.

H. Ogawa, M. Fugita, 1980, Land Use Pattern in a Nonmonocentric City. **Journal of Regional Science** 20, 455–475.

J. C. Ohls, 1975, Public Policy Toward Low Income Housing and Filtering in Housing Markets. **Journal of Urban Economics** 2, 144–171.

J. C. Ohls, R. C. Weisberg, M. J. White, 1974, The Effect of Zoning on Land Value. **Journal of Urban Economics** 1, 428–444.

Y. Oron, D. Pines, 1975, The Effect of Efficient Pricing of Air Pollution on Inter-Urban Land Use Pattern. **Environment and Planning A** 7, 293–299.

Y. Oron, D. Pines, E. Sheshinski, 1973, Optimum vs Equilibrium Land-Use Pattern and Congestion Toll. **Bell Journal of Economics and Management Science** 4, 619–636.

Y. Oron, D. Pines, E. Sheshinski, 1974, The Effect of Nuisances Associated with Urban Traffic on Suburbanization and Land Values. **Journal of Urban Economics** 1, 382–394.

J. M. Ortega, W. C. Rheinboldt, 1970, **Iterative Solution of Nonlinear Equations in Several Variables**. Academic Press, New York.

G. Orwell, 1949, **Nineteen Eighty-Four**.

A. de Palma, Y. Y. Papageorgiou, 1985, A Model of Heuristic Choice. Unpublished manuscript, Department of Geography, McMaster University, Hamilton, Ontario.

Y. Y. Papageorgiou, 1971, The Population Density and Rent Distribution Models within a Multicentre Framework. **Environment and Planning** 3, 267–282.

Y. Y. Papageorgiou, 1977, Fundamental Problems of Theoretical Planning. **Environment and Planning A** 9, 1329–1356.

Y. Y. Papageorgiou, 1978A, Spatial Externalities I: Theory. **Annals of the Association of American Geographers** 68, 465–476.

References

Y. Y. Papageorgiou, 1978B, Spatial Externalities II: Applications. **Annals of the Association of American Geographers** 68, 477–492.

Y. Y. Papageorgiou, 1979, Agglomeration. **Regional Science and Urban Economics** 9, 41–59.

Y. Y. Papageorgiou, 1980A, Social Values and Social Justice. **Economic Geography** 56, 110–119.

Y. Y. Papageorgiou, 1980B, On Sudden Urban Growth. **Environment and Planning A** 12, 1035–1050.

Y. Y. Papageorgiou, 1982, Some Thoughts About Theory in the Social Sciences. **Geographical Analysis** 14, 340–346.

Y. Y. Papageorgiou, 1987A, Spatial Public Goods 1: Theory. **Environment and Planning A** 19, 331–352.

Y. Y. Papageorgiou, 1987B, Spatial Public Goods 2: Applications. **Environment and Planning A** 19, 471–482.

Y. Y. Papageorgiou, T. R. Smith, 1983, Agglomeration as Local Instability of Spatially Uniform Steady-States. **Econometrica** 51, 1109–1119.

Y. Y. Papageorgiou, and J.- F. Thisse, 1985, Agglomeration as Spatial Interdependence Between Firms and Households. **Journal of Economic Theory** 37, 19–31.

M. J. Pauly, 1970, Optimality, "Public" Goods and Local Governments: A General Theoretical Analysis. **Journal of Political Economy** 78, 572–585.

A. C. Pigou, 1920, **The Economics of Welfare**. Macmillan, London.

D. Pines, 1975, On the Spatial Distribution of Household According to Income. **Economic Geography** 51, 142–149.

D. Pines and Y. Weiss, 1976, Land Improvement Projects and Land Values. **Journal of Urban Economics** 3, 1–13.

Plato, circa − 350, **Laws**.

A. M. Polinsky, S. Shavell, 1975, The Air Pollution and Property Value Debate. **Review of Economics and Statistics** 57, 100–104.

References

A. M. Polinsky, S. Shavell, 1976, Amenities and Property Values in a Model of an Urban Area. Journal of Public Economics 5, 119–129.

K. R. Popper, 1977, The Open Society and Its Enemies. Routledge and Kegan Paul, London.

R. Radner, 1975, Satisficing. Journal of Mathematical Economics 2, 253–262.

J. Rawls, 1971, A Theory of Justice. Harvard University Press, Cambridge, Mass.

J. Rawls, 1974, Some Reasons for the Maximin Principle. American Economic Review 64, 141–146.

C. E. Reid, 1977, Measuring Residential Decentralization of Blacks and Whites. Urban Studies 14, 353–357.

J. G. Riley, 1972, Optimal towns. Ph.D. thesis, Massachusetts Institute of Technology, Cambridge, Mass.

J. G. Riley, 1973, Gammaville: An Optimal Town. Journal of Economic Theory 6, 471–482.

J. G. Riley, 1974, Optimal Residential Density and Road Transportation. Journal of Urban Economics 1, 230–249.

A. J. Robson, 1976A, Cost–Benefit Analysis and the Use of Urban Land for Transportation. Journal of Urban Economics 3, 180–191.

A. J. Robson, 1976B, Two Models of Urban Air Pollution. Journal of Urban Economics 3, 264–284.

S. Rose–Ackermann, 1975, Racism and Urban Structure. Journal of Urban Economics 2, 85–103.

S. Rose–Ackermann, 1977, The Political Economy of a Racist Housing Market. Journal of Urban Economics 4, 150–169.

J.– J. Rousseau, 1755, Social Contract and Discourses.

D. L. Rubinfeld, 1978, Suburban Employment and Zoning: A General Equilibrium Analysis. Journal of Regional Science 18, 33–44.

C. P. Rydell, B. H. Stevens, 1968, Air Pollution and the Shape of Urban Areas. Journal of the American Institute of Planners 34, 50–51.

P. A. Samuelson, 1954, The Pure Theory of Public Expenditure. **Review of Economics and Statistics** 36, 387–389.

P. A. Samuelson, 1970, **Foundations of Economic Analysis**. Atheneum, New York.

I. W. Sandberg, 1975, Two Theorems on the Justification of the Multiservice Regulated Company. **The Bell Journal of Economics** 6, 346–356.

L. D. Schall, 1976, Urban Renewal Policy and Economic Efficiency. **American Economic Review** 66, 612–628.

T. C. Schelling, 1971, On the Ecology of Micromotives. **The Public Interest** 25, 61–98.

R. E. Schuler, 1974, The Interaction Between Local Government and Urban Residential Location. **American Economic Review** 64, 682–696.

R. E. Schuler, 1977, The Interaction Between Local Government and Urban Residential Location: Reply and Further Analysis. **American Economic Review** 66, 968–975.

U. Schweizer, P. Varaiya, J. Hartwick, 1976, General Equilibrium and Location Theory. **Journal of Urban Economics** 3, 285–303.

A. K. Sen, 1970, The Impossibility of a Paretian Liberal. **Journal of Political Economy** 78, 152–157.

A. K. Sen, 1973, **On Economic Inequality**. Clarendon Press, Oxford.

A. K. Sen, 1976, Liberty, Unanimity and Rights. **Economica** 43, 217–245.

A. K. Sen, 1977, Social Choice Theory: A Re-examination. **Econometrica** 45, 53–89.

E. P. Seskin, 1973, Residential Choice and Air Pollution: A General Equilibrium Model. **American Economic Review** 63, 960–967.

A. Shaked, 1982, Human Environment as a Local Public Good. **Journal of Mathematical Economics** 9, 275–283.

E. Sheshinski, 1973, Congestion and Optimum City Size. **American Economic Review, Papers and Proceedings** 63, 61–66.

References

B. Siegan, 1972, **Land-Use Without Zoning**. Lexington Books, Lexington, Mass.

H. Simon, 1957, **Models of Man**. Wiley, New York.

T. R. Smith, 1976, Set-Determined Process and the Growth of Spatial Structure. **Geographical Analysis** 8, 354–375.

R. M. Solow, 1972, Congestion, Density, and the Use of Land in Transportation. **The Swedish Journal of Economics** 74, 161–173.

R. M. Solow, 1973, Congestion Cost and the Use of Land for Streets. **Bell Journal of Economics and Management Science** 4, 602–618.

R. M. Solow, W. S. Vickrey, 1971, Land Use in a Long Narrow City. **Journal of Economic Theory** 3, 430–447.

D. A. Starrett, 1974, Principles of Optimal Location in a Large Homogeneous Area. **Journal of Economic Theory** 9, 418–448.

R. H. Strotz, 1965, Urban Transportation Parables. In J. Margolis (ed.) **The Public Economy of Urban Communities**, Johns Hopkins University Press, Baltimore, Md.

R. H. Strotz, 1968, The Use of Land Rent Changes to Measure the Benefits of Land Improvement. In J. Haring (ed.), **The New Economics of Regulated Industries: Rate-Making in a Dynamic Economy**, Economic Research Center, Occidential College, Los Angeles, Cal., 174–186.

R. H. Strotz, C. Wright, 1975, Spatial Adaptation to Urban Air Pollution. **Journal of Urban Economics** 2, 212–222.

C. Stuart, 1970, Search and the Spatial Organization of Trading. In S. A. Lippman, J. J. McCall (eds.), **Studies in the Economics of Search**, North-Holland, New York, 17–33.

W. J. Stull, 1974, Land Use and Zoning in the Urban Economy. **American Economic Review** 64, 337–347.

J. L. Sweeney, 1974, Quality, Commodity Hierarchies and Housing Markets. **Econometrica** 42, 147–167.

R. Thom, 1975, **Structural Stability and Morphogenesis**. W.A. Benjamin, Reading, Mass.

References

G. I. Thrall, 1980, The Consumption Theory of Land Rent. **Urban Geography** 1, 350–370.

G. I. Thrall, 1982, Public Goods, Externalities and the Consumption Theory of Land Rent. **Papers of the Regional Science Association** 50, 131–149.

Thucydides, circa − 397, History of the Peloponnesian War.

C. M. Tiebout, 1956, A Pure Theory of Local Expenditures. **Journal of Political Economy** 64, 416–424.

G. S. Tolley, 1974, The Welfare Economics of City Bigness. **Journal of Urban Economics** 1, 324–345.

J. H. von Thünen, 1826, **Die Isolierte Staadt in Beziehung auf Landwirtschaft und Nationaleconomie.**

H. Tulkens, 1978, Dynamic Processes for Public Goods: An Institution-Oriented Survey. **Journal of Public Economics** 9, 163–201.

United Nations, 1974, **Concise Report on the World Population Situation in 1970–75 and Its Long-Range Implications.** United Nations, New York.

R. J. Vaughan, 1975, "Optimum" Distribution of Population Within a Linear City. **Transportation Research** 9, 25–29.

W. S. Vickrey, 1969, Congestion Theory and Transport Investment. **American Economic Review** 59, 251–260.

V. C. Walsh, 1970, **Introduction to Contemporary Microeconomics.** McGraw-Hill, New York.

A. A. Walters, 1961, The Theory and Measurement of Private and Social Cost of Highway Congestion. **Econometrica** 29, 676–699.

W. C. Wheaton, 1974, A Comparative Static Analysis of Urban Spatial Structure. **Journal of Economic Theory** 9, 223–237.

W. C. Wheaton, 1976, On the Optimal Distribution of Income Among Cities. **Journal of Urban Economics** 3, 31–44.

W. C. Wheaton, 1977, Residential Decentralization, Land Rents, and the Benefits of Urban Transportation Investment. **American Economic Review** 67, 138–143.

References

W. C. Wheaton, 1978, Price-Induced Distortions in Urban Highway Investment. **Bell Journal of Economics** 9, 622–632.

W. C. Wheaton, 1982, Urban Spatial Development with Durable but Replaceable Capital. **Journal of Urban Economics** 12, 53–67.

M. J. White, 1975, The Effect of Zoning on the Size of Metropolitan Areas. **Journal of Urban Economics** 2, 279–290.

M. J. White, 1977, Urban Models of Race Discrimination. **Regional Science and Urban Economics** 7, 217–232.

J. H. Wile, 1975, The Interaction Between Local Government and Urban Location. **Working Paper 139**, Department of Economics, State University of New York at Stony Brook.

A. Williams, 1966, The Optimal Provision of Public Goods in a System of Local Government. **Journal of Political Economy** 74, 18–33.

A. G. Wilson, 1967, A Statistical Theory of Spatial Trip Distribution Models. **Transportation Research** 1, 253–269.

L. Wingo Jr., 1961, **Transportation and Urban Land.** Resources for the Future, Washington, D.C.

A. Wolinsky, 1983, Retail Trade Concentration Due to Consumers Imperfect Information. **The Bell Journal of Economics** 14, 275–283.

C. Wright, 1977, Financing Public Goods and Residential Location. **Urban Studies** 14, 51–58.

J. Yellin, 1974, Urban Population Distribution, Family Income and Social Prejudice: I. The Long Narrow City. **Journal of Urban Economics** 1, 21–47.

J. Yinger, 1976, Racial Prejudice and Racial Residential Segregation in an Urban Model. **Journal of Urban Economics** 3, 383–396.

Citation Index

W. Alonso, *2, 77, 82*
J. C. Amson, *319*(4), 320(3), 321(2)
A. Anas, *31, 117*(2)
Antiphon, *240*
R. J. Arnott, *31, 42, 100, 167, 168, 182, 288, 361, 441*(2), 443
K. J. Arrow, *58*(2), *75, 230,* 232, 233(2), *236, 237, 253*(2), 254(4), *257, 266, 307, 328, 331, 332, 333*
C. P. Averous, *441*
R. C. Baesemann, *42*
J. L. Barr, *338, 418, 441*
W. J. Baumol, *32, 220, 337*
M. J. Beckmann, *2*(2), *338, 361*

J. Bentham, *244*
L. van den Berg, *102, 133*
E. Berglas, *440*
B. J. L. Berry, *98, 133, 167, 208, 222, 224*
J. R. Bettman, *59*
H. Bleicher, *80,* 80
H. D. Block, *59, 331, 332, 333*
A. E. Boardman, *441*
E. Boruchov, *318, 361, 419*(3), *441, 441*(3), *442*
J. M. Buchanan, *257, 288, 417*
L. S. Burns, *133*
D. R. Capozza, *318*
A. Carrol, *167*
G. A. P. Carrothers, *338*
H. Carter, *42*

Index

E. Casetti, 2, 81(3), 82, *83*, 83, 84, 85(2), *98*, 98, 103, 104, 143, 144, 172(2), 177, 179, 182, *186*, *204*, 281, 283, 300(2), 301(4), 302, 319(2), 324, 332
J. R. Chamberlin, *440*
A. C. Chiang, *25*
W. Christaller, *31*, *93*, *287*
C. Clark, 80, *80*, 81, *133*
P. N. Courant, *182*, *338*(2), *378*, *402*, *403*
M. F. Dacey, *317*
P. Dasgupta, *257*
O. Davis, *402*, *403*
G. Debreu, *255*, *288*
J. Delafons, *402*
D. B. Diamond Jr., *182*
A. K. Dixit, 23, 24, *441*, *442*
C. A. Doxiadis, *185*, *198*
R. Drewett, *102*, *133*
J. Drèze, *361*
R. Dusansky, *287*
B. Ellickson, *440*
D. M. de Ferranti, *441*, *442*, 442
O. Fisch, *321*, *337*, *440*
F. R. Försund, *442*
M. Fujita, *31*, *42*
D. Gale, *43*
M. Getz, *182*
V. Ginsburgh, *99*, *330*, *334*, *337*, *339*
B. Greenwald, *442*
F. Grunberg, *333*
G. Haag, *7*

T. Hägerstrand, *337*
F. H. Hahn, *58*(2), *75*, *266*, 328
H. Haken, *337*
J. C. Harsanyi, *257*
J. Hartwick, *59*, *150*, *158*, *161*, *167*, *288*
M. Harwitz, *442*
E. Helpman, *338*, *401*(2), *402*, *404*, *418*, *419*(2), *441*, *442*
J. M. Henderson, *30*
J. V. Henderson, *3*, *31*, *205*, *338*, *440*, *441*(2)
W. Hildebrand, *57*
O. Hochman, *318*, *338*, *361*, *441*
S. Holtermann, *306*(2)
E. P. Howrey, *220*
W. von Humboldt, *233*, *287*(2)
L. Hurwicz, *331*, *332*, *333*
G. K. Ingram, *167*
W. Isard, *2*, *101*
Y. Kanemoto, *3*, *224*(2), *225*(3), *308*(2), *338*, *441*
C. R. Kern, *378*(2)
L. H. Klaasen, *102*, *133*
S. C. Kolm, *442*
M. Kraus, *338*, *441*
H. W. Kuhn, *9*, 9(4), 10(4), 22, 27, 78, 268, 440
M. Kurz, *307*
K. Lancaster, *287*, *440*
L. B. Lave, *338*, *441*(2)
A. C. Lea, *439*(2)
D. B. Lee Jr., *441*
L. Legey, *338*, *441*, *442*
D. Levhari, *257*, *305*

R. C. Lind, *182*
E. Lindhal, 27, *412*, *415*(2), *440*(2), 440
R. G. Lipsey, *287*
D. A. Livesey, *441*
W. H. Long, *77*
R. D. Luce, *378*
J. G. MacKinnon, *167, 168, 182*, *441*(2)
E. Malinvaud, *57, 58, 59, 99, 361*
R. D. Mandelker, *402*
Marcus Aurelius, *337*
J. Marschak, *57, 59*
K. Marx, *305, 308*
D. J. Mayston, *255*(2)
G. McCalden, *321*
M. McGuire, *440*
J. S. Mill, *233, 287*
D. E. Mills, *402, 403*
E. S. Mills, *2, 441, 442*, 442
J. A. Mirrlees, *59, 305, 307, 317*
T. Miyao, *339*
F. Modigliani, *333*
H. D. Mohring, *182*, *429*(3), *430*(2), *432*(6), *434*(2), *436*(2), *442, 443*
E. G. Moore, *317*
W. G. Moss, *402*
D. C. Mueller, *254*
R. A. Musgrave, *359*
R. F. Muth, *2, 31,* 61, *70,* *70*(3), *77,* 169, *170*(2), 261, 284, 300, 301, 424
Y. K. Ng, *440*

H. Nikaidô, *43*
R. Nozick, *255, 257*
W. H. Oakland, *440*
W. E. Oates, *32, 220, 337*
H. Ogawa, *42*
J. C. Ohls, *31, 402, 403*
Y. Oron, *257, 305, 338*(3), *401*
J. M. Ortega, *43*
G. Orwell, *283*
A. de Palma, *56, 59*
Y. Y. Papageorgiou, *31, 42*(3), *43*(2), *56*(2), *59, 99, 101, 203, 252, 257, 305, 328, 330, 334, 337*(3), *339, 361, 439*(2)
M. J. Pauly, *440*
A.C. Pigou, 271, 272, 392, 402
D. Pines, *167, 181, 182, 257, 305, 338*(4), *401*(2), *402, 404, 418, 419*(2), *441, 442*
Plato, *286, 286*(2)
A. M. Polinsky, *182*(3), 183
K. R. Popper, 240, *256*
R. E. Quandt, *30*
R. Radner, *59*
H. Raiffa, *378*
J. Rawls, *233, 256, 257*
C. E. Reid, *208*
W. C. Rheinboldt, *43*
J. G. Riley, *257, 338, 441*(2)
M. Ripper, *338, 441, 442*
A. J. Robson, *338, 353, 441*
S. Rose-Ackermann, *338*(2), *378*(2), *379*(2)
A. Rossi *102*

Index

J.-J. Rousseau, *240*
D. L. Rubinfeld, *182, 402*
C. P. Rydell, *338*
P. A. Samuelson, *134, 359, 360, 405*
I. W. Sandberg, *42, 43*
L. D. Schall, *31*
T. C. Schelling, *357, 377*
R. E. Schuler, *419*(2)
U. Schweizer, *59, 150, 158, 161, 167*
A. K. Sen, *253, 254*(3), *255*(3), *256, 257, 305*(2)

E. P. Seskin, *338*
A. Shaked, *42*
S. Shavell, *182*(3), 183
E. Sheshinski, *338*(2), *441, 442*
B. Siegan, *402*
J. W. Simmons, *98, 133, 167*
H. Simon, *59*
T. R. Smith, *42, 321*(3), *378*
R. M. Solow, *338*(3), *441*(3), *442*
D. A. Starrett, *42, 288*
B. H. Stevens, *338*
J. E. Stiglitz, *100*
R. H. Strotz, *9, 182, 338, 401, 402, 425, 427, 441, 442,* 442
C. Stuart, *42*
W. C. Stubblebine, *288*
W. J. Stull, *338, 402, 404*
J. L. Sweeney, *31*
R. J. Tennant, *98, 133, 167*

J.- F. Thisse, *99, 328, 330, 334, 337*(2), *339*
G. I. Thrall, *134, 418*
J. H. von Thünen, *2, 3, 4, 66*
Thucidides, *233, 255*
C. M. Tiebout, *31*
G. S. Tolley, *338*
A. W. Tucker, *9,* 9(4), 10(5), *22, 27, 78, 268, 440*
P. Varaiya, *59, 150, 158, 161, 167, 338, 441, 442*
R. J. Vaughan, *338*
W. S. Vickrey, *338, 441*(2), *442*
C. H. T. Vijverberg *102*
J. Walsh, *287*
V. C. Walsh, *254*
A. A. Walters, *441*
W. Weidlich, *7*
R. C. Weisberg, *402, 403*
Y. Weiss, *182*
W. C. Wheaton, *117, 118, 134, 167*(2), *168, 441*
M. J. White, *338, 378, 402*(2), *403*
J. H. Wile, *419*
A. Williams, *418*
A. G. Wilson, *338*
L. Wingo Jr., *2*
A. Wolinsky, *42*
C. Wright, *338, 401, 402, 418*
J. Yellin, *321*(2), *338, 377, 378*
J. Yinger, *317, 321, 338, 377*(3), *378*(3), *378*(2), *399*

DUE DATE			
~~OCT 3 0 1994~~			
~~DEC 1 9 1994~~			~~APR 2 3 1996~~
~~NOV 0 9 1995~~			
~~JAN 2 9 1996~~			
~~DEC 1 6 1995~~			
~~MAR 1 2 1996~~			
			Printed in USA